Physical Culture, Power, and the Body

During the past decade, there has been an outpouring of books on 'the body' in society, but none has focused as specifically as this one on physical culture – that is, cultural practices such as sport and dance within which the moving physical body is central.

The way in which bodies are emblematic of the social, mediate biological and social processes, are invested with power, and create social and cultural power are themes running throughout the book. It is intended to challenge old certainties about the body and physical culture and to investigate changing knowledge about the body and the ways in which it has been, and is, experienced, understood and transformed. Every essay in the collection throws light on how the body in physical culture is assigned meaning and influences identity.

Throughout the book, questions are raised about the character of the body, specifically the relations between the 'natural' body, the 'constructed' body and the 'alien' or 'virtual' body. The themes of the book are wide in scope, including:

- physical culture and the fascist body
- sport and the racialised body
- sport, medicine, health and the culture of risk
- the female Muslim sporting body, power, and politics
- technological bodies and virtual women
- experiencing the disabled sporting body
- embodied exhibitions of striptease and sport
- the social logic of sparring
- sport, girls and the neoliberal body.

Physical Culture, Power, and the Body aims to break down disciplinary boundaries in its theoretical approaches and its readership. The authors themselves come from different disciplinary backgrounds, demonstrating the widespread topicality of physical culture and the body. Their very varied contributions highlight the complexities, contradictions, and very indeterminacy of the body in physical culture.

Jennifer Hargreaves is Visiting Professor of Sport and Gender Politics at Brighton University, UK.

Patricia Vertinsky is Professor of Human Kinetics and Distinguished University Scholar at the University of British Columbia, Canada.

Routledge Critical Studies in Sport
Series Editors: Jennifer Hargreaves and Ian McDonald
University of Brighton

The Routledge Critical Studies in Sport series aims to lead the way in developing the multi-disciplinary field of Sport Studies by producing books that are interrogative, interventionist and innovative. By providing theoretically sophisticated and empirically grounded texts, the series will make sense of the changes and challenges facing sport globally. The series aspires to maintain the commitment and promise of the critical paradigm by contributing to a more inclusive and less exploitative culture of sport.

Also available in this series:

Understanding Lifestyle Sports
Consumption, identity and difference
Edited by Belinda Wheaton

Why Sports Morally Matter
William J Morgan

Fastest, Highest, Strongest
A critique of high-performance sport
Rob Beamish and Ian Ritchie

Sport, Sexualities and Queer/Theory
Edited by Jayne Caudwell

Physical Culture, Power, and the Body

Edited by Jennifer Hargreaves
and Patricia Vertinsky

 Routledge
Taylor & Francis Group

LONDON AND NEW YORK

First published 2007
by Routledge
2 Park Square, Milton Park, Abingdon, Oxon, OX14 4RN

Simultaneously published in the USA and Canada
by Routledge
270 Madison Ave, New York, NY 10016

Routledge is an imprint of the Taylor & Francis Group, an informa business

Typeset in Goudy by
RefineCatch Limited, Bungay, Suffolk
Printed and bound in Great Britain by
Cromwell Press, Trowbridge, Wiltshire

British Library Cataloguing in Publication Data
A catalogue record for this book is available from the British Library

Library of Congress Cataloging-in-Publication Data
   Physical culture, power, and the body / edited by Jennifer Hargreaves
and Patricia Vertinsky.
      p. cm – (Routledge critical studies in sport)
   Includes bibliographical references and index.
   1. Physical education and training—Social aspects. 2. Sports—Social
aspects. 3. Body, Human—Social aspects.   I. Hargreaves, Jennifer,
1937–II. Vertinsky, Patricia Anne, 1942–   III. Series.
   GV342.27.H37 2006
   306.4′83–dc22   2006015082

ISBN10: 0–415–36351–9 (hbk)
ISBN10: 0–415–36352–7 (pbk)
ISBN10: 0–203–01465–0 (ebk)

ISBN13: 978–0–415–36351–8 (hbk)
ISBN13: 978–0–415–36352–5 (pbk)
ISBN13: 978–0–203–01465–3 (ebk)

Contents

Illustrations

Contributors

Gamal Abdel-Shehid is Assistant Professor in the School of Kinesiology and Health Science at York University, Canada. His teaching and research interests include cultural studies of sport and leisure, popular culture in the black Diaspora, as well as queer and gender studies. He is the author of *Who Da' Man? Black Masculinities and Sporting Cultures*.

Jennifer Hargreaves is Visiting Professor of Sport and Gender Politics at the University of Brighton, in the UK. Among her many publications are the edited text, *Sport, Culture and Ideology* (1982); *Sporting Females: Critical Issues in the History and Sociology of Women's Sports* (1994), awarded the best sports sociology book of the year by the North American Society of Sports Sociology; and *Heroines of Sport: the Politics of Difference and Identity* (2000). In 2006, she received the Max and Reet Howell Award from the North American Society for Sport History (NASSH). Jennifer is joint editor of the book series, *Routledge Critical Studies in Sport* and co-editor of this book *Physical Culture, Power, and the Body*. She has worked as a guest professor in Germany, Hong Kong and Japan, lectures in venues around the world, does editorial work for journals and publishers, and consultancy work for sport organisations and the media.

Leslie Heywood is Professor of English and Sport Studies at State University of New York, Binghamton. She is the author of, among others, *Built to Win: The Female Athlete as Cultural Icon, Dedication to Hunger: The Anorexic Aesthetic in Modern Culture* and *Bodymakers: A Cultural Anatomy of Women's Bodybuilding*, and the sports memoir, *Pretty Good for a Girl*.

John Hoberman has been active in sports studies and sports journalism for thirty years. He is the author of *Sport and Political Ideology* (1984); *The Olympic Crisis: Sport, Politics and the Moral Order* (1986); *Mortal Engines: The Science of Performance and the Dehumanization of Sport* (1992); *Darwin's Athletes: How Sport has Damaged Black America and Preserved the Myth of Race* (1997); and *Testosterone Dreams: Rejuvenation, Aphrodisia, Doping* (2005). He is Professor of Germanic Studies at the University of Texas where he has taught courses on Race and Sport, and Race and

Medicine. Since 2001, he has been a visiting researcher in doping studies at the University of Southern Denmark.

Ian McDonald teaches sociology, politics and sport policy at the University of Brighton, UK. He has published widely on race and anti-racism in sport, the sporting body in India, and on the politics of sport policy. Ian is co-editor with Jennifer Hargreaves of the *Routledge Critical Studies in Sport* book series.

Kate O'Riordan is on a research secondment at the Centre for the Economic and Social Aspects of Genomics, Lancaster University, for three years, to work on the Flagship Project, *Media, Culture and Genomics*. She is seconded from the University of Sussex, where she is a Lecturer in Media Studies. Her research background is in digital media, and internet research and she has published on research ethics in this field. Previous work has included the representations of gendered bodies, technologies, sexualities and queer theory across a range of sites. She is currently working on intersections between biotechnology and information technology in media discourses. Recent book chapters include (2005) 'Changing Cyberspaces: Dystopia and Technological Excess'; with J. Doyle (2002) 'Virtually Visible: Female Cyberbodies and the Medical Imagination'; (2002) 'Windows on the Web: The Female Body and the Web Camera; (2001) 'Playing With Lara in Virtual Space'.

Beckie Ross is jointly appointed in Women's Studies and Sociology at University of British Columbia, Canada. Her teaching and research areas include feminist anti-racist qualitative methods, historical sociology, the family and nation-making, critical sexuality studies and critical sport studies. She has published articles in *Labour/Travail*, *Atlantis*, *Journal of Canadian Studies*, *Journal of Women's History*, and the *Journal of the History of Sexuality*. A chapter on women's athletics in the 1940s and 50s appears in *Disciplining Bodies in the Gymnasium: Memory, Monument, Modernism* (2004), and the chapter in this book is part of a larger book manuscript entitled *The Shake, the Rattle and the Pole: Vancouver's Striptease Past*.

Brett Smith is a lecturer in qualitative research and a member of the Qualitative Research Unit in the School of Health and Sport Sciences at the University of Exeter, UK. His current research focuses on men, sport and spinal cord injury. He is developing work on the lived experiences of becoming disabled through sport and the storied reconstruction of selves; the possibilities of narrative inquiry; and the pull of the body in storytelling.

Andrew C. Sparkes is Professor and Director of the Qualitative Research Unit in the School of Health and Sport Sciences, Exeter University, UK. His research interests include: performing bodies and identity/subjectivity formation; interrupted body projects and the narrative (re)construction of self; sporting auto/biographies; and the lives of marginalized individuals and groups. He seeks to explore the lived experience of embodiment via multiple forms of representation. He has published widely on these issues and is author of *Telling Tales in Sport and Physical Activity: A Qualitative Journey* (2002). He is also editor of *Auto/Biography: An International and Interdisciplinary Journal*.

Nancy Theberge is Professor at the University of Waterloo, Canada, where she holds a joint appointment in the Departments of Kinesiology and Sociology. She holds a Ph.D. in sociology from the University of Massachusetts at Amherst. She has published widely in the sociology of sport and the sociology of the body, and is the author of *Higher Goals: Women's Ice Hockey and the Politics of Gender* (State University of New York Press, 2000), winner of the North American Society for the Sociology of Sport Outstanding Book Award in 2001. She served as the Editor of the *Sociology of Sport Journal* from 2002 to 2004 and in 2005 received the Distinguished Service Award from the North American Society for the Sociology of Sport. Her current research is on the medicalization of the sporting body and the system of sport medicine professions in Canada.

Patricia Vertinsky is Professor of Human Kinetics and Distinguished University Scholar at the University of British Columbia, Canada. Her research programme focuses on the history of the gendered body, especially in relation to health and physical activity. She is the author of *The Eternally Wounded Woman: Doctors and Exercise in the Late Nineteenth Century* (1990, 1994); *Sites of Sport; Space, Place and Experience* (2004, with John Bale), *Disciplining the Body in the Gymnasium: Memory, Monument and Modernism* (2004, with Sherry McKay). Her ongoing projects include an investigation of Dartington Hall and a remarkable series of educators of the body who passed through there during the 1930s, and a study of the social construction of obesity in the twentieth century. She is past president of the North American Society of Sport History and Vice-President of the International Society for Physical Education and Sport History.

Loïc Wacquant is Professor of Sociology at the University of California, Berkeley, and Researcher at the Centre de sociologie européenne, Paris. His interests span comparative urban marginality, incarnation, ethnoracial domination, the penal state, and social theory and the politics of reason. His recent books include *Body and Soul: Notebooks of an Apprentice Boxer* (2004); *The Mystery of Ministry: Pierre Bourdieu and Democratic Politics* (ed.) (2005); *Das Janusgesicht der Ghettos und andere Essays* (2006); *Parias urbains: Ghetto, banlieues, État* (2006); and *Deadly Symbiosis: Race and the Rise of Neoliberal Penality* (2006). His ongoing investigations include a carnal anthropology of desire and a historical sociology of racial rule on three continents. He is co-founder and editor of the interdisciplinary journal *Ethnography*.

Acknowledgements

Our collaboration in editing this book was a natural outcome of our shared interest in the significance of the body in sport and exercise and of our professional communications and friendship over many years. Patricia was able to use her position as Distinguished Scholar in Residence at the Peter Wall Institute of Advanced Studies at the University of British Columbia to host a special conference in October 2004 for all the contributors. Financial support for the conference from the Social Science and Humanities Research Council of Canada and the Peter Wall Institute of Advanced Studies was much appreciated.

Particular thanks go to Patricia's two research assistants, Christiane Job and Ellexis Boyle, who helped with the planning of the conference and were on call throughout the event to make sure that everything ran smoothly and all our practical needs were catered for. All the people who came to the conference from the University of British Columbia and other local universities joined actively into the discussions about the book, resulting in a creative exchange of ideas.

Several of the chapters in the book are rich with original data resulting from interviews and communications with people who were generous with their time and willing to provide sensitive and personal information. We are grateful to all the research participants and to other people and organizations that facilitated the research processes.

Thanks also go to all the contributors to this text who made the difficult job of editing manageable by responding to requests and queries speedily and in good spirit; and we are most grateful to Mabel Yee who so efficiently did all the secretarial work, putting the book into the correct format and collating the original complete draft that was sent to Routledge.

Finally, our thanks go to Chris Crump for producing original art work for the cover of the book. He has symbolically captured some of the themes that run through the book – the relationship between the 'natural body', the constructed body, and the cyborg body in the main image, and the relation between the body and society in the depictions of historical sporting statues around a stadium for elite events.

Series editors' preface

Our bodies are implicated in everything we do – in birth, in death, in work and in leisure, whether we are young or old, rich or poor, men or women, heterosexual or bisexual, able-bodied or disabled, from the developed or the developing world, religious or atheist, members of a elite sports teams, or people who prefer hill climbing, and everything in between. These multiple identities, which are shaped by the different divisions and layers of society and our relations within them, are fundamentally and irredeemably embodied identities. A fascination with such infinite complexities of embodiment has spread in recent years throughout academia and is reflected in an escalation of publications about the social and cultural meanings attached to our bodies.

This collection of essays makes a key contribution to the field, being the first to concentrate specifically on physical culture by focusing on very diverse activities in which the physical, moving body is the primary focus. As co-editors of the Routledge Critical Studies in Sport series, we are delighted to both be included in its production: Jennifer Hargreaves as co-editor with Patricia Vertinsky and author of one of the chapters, and Ian McDonald as author of another chapter. We were both with the other contributors at a seminar in Vancouver in October 2004, convened specifically to encourage discussion and the exchange of ideas about the book's orientation and content. This is the second edited text in the Series where the contributors have been able to meet together prior to publication so that the book is more than a loose collection of essays, but one that has common themes and orientations.

So how, throughout this publication, do we make sense of the multiple images, complexities, and contradictions of disparate topics and fields, such as the body politics of fascism and Islam; the depiction of the bodies of young women and striptease artists in history and the present day; personal accounts of bodily feelings in boxing and disability; links between the nature of sport, the body and 'race'; the manipulation of, and dangers to the body in elite sport; and representations of the technologized body? The obvious starting point was to demonstrate the links between the personal body and the social body and to consider the significance of relations of power – in other words, in order to understand the historical and social construction of different bodies in different contexts, a key concern was to investigate links between the minute and personal aspects of the physical body, large-scale social arrangements, and the organization of power.

Another concern – which relates to all the books in our Series – was to link empirical material to theoretical ideas. In some chapters particular theorists and concepts are explicit, in other contributions, they are implicit. Common to them all is the critical stance – a rejection of essentially descriptive narrative, a deconstruction of the taken-for-granted, and a quest for the complexities of embodiment. The relation between 'nature' and culture, rather than a separation of the two, is another feature that runs through the book, as does the sense of contradiction between the emancipatory and repressive tendencies of the body.

If there is one particular characteristic of the book that most stands out it is that the human body – however 'natural', customary, and staid it might seem to each of us as individuals who live in it – is utterly indeterminate with continually shifting and irregular properties. In line with the understanding that the body is socially constructed, this book turns on its head the separation of Nature and Culture and the conventional mind-body dualism of Cartesian thought by providing examples of ways in which the body mediates biological processes and is essentially cultural and social. It provides confirmation that bodies are no longer exclusively the property of science and medicine, and the focus specifically on physical culture is an unusual and fascinating way of integrating physical and social bodies.

Given the focus on sport, it could be said that all books in this Series are organically linked to the body, but we think that a book that has the body as its *raison d'être* is important. It verifies that embodiment is partial and biased and highlights the significance of the body to issues of liberation and domination. We hope that this collection makes a worthy and distinctive contribution to analysing the politics of the (moving) body. Certainly, it is clear that studies of social experiences and manipulations of the body are needed for us to understand better what in the past we have taken for granted as something so personal such that we think we know all about it.

Jennifer Hargreaves (University of Brighton)
Ian McDonald (University of Brighton)
SERIES' EDITORS

1   Introduction

Jennifer Hargreaves and
Patricia Vertinsky

In October 2004, contributors to this book met together in the beautiful surroundings of the Peter Wall Institute of Advanced Studies at the University
of British Columbia in Vancouver, Canada.[1] As news of the meeting and the
topic spread around the university, what was initially conceived of as a closed
event blossomed into a conference with the same title as the book – *Physical
Culture, Power, and the Body* – that included faculty and graduate students
as well as some outsiders from other local universities. The attraction was
'*the body*'.

Except for the work of anthropologists, where the body has been prominent since the nineteenth century, very few academics from other fields have
shown an interest in the significance of the body and embodiment until
recent years. Sport historians and sociologists were some of the first, writing
about the sporting body since the 1970s,[2] but it was Bryan Turner who first
showed a concern to develop 'a genuine sociology of the body' when he
wrote *The Body and Society* in 1984. During the decade that followed, leading
up to the publication of the second edition of *The Body in Society* in 1996,
Turner claimed that there had been 'a flood of publications concerned with
the relationship between the body and society, the issue of embodiment with
relation to theories of social action, the body and feminist theory, and the
body and consumer culture' (p. 1). And now, another decade later, there is
a generalized and enthusiastic recognition of the cultural and social significance of embodiment in every aspect of life and culture among scholars
throughout the humanities and the social sciences, as well as in areas of
science and technology (Featherstone and Turner 1995: 2; Shilling 1993,
2005), paralleled by an explosion of interest in the body in popular culture.
Interest in the body is everywhere. The body matters.

This collection is part of this trend, but it has a particular orientation
that sets it apart from other publications for it focuses upon the neglected
issue of the body-in-movement. The outpouring of writings on the body has
had little to say specifically about *physical culture* (Kirk 1999), which is the
focus of this book. By physical culture we are referring to those activities
where the body itself – its anatomy, its physicality, and importantly its forms
of movement – is the very purpose, the raison d'être, of the activity. The

chapters in this book are concerned with a preoccupation with the body, a cultivation of the body by means of motor activity – in other words, our focus is on the active body; in the case of disability, the body that once *was* active (Chapter 8), and in the case of the technologized body, one that *suggests* humanity and immanent movement (Chapter 12). The book makes reference to a range of activities, including dance (Chapter 2), female striptease (Chapter 6), and various sports and other forms of physical recreation and exercise.

The different chapters cover different historical periods and social contexts, but a key feature of them all is the relation between the personal and the social body. This is fundamentally a relation of power linked to other key people, ethnicities, genders, histories, ideologies, religions, institutions, and politics. Taking account of the personal and the social derives from social constructionism, an approach which 'interprets the human body as a system of signs which stand for and express relations of power' (B. Turner 1996: 27) and uses deconstructivist techniques – essentially the techniques of questioning and critiquing the taken-for-granted in order to uncover mythologies and conflicts. B. Turner (ibid.) argues that, 'Deconstructivist techniques, anti-foundationalist epistemology and feminist theory have provided powerful tools for treating the body as a problematic text, that is as a fleshly discourse within which power relations in society can be interpreted and sustained. The critique of the text of the body therefore leads into a critique of power relations within society.'

In each of the chapters of this book, it is clear that the particular body in question is socially constructed – influenced, changed, adapted, reproduced according to social relations and social structures – and that integral to these processes are unequal relations of power. Even in the case of the paralyzed body which is physically unable to move and therefore appears to be resistant to social constructionism, in the very personal accounts of disabled ex-rugby players in Chapter 8, we can see how their experiences of bodily impairment are part of culture, how they are linked to the world outside their bodies by the immediacy of physiological and practical needs, and how their sense of time and feelings of loss are mediated by personal circumstances as well as the wider politics of disability. This *relation* between individual body processes and social processes has influenced the writing of each of the chapters in the book.

The nexus between the personal, the social, and relations of power is integral to the argument in Chapter 10 that the character of postmodern sport spills over into other aspects of personal and social life in society, described for this reason as a 'sportocracy'. The personal–social–power link is also very obvious in the case of embodiment and political interventions – such as in Nazi Germany, referred to in Chapters 2 and 3 – in the context of which two individuals, Rudolph Laban and Max Schmeling, negotiate political strictures and construct the dancing body and the boxing body, respectively. In the context of Islam (discussed in Chapter 4), politico-religious ideologies, tied to patriarchal domination, ensure that the personal lives and bodies of Muslim women are circumscribed by political and social structures of power; and in Chapter 11 the discussion focuses on how the concrete force of racist ideology is a major influence on the individual sporting careers of black athletes. The link between the personal and the social in the other chapters is made through examining: (i) the political and social processes that enable sport medicine to claim the athletic body as an object of practice and how medicalization is implicated in the construction of athletic identities (Chapter 9); (ii) the way in which the individual bodies of young women in the USA are represented in the publicity material of the Women's Sports Foundation (Chapter 5); (iii) the social and cultural milieu of post-war Canada that was the location for commercialized female striptease artists and elite sportswomen (Chapter 6); (iv) the ways in which technologies are intertwined with physical bodies by means of visual digital culture (Chapter 12); and, finally, (v) the experiences and attitudes of prize fighters in the USA – especially those concerning the boxer's body – that are influenced by the different dimensions of the boxing subculture and the social world outside (Chapter 7).

The examples of the body in physical culture outlined above are wide ranging. Each of the chapters confirms for us that the body has undeniable biological and physiological characteristics that appear as 'natural' and indisputable in commonsense thinking, but that these very personal and personalized beliefs are only experienced and understood within a social context. In other words, there is a clear relationship between the anatomy of the body and social roles, so that our bodies are at the same time part of nature and part of culture.

The concept of the 'natural' body is deconstructed throughout the book. In some of the chapters there is a very real sense in which the 'original' body is manipulated. Elite sport provides a context in which, through numerous performance-enhancing techniques, the character of the body is dramatically altered, appearing to be inauthentic and 'unnatural'. The most extreme examples of such bodily alienation took place in the German Democratic Republic (GDR) during the cold war, when a systematic hormonal high-dosage doping programme was promoted by the government. Women and adolescent girls were targeted because the amazing improvements in their sport performances greatly increased the medal count and national prestige. But very damaging side effects were widespread, grossly and often irreversibly changing body morphology and function. Girls experienced strong virilizing side effects, induced ambiguous sex characteristics, including androgenous facial features, excessive chest and pubic hair growth, lowering of the voice, and disturbances in libido. Liver damage, long-term amenorrhea, acne, and severe gynaecological disorders were regular occurrences (Franke and Berendonk 1997). The case of the GDR athletes is extreme, but other less damaging body-changing and performance-enhancing techniques remain endemic in elite sport. Although the medicalization of Canadian elite athletes, described in Chapter 9, is a far less dramatic and more 'humane' example of intense sport training procedures, claimed to be in keeping with the traditional amateur ideals of fair competition between 'natural' athletes, it is another level of the same 'culture of risk' based on body modification. Grosz (1994: x) claims that, 'The body has . . . remained colonized through the discursive practices of the natural sciences, particularly the discourses of biology and medicine.' If a continuum were drawn between the idealized 'natural' body at one end and the most extreme form of constructed body, then the technologized, virtual, alien body described in Chapter 12, would be at the latter end. Even in the case of cyborg bodies, there is a sense in which they are 'flesh and blood bodies' because they are imbued with human-like features, poses, clothes, and actions, so that there is confusion about what is 'real' and what is imaginery. Advances in technology have blurred the boundaries between body and machine. For example, in the case of amputee athletes with prosthetic legs, there is further confusion about authenticity and ownership of the body. The issue of body modification is not insular to physical culture and sport – society would be unrecognisable without the constant and systematic application of technology to bodies of all types and backgrounds and in all contexts. Shilling (2005: 173) argues that:

> The idea of 'technological bodies' . . . suggests not only that the work-based and other contexts in which we live have become more techno-logically dominated than ever before, but that productive techniques and knowledge have moved *inwards*, to invade, reconstruct and increasingly dominate the very contents of the body. This raises the possibility that the spatial and functional arrangements of the organic properties of our bodies have been altered in line with the structures of society, and to an extent which challenges conventional notions of what it is to be and to have a body.

The idea of the 'natural' body is a mythology, but it is an idea that is hung onto and reproduced, especially in contexts where the biological is used as an explanation for cultural inequalities and discrimination. Defined as biological determinism, this is a process that occurs in relation to gender and 'race' differences. In spite of evidence to the contrary, and for different reasons, both women and black Afro-Americans and Afro-Caribbeans are considered to be close to 'nature'. Over the years, their bodies have become the properties of science and medicine, tied to the idea of a 'fixed' 'natural' state whose sporting and exercising activities have been understood in terms of causal biological explanations. The female body has been conceptualized and repre-sented as 'natural' flesh embued with a caring, maternal, and gentle character, an identification that is used to restrict women's cultural roles. For example, Chapter 4 illustrates how in establishment male discourse, the association of Muslim women with nature is used to control their bodies and limit women's involvement in sport and exercise. The black male body has also been aligned with nature, but differently, through its association with brute strength, physicality, and innate athletic superiority, doubled with an implied intellectual inferiority. Examples of racial discrimination based on stereotypes of black male bodies in sport and the ideology of 'natural' superior black athletic prowess are explored in Chapter 11. There are similarities about the naturalizing of bodies in Chapter 10, where the commodification of the black body and black culture are explored as intrinsic to the idea of a 'sportocracy', characterized as a 'raciological' structure. It is not the actual biology or physiology of women or black men that is oppressive, but the meaning attached to their biologies within a specific social system and organization. And there is an added complexity to our understanding of gendered and racialized bodies. Gender and 'race' are not separate structures of difference, but intersect and overlap with others, such as age, class, and disability.

Bourdieu (1984) defines embodiment as a bearer of symbolic value that reflects social divisions – such as class, gender and racial divisions – and is integral to the maintenance of social inequalities. He uses the term habitus to describe 'a system of dispositions' or 'a way of being' that encompasses a 'predisposition, tendency, propensity, or inclination' relating to a person's social location (1995: 214). Bourdieu's concepts of habitus, field, and capital are very relevant to the sociology of dance, for example, despite the fact that he has been criticized for not directly addressing performance and movement experience (Shusterman 2002; Turner and Wainwright 2003). In the examples of physical culture in this book, we can recognize different ways in which social divisions based on unequal relations of power and domination are mediated through the body. Bourdieu maintains that the specific opposition between masculine and feminine, based on the body, constitutes 'the fundamental principle of division of the social and symbolic world' (1995: 93).

Specifically in relation to gendered relations of power and domination in the examples of physical culture referred to in this book, Judith Butler's concept of 'performativity' is helpful. Performativity refers to the idea of actively and intimately 'doing', 'sensing', and 'living' gender, which renders the notion of an innate or imposed gendered self inadequate. Butler (1993: xv) herself explains that, 'The view that gender is performative sought to show that what we take to be an internal essence of gender is manufactured through a sustained set of acts, posited through the gendered stylization of the body.' So gender for Judith Butler is, like sexuality, not 'naturally' ascribed, but a changing social construct, concretely expressed, but also fluid and changing through public performance. She argues that discourse produces: 'the regulatory norms of "sex" (that) work in performative fashion to constitute the materiality of bodies and, more specifically, to materialize the body's sex, to materialize sexual difference in the service of the consolidation of the heterosexual imperative' (1993: 2).

All bodies are essentially gendered and racialized in all forms of physical culture. And all gendered and racialized bodies result from relations of power. Because the focus in physical culture is on the body and the ways in which it moves and performs, the characteristics of masculine in relation to feminine bodies, and white in relation to black bodies are always visible and frequently exaggerated. Connell (1987: 85) has shown how 'The social definition of men as holders of power is translated not only into mental body-images and fantasies, but into muscle tensions, posture, the feel and texture of the body.' This characterization is especially clear in relation to the specifically hyper-masculine bodies of boxers portrayed in Chapters 3 and 7, and memories of the muscular and aggressive bodies of white male rugby players are essential to an understanding of their lived sense of post-accident disability portrayed in Chapter 8. Sexualized and commodified femininities are in different ways the focus of Chapters 5 and 6, and we are introduced to an exaggerated and idealized (and technologized) version of heterosexual femininity in Chapter 12. Body images of sexualized females reflect the changed meanings surrounding the body with the demise of industrial capitalism and the rise of leisure and consumerism society in which physical culture plays an important role (Davis 1997: 1–2). According to Baudrillard (1998: 144), it is sexuality itself which is offered for consumption, and he goes on to describe the body as 'the finest consumer object' as follows:

> its omnipresence (specifically the omnipresence of the female body . . .) in advertising, fashion and mass culture; the hygienic, dietetic, therapeutic cult which surrounds it, the obsession with youth, elegance, virility/femininity, treatments and regimes, and the sacrificial practices attaching to it all bear witness to the fact that the body has today become an *object of salvation*. It has literally taken over that moral and ideological function from the soul.
>
> (p. 129)

The idea of bodies as objects of salvation is especially relevant to the bodies of the young women in Chapter 5 who are portrayed as subjects for improvement in the marketing and publicity material of the WSF in the USA. Post-industrial culture focuses on physical culture for leisure and enjoyment, but also for the moral value and personal responsibility of keeping the body young and fit. The equating of fitness with goodness, followed by success, is signalled as an imperative pathway for the young women who are targeted. But if the body was not an object of constant attention and interpretation it could not be effective in this way as a means both of self-identification and social communication. B. Turner (1996: 27) points out that, 'Feminist writers have been concerned to reject the equation of the good body with the good person as the underlying principle of aesthetics in contemporary culture.' Feminist criticism is directed at the constant flow of commodified, fetishized, and idealized images of heterosexual femininity that fill new markets, and in particular with the obsession in publicity and advertising material with the explicit sexualization of the female body, often compared to pornographic representation (Hargreaves 1993).

In an attempt to capture the historical dimension of the body in society, B. Turner (1996: 1) uses the term 'somatic society', 'namely a society within which major political and personal problems are both problematized in the body and expressed through it'. We can see, then, that the body is change-able, malleable, according to private desires and troubles, public issues, and political demands. Bodies are part of a signifying process of meaning and identification. In the case of art and artistic movement such as dance, B. Turner (2005: 2) further raises the issue of the performing body and the complex relationship between performance, embodiment, and representa-tion. Dance, he points out, opens up an important research field in which we can study connections between the lived body in relation to state formation, national culture, and globalization. Dance has a natural language by which human beings convey meaning through organized performances, and it is this issue that we are drawn to in Chapter 2, which examines how Rudolph Laban's movement choirs and modern dance arrangements provided a powerful means for both celebrating existing social arrangements and cul-tural ideas and for imagining and advocating new ones. Dance, it is claimed, is 'corporeal politics', bringing people together in rhythmic affinity while expressing histories and embodied identities through movement (Turner 2005).

In the different forms of physical culture included in the book, we can see that the private body is made public and understood through its activities, movements and gestures, clothing and other accoutrements, and as a result of the social relations intrinsic to the activity. For example, in the case of the Chicago boxing club described in Chapter 7, the rituals of sparring, the physical appearance of the boxers, the 'body language', and the accompany-ing social interaction reflect an *inner* identity and communicate a *public* identity. The body has become, par excellence, a means of self-expression, described by Giddens (1991) as the essence of an 'identity project' which, in high modernity, has become hugely complex, incorporating and producing multiple identities. T. Turner (1994: 28) suggests that:

> This new 'life politics' (Giddens 1991) of personal identity has focused so largely on issues of bodiliness because . . . the appropriation of bodi-liness, in all its aspects, from sexuality and reproductive capacities to sensory powers and physical health, strength, and appearance, is the fundamental matrix, the material infrastructure, so to speak, of the pro-duction of personhood and social identity. What is at stake in the strug-gle for control of the body, in short, is control of the social relations of personal production.

The essential significance of the body lies in the intimate interconnectedness between the physical and the social dimensions of experience. Who we are, how we look and feel, what we do, our relations with others, our hurdles, struggles and aspirations, the organizations we belong to, and our under-standing of the social world, are all features of the politics of the body. In other words, we are embodied in every aspect of our everyday experiences. Dutton (1995: 11) describes how our lives and identities are centred on our bodies:

> What subject, after all, could be closer – either figuratively or literally – to our human concerns? The body is the focal point of our individual identity, in that we not only *have* but in a sense *are* our bodies: however distinct the body may be conceptually from the 'self' which experiences and knows it, that which experiences and knows is by its nature an *embodied* self, a self whose social identity and whose location in time and space are contained and defined by their individual embodiment.

In each contribution to this book it is possible to see how the body symbol-izes identity at the levels of both the personal and the social; how identity is constructed within the body, and how representations of the body specific-ally in physical culture are assigned meaning and influence identity. While theories relating to the social construction of the body proliferate, creative ethnographies of embodiment are less plentiful. One of the most graphic ways of understanding about bodily identities is to listen to personal stories (Sparkes and Silvennoinen 1999) – a research approach used in a number of chapters. Participant observation and autobiography are the methods used in Chapter 7 by Loïc Wacquant, allowing us to 'get under his skin' by means of his very personal, intense, and insightful feelings of body and selfhood as he works out and spars with professional boxers in a working-class subculture in Chicago. Andrew Sparkes and Brett Smith interrogate the life-histories of ex-rugby football players who have suffered spinal cord injuries, enabling the reader to understand their sense of body alienation and identifi-cation as disabled. These are methods that explore the connection between body, self, and identity. In Chapter 6 the very explicit and moving interview stories of strippers and professional female athletes illustrate clearly various aspects of identity linked to social differences such as class, ethnicity, femi-ninity, and sexuality, as well as to their identities as entertainers. Chapter 4 shows quite poignantly how the accounts of some Muslim women tell us about their struggle for identification and their sense of hybrid identity in the face of local–global disputes about their bodies. In Chapter 9, interviews with sport medicine practitioners working with elite Canadian athletes reveal how they construct their professional identities as they negotiate the 'dialectic between the cultures of risk and precaution' and the tensions between performance and health. Because these very personal stories have never been told before, they make available to us for the first time specific embodied practices that would otherwise have been hidden from history. Furthermore, allowing analysis to evolve from the narratives and locating them in specific contexts and historical periods results in a realistically authentic understanding of body and identity.

Another aspect of the body that is featured throughout the book is its very complex and contradictory character. At first glance physical culture appears to be a free, autonomous activity incorporating the body in ways that are personally enriching. But as we can see in different chapters, it is simultaneously a site of constraint and contestation. Referring to contemporary times, T. Turner (1994: 46) explains that, 'The body . . . has become the focus of fundamental contradictions between the emancipatory and repressive tendencies of the social, cultural and political order of contemporary capitalism.'

For Foucault (1979, 1980, 1981), the body is a site of discourses of power, an object of discipline and control. Burkitt (1999: 45), discusses Foucault's use of the term 'bio-power' – particularly relevant to Chapter 3 – as follows:

> A form of power exerted over the population and over the bodies of individuals, disciplining them and regulating them, and turning them into rational and calculable machines. Through bio-power, life is brought into the field of political calculation and manipulation and there develops a bio-politics of the population, fascism being one of the most extreme examples.

Referring to consumer culture, Foucault noted a shift in control of the body from control by repression to control by stimulation. The best examples in this book are Chapter 5, in which young women are enticed to exercise with the promise of securing well-toned, sexually attractive, good-looking and healthy bodies; and Chapter 9, where the chance of an Olympic medal will attract athletes to the rigours of elite training procedures at the expense of positive health and well-being. But Foucault fails to engage fully with the idea of the body as the source of consciousness, subjective will, and activity – the 'lived' body. Referring to Foucault, Csordas (1994: 12) asks the question, 'What about the body as a function of being-in-the-world, as in the work of Merleau-Ponty (1996) for whom embodiment is the existential condition of possibility for culture and self?' Lyon and Barbalet (1994: 50) introduce the concept of 'embodied agency', suggesting that, 'the current interest in the body in social theory generally fails to emphasize the body as agent' and 'The human capacity for social agency, to collectively and individually contribute to the making of the social world, comes precisely from the person's lived experience of embodiment.'

The examples of physical culture introduced in this book confirm the argument that although the body is subject to social power, it is not simply a passive recipient of it. For example, in Chapter 4, some Muslim women have negotiated for all-female venues and events in order to take part in sports of their choice, while other Muslim women have re-interpreted the Qur'an in order to take part in mainstream international competitions. In Chapter 6, both the striptease artists and top sportswomen articulate clearly how they present themselves in their respective activities in order to suit themselves. Embodied agency is accompanied by meanings, associated with desires, needs, and emotions. Participants cannot engage in physical culture simply as and when they like; they are constrained by circumstances and social inequalities, by ideologies, politics, and in ways that relate directly to the physical body. But agency arises from within regulatory practices and the body in physical culture can also be a site of relative freedom and personal empowerment.

Frank (1991: 47) makes the important point that:

> People construct and use their bodies, though they do not use them in conditions of their own choosing, and their constructions are overlaid with ideologies. But these ideologies are not fixed; as they are reproduced in body techniques and practices, so they are modified. The 'government of the body' is never fixed but always contains oppositional spaces.

The idea that embodiment is never neutral should be held in mind throughout the reading of this book. It is an idea that is confirmed through examples of the dialectic between body and society and between agency and constraint in specific instances of physical culture. The following descriptions of the chapters signal the range of usages of the body in physical culture covered in the book and the complexities of embodiment in physical culture in different historical, social, and political contexts.

With their focus on the dancing and sporting body, Chapters 2 and 3 both take on, in different ways, Foucault's complaint that the term 'fascism' is in need of historical analysis. 'There lies beneath the affirmation of the desire of the masses for fascism a historical problem which we have yet to secure the means of resolving' (Foucault 1980: 139).

Chapter themes and outlines

In Chapter 2, Vertinsky points out that while Susan Sontag in 'Fascinating Fascism' (1974: 79) has taken Leni Riefenstahl to task for her efforts to cast herself during Germany's Nazi years in the role of the individualist-artist defying philistine bureaucrats and censorship by the patron state, biographers of Germany's dance master Rudolf Laban have been more reticent. By all accounts Rudolf von Laban was an extraordinary man: a visionary, mystic, artist, modern dancer, choreographer, womanizer, charismatic teacher and theorist. Like Riefenstahl, who herself took classes in creative dance, he worked closely and willingly with the Nazis. It was only when he incurred Goebbel's displeasure on the eve of the 1936 Olympics that he felt compelled to flee, finding refuge at Dartington Hall in southwestern England.

In her chapter, Vertinsky examines Laban's later career in England and his impact upon the gendered world of physical education and modern dance in

British schools, while questioning the influence of his professional relationship with the Nazi leadership upon his approach to modern dance. Sontag suggests that, with the turn of the cultural wheel, it perhaps no longer matters whether Riefenstahl's Nazi past is viewed as acceptable or not, or whether we believe that her stated concern for simple beauty underlay all her work. Vertinsky argues, however, along with McDonald in the following chapter, that the extent to which the dancing, or sporting body, hinders or harbours a fascist aesthetic and ideology is worthy of investigation. She suggests that a critical view of Laban's work alerts us to provocative ways in which expressive movement and dance might be viewed as forms of kinaesthetic imagination capable of transmitting cultural (and political) memory through movement. From this perspective dance creators and their creations can be understood as unavoidably taking part in contests over the construction of gender and race, class and age, as well as struggles between political theories and regimes.

Laban elaborated the notion that modern dance could be a vehicle for conveying important ideas through choreographed public festivals and movement choirs which were ready receptacles for fascist propaganda and expressions of party devotion in the Third Reich. Is it possible, Vertinsky asks, that the creative dance activities promoted by Laban and his devoted assistants for British children during the postwar years were similarly infected with fascist aesthetics, or did the potency of his philosophy fade in the everyday context of the primary school gymnasium and the changing realities of educational policy and practice in the 1960s?

In Chapter 3, McDonald's interest in fascism centres on the male sporting body. Fascism certainly took the sporting body seriously, forcing consideration of the extent to which the dominant culture of sport autonomously but systematically produces bodily dispositions and cultural traits that are prone to fascist aesthetics and ideologies. This is a much rehearsed debate (Tannsjo 1998; Holowchak 2005), as are those drawing on issues surrounding the role of physical culture in Weimar and Nazi Germany, but McDonald provides a provocative and well-grounded analysis of the political somatics of fascism which shows us how fascism was, and continues to be, used as a powerful epithet in political debate.

To support his central contention that the sporting body is not inherently 'fascistoid' but rather takes on an ideological form that in particular contexts can either serve or undermine the political culture of fascism, he draws upon the example of boxer Max Schmeling whose triumphal victory over Joe Louis in New York in 1936 became the stuff of legends. Indeed, the Louis–Schmeling fights, with their extraordinary cultural and political significance, have been analyzed more than any other boxing matches in history. Shrewd enough never to have joined the Nazi party, in part because he was depending upon American (i.e. Jewish-managed) boxing for a lucrative career, Schmeling benefited from the patronage of the highest-ranking Nazis and the admiration of Hitler. Like Laban, he readily gave the Nazi salute and never appeared to have agonized over anything at the time. Till recently, their bio-graphers have given them both what Margolick (2005) calls 'an undeserved free pass', or have suffered what Judt (2005) claims is a case of Waldheimer's disease.[3] McDonald accepts that Schmeling was, at different points, both within and outside the Nazi camp and that this ambiguity shows how the sporting body possesses a degree of autonomy that enables a range of pos-sible articulations with fascism. From this perspective, the role of physical culture and sport in postwar contemporary fascisms remains a critical focus for students of the body. Fascism, he reminds us importantly, resonates inside our democracies as well as outside them.

Hargreaves continues the focus on politics and the body in Chapter 4. She addresses the sporting possibilities of Muslim women at a time when in-depth and nuanced understandings of the cultures and peoples of the Middle East are much needed by Western readers. She shows how the bodies of Muslim women in sport are experienced and mediated through different ideological interpretations of Islam, within the particular political arrange-ments of specific countries in ways that are coloured in varying degrees by patriarchal relations of power and control. This is a challenge given that struggles within Islamic societies over political, cultural, and social differ-ences 'are entangled within a history of imperialism and resentments against a modernity dominated by the same powers that have colonized the many worlds of Islam for more than a century (and continue to do so with the complicity of native elites)' (Dirlik 2005: 18). Diversity within Islam is both spatial and temporal – indeed Islam stands out for the impossibility of locat-ing it within identifiable boundaries (Huntington 1997). Hargreaves warns against monolithic assumptions about Islam and Muslim women's identities and their bodies, and reflects on one of the central questions facing women in Muslim societies: combining Islam and modernity without embracing Westernization in the creation of alternative modernities (see also, Ozyegin 2006).

An important issue for Hargreaves lies in the relationship between Islam, women's bodies, and feminism. The embeddedness of women's bodies in all areas of social life, she suggests, leads to a heightened self-consciousness among Muslim women about the ways in which they think about and use their bodies – specifically whether they want to or are able to enjoy the pleasures of sport and improved health through exercise. Feminists have generally not seen sport as a major theatre for gender politics and cultural transformation and this is particularly the case in Islamic societies where Muslim feminists have failed to construct a comprehensive politics of the female body, physical exercise, health, and well-being. Instead they have focused upon more pressing aspects of patriarchal control and the fraught relationship between conservative Islam and the West. In particular 'the capacity of images of the veiled Muslim female body to provoke intense reactions both from Muslims and non-Muslims, and to eclipse Muslim women's own diversity of voices and self-definition raises significant issues for feminist debate' (Macdonald 2006: 7). The symbolism of veiling which encloses the body and greatly restricts freedom of movement is integral to Muslim female identity yet is often seen to be directly at odds with the physicality of vigorous exercise and displays of muscle and power characterized by Western sporting femininities where fitness is increasingly seen as a feminist issue (Brabazon 2006). Islamic feminists, therefore, who are committed to operate within Shariah law, do not see eye to eye with secular feminists who seek to reduce the shackles constraining Muslim women from the healthy enjoyment of sport and exercise in places or circumstances of their choosing.

Muslim sport feminists have made significant gains for sporting women, however, and Hargreaves shows how their struggles and negotiations (albeit within an Islamic framework) have resulted in changes and advances for girls and women. Led by Faezah Hashemi, an outspoken advocate for girls' and women's rights to engage in sport, Iran has become (at least for now) the leading Muslim nation for women's sport. Muslim female Olympians, although few and far between, navigate complex clothing and modesty restrictions to overcome negative attitudes toward female sport and take pride in their achievements and their symbolic reconstruction of Muslim womanhood.

In Chapter 5, third-wave feminist Leslie Heywood introduces the new term 'Girl Studies' – a subdivision of Women's and Gender Studies – and examines the language of empire and globalization as it has 'produced' girls in the United States, with sport being used to further that particular form of production. She interrogates Hardt and Negri's claim that today's global empire is fundamentally different from older forms of imperialist and capitalist expansion built upon traditional arrangements of male power and control.[4] The new convergence of neo-liberal and feminist discourses has instead led, she claims, to a growing reliance upon self-policing and active participation in consumer culture that together construct girls in terms of a 'can-do' or 'girl power' model. Thus power, opportunities, and success are all expected to be modelled by the future girl who can take charge of her life and her body with 'all the sport she can do'. Indeed, sport becomes the place where girls learn to take personal responsibility for their own lives, including physical, economic, social, and sexual health. This is a big responsibility in a tumultuous world where American girls come from diverse communities presenting multiple barriers to achievement and offering very different chances in life. It is easy to see how the ideology of individualism and personal responsibility has a noticeable disregard for social systems and institutions for it hides both the material and the discursive forces shaping identity and the ways these gendered, raced, classed, and sexualized identities provide risk or benefits.

Heywood puts a critical eye to the Women's Sport Foundation's *GoGirlGo* programme, suggesting that its 'love yourself' message might be seen by some to be empty rhetoric in a culture that is constantly evaluating and judging and presenting idealized images against which girls have to compare themselves. Sport is touted as the panacea of all problems where the image of the female athlete does the cultural work of advertising equal opportunities and demonstrating that anyone can achieve this if they only work hard enough. For those urban girls who desperately need to be the recipients of fundamental social change, such programmes may help with personal change, but it is unlikely that they will change the political, economic, and cultural structures that surround them.

In Chapter 6, Ross takes up the image of the female athlete and her (supposedly) wholesome lifestyle and compares it with the sexualized persona of the female stripper in an era that preceded the popularity of lap dancing, champagne rooms, and stage fees. Focusing upon three decades in the mid-twentieth century she listens to the stories of a number of physically talented, sexy strippers in Vancouver, Canada. Viewing female striptease as embodied exhibition, she discusses the ways in which the dancers' tales about their craft, expertise, and physical talents unsettle the stubborn 'whore stigma' that she believes continues to conflate striptease with prostitution. Furthermore, she explores how women of colour, transsexuals, lesbians/ bisexuals, and several very large women cleverly subverted the industry's strict conventions of (white, straight, buxom) female physical beauty and desirability. It is tempting here, following from Hargreaves' focus on the Muslim veiled woman, to draw attention to Western traditions that read sexual availability against displays of the body and historical associations between unveiling and sexual fantasy – where a system of looking encouraged by the veil paradoxically turns the objects of the look into eroticized subjects (Naficy 2003).

Ross then investigates parallels between the identities and careers of professional striptease dancers and elite female athletes during the same period by focusing on their touring schedules, earning power, skill and training, and career trajectories. Acknowledging that the sexualization of the female athlete has a long and vexed history, she nonetheless underscores a potent contradiction. While postwar female 'bump and grinders' self-consciously and deliberately marketed and exploited their overtly sexualized persona on stage, they were (and still are) refused membership in the community of athletically trained female performers whose expertise and embodied exhibition of sporting skills were judged to uphold ideals of graceful, agile charming femininity, and by extension upstanding patriotic and hetero-normative womanhood indispensable to the health of the Nation. In other words, given the creative athleticism consistently displayed by female striptease dancers in the postwar era in Canada and elsewhere, Ross asks what was (and is) at stake in the persistent and pernicious material and discursive abjection of these performers.

It is interesting, in light of her analysis, to see the continuing popularity of burlesque in Vancouver, and reflect upon its staying power into the twenty-first century. Ross believes that it has a lot to do with the new hold of third-wave feminism – women want the same licence to be sexual that men have always had. As she shows so well in her chapter the idea of being empowered, beautiful, sexy, and smart is really appealing, and burlesque today continues to encourage this through making fun of traditional social stereotypes.

In Chapter 7 – an edited excerpt from *Body and Soul: Notebooks of an Apprentice Boxer* (2003) – Wacquant explicates 'the social machinery of sparring as a means of inculcating the pugilistic habitus'. He does so by positioning himself as a performer so that we can follow in an unusually intimate way the experiences, feelings, rituals and strategies of the boxer. This is an insider story about the physical and emotional aspects of sparring, especially the boxer's relation to his body which is described by Wacquant as the veritable 'subject' of pugilistic practice.

Much of the debate on boxing, Wacquant says, has tended to turn on the concerns of outsiders to the game, such as the reasons why people should not box as opposed to the reasons why they do it. It focuses on the negative determinants, from economic deprivation and school failure to family disorganization, racial prejudice, and social isolation, that allegedly funnel men into the ring by constricting other options. And it authoritatively imputes a host of individual motivations to boxers, such as a thirst for material success, worldly anger, or masculine pride. However, it seldom inquires into the collective dispositions that provide a public theatre of expression and incline some young men from working-class backgrounds to devote themselves to it.

Wacquant further describes how testimony about boxing, whether for or against it, is characteristically gleaned from the pronouncements of champions as described by sports writers. Only exceptionally do boxers and club fighters, prospects and contenders, journeymen and opponents, trial horses and bums who comprise the overwhelming majority of practitioners, and without whom the boxing economy would instantly collapse, speak of their own experiences. Boxing has been described by some as the most pitiless of sports, 'primarily about being and not giving hurt' (Oates 1987: 25), but, through Wacquant's eyes and those of his informers, it becomes the most dazzling sort of pugilistic dialogue, a 'fistic conversation', an ever-renewed duel where, at their best, body and mind function in total symbiosis.

Some years ago, Lennard Davis, in *Enforcing Normalcy* (1995: xi) claimed that 'disability is the bodily state that dare not speak its name in professional circles'. Because of this, he said, and the strong control of the subject by medical and psycho-social experts, disability is under-theorized and the connections between disability and the status quo under-explored. In Chapter 8, Sparkes and Smith address both these issues through their exploration of the use of narrative in their study of three men who suffered spinal cord injuries and 'crossed the border' to become disabled through playing the contact sport of rugby football union. The traumatic injury sustained by each was the result of one moment in their life that propelled them from the world of the able-bodied into the world of disability, which they continue to inhabit.

Sparkes and Smith seek to illuminate their stories about becoming and remaining disabled by focusing upon time – or rather the ways in which personal experiences of embodied time are framed by and embedded within larger socio-cultural constellations of meaning. Lives, they point out, have to be understood as lived within time, and time is experienced according to narrative. Living with a disability is living a life dominated by time and narratives – of past, present, or future – which then become the means by which biographical experience is given meaning. Identity is constructed via narrative, and the self in time can only exist as a narrative construction. From this perspective, the complex connections between narrative, time, and identity can play an important role in how we relate to ourselves and others as embodied beings in different contexts.

The authors draw from a number of disciplines to develop various concepts and frameworks for understanding time in order to reveal how this taken-for-granted aspect of embodiment and narrative plays a pivotal role in the process of autobiographical identity construction. They then make comparisons between the three men regarding their personal experiences of time at specific moments in their lives: pre-injury; immediately following injury; and as they live at the moment. To assist in this analysis they use Arthur Frank's framework of restitution (hope of returning to able-ness), chaos (life will never get better), and quest (acceptance) narratives to show how they operate to shape the post-injury experiences of each man in relation to their (now disabled) bodies. Finally, the implications of this complex process for the identity (re)construction of disabled men are discussed.

The difficulties provoked by traumatic events such as spinal cord injury focus particular attention upon the intimate connections among body, time, self, and society and the important role of narrative in how individuals make sense of these connections as they try to make sense of their own changed lives. Disability is tied to a process that defines us all and the narrative resources at our disposal within particular cultural settings intimately affect the ways we view the ideal of physical wholeness and the category of disability.

One of the most significant developments in sport over the last several decades has been the expanding power of medical knowledge in the production and regulation of sporting bodies. In Chapter 9, Theberge investigates this process by examining the role of sports medicine, including allied health professions such as physiotherapy and nutrition, in the construction of athletic bodies and athletic identities. Her particular interest lies in: analyzing professional discourses surrounding the scope and purpose of medical interventions in sport; the political and social processes that enable sports medicine to claim the athletic body as an object of practice; and how medicalization is implicated in the construction of athletic identities.

The negative correlation between competitive sport and a healthy body and the reduction of the sporting body to the level of a machine has long been acknowledged.[5] In Ancient Greece, Hippocratic treatises warned that athletes endangered their health by paradoxically being in too good a condition. Given that such a condition could not persist for long, and since it could not change for the better, it would inevitably change for the worse (Kuriyama 1999: 141). In *Sport: A Prison of Measured Time* (1978: 17) Brohm complained several decades ago about the way countries went about building up their sport arsenal and the dangers of an obsession with winning which could no longer conceal the fact that the risks of the game were on the increase and accidents were becoming alarmingly frequent:

> Every sport now involves a fantastic manipulation of human robots by doctors, psychologists, bio-chemists and trainers. The manufacturing of champions is no longer a craft but an industry calling on specialized laboratories, research institutes, training camps and experimental sports centres. Most top level athletes are reduced to the status of more or less voluntary guinea pigs.
>
> (p. 1189)

Indeed there is no denying that injury has now become an inescapable part, not only of the careers of elite sportsmen and women, but of all athletes, as a result of increasing specialization, intensity of training and resultant overuse of parts of the body. As a result the penetration of medical intervention in sport has deepened such that athletes are understood to require routine medical supervision, not because they have a clearly defined pathology but simply because they are athletes. As Safai (2005) points out, the growth, organization, and institutionalization of sports medicine as we recognize it today have occurred alongside the negation of the amateur athlete and widespread transformations in the production of high performance sport.

Theberge's particular focus in this growing culture of pain and injury is upon the clinical practice of sport medicine and the complex negotiations which take place between high-level athletes and health care practitioners in reconciling the tensions between performance and health. She concludes from the variety of practitioners with whom she spoke that they understand that health has a different meaning for high performance athletes than for the 'normal' population, and they adjust their practices accordingly.

Abdel-Shehid welcomes us to what he calls a 'sportocracy' in Chapter 10. By this he means that the complexity of human life is reduced to a metaphoric zero sum sporting competition where someone or some group's win is always some other group's or individual's loss. One could liken the situation to Marx's 'surplus extraction' from the bosses, or the colonial enrichment of the occupier, since sporting competition simply signals the winners and the losers. From this perspective, the camaraderie, national harmony and pursuit of excellence promised by sport is all just a myth – a prison, as Brohm (1976) tells us, of measured time, for the reality of elite competitive sport constitutes a huge blind spot for social consciousness.

Sport, Abdel-Shehid explains, naturalizes all of the bodies in its purview, endowing them with particular truths and a particular voice. Thus the spor-tocracy is able to accomplish two things: first it naturalizes the social body, or body politic; and secondly, it freezes individual bodies into immutable identity categories such as male, female, black, and white.

In particular, the sportocracy shores up ideas of 'race' through its ability to singularize and naturalize bodies. More often than not, this chapter argues, race refers to black subjects, such that the black male body in sport remains over-determined as hyper-masculine and overly sexualized – 'scene and not heard'. The way out of this singularity of gaze, suggests Abdel-Shehid, is to focus on the multiple and polyvalent nature of race in the contemporary world, to incorporate notions of hybridity and to try to bring an end to the innocent notion of the essential black subject. To move beyond the sporto-cracy, then, is to engage with dissonance and to seek ways of reading black masculinity as complex and beautiful. Seeing the beauty of black masculinity clearly troubles the notion that black masculinity is masculinity constantly at war – thus it might be used as a central plank with which to work against the sportocracy.

In Chapter 11, Hoberman continues the discussion that nothing handed down from the past could keep 'race' alive if we did not constantly reinvent and re-ritualize it to fit our own terrain (Fields 1982). Like Abdel-Shehid, he points to the significance of the traditional Western habit of identifying black people with their bodies and the consequences of black dominance in some high profile sports which has reinforced this identification. Using a rich array of popular and academic sources Hoberman discusses the signifi-cance of the black athlete as paradigmatic of his race through the tropes of evolutionary narratives and related 'truths' about racial athletic aptitudes. Then he documents their effects through a stream of scurrilous racist utter-ances in the marketplace of European sports venues where we are reminded how even the most primitive tenets of nineteenth-century racial anthropol-ogy continue to flourish in the sports cultures of the early twenty-first century. Neo-fascist French politician Jean-Marie Le Pen is offered as one such example. 'The best sprinters at the Olympic Games are black', he says, 'the best swimmers are white. Is it forbidden, illegal or immoral to state that those differences are real?'

The persistence of such aggressive racism and related violence obviously raises many very difficult questions and Hoberman seeks explanations by examining various debates about nature versus nurture that seem to force a choice between genetic and environmental explanations for human traits and behaviours. He looks at a variety of creative – one might almost call them desperate – coping strategies employed by white athletes to explain their apparent disadvantages in certain sports. And in a wide-ranging discus-sion of national and global environments he shows how, although racial folklore about athletic aptitudes flourishes or is more muted depending on the racial make-up of the population, the stereotypes of aggression, vio-lence, and primitiveness continue to be played out, sustaining sport's racial dimension in the twenty-first century. Race continues to be man's most dangerous myth.

Our final chapter completes Hoberman's evolutionary narrative by focusing on virtual bodies. Yet even here visions of biotechnologies continue to be invested in a parallel physical reductionism, intensified through digital forms. In her study of virtual bodies in popular digital culture, O'Riordan underscores how the human body, and the female body in particular, has traditionally been the marker of the natural. Indeed, naturalism has served as deceptively in the modern world as supernaturalism ever did in the past. Yet, although physical bodies, like the material world around them, really exist, 'by the very nature of their existence nothing is actually self evident in the nature of the body' (Lancaster 2003: 36). While the body has been conceptualized and represented as 'natural' flesh to be formed, it has also been socialized and conditioned by culture – a cultural tail wagging the biological dog so to speak. Furthermore, as O'Riordan points out in her chapter, the body has never been tame; the excess of the body is that which disrupts social structure, resists containment and thus remains under investigation in scientific discourses.

Understandings of the body have been continually mapped, imagined, contested, and transformed through imaging techniques in medicine, art, and visual culture. In the twentieth and twenty-first centuries the scopic regimes of digital imaging technologies have contributed to an ongoing technologization of the body – 'the conceptual wall between bodies and information increasingly bleeding as bodies and information continually graft themselves onto one another in a number of different cultural domains' (Thurtle and Mitchell 2004: 1). Through these regimes the body has been rendered simultaneously penetrable, opaque, malleable, wired, and networked. We have entered an era where signifying practices and embodiment are no longer practically and conceptually separate.

O'Riordan's central question focuses on how simulations of naturalized female bodies have been reproduced in cyberspaces through new information and commercial technologies. She underscores the significance of technologies of visual communication in this process of making the body subject to a scopic control and connection. Drawing on visual culture she outlines the ways in which technologies are intertwined with physical bodies, producing understandings of those bodies as structured through technologized networks. She uses examples of mediated and virtual bodies to illustrate her argument that the body is not only restructured but also both imprisoned and empowered by these transformations and technologizations. In many respects, she suggests, and the animated digital beauty Lara Croft is but one example, the frames for visualizing the female body in contemporary communication technologies and bio-technologies remain locked into a closer reiteration of the young, white, heterosexual, female body as the 'normal' female body. For game avatar Lara Croft, movement is central to her character and her sporting body has much in common with the growing popularity of the female form as active and toned, yet as O'Riordan shows, the contextual language used to present figures such as hers also signals a powerful force for normalization and containment. By means of cyberspace bodies, concepts of nature continue to be used in the performance of culture.

Conclusion

This book aims to challenge some of the old certainties about the body and provide insights into ways in which the body is experienced and under-stood and transformed. But understanding the body is fraught with difficulty because, as we can tell from the different chapters in this book, it is the very indeterminacy of the body that stands out as a major characteristic. Furthermore, it is clearly impossible to separate bodily experience from cultural meanings and it is the dialectic between the two that results in a shaping of the body by the social world and vice-versa. The permeation of the body with specific relations of power, its location within different polit-ical and cultural fields, and the ways in which it is manipulated and experi-enced through history, culture, and wider social discourses result in a huge number of variations, complexities, and contradictions. As a result, we can only understand the body as being multi-dimensional, constantly produced, *in process.*

In 1993, Shilling summarized his approach to the development of a soci-ology of the body by claiming that, 'The body is centrally implicated in questions of self-identity, the construction and maintenance of social inequalities, and the constitution and development of societies. It is far too important a subject for sociologists to leave to the natural sciences' (p. 204). It is certainly the case that since Shilling made this statement, what was at the time a still emerging sociology of the body has become firmly estab-lished in academia, attracting scholars from many disciplines. However, a feature of this development has been a certain elitism that has tended to prioritize highly theoretical and generalized discussions about the body, with particular attention being paid to postmodern thinking and theorizing, and to marginalize a wealth of material that has focused on the body *in movement* – specifically in physical culture. For example, although the soci-ologies of sport, dance, and education have developed in recent years into very sophisticated sub-disciplines of mainstream sociology, there are very few references to sport, dance, or physical education in the work character-ized as the sociology of the body. Shilling's publications (1993, 2003, 2005) are an exception in this respect. Furthermore, in empirical studies, the trend has been to focus on men's sports, such as boxing and body building – distinctive symbols of masculinity – and far less attention has been paid to women's bodies in sport and other forms of physical culture. What is also surprising is that although the central players in the sociology of the body have recognized the foundational contribution of modern feminism and feminist theories to the more generalized recognition of the significance of the body in social life, there has been a virtual silence about the work of sport feminists. There has been little acknowledgement, either, from mainstream feminists of the work of sport feminists, much of which since the 1970s has focused on the body, and specifically on the relationship between empirical material about the personal body and specific historical and social contexts.

In contrast to the unequal gender balance of most sociology of the body publications, *Physical Culture, Power, and the Body* has an equal gender balance, both in terms of content and contributors. This is an important innovation towards a better understanding of the gendered body. But we recognize that all the other social divisions, such as age, sexuality, different ethnicities, and disability should also be given equal attention and that there should be much more notice taken of bodies outside the Western world and of the specific effects of globalization processes on them. Developments in the sociology of the body are already shifting in this direction with an expanding corpus of work on bodies in other cultures and more publications that take account of the global level of analysis as well. However, it still remains the case that despite wide-ranging work on the materiality of the body in contemporary thought, the question of the body has not yet been posed as comprehensively as it could be (Wilson 2004). Looking to the future, there is a particular need for much more attention to be given to the body in the field of physical culture across the world.

Notes

1   In her role as Distinguished Scholar in Residence at the Peter Wall Institute of Advanced Studies at the University of British Columbia, Patricia Vertinsky facilitated and organized the conference. The contributors had an exceptional opportunity at the conference to interrogate the idea of the book, to share ideas among themselves and with an audience, and to have some input towards its final orientation.
2   The two editors of this collection were among the first sport feminists to focus on women's embodiment in relation to exercise and sport. These are among their best-known publications: Hargreaves 1994; Vertinsky 1990.
3   That is an inability to remember what you did during the war, named for Kurt Waldheim, Secretary General of the United Nations, Austria's President in 1986 in a country of under 7 million inhabitants where there were still more than 500,000 registered Nazis in Austria at the end of the war (Judt 2005).
4   For Marx and Engels, globalization was a potentially liberating revolutionary phenomenon subordinating men while also providing them with the opportunity to rebel against capitalism (Hardt and Negri 2000).
5   Adorno and Horkheimer (1971) described how the oarsmen who cannot speak to one another are each of them yoked in the same rhythm as the modern worker in a factory.

Bibliography

Adorno, T. and Horkheimer, M. (1971) *Dialectic of Enlightenment*, London: Allen Lane.

Baudrillard, J. (1998) *The Consumer Society: Myths and Structures*, London: Sage Publications.

Bourdieu, P. (1984) *Distinction: A Social Critique of the Judgement of Taste*, London: Routledge.

Bourdieu, P. (rep 1995) *Outline of a Theory of Practice*, trans. R. Nice, Cambridge: Cambridge University Press.

Brabazon, T. (2006) 'Fitness is a feminist issue', *Australian Feminist Studies*, 21(49): 65–83.

Brohm, J. M. (1978) *Sport: A Prison of Measured Time*, trans Ian Fraser, London: Ink Links Ltd.

Brown, N. and Szeman, I. (2002) 'Michael Hardt and Antonio Negri interviewed by Nicholas Brown and Imre Szeman', *Cultural Studies*, 16(2): 173–92.

Burkitt, I. (1999) *Bodies of Thought: Embodiment, Identity and Modernity*, London: Sage Publications.

Butler, J. (1993) *Bodies That Matter: On the Discursive Limits of 'Sex'*, New York: Routledge.

Connell, R. (1987) *Gender and Power*, Cambridge: Polity Press.

Csordas, T. (1994) 'Introduction: the body as representation and being-in-the-world', in Csordas, T. (ed.), *Embodiment and Experience: The Existential Ground of Culture and Self*, Cambridge: Cambridge University Press, 1–26.

Davis, K. (1997) *Embodied Practices: Feminist Perspectives on the Body*, London: Sage.

Davis, L.J. (1995) *Enforcing Normalcy: Disability, Deafness and the Body*, New York: Verso.

Dirlik, A. (2005) 'Performing the world: reality in the making of world histor(ies)', *German Historical Institute Bulletin*, 37(18): 9–25.

Dutton, K. (1995) *The Perfectible Body: The Western Ideal of Physical Development*, London: Cassell.

Featherstone, M. and B. S. Turner (March 1995) 'Body and society: an introduction', *Body and Society*, 1(1): 1–12.

Fields, B. J. (1982) 'Ideology and race in American history', in J.M. Kousser and J.M. McPherson (eds) *Region, Race and Reconstruction*, Oxford: Oxford University Press.

Foucault, M. (1979) *Discipline and Punish: The Birth of the Prison*, New York: Vintage.

Foucault, M. (1980) *Power/Knowledge: Selected Interviews and Other Writings, 1972–1977*, Colin Gordon (ed.), trans C. Gordon, L. Marshall, J. Mepham and K. Soper, New York: Pantheon Books.

Foucault, M. (1980) 'Body/Power', in C. Gordon (ed.), *Michel Foucault: Power/ Knowledge*, Brighton: Harvester.

Foucault, M. (1981) *The History of Sexuality. Vol.1: An Introduction*, Harmondsworth: Penguin.

Frank, A. (1991) 'For a sociology of the body: an analytical review', in M. Featherstone, M. Hepworth and B. Turner (eds), *The Body: Social Process and Cultural Theory*, London: Sage Publications, 36–102.

Franke, W. and Berendonk, B. (1997) 'Hormonal doping and androgenization of athletes: a secret program of the German Democratic Republic government', *Clinical Chemistry*, 43, 1262–79.

Giddens, A. (1991) *Modernity and Self-Identity*, Cambridge: Polity Press.

Grosz, E. (1994) *Volatile Bodies: Toward a Corporeal Feminism*, Bloomington and Indianapolis: Indiana University Press.

Hardt, M. and Negri. A. (2000) *Empire*, Cambridge, MA: Harvard University Press.

Hargreaves, J.A. (1993) 'Bodies matter! Images of sport and female sexualization', in C. Brackenridge (ed.), *Body Matters*, Leisure Studies Association Publication No. 47, 60–6.

Hargreaves, J.A. (1994) *Sporting Females: Critical Issues in the History and Sociology of Women's Sports*, London: Routledge.

Hargreaves, J.A. (2000) *Heroines of Sport: The Politics of Difference and Identity*, London: Routledge.

Holowchak, A. (2005) ' "Fascistoid" heroism revisited: a deontological twist to a recent debate', *Journal of the Philosophy of Sport*, 32: 96–104.

Huntington, S. P. (1997) *Clash of Civilizations and the Remaking of the World Order*, New York: Simon and Schuster.

Judt, T. (2005) *A History of Europe since 1945*, New York: The Penguin Press.

Kirk, D. (1999) 'Physical culture, physical education and relational analysis', *Sport, Education, and Society*, 4(1): 63–73.

Kuriyama, S. (1999) *The Expressiveness of the Body and the Divergence of Greek and Chinese Medicine*, New York: Zone Books.

Lancaster, R. N. (2003) *The Trouble with Nature. Sex in Science and Popular Culture*, Berkeley, CA: University of California Press.

Lyon, M. and J. Barbalet (1994) 'Society's body: emotion and "somatization" of social theory', in T. Csordas (ed.) *Embodiment and Experience: The Existential Ground of Culture and Self*, Cambridge: Cambridge University Press, 48–68.

Macdonald, M. (2006) 'Muslim women and the veil: problems of image and voice in media representations', *Feminist Media Studies*, 6(1): 7–23.

Margolick, D. (2005) *Beyond Glory: Joe Louis vs. Max Schmeling, and a World on the Brink*, London: Bloomsbury Press.

Naficy, H. (2003) 'Poetics and politics of the veil: voice and vision in Iranian post-revolutionary cinema', in D.A. Bailey and G. Tavadros (eds) *Veil: Veiling, Representations and Contemporary Art*, London: Institute of International Visual Arts.

Oates, J. C. (1987) *On Boxing*, New York: Doubleday.

Ozyegin, G. (2006) 'Review of gender, politics and Islam and new Pythian Voices: women building political capital in NGOs in the Middle East', *Gender and Society*, 20(1): 129–32.

Safai, P. (2005) 'The demise of sport medicine and the Science Council of Canada', *Sport History Review*, 36(2): 91–114.

Shilling, C. (1993) *The Body and Social Theory*, London: Sage Publications.

Shilling, C. (2003) *The Body and Social Theory*. 2nd edn, London: Sage Publications.

Shilling, C. (2005) *The Body in Culture, Technology and Society*, London: Sage Publications.

Shusterman, R. (2002) *Surface and Depth: Dialectics of Criticism and Culture*, Ithaca, NY: Cornell University Press.

Sontag, S. (1974) 'Fascinating Fascism', in *Under the Sign of Saturn*, Toronto: McGraw Hill Ryerson.

Sparkes, A. and M. Silvennoinen (eds) (1999) *Talking Bodies: Men's Narratives of the Body and Sport*, Jyväskylä, Finland: SoPhi.

Tannsjo, T. (1998) 'Is our admiration for sports heroes fascistoid?', *Journal of the Philosophy of Sport*, 25: 23–34.

Thurtle, P. and Mitchell, R. (2004) 'Data made flesh: the material poiesis of informatics', in R. Mitchell and P. Thurtle (eds) *Data Made Flesh: Embodying Information*, New York: Routledge.

Turner, B. (1984) *The Body and Society*, London: Sage Publications.

Turner, B. (1992) *Regulating Bodies: Essays in Medical Sociology*, London: Routledge.

Turner, B. (1996) *The Body and Society*, 2nd edn, London: Sage Publications.

Turner, B. (2005) 'Introduction: bodily performance: on aura and reproducibility', *Body and Society*, 11(4): 1–18.

Turner, B. and Wainwright, S. (2003) 'Corps de ballet: the case of the injured ballet dancer', *Sociology of Health and Illness*, 25(3): 269–88.

Turner, T. (1994) 'Bodies and anti-bodies: flesh and fetish in contemporary social theory', in T. Csordas (ed.) *Embodiment and Experience: The Existential Ground of Culture and Self*, Cambridge: Cambridge University Press, 27–47.

Vertinsky, P. (1990) *The Eternally Wounded Woman: Women, Exercise and Doctors in the Late Nineteenth Century*, Manchester: Manchester University Press.

Wacquant, L. (March 1995a) 'Pugs at work: bodily capital and bodily labour among professional boxers', *Body and Society*, 1(1): 65–94.

Wacquant, L. (March 1995b) 'Why men desire muscles', *Body and Society*, 1(1): 163–80.

Wilson, E. (2004) *Psychosomatic: Feminism and the Neurological Body*, Durham, NC and London: Duke University Press.

2 Movement practices and fascist infections

From dance under the swastika to movement education in the British primary school

Patricia Vertinsky

Introduction

In drawing our attention to the legacy of a fascist aesthetic that underpins the theatricals of contemporary politics, sports' scholars have quite logically focused on the hegemonic masculine sporting body (see, for example, Kruger 1999). Fascism certainly took the sporting body seriously, forcing considerations of the extent to which the dominant culture of sport autonomously but systematically produces bodily dispositions and cultural traits that are prone to fascist aesthetics and ideologies (McDonald 2006). Hitler famously expressed his total embrace of the masculine sporting body in *Mein Kampf*:

> In my castles a generation of young men will grow up who will be the terror of the world. I want forceful young men, majestic, awesome, fearless; without weakness or gentleness ... I want my young men to be strong and beautiful. They should have a physical preparation in all sports. I want them to be athletic. This is first and foremost.
>
> (Rauschning 1990: 100)

More recently, and in contrast to Norbert Elias's theorization of the civilizing process, George Bush's post 9/11 initiatives to instil a military spirit into the bodies of American citizens make it increasingly difficult to distinguish civilian from militarized bodies, in sport as well as the military. Gym culture, for example, has become a type of militarized labour where the desire to continually work out encompasses both the longing to consume and the yearning to surrender the body to state, God, or corporation. In this sense, says Bryan Turner (2003), charisma and sacred violence still pulsate today in the heart of human societies.

My intent in this chapter, however, is to shift the frame of reference from sport, masculinity, and violence to other embodied practices that more subtly might have the potential to be infected with fascist aesthetics using the example of modern dance, especially its incorporation into physical education in England in the years following WW2.[1] Although sport and dance are conventionally viewed in the west as residing within separate and even opposed cultural realms they share a common status as techniques of the body as well as the capacity to express and reformulate identities and meanings through their practised movements and scripted forms (Dyck and Archetti 2003: 1). One can argue that the embodied practices of dancers and athletes afford aesthetic and skilled accomplishment, but more critically they provide a powerful means for both celebrating existing social arrangements and cultural ideas and for imagining and advocating new ones. Both ballet and football, for example, are about movement, contact, lifting, carrying and falling, and rushing to and fro (Schechner 2002: 42). Performance theorist José Muñoz (1999: 14) claims that dance sets politics in motion, bringing people together in rhythmic affinity while expressing histories of embodied identities through movement. In this sense dance performances create, express, and articulate cultural and social knowledge: a way of being in the world. If embodied practices such as modern dance are both symptomatic and constitutive of social relations, informative ways of experiencing and knowing the world, then tracing the context within which they were nurtured and their diffusion from one group or area to another, along with the changes and reinscriptions that occur in this transmission, might illuminate shifting ideologies attached to bodily discourse, including the mediating effects of gender (Desmond 1997: 33).

We have sophisticated theoretical lenses through which to approach questions around the ideological moorings of physical culture practices. Marcel Mauss (1973), for example, wrote penetratingly of the social dimensions exhibited in particular styles of movement such as walking, swimming, and dancing. He was among the first to explicate the cultural importance of what he called 'techniques of the body', that is the ways in which, from society to society, people learn through education and imitation to use their bodies in a variety of instrumental ways.[2] In this sense, the inculcation of specific body techniques involves not only the transmission of knowledge and skills but can be linked to larger social processes and purposes and to the 'proselytizing of particular schemes of preference, valuation and meaning' (Dyck and Archetti 2003: 9). Pierre Bourdieu (1988: 80–2) further developed these ideas, taking Mauss's notion of 'habitus' and placing attention upon systems of habits and predispositions that become inculcated in the body in everyday life, along with the use of instruments or technologies. By understanding these habituations he felt that we could better comprehend the utilization of sports and organized forms of movement practices by authoritarian regimes, as well as the ways in which the articulation of movement signals group affiliation and group differences – whether consciously performed or not (see also Sterne 2003). Thus, empirically, he was particularly concerned with exploring how embodied actions structure how a person thinks, feels and acts, and how they become ingrained in an individual's psyche so that they act intuitively or unconsciously (Frew and McGillivray 2005).

Henning Eichberg (1997) has amply demonstrated how the prevailing notion of competitive sport is only one of many ways in which the moving physical body can be configured in modernity. He has attempted to recon-stitute the field of practices from which sport was historically singled out by focusing upon the relationships between sport and other kinds of body techniques such as dance and gymnastics. Michel Foucault (1980: 97), by attending to the ways in which power relations shape the culture of the body through biopower, and a wide range of disciplinary techniques, has helped us to realize more fully how the body has been brought increasingly within the orbit of professional power. He shows how in a number of ways 'subjects are gradually, progressively, really and materially constituted through a multiplicity of organisms, forces, energies, materials, desires [and] thoughts . . .'. Norman Bryson (1997) makes a persuasive Foucauldian case for examining sites where forms of dance have been central to the announcement and maintenance of operations of power leading to a broader theorization of how social meanings are constituted and contested through embodied practices. And, of course, issues of gender are integral to all these theories and to any examination of embodied practices such as dance and physical education, given that movement serves as a marker not only for the production of gender, but also racial, ethnic, class, sexual, and national iden-tities. Indeed, dance is a practice that often accentuates gendered conventions while also revealing racialized practices and cultural mores around sexuality.

My chapter, then, steps into the gendered world of modern dance and physical education through a critical examination of the work and influence of Rudolf von Laban, Germany's most famous theorist of modern expres-sive dance (*Ausdruckstanz*) in the first half of the twentieth century, as a way to examine how ideas and belief systems become embedded in (or infect) particular systems of embodied practices. By all accounts, Rudolf von Laban (1879–1958) was an extraordinary man – a visionary, a mystic, artist, dancer, choreographer, womanizer, charismatic teacher, and theorist. He led an extraordinary life, one intimately bound up with the political, social, and cultural upheavals that formed the turbulent backdrop of modern Europe. Yet surprisingly, in the decades following his death in 1958, few of his pupils or scholars have attempted to analyze his work, which has tended to evoke either unconditional support or immediate criticism. Laban worked closely and willingly with the Nazis as Germany's dance master before incurring Goebbels' displeasure on the eve of the Berlin Olympics. He became one of a number of Hitler's émigrés who were given refuge at Dartington Hall, a unique arts and educational community in the Devonshire countryside of southwestern England set up by Leonard and Dorothy Elmhirst in 1925.[3] The progressive Dartington ethos and Laban's later emphasis upon modern dance, educational gymnastics, and movement as an educational force – especially the eager cooptation of his work by female physical educators – had a widespread and relatively unexamined impact upon British primary schools in the two decades after WW2. Those female physical educators who interpreted and promoted Laban's complex and often mystical views were intensely aware of the significant role movement could play in everyday living and behaviour. They believed that something of the personality of the doer was revealed in every movement task, making the human body a channel of expression and medium for serving the group as a whole. They encouraged both the senses of selfhood and citizenship to be nurtured through their teaching of movement practices tied to Laban's theory and methods.

It is axiomatic that the field of movement is given form and substance through the interactions of individuals and groups in particular time–space localities (Kirk 1992). One can see how powerful ideas were constructed around particular embodied practices in different contexts and in response to a range of very different circumstances when one tries to look at the political ground trodden by Laban in Germany and that of his physical education followers in England. *Ausdruckstanz* embodied a cluster of ideologies that had dominated German thought during the nineteenth century, including the notion of art as the handmaiden of politics. Laban elaborated the notion that modern dance could be a vehicle for conveying important ideas through choreographed public festivals and movement choirs which were ready receptacles for fascist propaganda and expressions of party devotion in the Third Reich. But, as a reluctant émigré to England in the late 1930s, he was pressed to rely on the training of predominantly female physical educators to earn a living. When the British primary school child became the thrilling object of the gaze of their authority, with the belief that the crafting of moving bodies along Laban's principles was transformational, it seems appropriate to ask whose political ground they were treading, and whose mystic cannons they were firing in the primary school gymnasium. Certainly, male physical educators of the time had their own doubts about the 'credibility' of Laban-inspired modern dance and its derivative educational gymnastics, and contributed to a stormy gendered debate around control over content and method in physical education.

Laban's path to Dartington

> How can one associate the choreographer that was with the industrialist [and movement specialist] he became? In 1936 he was the internationally acclaimed Director of Dance in Berlin at the height of his career. Two years later he was a disillusioned and penniless refugee at Dartington Hall in the English countryside.
>
> (Hodgson 2001: 8)

Laban's path to Dartington was clearly a troubled one. Unlike many German writers and artists, he remained in Germany during the Third Reich and came to terms with National Socialism before finally falling out of favour with Joseph Goebbels in 1936. He was not, of course, the only artist or modern dancer who was complicit with the Nazis, and the association between *Ausdruckstanz* and National Socialism has come under vigorous investigation concerning the connections which can be drawn between artistic form and political ideology.[4] Susan Sontag (1974: 85), for example, has long complained about efforts to 'rehabilitate' the reputation of filmmaker Leni Riefenstahl by suggesting that she could hardly claim an absent-minded acceptance of propaganda in her desire to portray 'pure beauty' independent of the material world. Any screening of *Triumph of the Will* negates the possibility of that filmmaker having an aesthetic conception independent of propaganda. Turning to Laban, whose star pupil Mary Wigman was one of Riefenstahl's early dance teachers, Marion Kant (2002: 44) insists that Laban's involvement with the Third Reich (and its effects upon his later work) needs to be taken more seriously and not ignored as an embarrassing episode or mental lapse. This has been made more difficult says Toepfer (1997: 99) by the fact that 'Laban fabricated a powerful mystique and his disciples have perpetuated an aura of mystery surrounding him with a rhetoric that is sometimes even murkier than his own'. Kant further insists that the 'Laban legacy' was tainted by his years under Nazism even though elaborate explanations have tended to exonerate him of intentional attachment and collaboration with Nazi views.

By his own account, Laban took his ideology with him when he fled to Dartington Hall, from where he was helped to 'sell its parts' in the British schools (Kant 2002: 59). We cannot assume that he simply abandoned his mystical religious commitment, his occult and racist views, his reactionary politics, or that his ideas and belief systems, nurtured in nineteenth-century German Romanticism, were not deeply embedded in the modern dance practices his pupils and supporters found so promising for the education of the British body. Furthermore, Laban's powerful gift for motivating people (especially his women disciples) to pursue ideals that are not easily understood needs to be considered further. 'After a session with Laban', said Joan Littlewood (1994: 72–3), an important figure in modern theatre in Britain, 'you began to look at the world with different eyes, as if he had changed its colors or its shapes.'

Laban's early years, the road to Berlin and 'German dance' in the shadow of Nazi Germany

Born in 1879 to a well-off military family in Bratislava, Laban was a man of his time. He wrote later of his love for sports and physical exertion from his earliest years, and his fascination at observing people's movements, especially in natural surroundings (Laban 1935: 16). His wanderings took him to the centres of artistic thought during times of great debate concerning the nature of aesthetic experience (Foster 1977: 46). In Paris he became caught up in the artistic ferment of the avant-garde where artists sought experimental modes of expression through movement to portray 'the new man' (Preston-Dunlop 1994: 110). Dancing especially was celebrated as an erotically charged and intoxicating activity in a Nietzschean sense on a par with war and sports. In this milieu he painted in his studio in Montparnasse, contemplated Delsarte's approach to gesture and movement and became deeply influenced by Kandinsky's (1911) theories around movement and abstractions in art.

In 1912, Laban visited Dalcroze's rhythmic institute in Hellerau, near Dresden, before leaving to Ascona, a centre of counterculture in the Swiss mountains overlooking Lake Maggiore where artists such as Paul Klee and Dadaist Hugo Ball communicated with an assortment of rebels against contemporary culture and the perceived oppressions of city, industry, and technology.[5] He practised there as dance teacher and psychosomatic healer organizing a *Schule für Lebenskunst* (School for the Art of Life) on Monte Verità where his followers could get in touch with nature, renounce 'civilizational influences' and mount festive celebrations of the spiritual life.[6] Man, he proclaimed in Nietzschean terms, must grow beyond his everyday existence to reach a state of collective 'festive' being through dance and movement practices, which included a large dose of nudism, sexual adventure, and nature worship (Koegler 1974: 4).[7] In one of his earlier choreographed dances *Sang an die Sonne* (Song to the Sun), he encouraged his pupils to dance naked and barefoot to the rising and setting sun in a mystic encounter with nature (Wollen 1995: 159). It was during this period, says Toepfer (1997: 99), that Laban perfected his strategy of ensuring the legacy of his pedagogical ideas by cultivating powerful erotic-physical relations with his female students. 'Come hell or high water I would have done anything for Laban at that time', said Mary Wigman (Sorrell 1973: 43).

With the outbreak of WW1, Laban, now penniless and ill, moved to Zurich with his second wife, Maja Lederer, their children and his mistress, Suzy Perrottet. Here he engaged with the early flowering of Dada, the secret seductiveness of Freemasonry and almost died of influenza, before leaving hurriedly as a result of debts and his dubious reputation for womanizing and dabbling in occult ritualistic Masonic activities.[8] He fared better, however, in Germany and his choreographic career and production of dance symphonies and movement choirs began to blossom during the 1920s and early 30s.[9] By 1927 he had founded at least nine Laban dance schools in various European cities led by his former, mostly female, pupils. He had also written several books in German to explain his views on movement and dance including his system of dance notation which, assisted by Albrecht Knust, was published in 1928 as *Schrifttanz*.[10]

By 1930, his growing reputation landed him the two most prestigious jobs in dance choreography in Germany – one at the Bayreuth Wagner Festival and the other as Director of Movement at the Berlin state theatres. Wagner, said Laban (1975: 174–5) was a decisive influence on his approach to movement. 'My time under his direction was a time of unclouded joy and inspiration ... The greatest German dramatist has shown us dancers what we have to do.' Now acknowledged as a leader of the 'New German Dance' (the new term for *Ausdruckstanz*) he began work on his autobiography and applied for German nationality – all in the shadow of the nazification of Germany.

The Nazis were not slow to recognize the political potential of Laban's talent for choreographing huge operatic-dance spectacles and mass movement choirs and in 1934 Goebbels' Ministry for Enlightenment and Propaganda hired Laban to be the Director of the Deutsche Tanzbühne (German Dance Stage). This effectively placed him in charge of dance and movement throughout Germany and allowed him to remove amateur dance from his rival Rudolf Bode's League for the Struggle for German Culture, which promoted massed physical training efforts under the slogan 'Strength through Joy'.[11] His position gave him free rein to mount dance festivals and work on large-scale projects, including an international dance competition on the eve of the 1936 Berlin Olympics. His most ambitious project was a dance pageant to inaugurate an Olympiad of the Arts and when he unveiled his epic spectacle *Vom Tauwind und der neuen Freude* ('Of the Spring Wind and the New Joy') it was a celebratory ritual of music and movement redolent of the films of Leni Riefenstahl. Though Laban claimed it was designed to celebrate National Socialism it apparently did not appeal to Goebbels who attended the dress rehearsal and abruptly cancelled it. 'I do not like it', he wrote in his diary. 'Dance rehearsal freely based on Nietzsche, a bad, contrived and affected piece' (Müller and Stockemann 1993: 166).[12]

Stories differ on the exact nature of Laban's fate with the Hitler regime. He was placed under house arrest, declared a non-person with his work branded hostile to the state, and his earlier freemasonry activities denounced (Segel 1998: 87). A campaign against him in the press hinted at homosexual activities. Crushed, he eventually left Germany and headed for exile in Paris from where he was rescued by his former pupil Kurt Jooss and brought to Dartington. He never set foot in Germany again.

Laban at Dartington Hall

Despite his welcome at Dartington, Laban was depressed when he arrived and remained in ill health for most of the rest of his life. He had no money and little influence. His prospects were bleak considering his German citizenship, suspicions about his collaboration with the Nazis, his passion for 'German dance' with all its connotations, his lack of formal education and his very limited grasp of the English language. He confided wearily to his rescuer Jooss, 'I care very little whether I see a moving, dancing body ever again.'[13]

Yet within a few years, Laban's movement approach had taken the female physical education world by storm and, by the late 1950s, modern educational dance and educational gymnastics were well established in many teacher-training colleges and schools. In some respects the shift to a framework incorporating Laban's movement techniques was a perfect fit for the broader educational ideals of the time, especially Dewey's views on child-centred education and Froebel's work on creativity in the kindergarten (as well as prevalent assumptions concerning girls' schooling in general).[14] Though Joan Littlewood (1994) claimed that Laban was sidetracked into education by Lisa Ullmann, a former pupil and young German dance teacher he met at Dartington who adopted the role of his helpmate (and constant companion for the rest of his life), his ideas nevertheless had a significant impact upon education and within the physical education profession.[15] His biographer and devoted pupil claimed that 'Intuitively he knew what educationists around him needed and was able to supply it, albeit through Ullmann's assistance' (Preston-Dunlop, quoted in Foster 1977: 33).

In any case, Laban's influence on the British educational scene had preceded him through the 'missionary' work of a scattered group of women who already had some experience of continental developments in modern dance (Willson 1997: 9). An article describing his views on dance appeared in the *Journal of School Hygiene and Physical Education* as early as 1924. Sylvia Bodner, who was to become President of the Laban Art of Movement Guild, had worked with his movement choirs in Germany during the 1920s. Lesley Burrowes learned of Laban's ideas from Mary Wigman and formed a studio in London in 1932 where one of her early pupils was Joan Goodrich from Bedford Physical Education Training College for Women.[16] Goodrich, who had studied with Mary Wigman in Dresden in 1933,[17] recommended Burrowes' London studio to Diana Jordan, who thereafter published the first movement education book for British teachers in 1938, *The Dance as Education*. As dance organizer for the West Riding of Yorkshire, Jordan (1938: 62) was instrumental in promoting modern dance in girls' schools and in supporting Laban and Ullmann's earliest ventures to make a living in the world of physical education.[18] Deploring 'copy dancing' and the series of exercises in schools typically masquerading as dance, she argued that the teaching of 'movement as expression' must be the basis of dance. And while she agreed that Laban laid no claim to being an educator, she enthused that 'one quickly realizes he knows more than many professional educationists about the process of education'. Nodded her contemporaries, 'Diana understands much more than most people the backbone of Laban's thinking' (Salter 1980: 35).

Laban's Dartington location was a powerful stimulus for it already had an international reputation as an experimental centre for the arts and progressive educational thought. These experiments, reflecting the inspiration Leonard Elmhirst drew from his mentor Nobel laureate Rabindranath Tagore, were designed to combat the encroachment of modernity on rural traditions with some of the same spiritual and educational values as those found at Monte Verità, though without some of the bohemian excesses of the earlier communal experiment. Reflecting on the inter-war years, Victor Bonham-Carter (1958: 132) remembered the sheer vitality and force of this phase of the Dartington estate's activities:

People felt that Dartington was the New Eden from which people would radiate like rays from a rainbow . . . It was somehow both absurd and at the same time extremely moving. And one was encouraged to feel part of a generation, of a whole concept that was going to take over the world in some way at some future point.

(Punch 1977: 20)

The school that was established at Dartington became one of the most experimental and best-known co-educational schools in England. Its radicalism was in direct relation to its rejection of the values and practices upholding the Arnoldian legacy based on the classics, chapel, organized sport, and prefects, along with its complex apparatus of control. Nicknamed the 'village school of the Bloomsbury set' Dartington boasted among its patrons Bertrand and Dora Russell, Aldous Huxley, Ernst Freud and many other literary and artistic clients who often mingled with the residents at Dartington and aired their views.[19]

Laban profited from this changing, more experimental, climate in education when he came to promote his views on movement and expressive dance as desirable forms of schooling. At Dartington he found himself in the midst of a group of liberal intelligentsia whose communitarian, antiinstitutional, and anti-authoritarian views he might have recognized from his earlier Weimar days. In their reaction to traditional Victorian values and the trauma of WW1 and economic depression, they had a somewhat janus-like approach to social change: on the one hand welcoming innovation and modernity, on the other, seeking to preserve a cultural and rural heritage from the encroachment of industrial development and military challenges.[20] Profoundly spiritual, the new education ethos was aimed, above all, at preserving and developing the spiritual power of the child. 'The free infant, the handmaiden of the new era, would be granted the freedom to flower naturally in a remote bucolic retreat' (Punch 1977: 12). It was a very Labanite phrase.

While Laban had little to do with the two hundred or so children at the Dartington school during his recuperation at the Hall (as indeed he had little to do with his own several children), the dance and theatre activities which were ever present among the eclectic Dartington community's activities attracted his attention. In fact, when he arrived, three schools of modern dance were resident at Dartington. In addition to the Jooss-Leeder School, Louise Soelberg taught Dalcroze's Eurhythmic system and Margaret Barr led a small group inspired by Martha Graham's ideas. Not surprisingly, given their adherence to different systems, relations among the groups were often strained and Laban saw his opportunity to take over. In a letter to Leonard Elmhirst on 10 March 1939, Laban outlined a plan for a work and education centre for dance to bring them together under his rubric. 'It would be a splendid idea to join to the marvellous unfolding of the professional dancing at Dartington an organization of the modern dance chorus.'[21]

The document closely reflected his earlier plans to develop a State Dance College in Nazi Germany dedicated to the 'New German Dance'. Inside that file at Dartington, suggests Willson (1997: 17) 'lay all the elements of what Laban hoped for and tried to bring about'. War intervened, however, and there is no record of any response to Laban's ideas from Leonard or Dorothy Elmhirst. Nor is there any record of Leonard's response to another letter from Laban enclosing a copy of the programme of his festival dance project which had been cancelled by Goebbels as an example of the 'new way of body-mind training for laymen' that he had in mind to set up at Dartington.[22]

From Ling to Laban: the diffusion of modern educational dance, educational gymnastics, and movement education

When wartime exigencies forced Laban and Ullmann (as German aliens) to leave Dartington, Lisa sought work opportunities for them both in Manchester through their contacts with physical education teachers.[23] These were made easier as interest in interpretive movement (at least among some women educators) increasingly nudged aside the more rigid Swedish system of gymnastics, which had been the hallmark of professional female physical educators since the late 1890s.[24] This therapeutically oriented system, as Sheila Fletcher (1984: 55) has pointed out, was an important platform of the early British physical education training colleges, which were dominated by women who promoted the practice of Ling's scientific gymnastic system over the drills and formal calisthenics of earlier days. The system was promoted by the Ling Physical Education Association set up by female physical educators in 1899 as a national professional body to steer physical education toward Swedish gymnastics and to oversee teacher training.[25] Holiday courses for teachers were central to the founding objectives of the association and it was through this mechanism, as well as at special training courses, annual conferences, and in publications that Laban (largely through Ullmann) profiled his expressive and rhythmic movement concepts as an alternative to the 'holy principles of Ling', which focused so rigidly on orderly, corrective, and remedial aspects of exercise.[26]

The new challenges to Swedish gymnastics highlighted the growing importance of psychology in educational thinking that demanded more attention be paid to the mind while training the body. Whereas gymnastics focused on the qualitative evaluation of bodily strength and health, dance was seen to provide a medium for expression and emotion. Modern dance aimed at 'the beneficial effects of the creative activity of dancing upon the personality of the pupil', said Laban (1948: 11), 'for movement exerts a stimulating power on the activities of the mind'. Vague though it was, the idea of freeing the expressive body from rigid training and bounded spaces fitted well with the child-centred ethos of post-war England and a renewed focus on the Arts where every child could be a dancer. And although Laban had abandoned movement choirs in Germany, he still regarded guided group interaction and improvisation as central to the development of personal, social, and kinaesthetic awareness.

The Ling Association Conference in 1941 was a major platform for the expansion of modern educational dance in schools (as Laban's modern dance now became called) along with its derivative educational gymnastics, and it occurred as the Association attempted to continue its work during the austerity of wartime conditions (as well as to avoid pressures from the government to organize physical recreation into a more militaristic form).[27] Laban was the star of the conference convened by Joan Goodrich with his claim that modern dance was a type of movement useful in the schools and satisfying to mind, soul, and body. The conference organizers went on to request that the Board of Education officially promote modern educational dance in the schools while its practitioners explained it to the readers of the *Journal of Physical Education*.[28] A three-week holiday course on modern dance followed as Ullmann sought to increase their opportunities in the teacher-training domain. It was the first of 26 to be held during the next 20 years (Willson 1997: 23). In 1945, she opened the Art of Movement Studio in Manchester which became the training centre for Laban's movement concepts through a one-year supplementary training course for teachers. Shortly thereafter she helped set up the Laban Art of Movement Guild to act as a forum for the dissemination of his ideas. A year later, Laban published *Modern Educational Dance* (1946), 'the most widely read and arguably the most influential of his writings on movement and dance' (Segel 1998: 187). It was reprinted five times.

As Preston-Dunlop (1998: 219) points out, however, the problem of a close association between physical education and dance, well known to Laban in Germany, had already begun to surface. Inexperienced physical education teachers were not Laban's preferred material nor were they potential dance professionals. It was Ullmann who learned to organize the dance classes at the level of the needs of the physical education teachers, while Laban pursued the opportunity to promote his movement ideas in industrial settings with Frederick Lawrence, a management efficiency consultant.[29] She was the one who implemented her version of his ideas, Laban being 'too catholic in his intellectual and artistic concerns to devote himself exclusively to the pursuit of teacher training' (Willson 1998: 38). His influence occurred without his personal touch, and this would lead to schisms among those who interpreted his views with different degrees of rigidity (Brinson 1991: 65–6). Ullmann in particular was charged with both vagueness and inflexibility. 'Lisa's trouble', said Leonard Elmhirst somewhat uncharitably, 'was the strict limitations of her own horizon so that her technique was way ahead of her capacity to use it in an artistically meaningful way.' What this meant, some thought was 'the replacing of Laban's Bohemian outlook by an ultra conformist schoolmistresses' circle' (Foster 1977: 75–6).

Gender struggles over content and method in physical education and dance

Gender issues were at the heart of the emerging conflicts in physical education and dance (and in many respects they have remained so). As early as 1943, articles on Laban's educational work appearing in the *Journal of Physical Education* were being met with critiques that his ideas were 'over the top' (Preston-Dunlop 1998: 226). The critiques came mainly (though not exclusively) from male physical educators who were less interested in creativity and movement than they were in skill training and competitive games. Indeed, the broader the claims for modern educational dance and educational gymnastics in the schools, the more sceptical and antagonistic became the male specialists (McIntosh 1968: 261). Foster (1977: 103) suggests that Laban influenced the education of girls and young children far more than boys because of the historical accident that his early influence took place during the war years when men were still largely focused upon the military and armed combat. But the issues lay far deeper than this. Gender divisions were a defining characteristic of the physical education profession in England from its beginnings in the 1880s, affecting the very constitution of the form the subject took in schools and higher education, especially the nature of activities taught to boys and girls (Kirk 2002: 25). It was within the 'tight little specialized empire' of professional female physical educators who commanded the field of physical education that Laban's ideas flourished and eventually trumped Swedish gymnastics (Fletcher 1984: 5). It was they who helped to adapt educational gymnastics from modern dance and promote it widely within the prevailing holistic, child-centred progressivism, such that by the end of the 1950s educational gymnastics were thriving.[30] Ruth Morison from the I.M. Marsh College of Physical Education played a leadership role with her booklet, *Educational Gymnastics* (1956) in which she underscored that there was no set of progressions in this form of gymnastics, no definite starting point or step-by-step progress to the goal. Everyone, she applauded, was encouraged to work in her own time and to her own limit.

Male antagonism to such views was increasingly vocal.[31] The main complaint was that educational gymnastics and basic movement education focused on learning through discovery which failed to provide an adequate grounding in skill development or competitive games. Male physical educators blamed the personal influence of Laban over a 'mystic cult of female groupies' who were overcome by Laban's personal charm (Fletcher 1984: 136). While he was able to fruitfully combine the two approaches in his work as an industry consultant organizing rhythmic movements for workers to deploy effort in lifting and carrying, physical educators were less successful in promoting their methods.[32] Lisa Ullmann may have contributed to these difficulties for she stuck close to Laban, tirelessly shouldering the burden of proselytizing his ideas as she understood them. But as Leonard Elmhirst pointed out, she firmly discouraged discussion between female physical educators and Laban, keeping him at arm's length from any woman she thought might catch his eye and regarding those who did with a certain feline antagonism.[33]

While Sheila Fletcher (1984) and David Kirk (2002) have both documented the gender struggles around the teaching of Laban-related movement in the schools and teacher training colleges during the 1950s and 60s, I experienced them personally as a young physical education student at Birmingham University and later as a teacher at a large grammar school in north-east England. At Birmingham, David Munrow and Barbara Knapp took a firm stand on the issue. In *Pure and Applied Gymnastics* (1955), our textbook in his course, Munrow (1955: 276) developed a thorough critique of the progressive trend in physical education epitomized by movement education. 'Women physical educators', he said, 'had diluted traditional gymnastic skills by substituting generalized body awareness as a foundation for more specific movement learning.' In this sense they had overlooked the important competitive environment necessary for achieving sports skills and ability in games. Skill learning was specific, wrote his colleague Barbara Knapp (1963) in support of his views, hence repeated, directed practice was the key to mastery. Movement education could not, therefore, serve the purposes of systematic skill development. Thus while Munrow could accept 'Movement' as one facet of a broader programme of physical activities and their related skills (and indeed mandated it for the women undergraduates in his programme), he was alarmed to see movement training 'dressed in the guise of the mother of physical education'.[34] As male physical educators pushed for a focus upon increased competition and a more scientific approach to skill acquisition, tests and measurements, and strength and endurance activities, female physical educators distanced themselves from what they saw as authoritarian pedagogic practices designed to train solely for the acquisition of discrete motor skills (Lathrop and Murray 1996).

Furthermore, the whole context of physical education in the schools and in higher education was changing. Energized by the ending of the war, male physical educators looked beyond the gymnasium to the playing fields and adventurous outdoor activity options. With the rapid increase in secondary level schooling and a burgeoning demand for teachers, male physical educators soon gained the majority within the formerly female dominated profession and they championed the sports and games that had been played in elite British public schools since the nineteenth century that were now part of the fabric of the average Englishman's leisure (Jones 1987). 'We are a games playing nation', said Hugh Brown (1958: 92), Director of the all-male Scottish School of Physical Education between 1958 and 1974, 'and now we are recognizing this'. By emulating public school traditions and applying new scientific knowledge in motor learning and exercise physiology, male physical educators simultaneously enhanced their professional status in relation to their female peers (Bailey and Vamplew 1999: 82).

As well, the nature of teacher education was changing as degree programmes took precedence over diploma courses at the physical education
teacher education colleges, effectively ending their near monopoly of the
last half-century. The net result was the ascendancy of (mostly) male physical
educators who gained positions of authority in the secondary schools and
in the new BA and BEd degree courses where they promoted the scientific
acquisition of skills and the technology of fitness development. Men, said
Munrow (1956: 2), who had become the first Director of the Physical
Education degree programme at Birmingham University, 'could not at the
moment subscribe to a general account of movement training'. Marjorie
Randall (1956: 15) was one of a number to respond by invoking the qualities
of Laban's movement and suggesting 'the masculine approach [articulated
by Munrow] has become largely outmoded so far as women's work is
concerned'.

It was ironic that the rise of feminism in the second half of the century
coincided with the dissipation of the female tradition, as physical education
for women developed by women increasingly came to be controlled by
men. A feminine focus on educational dance and basic movement in physical education slowly lost its status as it became increasingly identified
with young children in the primary schools and a concern with the non-
competitive and creative aspects of the child-centred movement. A strong
emphasis upon nurturing young children and girls further underscored the
underlying premise of the early female founders of a physical education
profession that was designed to enhance traditional women's roles as wives
and mothers (Randall 1956: 19).

Taken as a whole, therefore, the child-centred progressivism within which
Laban-inspired movement education found such fertile ground at Dartington
during the 1940s and 50s received diminishing support in light of the changing realities of educational policy and practice in the 1960s. Worse, says
Fletcher (1984: 138–9), 'a form of movement/anti-movement sex war went
on right through the 1960s and still had steam at the end of the decade to
inspire the kind of comment, let us please, in the women's P.E. world, come
down to earth from these Labanite clouds'. Scrutinizing school physical
education practices in the mid 1970s, Whitehead and Hendry (1976: 26)
barely mentioned Laban and modern educational dance suggesting that 'if
teachers really believed in the values of the work as claimed by authorities in
dance, they would be teaching a great deal more than was seen in this study'.
Dance, it seemed, remained the Cinderella of education.

In any case, Laban himself was turning away from a focus on education
which he was happy to leave to Ullmann and her group of female teachers.
He said he was not comfortable with too didactic a point of view. 'My tools
can be better or worse than other peoples' and more suitable for some people
than for others. They are in no way a means to establish a method . . . or to
attract people to "Labanism" to form Labanites or Laban folk and all this
nonsense' (quoted in Ullmann 1957; see also Maletic 1987: 182). Modern

dance holiday courses maintained the teacher training link (and the main source of income), but at the one held at Dartington Hall in 1952 it was obvious that there was a clear division between the basic movement course for teachers taught by the physical educators and the special dance courses taught by Laban, one of which was specifically for men. In this course, Laban reconstructed *The Swinging Cathedral*, first choreographed and performed in Germany in 1922, and he included among the performers the Elmhirst's youngest son, Bill.

Bill's involvement with Laban's work grew from this point and he was largely responsible for buying the estate in Addlestone, Surrey to which Laban and Ullmann would transfer the Art of Movement Studio. Laban was entranced with the new site and its rural outlook, says Preston-Dunlop (1998: 261), who accompanied them to teach in the new studio. 'A modern day Ascona lay at the back of his mind . . . and the association with Darting-ton was now closer than ever.' Concerned with the future of Laban's creative work, independent of Ullmann's focus on teachers, Leonard Elmhirst set up a Trust so that Laban could pursue his research on dance notation, choreol-ogy, and the therapeutic aspects of movement that increasingly interested him. He might have died in peace had not the suicide of Allar, son of one of his mistresses whom he had abandoned in childhood, and who came to visit him in Addlestone, affected him rather profoundly shortly before his death on 1 July 1958. And Laban's death was a personal tragedy for Lisa Ullmann who continued work at the Art of Movement Studio until her retirement in 1972.[35] 'When he died I do not think she ever recovered', said one of her colleagues (Stephenson 1985: 7). For the rest of her life she acted as ambas-sador and strict guardian of Laban's work and papers even while modern educational dance, educational gymnastics, and movement education lost their prominence in British schools.

The ideological moorings of embodied practices

> The body plays what it believes and it 'enact[s]' the past, bringing it back to life.
>
> (Bourdieu 1990: 73)

It is a complicated matter attempting to disentangle bodily practices from their ideological moorings, especially where Rudolf Laban is concerned.[36] A decade after his death, dance historian Kirstein (1969) tried to explain how Laban was a powerfully infused individualistic dance-composer, a Nietszchean theorist and a Wagnerian innovator dedicated to quasi-mystical attempts to enforce the unique supremacy of movement as movement. He was clearly a man of astonishing variety, Bohemian by temperament, highly creative, relatively uneducated, and very ambitious leaving abun-dant if contradictory documentation of his ambitious enterprises. Irene Champernowne (quoted in Hodgson 2001: 78), a Jungian therapist who worked with Laban in England, described him as being 'very close to the archetype of a trickster . . . an opportunist in a way and a bit of a wizard . . . manipulating life'. 'It was a bit of genius too', she added. And throughout his life, Laban charmed (especially women, though he had several wives, many mistresses and never seems to have had time for the many children born of his relationships). Sigurd Leeder believed his magnetism was such that no woman was safe with him (Green 1986: 92). Kurt Jooss saw him as a God: 'He had a radiance . . . such an extraordinary personality that everyone became intoxicated by him.'[37]

But, as we have seen, he was also a tardy and reluctant Hitler émigré, a seemingly willing participant in the Nazis' social experiments using community dance and festival as an unpalatable social control mechanism – a fascist instrument in the toolbox of National Socialism. Laban did not participate accidentally in the Nazi regime. His theory of dance and community disposed him to arrive at the same Völkish ideas as the Nazis. He was particularly adept at working with crowds. He knew that the appeal of mass movement spectacles lay in their power to turn simple physical action into a power for building group identity around totalitarian ends (Mandell 1984). While Toepfer (1997: 301) reminds us that it is misleading 'to assume that the mass movement aesthetic inherently embodied a totalitarian vision of communal identity', the emotional effects of the dance displays in enhancing an idealized sense of belonging to a community were powerful. Could Laban fail to see or feel the enormous attraction of fascist celebrations and the overwhelming impact on participants? (Theweleit 1987: 430). Was he blind to the impact that Walter Benjamin could see all too clearly, that fascism might help the masses express themselves but it certainly did not help them to gain their rights?[38]

Laban's biographers have tended to paint a sympathetic portrait of a gifted but pained man who cooperated willingly though unthinkingly with the Nazis, seeing the regime as a problem to be circumvented, as one of the constant stream of problems in his life's work (Preston-Dunlop 1989: 123). Vera Maletic (1987: 123) claims that Laban was 'lured into the framework of Nazi spectacles'. John Hodgson (2001: 38) saw him as an innocent despite his mature years: 'an artist disdaining interest in politics in order to continue his creative work'. Perhaps, said Daniel Snowman (2002: 80), he had been naïve to believe that an artist like himself, so wedded to ideas of free expression, could survive under the Third Reich. 'Or perhaps some of his ideas, rooted as they were in the quasi-mystical integration of body, mind and soul, did genuinely correspond with those of Nazism'. Mary Wigman (who also worked willingly with the Nazis but keenly felt a lack of appreciation and support from Laban in those years) was less forgiving. 'There hovers the figure of Laban, juggling between his ideals, three-quarters of which are already lost, and a wish to survive and what one would call collaboration.'[39]

Certainly, Laban (1935: 145) did not publicly protest. It remains something of a mystery, says Hodgson (2001: 39) why a man of such idealism could brush away so many signs of Nazi atrocities. He routinely used the Heil Hitler greeting and obeyed requests to remove Jewish pupils and dancers from his companies. While he never joined the Nazi party he compromised again and again, confessing in a letter to his friend Marie Luise Lieschke that he was genuinely fond of German culture. Wherever German was spoken, he said, 'I felt at home'. There is no mention in his 1935 autobiography, *Ein Leben für den Tanz* (A Life for Dance) of any anguish over Nazi atrocities and the racist views he expressed there about the 'grotesque and unoriginal style' of Black American jazz dance were clearly supportive of Nazi views. I doubt, he said, whether the negro is capable of inventing any dance at all.[40] He worked willingly with Goebbels who wrote in his diary, 'Laban does his job well' (Preston-Dunlop 1998: 192). On 5 November 1935, Laban obtained German nationality after four years of paper work and he continued to insist that there was a future for dance in Germany, joining Wigman in renaming *Ausdruckstanz* 'German Dance' to reflect its perceived pure origins in the German *Volk* (Hodgson 2001: 131). 'We want to bring to the national community the germ of pleasure which we feel in our art. We want to place our means of expression and the language of our eager energy in the service of the great tasks which our nation is fulfilling and to which our leader is showing the way with unmistakable clarity' (Laban 1934: 5). It was not until after his fall from grace that he admitted for the first time that he was ashamed of being German.

Perhaps one must agree with Kant (2002: 43, 59) who concludes that 'there is no safe guide through the complex and confusing mindscape of Laban'. Analyzing his many writings she proposes that Laban's view of modern dance as a religious activity derived from mystical Freemasonry and focused on spiritual transcendence provides the glue or clue to understand all his undertakings, from Ascona to Berlin, to Dartington and Addlestone. If, as she shows, Laban's modern dance was a part of a carefully devised quasi-religious cultic belief system derived from the secret Masonic order of *Ordo Templi Orientis* with its links to all sorts of Rosicrucian, Eastern philosophies and Western ritualistic elements, then 'we need to rethink the entire history of its development, for it is these ideas which have seeped into the way dance is done, thought, written or spoken about'. In many respects, what Laban tested at Monte Verità was the same kind of practice repeated in Germany and then brought to England. Long after his death, Lisa Ullmann (1975: 89) herself wrote (in the annotation to Laban's autobiography) that developments at Ascona through to the present could be regarded as one coherent lineage.

When one seeks to find meaningful connections from Monte Verità to Dartington Hall they are there in abundance though one is constantly taken aback at the contradictions inherent in both communities. Monte Verità was sold in 1920 and Laban's dance commune broke up, but many of the kinds of utopian ideas around 'wholeness', the alternative life, the restorative power of nature, nudity, and the creative arts found a place in

Leonard Elmhirst's experimental community project at Dartington Hall. Rabindranath Tagore was Leonard's muse and the inspiration behind the Elmhirsts' purchase of Dartington in 1925. His school in India, much admired by Gandhi, became the model (albeit a vague one) for the Elmhirsts' joint experiment at Dartington where Laban would arrive some years later. (In fact Leonard sent Tagore's draft on his ideas about movement and physical education to Laban for comment and Laban was familiar with Tagore's poems which had been recited and danced to at Monte Verità.)[41] Dorothy Elmhirst, in particular, encouraged the arts, and her keen interest in (and financial support of) Jungian psychotherapy was extended through Irene Champernowne, who would later link up with Laban to develop movement therapies. To Dartington's founders, dance seemed particularly appropriate as a medium to recreate the traditional village atmosphere of festival and community, and professionals such as Laban were welcomed in to foster it. What was not acknowledged, of course, was the other side of Monte Verità, where the activities of life philosophers such as Laban could be seen as 'in one sense of the phrase a precursor of Nazism'. Green (1986: 238, 245) points to the conservative, irrational 'völkish' ideas expressed in Laban's work and writings, his focus upon the culture of massed group body movements which would be actively promoted by the Nazi regime, his virulently racist language and views, and his many flattering references to Wagner, which could 'surely be taken as tokens of loyalty to official Nazi taste'.

It was, however, the views on child centred and holistic education fostered in Dartington School that became the main vehicle for Laban's modern dance and movement education in the schools, and a string of his former female pupils who would implement them. Laban himself was a late and reluctant entrant to the educational world. He always needed people to take up his ideas and implement them, and he always found them – a sign perhaps that it was the man who impressed more than the theory. Their enthusiasm for promoting the 'master's work' was unbounded, but it is hard to see how the modern dance practices they fashioned in the schools were either indelibly tainted with reactionary politics, fascist ideologies, and secret cultic mysticisms or that they comprised the national revolution portended by Diana Jordan. How many young teachers had the slightest idea about the mystical 'thread' that Lisa Ullmann claimed tied Laban's many ideas together, and its significations?[42] More likely they saw the potential for modern educational dance (and movement education) to provide a means for healthy exercise and effective movement in refreshing contrast to formal gymnastics, repetitive sports skills, and forms of dance such as ballet, which was exemplified by the firm discipline placed on the body by industrial society. They may have enjoyed the idea that modern dance characterized the resistance of the body to such disciplining but they were wrong in thinking that it promised a mechanism for female physical educators to sustain their leadership in a profession slipping out of their grasp as male-oriented competitive sport, changing disciplinary paradigms, and scientific research on

motor development and skill training gained ascendancy in physical education. Dance as art all too easily lost ground in a subject-centred scientific
curriculum and it would take decades before dance began to be welcomed
back into the schools, not as part of physical education but on the heels of a
regeneration of the creative arts in education in the twenty-first century.

How then can we assess the nature and impact of Laban's movement
education and modern educational dance upon the education of the British
child? Diana Jordan and her colleagues felt that Laban had opened the flood-
gates of an ecstatic world for teachers of movement and their young charges,
inculcating them with techniques of the body which might signal group
affiliation, set politics in motion; ideologies systematically deposited in the
neuromusculature of the dancer's body (Goellner and Murphy 1995: 23).
Male commentators such as Gordon Curl (1967: 157), although fascinated
with the man, concluded by the late 1960s that 'the mystical, magical and
occult ideas which impregnate all of Laban's work render his philosophy and
theories totally unsuitable [as well as incomprehensible] for present day educational practices'. Certainly 'Laban lived in the service of his overriding
oeuvre', with little consideration for his female colleagues who did all his
drudge work (Jeschke 2000: 204). It was they who took modern dance and
educational gymnastics to the playgrounds and gymnasiums of schools in
Manchester and Birmingham, far removed in space and time from the pedagogical province of Monte Verità and the mass choreographies of moving
bodies in Berlin and Munich. Given Mauss's formulation that the body is a
territory upon which particular body techniques are inscribed, one can see
how it can become a site for the production of a certain physical intensity
that potentially has important ideological effects. Yet if Laban was trying to
re-route the express of historical progress through the bodies of English
schoolchildren his success was doubtful at best, even though his followers
did help to chart alternative routes for physical education in the culture of
British schools, at least for girls. While Sontag saw the force of Riefenstahl's
work precisely in the continuity of its political and aesthetic ideas, the
potency of the fascist aesthetic of Laban's dance philosophy surely faded in
the everyday context of the British primary school gymnasium. Unable to
transform the world through the art and religion of dance, Laban nevertheless contributed in substantial ways to our contemporary cult of the body
which has become both a widespread ideology and a growing industry. Furthermore, we need to remember that performance itself, as Jon McKenzie
(2001: 18) has pointed out, is not necessarily subversive even though it must
be understood as an emergent sub-stratum of power and knowledge. On the
other hand there is ample evidence to show how ballet, for example, has
disseminated, transmitted, and contested social and political attitudes from
the seventeenth century onwards (Roach 1996). In addition, a critical view
of Laban's work alerts us to provocative ways in which expressive move-
ment/dance might be viewed as mnemonic reserves, or forms of kinaesthetic
imagination capable of transmitting cultural (and political) memory through

movement. As Linda Tomko (1999: xv) points out in one of a surge of new and interesting studies around the broad domain of movement practices, what consideration of dance brings to a discussion of the social and ideo-logical underpinnings of embodied practices is the cry to recognize bodies as powerful sites for social and political contestation. 'Dance creators and cre-ations can be understood as unavoidably taking part in contests over the con-struction of gender and race, conflicts among classes and age groups, struggles between political theories and regimes – meaning-making systems all.'

Acknowledgements

I would like to thank the Social Science and Humanities Research Council of Canada for its generous support of this research as well as the helpful archivists at Dartington Hall, The Laban Centre for Movement and Dance in London, the Hodgson/Laban Archives at the Brotherton Library, Leeds University and the Laban Archives at the National Research Centre for Dance at the University of Surrey, Guildford. Part of this chapter can be found in 'Schooling the Dance: from dance under the swastika to movement education in the British school', *Journal of Sport History*, 31(3): 273–95, which kindly grants permission to reprint the material.

Notes

1 I use the word infection here meaning 'to imbue with some pernicious beliefs or opinions, to affect so as to influence feeling or action unfavourably' (*Websters Encyclopedic Dictionary*). I use the word fascism as a manifestation of authoritar-ian practices or inclinations linked to right-wing dictatorships or political parties such as Hitler's Third Reich although, as Lukacs (2005: 118) reminds us, fascism was largely an Italian phenomenon focused on the primary importance of the state.

2 As David Kirk (1993: 17) has pointed out, physical education, sport, and various forms of dance are all highly institutionalized and codified sets of practices which school the body, but they are only extensions and elaborations of the everyday activities of walking, running, and throwing that Mauss conceived of as essential to 'normal' existence in any particular society.

3 Dorothy Whitney Straight Elmhirst was an immensely rich and well-connected American heiress, and Leonard an idealistic English squire who had worked with Rabindranath Tagore in India. Together they established an arts and educational community inspired by an ethos similar to the Bauhaus at Dartington Hall. Among the last substantial private patrons of the arts in England their goal was to enable a new flowering of the arts that could transform a society impoverished by industrialization and secularization (Young 1996).

4 *Ausdruckstanz* argues Müller (1985: 13) was not a label for a single dance ideology with a clearly defined technique or method. It was a collective term for some highly contradictory dance forms ranging from expressive to those making polit-ical statements. For a discussion of the issues, see Burt 1998, Kew 2001 and Manning 1995: 175, who point out that it is important to note that the division between dancers who collaborated with Nazi Germany and those who left did not necessarily result from differing ethnic origins.

5 Emil Jaques-Dalcroze developed a series of gymnastic exercises designed to help students build up a sense of rhythm. His work was brought to England before Laban and acted as a platform from which Laban's work could develop (Foster 1977: 57). Hellerau was a centre of artistic pursuits and A.S. Neill worked there before returning to England to open Summerhill School. Hall (1953) attributes Dalcroze's influence on Laban to his mistress, Suzanne Perrottet, a Dalcroze pupil and one of the first rhythmicians. Both Laban and his star pupil Mary Wigman, however, came to consider Eurhythmics limited, too wooden, and lacking in dance and expression. Wigman took the best of the system and developed 'dance gymnastics'.

6 See Green 1986. D.H. Lawrence, Isadora Duncan, and Herman Hesse were among the many visitors at Monte Verità. For a discussion of D.H. Lawrence's work and its relation to the fascist body, see Guttmann 1999 and Newhall 2002.

7 Nietzsche prefigured life as an experience lived beyond conventional boundaries and which celebrated dance in particular. We should consider every day lost on which we have not danced at least once, he said in *Thus Spake Zarathustra* (cited in Ascheim 1992: 59).

8 According to Foster (1977: 15), the Masons helped Laban financially and he set up a secretive section of a Lodge for Women, but he also seems to have run into debt and created other problems for the Masons – a reputation which followed him.

9 One of his early pupils there was Kurt Jooss who became a theatre choreographer at Munster and eventually left with his dance company to Dartington Hall as Nazi belligerence toward his Jewish artists grew. Jooss became an outstanding choreographer combining insights from classical ballet and Laban's approach to movement (Adamson and Lidbury 1994).

10 Knust went on to promulgate Laban's system of notation at Bedford Physical Education Training College for Women in the UK and to introduce his ideas to the Imperial Society of Teachers of Dancing (Hodgson 2001: 102).

11 Bode was hired by the RKK to oversee massed physical training in Germany with the motto 'Strength through Joy'. Initially Laban schools became subject to Bode's organization and aims (Preston-Dunlop 1998: 190).

12 See also Kew (2001: 82) who suggests that the problem was that the epic spectacle did not sufficiently encode Nazi martial values or promote the Fuhrer cult.

13 Kurt Jooss interview with John Hodgson, October 1975, Laban Archives.

14 Scraton (1992: 42). Shortly after WW2 a White Paper entitled *Educational Reconstruction* suggested that primary education must foster the holistic potentialities of the child, their imagination, energy, and spirits. Learning by doing was especially important (Stone, 1949).

15 Littlewood maintains in *Joan's Book* that Lisa sidetracked him into education so that she could get acceptance by the education authorities, a steady income, and a regular life for Laban with no (womanly) temptations. In Toepfer's (1997: 99–101) view, however, Laban was neither a great artist nor a great theorist but rather a powerfully motivating teacher whose true medium was not the theatre but the school, the demonstration, the act of instruction.

16 Bedford Physical Education Training College for Women was at the heart of dance innovations. Revived Greek Dance associated with Ruby Ginner and the pioneering work of Isadora Duncan was introduced in 1914, including less formal and lyrical approaches to movement. Richard Smart (2001: 138) points out that the success of modern dance in its earliest stages owed much to the influence of Margaret Stansfield, the Head of Bedford, who was instrumental in sending her teachers to study with Laban's pupils in Germany. Freda Colville was the first teacher sent by Bedford to study Laban's techniques in Vienna. Eileen Harper established an experimental scheme of modern dance at Brighton around the same time. Betty Meredith-Jones was teaching at Homerton College;

Ruth Foster, Else Palmer and Myfanwy Dewey were others promoting dance in their role as inspectors and organizers in the educational system (Willson 1997: 11).

17 This was at a time one might note when Kurt Jooss and other dancers had already fled Germany.

18 See also Ruth Morison who promoted Laban-type ideas in the 1933 *Syllabus of Physical Training*.

19 Stephen Spender, an acute observer of the Bloomsbury group, considered the group to be 'the most constructive and creative influence on English taste between the two wars. It was a group suggests Snowman' (2002: 48, 53) that acted as a bridge between the somewhat circumscribed world of Little Englandism and the wider aesthetic currents of Europe during the inter-war years. Bertrand Russell is loosely grouped with Bloomsbury for his Cambridge education brought him close to a number of members of the group. He and his wife Dora had founded an alternative school at Beacon Hill before taking their children to Dartington Hall.

20 See, for example, Clough's *Britain and the Beast* (1934). The book was said to be a doughty champion of the beauty of rural England against the beast of unseemly urban development . . . and industrialism with all its foul habits of spoliation. In the preface (vi) Baden-Powell said he would like to make *Britain and the Beast* compulsory reading at all teacher training colleges.

21 Laban to Leonard Elmhirst, 10 March 1939, Dartington Archives, High Cross House.

22 Letter from Laban to Leonard Elmhirst, 10 March 1939. E (L) 45 16 Education 3/IV/36, National Research Council for Dance Archives, Surrey University, England.

23 Dorothy Elmhirst looked for an opportunity to find Laban work in the New School of Social Research in New York (which she had founded with her first husband) but it was unsuccessful because work could not also be found for Lisa.

24 Invented by Per Henrik Ling earlier in the nineteenth century, the Swedish system was developed into a system of physical training in Stockholm where a series of specific remedial exercises systematically and to military commands were performed by each part of the body in turn.

25 The Ling Physical Education Association ceased to be an examining body after 1932 when the University of London developed a diploma for physical education teachers (Bailey and Vamplew 1999: 34).

26 Holiday courses and summer schools had been the key ingredient of dance education programmes in the Weimar period. For many Laban schools it was the annual meeting point (Preston-Dunlop and Lahusen 1990: 48).

27 For example, the President of the Association criticized government plans for keep fit and organized recreation as 'Hitlerite and Christian Fascist'.

28 *Ling Association Booklet* (1941). It was in this discussion that Movement began to be spelled with a capital M. See McIntosh (1968: 260).

29 Laban's revolutionary effort analysis in industrial contexts helping workers with their movement tasks was organized in Laban/Lawrence *Industrial Rhythm* (1942) and later as *Effort* (1947).

30 The child-centred curricula, *Moving and Growing* and *Planning the Programme* were published in the early 1950s to replace the old *Syllabus of Physical Training* issued by the Board of Education in 1933. Though Laban was not mentioned by name, his influence on the documents was very clear.

31 See Willson (1997: 31) where Myfanwy Dewey wrote 'I felt sure that if one just wrote an extremely eulogistic rhapsody on your system, which to my mind is utterly astounding and alone could revolutionize our education and turn it into something living and vitally important, the remark would just be made by my men colleagues "another of those unbalanced women".'

32 See Randall (1961) for a discussion of the problem of separating gymnastics from dance.

33 Letter from L.K. Elmhirst to Foster (1972: 20). Geraldine Stephenson (1985 : 7) remembered, 'I had never seen anyone move as Lisa did. Anatomically her body was squat, broad hipped and unlikely material for a dancer. But when she was with Laban . . . she flowed in all directions.'

34 A.D. Munrow, quoted in McIntosh (1968: 268). At Birmingham, our dance instructor and teacher trainer was Christine Roberts who, in the eyes of her students, was a dedicated Labanist. Perhaps with an eye to her job, therefore she had written in the *Journal of Physical Education* (1953: 93) that 'some of us view with alarm the tendency to claim too much from movement training. Movement training cannot take the place of systematic instruction in skills.'

35 At this time it became the Laban Center for Movement and Dance directed by Marion North who shifted the focus away from education to a broader range of concerns.

36 David Caute (2003) has recently asked the same question of ballet during the Cold War. Was cold war cultural conflict to be found within the art, craft, and vision of ballet itself and what form did the clash between modernism and realism, the abstract and the concrete, assume? His conclusion is that multiple viewpoints are essential for approaching the topic.

37 Kurt Jooss, interview with John Hodgson, October 1973. Despite these statements however there is a letter in the archives from Dorothy Elmhirst to Jooss at Dartington chiding him for not making good use of Laban's talents, 20 January 1941, NRCD Archives, Surrey University, E (L) 23–2.

38 The relationship between German body culture and the rise of the Third Reich is complex, as is Laban's connecting role. Suggestions have been made that the mysticism and irrationalism of *Ausdruckstanz* and its links with the antirational nature of Expressionism in some ways facilitated the rise of fascism (Herman and Trommier 1978). Also, Green (1986: 245) describes how in many ways 'the Asconan enthusiasm led straight to Nuremberg'.

39 Preston-Dunlop (1998: 194,30) suggests that Laban's rejection of Wigman as a lover turned gradually into an uncontrolled sense of injustice during the next 20 years, which proved to be dangerous to German dance.

40 Wollen (1995: 171) describes how a splitting took place in his thinking between healthy and unhealthy primitivism, with Native American dancers, like the whirling dervishes, seen as kind of honorary Greeks.

41 Tagore (1961: 101–11). Tagore's 'Rousseauian' idea was to use education to recreate village life in rural India where villages could re-establish their social balance and their traditions. He especially focused on the importance of expressing thoughts and feelings in physical movement. Children must dance, he said. Whenever they are stirred emotionally or feel receptive to thought they need an appropriate accompaniment of physical movement.

42 Lisa Ullmann told Foster (1977: 33) that Laban once told her, 'in 200 years they will understand'.

Bibliography

Adamson, A. and Lidbury, C. (1994) *Kurt Jooss: 60 Years of The Green Table*, Birmingham: Birmingham University Press.

Ascheim, S. (1992) *The Nietzsche Legacy in Germany, 1890–1990*, Berkeley, CA: University of California Press.

Bailey, S. and Vamplew, W. (1999) *100 Years of Physical Education, 1899–1999*, Warwick: Warwick Printing Press.

Benjamin W. (1973) 'The work of art in the age of mechanical reproduction', *Illuminations*, London: Collins/Fontana.

Bonham-Carter, V. (ed.) (1958) *Dartington Hall: The History of an Experiment*, London: Phoenix House Ltd.

Bourdieu, P. (1988) 'A program for the comparative sociology of sport', in S. Kang, J. MacAloon and R. DaMatta (eds), *The Olympics and Cultural Exchange: The Papers of the First International Conference on the Olympics and East/West and South/North Cultural Exchange in the World System*, Seoul: Hanyang University Press.

Bourdieu, P. (1990) *The Logic of Practice*, trans R. Nice, Stanford, CA: Stanford University Press.

Brinson, P. (1991) *Dance as Education. Towards a National Dance Culture*, London: The Falmer Press.

Brown, H.C. (1958) 'The training of the man teacher of physical education', *Physical Education*, 50(151): 91–4.

Bryson, N. (1997) 'Cultural studies and dance history', in J.C. Desmond (ed.), *Meaning in Motion: New Cultural Studies of Dance*, Durham, NC and London: Duke University Press.

Burt, R. (1998) *Alien Bodies. Representations of Modernity: 'Race' and Nation in Early Modern Dance*, London and New York: Routledge.

Caute, D. (2003) *The Dancer Defects. The Struggle for Cultural Supremacy During the Cold War*, Oxford: Oxford University Press.

Clough, W.E. (ed.) (1934) *Britain and the Beast*, London: Reader's Union, The Temple Press.

Curl, G. (1967) 'Rudolf Laban', unpublished MEd. Thesis, University of Leicester; in Hodgson Archives, Brotherton Library, Leeds University.

Curry, W.B. (1947) *Education for Sanity*, London: Heinemann.

Desmond, J.C. (1997) 'Embodying difference: issues in dance and cultural studies', in J.C. Desmond (ed.), *Meaning in Motion: New Cultural Studies of Dance*, Durham, NC and London: Duke University Press.

Dyck, N and Archetti, E.P. (eds) (2003) *Sport, Dance and Embodied Identities*, Oxford: Berg.

Eichberg, H. (1997) 'Body culture as paradigm: the Danish sociology of sport', in J. Bale and C. Philo (eds), *Henning Eichberg. Body Cultures: Essays on Sport, Spaces and Identity*, New York: Routledge.

Fletcher, S. (1984) *Women First: The Female Tradition in English Physical Education 1880–1980*, London: Athlone Press.

Foster, J. (1977) *The Influences of Rudolf Laban*, London: Lepus Books.

Foucault, M. (1980) *The History of Sexuality, An Introduction, vol. I*, New York: Vintage Books.

Frew, M. and McGillivray, D. (2005) 'Health clubs and body politics: aesthetics and the quest for physical capital', *Leisure Studies*, 24(2): 161–75.

Goellner, E.W. and Murphy, J.S. (eds) (1995) *Bodies of the Text. Dance as Theory, Literature on Dance*, New Brunswick, NJ: Rutgers University Press.

Green, M. (1986) *Mountain of Truth: The Counter-Culture Begins: Ascona 1900–1920*, Hanover, NH: University Press of New England.

Guttmann, A. (1999) 'Sacred, inspired authority: D.H. Lawrence, literature and the fascist body', *International Journal of the History of Sport*, 16(2): 169–79.

Hall, F. (1953) *An Anatomy of Ballet*, London: Andrew Melrose.

Harmitage, J. (2003) 'Militarized bodies: an introduction', *Body and Society*, 9(4): 1–12.

Herman, J. and Trommier, F. (1978) *Die Kultur der Weimarer Republik*, Munich: Nymphenburger, Verlagshandlung.

Hodgson, J. (2001) *Mastering Movement. The Life and Work of Rudolf Laban*, New York: Routledge.

Jeschke, C. (2000) 'Review of Valerie Preston-Dunlop's Rudolf Laban: an extraordinary life', *Dance Research*, 18(1): 100–7.

Jones, S.G. (1987) 'State intervention in sport and leisure in Britain between the wars', *Journal of Contemporary History*, 22: 163–82.

Jordan, D. (1938) *The Dance as Education*, Oxford: Oxford University Press.

Journal of School Hygiene and Physical Education (July 1926), 16: 139.

Kandinsky, W. (1977, first pub 1911) *Concerning the Spiritual in Art*, trans. M.T.H. Sadler, New York: Dover Publications.

Kant, M. (2002) 'Laban's secret religion', *Discourses in Dance*, 1(2): 43–62.

Kew, C. (2001) 'From Weimar movement choir to Nazi community dance: the rise and fall of Rudolf Laban's festkultur', *Dance Research*, 2(1): 73–96.

Kirk, D. (1992) 'Curriculum history in physical education', in A. Sparkes (ed.), *Research in Physical Education and Sport: Exploring Alternative Visions*, London: The Falmer Press.

Kirk, D. (1993) *The Body, Schooling and Culture*, Geelong, Vic: Deakin University Press.

Kirk, D. (2002) 'Physical education: a gendered history', in D. Penney (ed.), *Gender and Physical Education. Contemporary Issues and Future Directions*, London, Routledge.

Kirstein, L. (1969) *A Short History of Classic Theoretical Dancing* (3rd edn), New York: Dance Horizons Republication.

Knapp, B. (1963) *Skills in Sport*, London: Routledge and Kegan Paul.

Koegler, H. (1974) 'In the shadow of the Swastika: dance in Germany, 1927–36', *Dance Perspectives*, 57: 3–48.

Kruger, A. (1999) 'Breeding, rearing and preparing the Aryan body: creating supermen the Nazi way', *International Journal of Sport History*, 16(2): 42–68.

Laban, R. (1934) *Deutsche Tanzfestspiele*, Dresden: C. Reissner Verlag.

Laban, R. (1948) *Modern Educational Dance*, London: Macdonald and Evans.

Laban, R. (1975, first published 1935) *A Life for Dance*, trans and annotated by Lisa Ullmann, London: Macdonald and Evans.

Laban, R. and Lawrence, F.C. (1942) *Laban Lawrence Industrial Rythmn/and Lilt in Labour*, Manchester: Paton, Lawrence and Co.

Laban, R. and Lawrence, F.C. (1947) *Effort*, London: Macdonald and Evans.

Lathrop, A.H. and Murray, N.R. (1996) 'Movement education: relevance in the postmodern age', *International Journal of Physical Education*, 33(2): 70–5.

Littlewood, J. (1994) *Joan's Book. Peculiar History As She Tells It*, London: Methuen.

Lukacs. J. (2005) *Democracy and Populism. Fear and Hatred*, New Haven, CT: Yale University Press.

Mackenzie, M. (2003) 'From Athens to Berlin: The 1936 Olympics and Leni Riefenstahl's Olympia', *Cultural Inquiry*, 29: 302–37.

Maletic, V. (1987) *Body–Space–Expression. The Development of Rudolf Laban's Movement and Dance Concepts*, Amsterdam: Mouton de Gruyter.

Mandell, R. (1984) *Sport. A Cultural History*, New York: Columbia University Press.

Manning, S.A. (1995) 'Modern dance in the Third Reich: six positions and a coda', in S. Leigh Foster (ed.), *Choreographing History*, Bloomington, IN: Indiana University Press.

Mauss, M. (1973) 'Techniques of the body', *Economy and Society*, 2(1): 70–88 (orig. published in French in 1935).

McDonald, I. (2006) 'Political somatics: fascism, physical culture and the sporting body', in J. Hargreaves and P. Vertinsky (eds), *Physical Culture, Power and the Body*, London: Routledge.

McIntosh, P.C. (1968) *Physical Education in England since 1800*, London: G. Bell and Sons.

McKenzie, J. (2001) *Perform or Else. From Discipline to Performance*, New York: Routledge.

McNeill, H. (1995) *Keeping Together in Time: Dance and Drill in Human History*, Cambridge: Cambridge University Press.

Morison, R. (1956) *Educational Gymnastics*, Liverpool: Speirs and Gledsdale Ltd.

Müller, H. (1985) *Jooss: Dokumentation von Anna und Hermann Markard*, Köln: Ballet-Buhnen-Verlag.

Müller, H. and Stockemann, P. (1993) *Jeder Mensch ist ein Tänzer*, Giessen: Anabas-Verlag.

Muñoz, J.E. (1999) *Disidentifications: Queers of Color and the Performance of Politics*, Minneapolis, MN: University of Minnesota Press.

Munrow, A.D. (1955) *Pure and Applied Gymnastics*, London: Arnold.

Munrow, A.D. (1956) 'Gymnastics in the secondary school', *The Leaflet*, 57(1): 2.

Newhall, M.A.S. (2002) 'Uniform bodies: mass movement and modern totalitarianism', *Dance Research Journal*, 34(1): 27–51.

Preston-Dunlop, V. (1989) 'Laban and the Nazis', *Dance Theatre Journal*, 6: 155–68.

Preston-Dunlop, V. (1994) 'Laban, Schoenburg and Kandinsky, 1899–1938', in L. Louppe (ed.), *Traces of Dance, Drawings and Notations of Choreographers*, trans B. Holmes and P. Carrier, Paris: Editions Dis Vir.

Preston-Dunlop, V. (1998) *Rudolf Laban: An Extraordinary Life*, London: Dance Books.

Preston-Dunlop, V. and Lahusen, S. (eds) (1990). *Schrifttanz, A view of German Dance in the Weimar Republic*, London: Dance Books.

Punch, M. (1977) *Progressive Retreat: A Sociological Study of Dartington High School, 1926–57, and Some of its Pupils*, Cambridge: Cambridge University Press.

Randall, M. (1956) 'The movement approach – a need for clarification', *Physical Education*, 48(145); 15–17.

Randall, M. (1961) *Basic Movement. A New Approach to Gymnastics*, London: G. Bell and Sons.

Rauschning, H. (1990) 'Gespräche mit Hitler (1940)', repr. in H. Kanz (ed.) *Der Nationalsozialismus als pädagogisches Problem. Deutsche Erziehungsgeschichte, 1933–1945*, 2nd edn, Frankfurt/M: Lang.

Roach, J. (1996) *Cities of the Dead. Circum-Atlantic Performance*, New York: Columbia University Press, 1996.

Roberts, C. (1953) 'Movement Training for Girls', *Journal of Physical Education*, 45(136): 93–6.

Salter, A. (ed.) (1980) *The Laban Centenary Symposium Report, 1979*, Goldsmiths College, University of London: Laban Center for Movement and Dance.

Schechner, R. (2002) *Performance Studies*, New York: Routledge.

Scraton, S. (1992) *Shaping up to Womanhood. Gender and Girls' Physical Education*, Buckingham: Open University Press.

Segel, H.B. (1998) *Body Ascendant: Modernism and the Physical Imperative*, Baltimore, MD: The Johns Hopkins Press.

Smart, R. (2001) 'At the heart of a new profession: Margaret Stansfield, a radical English educationist', in J.A. Mangan and F. Hong (eds), *Freeing the Female Body: Inspirational Icons*, London: Frank Cass.

Snowman, D. (2002) *The Hitler Émigrés: The Cultural Impact in Britain of Refugees From Nazism*, London: Chatto and Windus.

Sontag, S. (1974) 'Fascinating Fascism', in *Under the Sign of Saturn*, Toronto: McGraw Hill Ryerson.

Sorrell, W. (ed.) (1973) *The Mary Wigman Book. Her Writings*. Middleton, CT: Wesleyan University Press.

Stephenson, G. (1985) 'Reminiscences of Lisa', in *Memory of Lisa Ullmann*, Goldsmiths College, University of London: Laban Centre for Movement and Dance.

Sterne, J. (2003) 'Bourdieu, technique and technology', *Cultural Studies*, 17(3/4): 367–89.

Stone, L.A. (1949) *Story of a School*, London: HMSO.

Tagore, R. (1961) 'The art of movement', in L. Elmhirst (ed.) *Rabindranath Tagore. Pioneer in Education*, London: John Murray.

Theweleit, K. (1987) *Male Fantasies*, vol. 1, *Women, Floods, Bodies, History*, Minneapolis, MN: University of Minnesota Press.

Toepfer, K. (1997) *Empire of Ecstasy. Nudity and Movement in German Body Culture, 1910–1935*, Berkeley, CA: University of California.

Tomko, L.J. (1999) *Dancing Class. Gender, Ethnicity and Social Divides in American Dance, 1890–1920*, Bloomington, IN: Indiana University Press.

Turner, B. (2003) 'Warrior charisma and the spiritualization of violence', *Body and Society*, 9(4): 93–108.

Ullmann, L. (1957) 'Comments by R. Laban', unpublished manuscript, Laban Archives, Creekside, London.

Whitehead, N.J. and Hendry, L.B. (1976) *Teaching Physical Education in England – Description and Analysis*, London: Lepus Books.

Willson, F.M.G. (1997) *In Just Order Move. The Progress of the Laban Center for Movement and Dance, 1946–1996*, London: The Athlone Press.

Wollen, P. (1995) 'Tales of total art and dreams of the Total Museum', in L. Cooke and P. Wollen (eds), *Visual Display. Culture Beyond Appearances*, Dia Center for the Arts, Seattle, OR: Bay Press.

Young, M. (1996) *The Elmhirsts of Dartington*, Totnes, Devon: Dartington Hall Trust.

3 Political somatics
Fascism, physical culture, and the sporting body

Ian McDonald

Introduction

Max Schmeling, the world heavyweight boxing champion of the 1930s, died on 2 February 2005, just a few months short of his hundredth birthday. For many people, Schmeling will be forever associated with the Nazi regime. It was in 1936, despite being past his physical prime, that Schmeling defied his advancing years and his rank outsider status to beat the formidable and much younger Joe Louis, in New York. As a result, Schmeling was held up by the Nazi regime in Germany as an 'Aryan Superman'. Louis may have been stronger, a more accomplished boxer maybe, but for the Nazis, Schmeling had demonstrated a deeper and more enduring power – 'a triumph of the will'. Propaganda Minister Goebbels immediately sent his congratulations, 'I know you fought for Germany; that it was a German victory. We are proud of you. Heil Hitler!' (Mandell 1972: 120). Recognizing the propaganda value of this unexpected victory, Goebbels sanctioned the making of *Max Schmeling's Victory – a German Victory*, a film that was shown to packed cinemas (Lewis 2005). Soon after returning to Berlin, Schmeling was feted by Adolf Hitler in the Reich Chancellery (Mandell 1972: 121). For his part, Schmeling played the role of a reliable ambassador for Germany at a time of increasing international hostility. He never publicly criticized Hitler even when the persecution of Germany's Jews became clear (Margolick 2005). But the story does not end there, for Max Schmeling was not a Nazi.

The countless obituaries following his death did not portray Schmeling simply as the Nazi boxing champion. Rather, it was Schmeling's heroism outside the boxing ring, as much as inside it, that was commemorated and celebrated. When the Nazis came to power, Schmeling did not succumb to pressure: he declined to join the National Socialists; he refused to replace his Jewish trainer, the flamboyant Joe Jacobs; and he did not divorce his Czech-born wife, the film star Anny Ondra. But it was the actions taken to shelter Jews fleeing from their Nazi persecutors that seem to have marked him out as a hero, risking not only status and reputation, but also his life. This information was to emerge late in his life when two Jewish brothers told of how Schmeling hid them during a dark November night in 1938, when the

Nazis went on a rampage against Jews in what became known as *Kristallnacht* (Night of Broken Glass), described by Bauman (1989: 89) as, in effect, 'The beginning of the Holocaust'. Schmeling also helped the brothers flee to the USA, where they were to rebuild their lives as successful hoteliers (Lewis 2005). Famously, Schmeling not only survived the war and the downfall of the maleficent Nazi regime, but he went on to become friends with Joe Louis, often sending money to his erstwhile opponent who was enduring hard times in another land of racial prejudice and persecution. However, Schmeling's heroism has to be read carefully. Margolick (2005) has argued that the representation of Schmeling as a heroic anti-Nazi is as much a caricature as accusations that he was an ardent supporter of Hitler. Schmeling's relationship to the Nazi regime was decidedly ambiguous, born out of a mixture of self-interest, self-preservation, and self-respect. Thus, while he never publicly declared a position either *for* or *against* the regime, at different points he was sometimes *inside* and occasionally *outside* the Nazi camp.

In relation to the political somatic of fascism, the story of Max Schmeling is apposite. The central contention of this chapter is that while the sporting body is not inherently pro- or anti-fascist, it is nevertheless an ideological form that in particular contexts can either serve or undermine the political culture of fascism. While all physical culture and sport is, of course, ineluctably ideological, it is acutely so under fascism (Hoberman 1984). As Mangan has noted, 'The reasons are not hard to find. Sport develops muscle and muscle is equated with power – literally and metaphorically' (2000: 1). However, the ambiguous place of Schmeling in German political and sporting history points towards a more complex sporting political somatic. Though it highlights the ideological potency of the specifically *male* body within fascist discourse, it suggests that the sporting body possesses a degree of autonomy that enables a range of possible articulations with fascism.

In this chapter, my concern is with the politics of these somatic articulations: that is the extent to which the sporting body hinders or harbours a fascist aesthetic and ideology. It will also examine the pivotal role of physical culture in the construction of a fascist body 'habitus' (Bourdieu 1984). The first part of this chapter outlines the significance of the body in theorizing fascism. The second part examines the place of physical culture in the development of a fascist body and mentality. It draws on the debates surrounding the role of physical culture in Weimar and Nazi Germany. This is followed by a discussion of the role of the fascist state in promoting sport in inter-war Germany and Italy, focusing on a conceptual mapping of the different relationships between the fascist state and sport policy. The chapter concludes with some thoughts on the ways in which we might think about fascism and the contemporary sporting body. Paul Gilroy's (2000) assertion that it is necessary to analyze the extent to which fascism resides within liberal democracies, as well as outside and against them, is related to the field of sport.

Understanding fascism and the body

Academic research on fascism has burgeoned since the 1970s. The main thrust of what has been labelled 'Fascist Studies' (Griffin 1995) is the desire to disambiguate the political, cultural, and ideological nature of fascism after the trauma of the Second World War. Such were the horrors of Nazi Germany and fascist Italy that it was widely felt that to study fascism 'dispassionately' was to condone totalitarianism. It was against just such an ostrich-like stance that Michel Foucault was provoked into claiming that, 'The non-analysis of fascism is one of the most important political facts of the past thirty years. It enables fascism to be used as a floating signifier, whose function is essentially that of denunciation' (Foucault, cited in Gilroy 2000: 138). However, even though 'non-analysis' is no longer an issue, fascism continues to be used as a powerful epithet in political debate. While this may confirm fascism's pariah status in mainstream liberal democratic politics, it also makes its contemporary forms and manifestations difficult to pin down as neo-fascist ideologues and movements tactically adopt the garb of mainstream political language and presentation in their attempt to gain political advantage.

The term 'fascism' originated with Mussolini in 1919. As a mass movement, fascism first emerged out of, and as a reaction against, the wave of proletarian revolutions sweeping Europe after the turmoil of the First World War, a period of acute social crisis. However, as a form of political behaviour and ideology, fascism is not just a phenomenon of historical interest restricted to Italy or even to the range of regimes that emerged in inter-war Europe. While acknowledging the distinctiveness of national political cultures, for the purposes of this chapter I will interpret fascism as a generic term not only to describe the fascist and Nazi regimes of interwar Italy and Germany, but also as an ever-present potentiality within capitalist social relations. Therefore I capitalize Fascism when referring to the Italian movement, party and regime, and leave fascism in the lower case when I refer to the general phenomenon.

Fascism has been analyzed from a number of competing and complementary paradigms. In his survey of the field, Dave Renton (1999: 18–19) identifies the following approaches to studying fascism: psychological definitions that concentrate on the features of the authoritarian personality; Weberian definitions that link fascism to the crisis of the petty bourgeoisie; 'idealist' theories that examine the mythical and ideological character of fascism; structuralist theories that view fascism as a political response to the failure of economic development; and Marxist theories that stress the anti-proletarian and anti-democratic ideology of fascism as a mass movement based on the petty bourgeoisie, but appealing to large numbers of the 'politically homeless . . . the socially uprooted, the destitute and the disillusioned' (Zetkin, cited in Renton 1999: 102). Crucially, fascism cannot be understood in the abstract as a set of ideas alone, but neither can it be reduced to material circumstances. As Renton (1999: 106) summarizes:

Should the essence of fascism be found in the realm of ideas, or in the historical conditions which gave rise to it? . . . neither alone will suffice. Fascism is primarily a form of political mobilisation, shaped by a distinctive relationship between a particular ideology and a specific form of mass movement. It is the relationship between the ideology and the movement which is key to an understanding of fascism.

But how are we to understand the political somatic of fascism? Specifically, what is the relationship between sporting bodies and fascism as an ideology and as a reactionary mass movement? Unfortunately, the body, and especially the sporting body, has rarely been explicitly theorized in the canonical studies of fascism. Even in more recent studies, such as the otherwise exemplary *The Anatomy of Fascism* by Robert Paxton (2005), the body is only briefly mentioned, and sport is referred to in passing. The significance of sporting events like the 1936 Olympics in Berlin is completely ignored. And yet, such omissions are belied by the emphasis on the visceral nature of fascism outlined by Paxton (2005: 218) in his useful if rather expansive definition:

> Fascism is a form of political behaviour marked by obsessive preoccupation with community decline, *humiliation*, or victim-hood and by compensatory cults of *unity, energy, and purity*, in which a mass-based party of committed nationalist militants, working in uneasy but effective collaboration with traditional elites, abandons democratic liberties and pursues with *redemptive violence* and without ethical or legal restraints goals of *internal cleansing and external expansion* [italics added for emphasis].

Unfortunately, the omission of the body, *sui generis*, is not unusual in accounts of fascism. Thus, in *A History of Fascism* (Payne 1995), acclaimed as the 'most authoritative narrative history of all fascist movements and regimes' (Paxton 2005: 221), Stanley Payne constructs a descriptive typology that identifies the key characteristics of all the interwar fascist movements, based on three elements consisting of (i) fascist negations, (ii) fascist goals and (iii) fascist style and organization (1995: 7). His theoretical framework has the virtue of clarity but fails to theorize the significance of the body. Therefore what follows is an outline of, and a commentary on, Payne's schematic framework, but with the body inserted into the analysis, so providing a more appropriate theoretical framework for developing an understanding of the relationship between physical culture, the sporting body and fascism.

(i) Fascist negations

Fascism is based on a series of negations: anti-liberalism, anti-communism, and anti-conservatism. Payne argues that it is through these ideological negations that fascism derives much of its cachet as 'a form of revolutionary ultranationalism' (1995: 14). However, the revolutionary credentials of fascism have been challenged by contemporary theorists: 'They left the distribution of property and economic and social hierarchy largely intact . . . They did want a socioeconomic revolution' declares Paxton (2005: 141–2), while Slavoj Žižek (1999: 200) argues that fascism's revolutionary *rhetoric* conceals its actual conservative social role:

> Fascism emphatically does *not* pass the criterion of the act. Fascist 'Revolution' is, on the contrary, the paradigmatic case of a pseudo-Event . . . of a spectacular turmoil destined to conceal the fact that, on the most fundamental level (that of the relations of production), *nothing really changes*. The Fascist Revolution is thus the answer to the question: what do we have to change so that, ultimately, nothing will really change?

Far from representing a break with capitalist social relations, fascism is an inherent potential within capitalist modernity: as Colin Sparks comments, the 'normalcy' of social democracy 'needs to be qualified by the clear understanding that fascism is in no way abnormal' (1980: 14). Notwithstanding these caveats, there was a revolutionary dimension to fascism. As noted by Colin Mercer: 'Fascism's discourse of revolution was pitched not at the level of fundamental transformation of economic and social relations, but rather at the level of a pervasive *symbolism*' (Mercer 1986: 223). This symbolism was visually expressed through mass meetings and marches, where the goal was 'to envelope the participant in a mystique and community of ritual that appealed to the aesthetic and the spiritual sense as well as the political' (Payne 1995: 12) to affect what Paxton calls a 'revolution of the soul' (2005: 142). It is through symbolic representations that the masses are organized and mobilized under the banner of fascism, resulting as Walter Benjamin (1973: 243) pointed out, in the aestheticization of political life:

> Fascism attempts to organise the newly created proletarian masses without affecting the property structure which the masses strive to eliminate. Fascism sees its salvation in giving these masses not their right, but instead a chance to express themselves . . . The logical result of fascism is the introduction of aesthetics into political life.

An understanding of fascism as an embodied ideology is premised on an aesthetically driven externalization of the emotions, pointing to the critical significance of physicality and movement in fascist politics. Unlike the other ideological 'isms': conservatism, liberalism and socialism; fascism eschewed rational argument and the authority of great thinkers, in favour of appealing mainly to the 'soul' of the masses by the use of ritual, carefully stage-managed ceremonies, and intensely charged rhetoric. As Paxton observes, in this sense fascism was 'a new invention created afresh for the era of mass politics' (2005: 16), an era that was above all, a 'visual age to be dominated by visual culture' (Payne 1995: 13). Fascist leaders attempted to elevate the masses into a new realm of politics, 'that they would experience sensually: the warmth of belonging to a race now fully aware of its identity, historic destiny, and power; the excitement of participating in a vast collective enterprise' (Paxton 2005: 17). To the extent that reasoned debate was replaced with the authority of immediate sensual experience, fascism succeeded in introducing 'aesthetics into political life'. And the ultimate fascist aesthetic experience was war, which brings us back to Stanley Payne and the second element of his theory of fascism: fascist goals.

(ii) Fascist goals

According to Payne (1995: 9), 'Fascists were even more vague about the shape of their ultimate utopia than were members of most other revolutionary groups, because the reliance on vitalism and dynamism produced a mode of "permanent revolution".' However, he concedes that for some forms of fascism, and Germany would be the prime example, the goal is the creation of a nationalist authoritarian state and the creation of an expansive Empire through war and conquest. These goals derive from conditions of its growth. Fascist regimes emerge out of and as a response to economic crises. Indeed it is precisely the ideological incoherence and consequent fragility of fascism that allows it to survive and thrive in conditions of crisis. Fascism is a product of a crisis, but also heightens the crisis to apocalyptic levels in order to keep the nation on a permanent war footing and a constant state of mobilization. Commitment, mobilisation and movement of people on the streets, and of armies in war, are its lifeblood. Sam Rohdie's (1995: 98) comments about Pier Paolo Pasolini's films, *Trilogia della vita* and *Salo* (more will be said about *Salo* later) are equally apposite to fascism generally, 'It is death which motivates the life and movement of the films.'

(iii) Fascist style and organization

The third strand outlined by Payne is concerned with fascist style and organization. Fascist style is rooted in violence, youthful exuberance, the exaltation of war, and an aggressive masculinity. Payne (1995: 13) notes that only fascism 'made a perpetual fetish of the virility of the movement and its program and style, stemming no doubt from the fascist militarization of politics and the need for constant struggle'. Aggressive masculinity is fundamental to fascist reality. It represents, according to Griffin (1993: 198), a 'radical misogyny of flight from the feminine, manifesting itself in a pathological fear of being engulfed by anything in external reality associated with softness, with dissolution, or the uncontrollable'. Certainly the politics of gender in fascist discourse are stark, 'Feminized men are as repellent to the fascist mentality as masculine women' (Benjamin and Rabinbach 1989: xix); as one Italian Fascist politician proclaimed, 'War is to men what maternity is to women' (Bruno Biancini in a speech to Parliament in 1934, cited in Paxton 2005: 156). At the risk of simplifying the complex interactions between fascism and women, it can be argued that the extreme patriarchy of fascism ensured the explicit subjugation of most women in Germany and Italy (Passmore 2003). This is not to suggest that many women did not embrace the fascist cause, millions did, some as soldiers, so that 'alongside the image of women as mother and wife exists an image of women as *fighters* for the nation' (Neocleous 1997: 80). However, the dominant tendency in fascist movements was anti-feminist (Renton 2001) and therefore was 'inhospitable to women' (Passmore 2003: 268).

In Italy, women faced the double burden of the fascist state and the Church who combined in discouraging women from participating in public life, including sport. 'For girls, sport was deemed a secondary occupation, advisable during adolescence to prepare them for their future role as strong healthy mothers' (Dogliani 2001: 330). The isolated but celebrated case of Tresbisonda 'Ondina' Valla, the first female, indeed the only Italian to win gold medals in athletics in the 1936 Berlin Olympics, was the exception that proved the rule for women in Italy. Though Valla's success was used by Mussolini to project 'the Fascist Superman *and* Superwoman', it was still the case that 'Ordinary fascist women . . . remained the prisoners of gender ideology' (Gori 2001: 192–3). In Fascist Italy, pronouncements were made that women should stay in the home and address the problem of low birth rates: as Victoria de Grazia quipped, 'Ultimately, childbirth was the best exercise, of course' (cited in Martin 2004: 36). In Germany, contraception was banned and feminism was described as an alien, Jewish invention (Renton 1999: 85–6). In postwar Europe, fascist parties in Italy, France, and Germany still called for women to return to the home in order to produce children for the nation (Durham 1989: 13, 20, 110).

Fascist style and organization is also concerned with the mass mobilization and the militarization of the people. Fascism is not an ideology that is based on belief, rather, it is an ideology that is performed. It is, to paraphrase Nietzsche, a philosophy of activism, expressed and directed towards the leader as the embodiment of the nation and its people. The cult of the leader as the embodiment of fascism has been widely noted, especially in the case of Mussolini (Gori 2000), but as Griffin (1995) has noted, the political somatic of fascism extend to the people as a whole, or more pertinently, to the people as a 'race' and nation. For Griffin, the creation of a 'new man' via a process of national rejuvenation is central to the fascist project. The young, virile, and athletic 'new man' constitutes the fundamental building block for the creation of a new society. Following the philosophy of *Organicism* popularized by Herbert Spencer in the mid nineteenth century (Sabine and Thorson 1973), the individual body and the social body are conjoined to form the body-politic. The health of the state is organically tied to the individual soul and body in a process that is expressed in radical forms of cultural nationalism. Griffin (1995: 3–4) labels this a 'palingenetic [rebirth] form of populist ultra-nationalism', which 'crystallizes in the image of the national community, once purged and rejuvenated, rising phoenix-like from the ashes of a morally bankrupt state system and the decadent culture associated with it'. The concept of palingenetic populist ultra-nationalism places the body in a pivotal position within fascist methodology, an approach that I found useful in previous research on the politics of the body and fascism in India (McDonald 1999). Quite how the body is positioned within fascist philosophy, politics and practices will depend on the concrete mani-festation of the body in society. Thus the military body, the labouring body, the dancing body, and the sporting body will each possess a distinctiveness that will be reflected in their multi-faceted relationship to fascism.

Sport as physical culture and the (disembodied) fascist habitus

Sport is not a unitary concept. It can take different forms with distinct values and structures, producing as a consequence particular meanings and bodily practices. Henning Eichberg (1998) offers a useful analytical approach to understand sport as a differentiated concept, by placing it under the rubric of body culture. Thus, according to Eichberg, what is often assumed to be *the* definition of sport: the mass mediated, rule-bound competitive performances, is actually *a* definition, albeit a dominant one in Western and developed societies with its own historical trajectory rooted in industrializing British society (Holt 1990). 'High performance sport' is relativized by Eichberg as one dimension of body culture in modernity.

The second dimension in Eichberg's trialectical model is 'fitness sport': those activities that may or may not be competitive, but are enacted or performed for the social and psychological benefit of the individual. While high performance sport is based on the ethos of production – of results and of performances – fitness sport is premised on a recreational ethos – of the social, physical, and psychological benefits to the individual. The third dimension is referred to as 'body experience'. These are expressive and sen-suous forms of physical activity that offer the potential for transgression and transcendence. Lifestyle sports that emerged against the grain of insti-tutionalized and competitive sports, such as windsurfing and skateboarding, could be considered examples of 'body experience' (Wheaton 2004). The different logics of high performance sport, fitness sport, and body culture (based on production, reproduction, and experience respectively), each offer a distinct set of limitations and possibilities for individual expression, empowerment, and political exploitation. The trialectic of sport is a useful analytical model from which to approach the study of fascism and sport during the inter-war period.

The development of sport and physical culture during inter-war fascism can be divided into two phases. The first phase, in the 1920s in Italy and from 1933 to 1937 in Germany centred on the role of 'body experience' and 'fitness sport'. The development of 'high performance sport' systems emerged only later, but was soon to dominate the sporting culture of inter-war Italy and Germany from the mid 1920s and mid 1930s respectively. But prior to the take-over of high performance competitive sport, a major concern was to mould the population into ideal fascist citizens and soldiers. Physical education programmes for the young were developed based on the presumed transferable qualities of 'fitness sport' and 'body experience'. During this period, there was even an antipathy to high performance sport amongst fascist ideologues. In Germany, physical culture theorist, Alfred Baeumler, dismissed sports as a foreign import and for encouraging individualism rather than community feelings. Baeumler argued that, 'it is revealed from the *volkisch* thought that we cannot speak of the body per se, or of the body of the individual as an *individual*, but rather of the body of the individual in relation to the total-body of the Volk' (cited in Magdalinski 1995: 67). Care of the body and its presentation was declared a matter of public and therefore political importance. And it is precisely the relationship between corporeal autonomy and collective determination, between the individual and the community, that shaped the development of physical culture in the first phase of fascist rule.

The problematic of the body, identity, and modernity was writ large in pre-Nazi Germany. In the latter part of the nineteenth century, Friedrich Lang (1778–1852) used physical activities as a means of inculcating a strong sense of national identity in creating the *Turnen* movement (Ueberhorst 1979). Based on 'a mystical, integral nationalism founded on the racial doctrine of a transcendental German essence' (Toepfer 1997: 100–1), the *Turnen* movement was geared towards preparing the bodies of German youth to wage war against Napoleon. However, in pre-Nazi Germany, arguably the most forbidding form of physical training for fascistic political ends was instigated in the *Freikorps*, the armed counter-revolutionary groups that were made up largely of soldiers demobilized in 1918.

In *Male Fantasies*, Klaus Theweleit (1989) graphically illustrates the brutal physical training in the *Freikorps*. It was designed to create the ideal fascist habitus: masculinized, militarized, and machinized. In 'focussing on two materialities repressed within conventional Marxism, the body and the word' (Carter and Turner 1986: 210), Theweleit presents a vivid account of the central importance of the body in fascist methodology. Indeed, 'It is this single-minded attention to the physical, the corporeal and the sensuous' note Benjamin and Rabinbach in their foreword to *Male Fantasies*, 'that provides the most original and provocative impulse for this work' (1989: xii). Drawing heavily, though by no means exclusively, on Deleuze and Guttari's conception of 'desiring-production', Theweleit presents a psychoanalytical reading of the memoirs, diaries, letters, and fictional writings produced by men who were members of the *Freikorps*. Across these writings Theweleit sets out to chart the territories of a fascistic male *desire*, expressed in the brutal training regimes of the *Freikorps*.

For the soldiers in the *Freikorps* experiencing the most extreme and brutal regime, masochism takes on a sado-masochistic slant. Intense emotional attachments between officers and soldiers, based on a mixture of sublimated sexual tenderness and violence, were formed. Here is a telling account of one soldier who recalls an incident in which he receives, *nay*, desires physical punishment.

> Glasmacher stepped forward, took me by the arm, and led me over to the table. I climbed up, not without difficulty, and lay down on my stomach. Glasmacher took my head in his hands, pressed my eyes shut, and forced my skull hard against the surface of the table. I gritted my teeth and tensed my whole body . . . The first blow whistled. I jerked upward, but Glasmacher held me tight; the blows rained down on my back, shoulders, legs, a frenzied fire of hard, smacking blows. My hands were tightly gripped around the edge of the table, I beat out a rhythm with my knees, shins, and toes in an attempt to expel the excruciating pain. Now all the torment seemed to move through my body and implant itself in the table, again and again my hips and loins slammed against the wood and made it shudder; every blow recharged the bundle of muscles and skin, blood and bones and sinews, with slingshot force, till my whole body stretched under tension and threat- ened to burst in its lower regions. I gave my head over entirely to Glasmacher's hands, wrenched myself shut, and finally lay still and moaning. 'Stop!' Corporal First Class Glocken commanded, and the assembled company jumped back instantly. I slid slowly from the table. Glasmacher stepped up to proffer his hand, and said, 'Peace! The affair is closed'.
>
> (Theweleit 1989: 150)

The sado-masochistic tenor of this account exemplifies the importance of an anti-erotic sexuality in fascist culture. The connections between sexual perversion, fascist power, and the body are dissected in the visually stunning and brutally detailed film, *Salo or 120 Days of Sodom* directed by Pier Paolo Pasolini (1974). In *Salo*, the bodies of the young are humiliated, besmirched, torn apart, violated, entered, solely for the pleasure of the bodies of the decadent old (the judge, the banker, the duke, and the priest). The 'society' formed by the fascist libertines in their mansion is cut off from the outside world. Laws are created that are absolute and totalitarian, to the extent of governing all aspects of bodily functions. For the young captives to defecate without permission was a crime, as it was to have sexual intercourse, espe- cially if it was heterosexual sex. Punishment was meted out against the body: all of its surfaces, openings, functions, and desires. As Sam Rohdie (1995: 48) argues, 'In it fascism and capitalism are triumphant. Reason dominates to the point of the complete destruction of all that is pure and innocent. Reason turns into the horror of a demonic, fascist unreason.'

Does a concomitant 'rule and madness of reason' (Rohdie 1995: 80) and 'sado-masochism' underpin high performance sport? According to Jean Marie Brohm, sport is a 'Prison of Measured Time' that 'replaces libidinal pleasure with the masochistic pleasure obtained from movement' (1989: 50). It may partly account for the ease with which the fascist states of inter-war Europe eventually embraced and promoted the culture of high performance sport. Hitler's support for boxing – singled out in *Mein Kampf* as an indispensable part of the school sport curriculum – signals a masochistic function of sport in the quest for hardness:

> There is no sport that so much as this one promotes the spirit of attack, demands lightning decisions, and trains the body in steel dexterity . . . above all the young healthy body must learn to suffer blows . . . it is not the function of the folkish state to breed a colony of peaceful aesthetes and physical degenerates. And so sport does not exist only to make the individual strong, agile and bold; it should also toughen and teach him to bear hardships.
>
> (Hitler [1925] 1961: 410)

The aim of fascist socialization in the *Freikorps* was to create a body-machine, 'the acknowledged "utopia" of the fascist warrior' (Benjamin and Rabinbach 1989: xix). The individual fascist only has meaning insofar as he is an embodied component of a machinic social whole, as represented in the mass ranks of marching soldiers. The notion of personal identity is oxymoronic. Identity is experienced, emoted, and collective, rather than individual, reflective, and autonomous. The effect of the individual 'body-machine' being absorbed into the machinic social whole is that the soldier, paradoxically, is disembodied as Theweleit describes:

> A single sword hurled itself upward, flashed and dropped deep to the ground: the earth turned to dust under hundreds of marching feet; the earth rumbled and groaned; two hundred fifty men were passing, touching close to one another, two hundred fifty rifles on their shoulders, a line sequence straight as an arrow above a line of helmets, shoulders, knapsacks straight as an arrow; two hundred fifty hands hissing back and forth; two hundred fifty legs tearing bodies onward in cruel, relentless rhythm . . . The soldiers limbs are described as if severed from their bodies; they are fused together to form new totalities. The leg of the individual has a closer functional connection to the leg of his neighbor than to his own torso. *In the machine, then, new body-totalities are formed: bodies no longer identical with the bodies of individual human beings . . . Each individual totality-component moves in*

precise unison with every other: 'One troop, one man, one rhythm' [italics added for emphasis].

(Theweleit 1989: 154)

While the extreme training regimes of the *Freikorps* may have met the demands for developing a hard cadre of fascists, it was not a feasible means of engaging the mass of the population. For this task, German fascism drew on an apparently more unlikely source for ideas – the mass physical culture movement of the Weimar period. The physical culture movements of Weimar society were part of a remarkable period in European history of politicization, experimentation, and innovation of the moving body. This multifarious movement raised complex questions to do with issues of freedom and constraint underpinned by a concern with the interplay between the body and the soul, spirit, and consciousness. In Weimar Germany, it was the expressive dance movement that led the way in exploring such issues, which made their mark on society with elaborately choreographed public festivals. Modern expressive dance offered exciting possibilities for critical and artistic expression. For choreographers, such as Rudolf von Laban, the sensuousness of individual movement resulted from free movement (often of the nude body), set within an orchestrated framework of collective activity. Laban was interested in communal identity, but experimented with how a group could maintain a unity while containing all manner of different, individualized movements (Maletic 1987). The key lay in bounded improvisation: 'The improvisational dimension revealed how a group heightened individual freedom' (Toepfer 1997: 302).

Modern expressive dance and other forms of physical culture like rhythmic gymnastics challenged traditional hierarchies of high and low culture. They were concerned with the liberating aspects of body culture, and insofar as this was the case, were associated with leftist politics. For example, Eichberg's (1997) study of *Thingspiel*: an expressionistic multi-media genre designed for open-air performance employing speech choirs, movement choirs, singing choirs, narrators, and elaborate sets involving banners marches, loudspeakers, spotlights, and projections, showed that they were a notable feature of the First International Workers Olympics in Frankfurt in 1925. The centrepiece of a festival of gymnastics in Nuremburg in 1929 was a production involving 66,000 working men and women in a spectacular drama of a proletarian storm troop that 'takes up the fight to free all intellectually, economically, socially, and politically enslaved people from their bondage' (Eichberg 1997: 318). A festival play was also created for the Second Workers Olympics in Vienna in 1931: 5,000 performers dramatized the 'revolutionary awakening' of the proletariat against 'the oppressive ages of industrial servitude' (Eichberg 1997: 143–4).

And yet this very same diverse body culture has been held responsible for the rise of the Third Reich. How is this so? It is an accusation that has been raised because of the apparent continuities between Weimer body culture and Nazi physical culture. The Nazis adopted lay-movement choir techniques in the production of numerous propaganda spectacles. In particular, the techniques of *Thingspiel* were employed to dramatic effect in the opening and closing ceremonies of the 1936 Olympic Games captured by Leni Riefenstahl in her landmark documentary *Olympia* (Sontag 1983). However, while the techniques and forms may have been similar, the themes and content of the mass spectacles changed under the Nazis: for example one of the last mass spectacles was staged in a Munich stadium and paired 'manly strength' with 'womanly grace' in gigantic folk dances and marches involving 1,000 girls and several thousand uniformed men, and concluded with a monumental hymnic surge toward the swastika (Eichberg 1997). Toepfer is concerned to counter the accusation that Weimar body culture was culpable for Nazi physical culture. His argument is that physical culture is essentially catholic in orientation, and any a priori association between it and political ideology is erroneous. It is primarily context and content, not form and technique, that define politics. Hence, mass movements could be directed to achieve liberation, or to serve regimentation:

> The same mass movement devices can make a swastika or a star; totalitarianism is not inherent in either . . . However, the swastika rather than the star became a totalitarian symbol because it urged people to act on behalf of a community that invariably valued sameness over difference.
>
> (Toepfer 1997: 319–20)

Though in no sense a leftist, Laban was nonetheless preoccupied in dance with the dialectical relationship between the power of the collective and individual freedom of expression. Laban, like Lang before him, was undoubtedly influenced by mysticism in critiquing modernity, which according to Vertinsky (this volume) facilitated Laban's rise to prominence, albeit short-lived, under Nazi rule. Certainly, Laban's choreography shared a reverence for action with the militarized, machine-precise synchronizations of the Nazi mass performance aesthetic that came after him, but Toepfer insists that Laban always allowed for an expression of 'difference' that ran counter to the totalitarianism in Nazi physical culture. For Laban, a dancer is a person 'who combines a clear mind, deep feelings, and a strong will to a harmonious well balanced whole, the parts of which are in constant flux' (cited in Kruger 1991: 148). Both Nazi physical culture and Laban's philosophy of dance were framed by a notion of totality, but for the latter, totality is the framework for 'flux' and the expression of difference, whereas for the former, totality is a means of suffocating difference and imposing sameness. Therefore, the 'difference-sameness' binary is a rather prosaic way of marking a key aspect of fascist physical culture. Sameness speaks of the way in which the individual is not merely subordinated to the whole but completely absorbed. Difference permits for a dialectical growth of both individual *and* collective empowerment, indeed one is dependent on, and the precondition for, the other. It is therefore around the dichotomy of 'sameness' and 'difference' that nostalgic romanticism of Lang can be distinguished from the critical mysticism of Laban.

Fascist regimes and sport policy: expediency, antinomy, and ambiguity

In understanding the relationship between the fascist state and sport policy, it is necessary first of all to recognize that we are not simply studying fascist ideology, but the fascist *state*. The state is key here because, irrespective of its political hue, be it liberal-democratic or totalitarian, the modern state performs certain functions that are common to all states. The role of *any* modern state, communist or capitalist, liberal or totalitarian, is to maintain and reproduce dominant social relations by a mixture of coercion and consent. Historically, sport has tended to be assigned the role of reproducing consent, primarily through encouraging social integration and promoting national pride. Indeed, all states display a remarkably similar attitude to sport irrespective of political ideology. Sport policy in the inter-war states of Italy and Germany was explicable in terms of social integration and national pride, but its fascistic nature was evidenced in the zeal and aggression with which it increasingly pursued these objectives after an initial period of indecisiveness (Arnaud and Riordan 1998; Riordan and Kruger 1999). In Germany for example, there was certainly 'no blueprint for sport and physical education' (Magdalinski 1995: 61) when the National Socialists came to power in Germany in 1933: 'As a fighting organization they had spent so much time and effort on getting to power that many of their aims in "minor" fields such as leisure and sport were not clearly defined' (Kruger 1987: 12–13). Without a clear philosophy, sport policy was shaped by the needs of the fascist state at any particular time.

> When the Nazis came to power . . . they ripped up the famous cinder track of their stadium and planted oak trees on the track. The track for them had been the instrument of foreign (British) influence, the stopwatch a symbol of the pressure on athletes to race against each other instead of all together for the betterment of the German race. The German oak, the symbol of Jahn, the Turnvater, stood for paramilitary training . . . only six weeks later – the trees were all gone. Training was intensified as athletic success was to demonstrate the superiority of the Ayran race and the fatherland.
>
> (Kruger 1999: 68–9)

Expedience rather than principle determined Nazi state policy on sport, hence the early twists and turns with the government switching from hostility to encouragement in accordance with the need of the fascist regime. Also in Fascist Italy, Benito Mussolini's own self-conscious physicality is well known

(Hoberman 1984), as is his regime's promotion of physical and militarist exercises to mould a population in a ready state of war preparedness (Teja 1998). Again, it was political expediency that led the Fascist party to shift towards a competitive sport and state-run elite sports system in 1928, a full five years after taking power, when promoting and spreading fascist ideology abroad became a priority. The Italian sports system was controlled by the party and accrued clear political benefits: initially for strengthening a race of 'soldier-citizens', then later for diverting and mobilizing the masses into supporting the Italian national team, which were now synonymous with the fascist regime; and abroad through enhancing Italian prestige (Dogliani 2001). The victorious campaigns at the World Cup Finals in Italy in 1934 and 1938, allied to Italy's Olympic successes in sports like boxing and cycling, certainly contributed to the popularity of Mussolini (Martin 2004). The benefits derived from such successes could not have been lost on the newly installed German National Socialists who were debating what attitude to take to hosting the Olympic Games which had already been awarded to Berlin prior to their ascent to power (Hart-Davis 1986; Mandell 1972).

After some prevarication, the National Socialists took their cue from the Italian model and promptly adopted a centralized sports system, initially under government control and then, after 1938, under Party control. They embraced high performance sport without reservation, employing the latest coaching techniques, technology, sports medicine, and engaged in sports selection procedures and developed sports schools, building on an efficiently organized sporting system inherited from the Weimar Republic (Germany had come second in the 1928 Olympic Games). Certainly, Germany's unexpected victory (with Italy third) at the 1936 Berlin Olympics demonstrated to the German people and the world what a strong, unified Germany could achieve under National Socialism and Adolf Hitler. The ready exploitation of sport by fascist regimes has lent credence to analyses that stress the fascistic nature of sport itself. As Jean-Marie Brohm (1989: 180) argues:

> Sport is a means of militarising and regimenting youth. Hitler, Mussolini, Franco, Petain, and de Gaulle all used or use sport to regiment youth in their efforts to put out the flame of proletarian revolution. Sport serves this purpose by developing *a standardised image of the body*, regulating the way the adolescent relates to his or her own body and seeking to establish the ideology of the body as a sort of automated machine. As a 'character school', sport creates authoritarian, aggressive, narcissistic and obedient character types . . . sport contributes to the militarisation of youth with the aim of reinforcing the nation's military potential and preparing for imperialist war.

The militarization of youth that Brohm refers to occurred in Germany through the Hitler Youth Movement. This was a mass organization of girls and boys. Already in 1933, 2.3 million or 30.5 per cent of the young people were members. By 1939, following a decree that obligated all youths to join up, membership soared to 98.1 per cent of 10- to 18-year-olds (Kater 2004: 23). The most common activities in Hitler Youth involved pre-military forms of training, such as camping and trekking, with war games played out complete with the rituals of a real military camp. This ensured a smooth transition for the eighteen-year-old youths into the armed forces. Sport was a major part of this pre-military training, especially boxing, Hitler's preferred activity, but also swimming, fencing, calisthetics, soccer, and shooting. It was declared that sports were played for two reasons: as a means of training the body for combat (rather than for competitive purposes), and as a means of developing a sense of community. However the reality was that, like the *Freikorps*, they were often brutalizing. In his fascinating study of the Hitler Youth, Michael Kater argues that they operated according to Social Darwinist principles of the superiority of the fittest, where the elder and more powerful youths would use sports and drill to humiliate the weaker and the younger. Just like the *Freikorps*, the aim was to depersonalize the youth and make them totally malleable. The individual and group sadism, done in the name of 'training the body for combat' and to develop a sense of 'community' could result in the needless loss of life.

> There were forced tests of courage such as making youths jump from five-meter boards into water, often when they could not swim, making them climb up the side of ravines without proper support, and forcing them to perform endless knee-bends. In one camp, a non-swimmer drowned in the deep end of a swimming pool.
>
> (Kater 2004: 31)

Kater's accounts of the sporting activities of the Hitler Youth lends support to Hoberman's (1984) argument that there are close affinities between fascism and sport: that they share a competitive aggressiveness, a self-conscious physicality, an ascetic indifference to pain, a disregard of ethical concerns, and an obedience to authority. However, in a later article (Hoberman 1999) noted that while all the foregoing are features 'high-performance sport', that there are also important differences. High performance sport also promotes individualism, egotism, specialization, materialism, and winning: ideological traits that do not sit easily with fascism. For Alfred Baeumler, the Nazi physical culture theorist, the main problem with high performance sport was the principle of achievement. Magdalinski (1995: 69) summarized Baeumler's discontent with sport thus, 'Rather than competing for the good of the Volk they concentrated on their own abilities.'

Each of the contributions to the critical work on fascism and sport outlined above by Kruger (who focuses on expediencies), Brohm (who emphasizes affinities), and Hoberman (who reminds us of certain antinomies), identify critical aspects of the fascist-sport nexus, and *taken together*, highlight the importance of conceptualizing fascism as a dynamic social movement born out of a shifting interplay between ideology and practical politics, specifically between the exigencies of regime building and politico-economic vicissitudes of capitalism. Such a multi-faceted approach reveals the decidedly ambiguous, rather than the structurally supine, nature of high performance sport under fascism.

Concluding thoughts

Up until the early 1970s fascism was confined to the fringes of European political life. Yet sixty years after millions of Jews and other minorities were slaughtered in the Holocaust and millions of soldiers and citizens were killed in the Second World War, fascism appears to be on the rise once more in many major European countries: notably France, Austria, Italy, Germany, and especially the Balkans. The taboos surrounding declarations of support for fascism have been circumvented by repackaging fascism in the language of national pride, cultivating a moderate façade to the general public, while privately polishing the 'iron fist inside the velvet glove'. As Paxton quips, 'There is no sartorial litmus test for fascism' (2005: 174). Fascism's attempt to morph into something politically palatable underlines the salience of Gilroy's injunction to 'Know exactly where fascism begins, updating ourselves as to what [fascists] look, sound and feel like, and explore the inevitable continuities between the normal orders of democratic governance and their revolutionary repudiation' (2000: 145). Yet it would be a mistake to exaggerate the influence of fascism in political life. Certainly in relation to fascist uses of sport, it would be accurate to say that the main narrative peaked before the demise of Hitler and Mussolini's regimes. Certainly, Franco's well-documented patronage of Real Madrid football club in post-war Spain (Burns 1998) paled in political and cultural significance when compared to the sporting policies pursued by inter-war fascist regimes.

A historical study of how sport was used by fascist regimes is important, but a fuller understanding of fascism and sport must necessarily shift to a study of its legacies within contemporary political and sporting culture. As Gilroy (2000: 175) states,

> Physical strength, sport, combat, competition and their accompanying values may not be the core components in a generic fascist aesthetic. But the way they present the relationship between national and racial identity and physical embodiment lies at the center of what distinguished the fascist movements of the past and what remains fascistic in their influence on contemporary culture.

Some commentators have discussed what they see as a fascistic aesthetic, inspired by Riefenstahlian techniques, that underpins a body-obsessed contemporary visual culture (Sontag 1983). There is considerable analytical and empirical scope contained within these questions. The Swedish philosopher, Torbjorn Tannsjo asserts that the veneration of sporting winners is symptomatic of a 'fascistoid' mentality in contemporary culture. He argues that the 'hard core of Nazism was not nationalism, or chauvinism', as is often assumed, but 'a contempt for weakness' (Tannsjo 1998: 26) and an adoration of strength. According to Tannsjo, the approbation accorded to Olympic winners, irrespective of their national identity, is evidence of an incipient 'fascistic' mentality. Given the cultural ubiquity of modern mediated sport, Tannsjo has raised a pertinent if contentious debate, which has already been joined by Tamburrini (1998), who criticizes Tannsjo's position, and Holowchak (2005), who is more sympathetic to it.

Some commentators have discussed what they see as a fascistic aesthetic, inspired by Riefenstahlian techniques, that underpin a body-obsessed contemporary visual culture (Sontag 1983). Indeed, Pronger explores the possibilities, limitations, and significations of the body in 'risk society', arguing that, 'The widespread promotion of exercise and fitness reasserts the cultural logic of fear and domination in the face of the profound failure of modernity to deliver on its promise of control' (Pronger 2002: 178). The logic of capitalist ideology directs the longing for control promised by achieving the ideal body into exercising and dieting technologies that may or may not produce the taut muscular ideal, but ultimately reflects an acutely limited, indeed fascistic imagination of what is possible and desirable. Pronger presents a compelling argument, highlighting how fascism resonates inside our democracies as well as outside them.

This chapter has argued that both liberation and regimentation are immanent to sport and physical culture. It confirms Adorno's assessment, originally made in 1966 (2003: 24), that:

> Sport is ambiguous. On the one hand, it can have an anti-barbaric and anti-sadistic effect by means of fair play, a spirit of chivalry, and consideration for the weak. On the other hand, in many of its varieties and practices it can promote aggression, brutality and sadism, above all in people who do not expose themselves to the exertion and discipline required by sports but instead merely watch: that is those who regularly shout from the sidelines.

No doubt Max Schmeling would have concurred with this statement, for he embodied these ambiguities in a sport characterized simultaneously by chivalry and brutality. Although he was not a Nazi, the extent to which Schmeling gave succour to Hitler's regime in navigating his sporting career under the strictures of Nazi control will no doubt continue to be subject to much debate. However, it is the very ambiguity of sport that alleviates the need for any defensiveness against those who raise the spectre of fascism. While it is the case that a critique of the 'fascistic' lurking inside our sporting bodies is an exercise in delineating how the body is used in certain ways to quell individual freedom and to further oppression, the point is not to simply decry sport. In identifying 'brutality' and 'sadism' in sport, critique implicitly points towards the 'anti-barbaric and anti-sadistic' potential of sport and physical culture. The aim of 'critique' is 'to pull reality towards what it ought to be, what is immanent to it' (How 2003: 5). Herbert Marcuse referred to critique as a form of negative thinking:

> Negative thinking draws whatever force it may have from its empirical base: the actual human condition in the given society, and the given possibilities to transcend this condition, to enlarge the realm of freedom. In this sense, negative thinking is by virtue of its own internal concepts 'positive'; oriented towards, and comprehending a future which is 'contained' in the present . . . Negative thinking, and the praxis guided by it, is the positive and positing effort to prevent this utter negativity.
>
> (Marcuse 1969: 89)

If fascism represents 'utter negativity' in sport, then critical analysis can play its part in negating this negativity. In so doing, it points a torch light on the nature of modern sport: its institutional structures, values, and practices; and prompts us to question whether and how sport can be redeemed.

Acknowledgements

Thanks to Jenny Hargreaves and Patricia Vertinsky, exemplary editors both.

Bibliography

Adorno, T. (2003) 'Education after Auschwitz', in R. Tiedemann (ed.) Can One Live After Auschwitz: A Philosophical Reader, 19–33, Stanford, CA: Stanford University Press.

Arnaud, P. and Riordan, J. (eds.) (1998) Sport and International Politics: The Impact of Fascism and Communism on Sport, London: E. & F.N. Spon.

Bauman, Z. (1989) Modernity and the Holocaust, New York: Cornell University Press.

Benjamin W. (1973) 'The work of art in the age of mechanical reproduction', in Illuminations, London: Collins/Fontana.

Benjamin, J. and Rabinbach, A. (1989) 'Foreword', in K. Theweleit, Male Fantasies, vol. II, Cambridge: Polity Press.

Bourdieu, P. (1984) Distinction: A Social Critique of the Judgement of Taste, London: Routledge.

Brohm, J.M. (1989) Sport: A Prison of Measured Time, London: Pluto Press.

Burns, J. (1998) Barca: A People's Passion, London: Bloomsbury.

Carr, G.A. (1979) 'The synchronization of sport and physical education under national socialism', Canadian Journal of History of Sport and PE, 10(21): 15–35.

Carter, E. and Turner, C. (1986) 'Political somatics: notes on Klaus Theweleit's male fantasies', in V. Burgin, J. Donald, and C. Kaplan (eds) *Formations of Fantasy*, London: Methuen.

Dogliani, P. (2001) 'Sport and fascism', *Journal of Modern Italian Studies*, 5(3): 326–43.

Durham, M. (1989) *Women and Fascism*, London: Routledge.

Eichberg, H. (1977) 'The Nazi thingspiel: theatre for the masses in fascism and popular culture', *New German Critique*, 11: 133–50.

Eichberg, H. (1998) 'Body culture as paradigm: the Danish sociology of sport', in J. Bale and C. Philo (eds), *Henning Eichberg. Body Cultures: Essays on Sport, Spaces and Identity*, New York: Routledge.

Gilroy, P. (2000) *Between Camps: Race, Identity and Nationalism at the End of the Colour Line*, London: Allen Lane.

Gori, G. (2000) 'Model of masculinity: Mussolini, the "new Italian" of the fascist era', in J.A. Mangan (ed.) *Shaping the Superman: Fascist Body as Political Icon – Aryan Fascism*, London: Frank Cass.

Gori, G. (2001) 'A glittering icon of fascist femininity: Trebisonda "Ondina" Valla', *The International Journal of the History of Sport*, 18 (1): 173–95.

Griffin, R. (1993) *The Nature of Fascism*, London: Pinter Publishers.

Griffin, R. (ed.) (1995) *Fascism*, Oxford: Oxford University Press.

Hart-Davis, D. (1986) *Hitler's Games*, New York: Harper and Row Press.

Hitler, A. (1925) (1961) *Mein Kampf*, Boston, MA: Houghton Mifflin.

Hoberman, J. (1984) *Sport and Political Ideology*, Austin, TX: University of Texas Press.

Hoberman, J. (1999) 'Primacy of performance: superman not superathlete', in J.A. Mangan (ed.) *Shaping the Superman: Fascist Body as Political Icon – Aryan Fascism*, 69–85, London: Frank Cass.

Hoch, P. (1972) *Rip off the Big Game*, New York: Anchor Books.

Holowchak, A. (2005) ' "Fascistoid" heroism revisited: a deontological twist to a recent debate', *Journal of the Philosophy of Sport*, 32(1): 96–105.

Holt, R. (1990) *Sport and the British*, Oxford: Oxford University Press.

How, A. (2003) *Critical Theory*, Basingstoke: Palgrave Macmillan.

Kater, M. (2004) *Hitler Youth*, Cambridge, MA: Harvard University Press.

Kruger, A. (1987) '*Sieg heil* to the most glorious era of German sport: continuity and change in the modern German sports movement', *International Journal of the History of Sport*, 4 (1): 5–20.

Kruger, A. (1991) 'There goes this art of manliness: naturism and racial hygiene in Germany', *Journal of Sport History*, 18 (1): 135–58.

Kruger, A. (1999) 'Strength through joy: the culture of consent under fascism, nazism and francoism', in J. Riordan and A. Kruger (eds) *The International Politics of Sport in the Twentieth Century*, 67–89, London: E. & F.N. Spon.

Lewis, M. (2005) 'Max Schmeling', Obituary in *The Guardian* newspaper, 5 February www.guardian.co.uk/obituaries/story/0,,1406354,00.html (accessed 5 February 2005).

Magdalinski, T. (1995) 'Beyond Hitler: Alfred Baeumler, ideology and physical education in the Third Reich', *Sporting Traditions*, 11(2): 61–79.

Maletic, V. (1987) *Body–Space–Expression. The Development of Rudolf Laban's Movement and Dance Concepts*, Amsterdam: Mouton de Gruyter.

Mandell, R. (1972) *The Nazi Olympics*, London: Macmillan.

Mangan, J.A. (ed.) (1999) *Shaping the Superman: Fascist Body as Political Icon – Aryan Fascism*, London: Frank Cass.

Mangan, J.A. (2000) 'Global fascism and the male body: ambitions, similarities and dissimilarities', in J.A. Mangan (ed.) *Superman Supreme: Fascist Body as Political Icon – Global Fascism*, London: Frank Cass.

Marcuse, H. (1969) *An Essay on Liberation*, Harmondsworth: Penguin.

Margolick, D. (2005) *Beyond Glory: Joe Louis vs. Max Schmeling, and a World on the Brink*, London: Bloomsbury Press.

Martin, S. (2004) *Football and Fascism*, Oxford: Berg.

McDonald, I. (1999) ' "Physiological patriots"? The politics of physical culture and Hindu nationalism in India', *International Review for the Sociology of Sport*, 34(4): 343–58.

Mercer, C. (1986) 'Fascist ideology', in J. Donald and S. Hall (eds) *Politics and Ideology*, Milton Keynes: Open University Press.

Neocleous, M. (1997) *Fascism*, Buckingham: Open University Press.

Passmore, K. (ed.) (2003) *Women, Gender and Fascism in Europe, 1919–45*, Manchester: Manchester University Press.

Paxton, R. (2005) *The Anatomy of Fascism*, New Delhi: Penguin Books.

Payne, S. (1980) *Fascism: Comparisons and Definitions*, Madison, WI: University of Wisconsin Press.

Payne, S. (1995) *A History of Fascism, 1914–1945*, London: UCL Press.

Pronger, B. (2002) *Body Fascism: Salvation in the Technology of Physical Fitness*, Toronto: University of Toronto Press.

Renton, D. (1999) *Fascism: Theory and Practice*, London: Pluto Press.

Renton, D. (2001) 'Women and fascism: a critique', *Socialist History*, 20: 72–83.

Riordan, J. and Kruger, A. (eds) (1999) *The International Politics of Sport in the Twentieth Century*, London: E. & F.N. Spon.

Rohdie, S. (1995) *The Passion of Pier Paolo Pasolini*, London: British Film Institute.

Sabine, G.H. and Thorson, T.L. (1973, 4th edn) *A History of Political Thought*, Hinsdale, IL: Dryden Press.

Sontag, S. (1983) 'Fascinating fascism', in *Under the Sign of Saturn*, Toronto: McGraw Hill Ryerson.

Sparks, C. (1980) *Never Again!: The Hows and Whys of Stopping Fascism*, London: Bookmarks.

Tamburrini, C. (1998) 'Sports fascism and the market', *Journal of the Philosophy of Sport*, 25(1): 35–47.

Tannsjo, T. (1998) 'Is our admiration for sports heroes fascistoid', *Journal of the Philosophy of Sport*, 25(1): 23–34.

Teja, A. (1998) 'Italian sport and international relations under fascism', in P. Arnaud and J. Riordan (eds) *Sport and International Politics: The impact of Fascism and Communism on Sport*, London: E. & F.N. Spon.

Theweleit, K. (1989) *Male Fantasies Vol. II: Male Bodies; Psychoanalyzing the White Terror*, Cambridge: Polity Press

Toepfer, K. (1997) *Empire of Ecstasy. Nudity and Movement in German Body Culture, 1910–1935*, Berkeley, CA: University of California.

Ueberhorst, H. (1979) 'Jahn's historical significance', *Canadian Journal of History of Sport and PE*, 10 (1): 7–14.

Vertinsky, P. (2006) 'Movement practices and fascist infections: from dance under the swastika to movement education in the British school', in J. Hargreaves and P. Vertinsky (eds), *Physical Culture, Power and the Body*, London: Routledge.

Wheaton, B. (ed.) (2004) *Lifestyle Sport: The Politics of Identity and Difference*, London: Routledge.

Zizěk, S. (1999) *The Ticklish Subject: The Absent Centre of Political Ontology*, London: Verso.

ırt, exercise, and the ıale Muslim body

gotiating Islam, politics, and ıııale power

Jennifer Hargreaves

Introduction

The sense that each of us has of our body is deeply personal, emotional, and physical. It is a sort of primordial corporeal consciousness, a sense of ownership of, and meaning ascribed to our physiological selves and inseparable from a more general sense of self. These very intimate feelings of body and selfhood are at the same time social products, constituted by, and located in culture. This fascinating inter-relationship between personal bodies and culture is explored throughout this chapter. More specifically, the focus is on the bodies of Muslim women in sport[1] and physical recreation. The countries of the Middle East provide the major context.

However, Muslim women in the Middle East are not a homogeneous group, and treating Muslim culture as uniform mystifies the multiple ways in which women interpret Islam and live their lives. The bodies of Muslim women in sport are experienced and mediated through different ideological interpretations of Islam, within the particular political arrangements of specific countries, and in ways that are penetrated to various extents by patriarchal relations of power and control. Further, the empirical evidence collected for this chapter shows how 'the idea of the unity of body, person and consciousness is the result of a protracted historical process' (a claim made by Marcel Mauss, cited in Turner 1984: 56).

The idea that Muslim women experience their bodies and their lives in a local Islamic vacuum is also false. The bodies of Muslim women are regulated within the broader context of local–global tensions and in relation to Western femininities and sexual politics. Muslim women are influenced by Western images of female sport through the media, advertizing, and travel. Their bodies are, therefore, symbolized, represented, and interpreted in relation to the personal and social worlds of Western 'outsiders', as well as to those living in Islamic communities.

Images of Western sportswomen are a significant part of the political tug-of-war over women's bodies. Conservative Muslim clerics view immodest dress – and specifically body-hugging, sexualized sportswear – as thoroughly immodest and symbolic of the corrupt values and practices of the West.

Westerners in general believe women's sports reflect freedom of choice, gender equality, and the democratic values supposedly intrinsic to Western culture. Because female modesty (*hijab*) is fundamental and precious to all Muslims, Muslim women are anxious about exercising in public venues, and bans have been placed on their participation in mixed sports (notably the Olympic Games – see Hargreaves 2000: 71–4).

However, a straightforward comparison between Islam and the West is misleading – the reality is highly complex. Although in countries such as Iran and Saudi Arabia women are mandated to wear the veil in public and many of them feel angry, repressed, and resistant, they are fearful of showing their opposition and troubled that their anti-fundamentalist sentiments will be interpreted as anti-Islamic ones and used to fuel Western Islamophobia (Mahl 1995: 14). But other Muslim women hold a positive view of *hijab* – for them, wearing the veil is a deliberate choice, a politicized act, rather than a question of male power. They interpret 'unveiling' and taking part in sport as a new form of imperial control (Kanneh 1995). It is also the case that many Muslim women have no interest whatsoever in sport or physical recreation of any sort, and married women are typically more concerned about family responsibilities than going for a jog and keeping fit. For most women from the lower classes or who are immigrant workers, participation is not even an option. Throughout modern times, sport and other recreational forms of exercise have never been an organic feature of the cultural history of Muslim women (Al-Hadair 2004).

The bodies of Muslim women are at the very core of self–society/personal–social/local–global dialectics and women's feelings about themselves and their identities as Muslims are reflected in their participation – or non-participation – in sport and exercise. But this is not a passive process. Muslim women are constantly negotiating and re-negotiating the usages of their bodies, and agency is a central feature of the extent and variety of their participation in sport.

Turner's claim (1984: 39) that, 'The body lies at the centre of political struggles, in the sense that different roles and identities, such as gender identity and personality and patriarchy are inserted into physiology' is directly relevant to the bodies of Muslim women. However, although the 'traditional' female body has been a pivot of cultural and political control for conservative Islam, Muslim feminists have failed to construct a comprehensive politics of the female body, physical exercise, health and well-being. Their agenda has included aspects of patriarchal control that are considered to be more pressing (Karam 1998; Mernissi 1991; Walter and Al-Faisal 2005). In this chapter there is an attempt to understand how male authority is transmitted through the bodies of Muslim sportswomen, facilitating the continuity of male power, and also, in contradiction, how sport can provide a context for freeing the female Muslim body from male power.

Islam, veiling the body, and male power

Over the past 100 years Islam has been the fastest-growing religion in the world and as well as having a long history in predominantly Muslim societies, it has captivated the hearts and imaginations of increasing numbers of people in the West (Gellner 1994: xi). But Islam is more than just a religion: it is an interpretation of the world, a style of thinking, 'a total way of life that affects all aspects of being: public, private, and spiritual' (Goodwin 1994: 7). Although there are different Islamic ideologies, attitudes to women's bodies are pivotal in the mix of religion, politics, and culture. Women's bodies are also central in the construction of a diasporic, truly global 'Muslim society', replacing 'nation' as the basis for identity and authenticity. The imbeddedness of their bodies in all areas of social life leads to a special self-consciousness among Muslim women about the ways in which they think about and use their bodies – specifically whether they want to, or can, enjoy the pleasures of sport and improved health through exercise.

Discourses of the Muslim female body are also at the very heart of theological struggles between Islamic fundamentalists (Islamists) and more moderate Islamic and secular ideologues, fuelled by global politics, and signalling the essentially complex and unstable nature of the female Muslim body in sport. Islamists, in particular, portray Muslim women as especially vulnerable to the dominating influences of a postmodern Western culture that promotes 'youth, change and consumerism' and emphasizes 'noise, movement and speed' (Ahmed and Donnan 1994: 13), and they use Muslim women in defence of 'local' traditional Islamic culture that they contend will otherwise be wiped out (Mernissi 1991: 17). Female sports and exercise in the West have adapted to the individualism of postmodernity: to its obsession with the physical body, its movements in space and time, and its 'look', as well as to the rituals and corruption of sporting elitism and performance-enhancement. By contrast, the most conspicuous symbol of ethical traditional Islamic culture and female modesty, dominant in Islamic thinking, is the veiled woman.

In Islamic societies there are various processes of female body regulation, but it is the exterior (veiled/covered) female body and its representation in public that has become central to both local/Islamic definitions of Muslim womanhood and global/Western ones. Veiling is a stark example of the way in which very private bodies can be socially constructed as gendered bodies and socially appropriated, confirming the link between the personal and the social. During the past quarter of a century, very narrow and rigid interpretations of religious modesty demanding extensive body covering, fostered under the influence of Islamism, have become increasingly influential throughout the Muslim world. Although there are different forms of Islamism, it is an essentially anti-colonial, anti-American resurgence of ethnic politics that attempts to unify in religious terms around the Qur'an and Hadith[2] (Halliday 1994; Mernissi 1991). Islamists make claim to an 'essential'

Islam, using politics to legitimize their ideals. They revolt against the secular modernising state, make ideological appeals to 'traditional' values, and are obsessed with the control of women. Leila Ahmed (1992: 225) argues vehemently that establishment Islam is 'authoritarian, implacably androcentric, and hostile to women', and 'has been and continues to be the established version of Islam, the Islam of the politically powerful'. She goes on to say that,

> Women's freedom of movement within the areas in which they reside, women's dress, women's rights to travel and to work and to choose where to work, are strictly supervised and controlled in several Middle Eastern countries today, most stringently in Saudi Arabia, but elsewhere as well.
>
> (p. 231)

The idea that women are 'naturally' inferior, perpetrated by powerful male politico-religious ideologues and disseminated in concrete ways throughout society, deludes women into believing in gender biologism so they become captives of the state and of individual family men, leading Karam (1998: 29) to claim that 'Islamists, both male and female, are . . . using the body as a site of power; whence their views on veiling'.

The history of Iran encapsulates the way in which women are at the centre of changes in the relation between religion and the state. When the secularist Shah Reza Khan Pahlavi was in power in the 1930s, he outlawed the *hijab* in order to Westernize Iranian society. Women joined sports clubs and wore bikinis on the beaches (Hargreaves 2000: 54). Then, at the time of the 1979 Revolution, and the setting up of a theocratic state under the Ayatollah Khomeini, the Westernization of Iranian society was reversed (Roberts 1980; Tohidi 1991) and a firm precedent was established for the overthrow of other secular Muslim states. Women's bodies were at the forefront of the Ayatollah's sweeping changes to eliminate all things Western. He demanded that, 'no part of a woman's body may be seen except her face and the part of her hand between the wrist to the tip of her fingers' (Tohidi 1991: 253) and so the black *abaya* – a long black cloak with arm slits – became obligatory, and sex-segregation in all public areas of Iranian society was lawfully imposed. The most extreme fundamentalist politico-religious ideology demands that the entire female body, including face and hands, is covered so that it is completely hidden from public gaze, symbolizing the 'absolute purity' of Islamic culture. A version of this, known as the *burqah* – material that drapes the body from head to toe with a type of face mask that covers the eyes – was imposed on Afghan women when the Taliban were in power. But in Kuwait – considered to be the moderate face of Islam – 'decent' non-provocative Western dress with no veil is tolerated in public places (Al-Hadair 2004; Hargreaves 2000). The degree of veiling is like litmus paper, varying according to the influence of Islamists. For example, following the 1990 Iraqi invasion of Kuwait, when Islamism became more influential as Kuwaiti refugees who had fled to more conservative countries, such as Saudi Arabia, returned home (Al Hadair 2004: 35), there was a marked increase in the numbers of veiled women than in previous years; and then, following the bombing of the World Trade Centre in New York, in 2001, anti-Western feeling in Kuwait resulted in a further increase of Islamism and the veiling of even more women than before. In the present climate of global politics, there is an ideological pressure on Muslim women to demonstrate solidarity with Islamic tradition and rejection of Western culture.

The symbolism of veiling which encloses the body, protecting it from view and preventing freedom of movement, is integral to Muslim female identity. It is directly at odds with the sheer physicality of vigorous exercise, and the displays of muscle and power that characterize contemporary Western sporting femininities (Hargreaves 1993). Very few Muslim women participate in sport and exercise and almost exclusively in female-only spaces, so the general impression of women as private, separate, and characteristically unphysical is maintained.

Critics of Islamism argue that the imperatives for women to veil arise because there is 'confusion between Islam as a belief, as a personal choice, and Islam as law, as state religion' (Mernissi 1991: 21), and that, 'The movement, largely funded by the Saudis and Kuwait, is pushing a doctrine that is antiwoman, anti-intellectual, anti-progress, and anti-science' (Badawi, cited in Goodwin 1994: 27). The power of Islamism derives from starkly uneven gender relations of power in religion, politics, and people's personal lives (Karam 1998; Mernissi 1991) to the extent that women lose freedoms that they have previously enjoyed, only gaining some autonomy when there are more liberal, secular political leaders.

Large numbers of Muslim women believe veiling 'exemplifies the Islamic requirement of modesty . . . and (obedience) to God'. Others argue that it 'detracts from patriarchal prioritization of women's physical and sexual attractiveness (and) . . . provides resistance to a perceived Western consumerism in which money and energy are constantly spent in keeping up with changing fashions that in reality keep women hostage to their appearance and to the market' (Shaikh 2003: 152–3). In contradiction, those who explicitly oppose fundamentalism argue that, 'There has never been an Islamic obligation for women to cover at any time. In fact, veiling the face is an innovation that has no foundation whatsoever in Islam . . . and even in Saudi Arabia the covering of women from head to toe is recent; it was not required before the discovery of oil' (Badawi, cited in Goodwin 1994: 30). Mernissi (1993: 85–101) explains that the literal meaning of *hijab* is a barrier or spatial dimension that led to the 'splitting of Muslim space' between men and women, and between public and private space which today is used as 'a weapon of male resistance to women'.

Islamic discourses about Muslim women and their bodies are multiple and complex, claimed by Karam (1998: 22) to be 'part-and-parcel of post-modernity . . . and the recognition of the non-universality of Western discourse, of the ability to think difference in a different way'. Attitudes to sport and other physical activities for females have become unavoidable features of these discourses, and the strengthening of Islamism is setting back the chances of women taking up these activities. This politicization of women's bodies and the banning of women from decision-making roles in politics is blocking proper representation of women's affairs and wishes and the potential to change gender inequalities in life and sport. For example, liberal women in Iran described the 2004 parliamentary elections as a sham because hundreds of reformist candidates were disqualified from standing (Schlein 2004); in Saudi Arabia elections were held for the first time in 2005, but although women had expected to vote, they were banned from the poll as a result of Islamist influence (Walter and al-Faisal 2005); also in 2005, in Egypt, The Muslim Brotherhood (a fundamentalist organization using the slogan 'Islam is the solution') became the main opposition in the parliamentary elections even although Egypt's constitution forbids parties based on religion, ethnicity, or gender (Tisdall 2005); and in Iraq, with its official pronouncement about shedding a history of female oppression and establishing a nation in which a woman's voice matters as much as a man's, the growing Islamization of the new government elected in 2005 has reduced the chances of Iraqi women gaining social and cultural autonomy (Carroll and Borger 2005; Mahdi and Carroll 2005).

Sardar (2002: 11) argues that the real Islam is a religion of peace with multiple, negotiated interpretations of the Qur'an and that literalist, monolithic interpretations are misreadings. As a result, liberal Muslims find themselves trapped between 'aggressive globalization and equally aggressive traditionalism' and 'as individuals and communities, Muslims need to reclaim agency' (p. 13). However, Shaikh (2003: 154) cautions that:

> homogenization, generalization, and objectification of Muslim women result in the perpetuation of dominant patriarchal and colonial discourses that freeze women and the colonized into rigid categories. Such approaches suppress the ways in which particular groups of women challenge, subvert, and resist patriarchy at various points.

Muslim feminisms, complexities, and sport

Throughout the Muslim world individual women and groups of women have challenged, subverted, and resisted gender inequalities and patriarchal discrimination. Collectively, they are characterized as Muslim feminists (Tohidi 1991, 2002), and yet they have had different and sometimes conflicting approaches shaped by specific historical, political, and cultural contexts (Moghadam 2002). The situation is made more complex because 'there are also some Muslim women who have internalized the patriarchal dimension of their heritage and become its proponents' (Islamists), alongside those 'who have exited the religious tradition as a response to patriarchal realities' (secular), as well as some Muslim leaders (all men) who 'contest sexism and resist the masculinist bias of inherited traditions' (Shaikh 2003: 148).

Muslim feminists share the same starting point: that men discriminate against women and justify their actions by mis-interpreting the Qur'an. It is argued further that women's interests conflict with those of a male elite, and that the state has been an important sustainer of patriarchy (Mernissi 1993). Referring to the situation in Iran, which is relevant to other countries in the Middle East, Moghadam (2002) suggests that Muslim feminists fall into two opposing camps – Islamic feminists and secular feminists – with overlap and ambiguity between them. The main difference is that Islamic feminists explore the possibilities of operating within an Islamic paradigm according to Shariah[3] law (Badran 2002), whereas secular feminists argue for a separation of religion and the state, and freedom of religious affiliation (Moghissi 1999).

Nasra Nomani (2005) is one of an international group of women who, in October 2005, attended the first International Congress on Islamic Feminism hoping that it will become a global movement to liberate Muslim women (Tremlett 2005). It is already the most rapidly growing feminist movement among Muslim women across the world – in countries with Muslim majorities, established minority communities, or convert communities in the West – and its membership is boosted through the increasing frequency of cyberspace activity. Islamic feminists claim that the possibility for gender equality exists in the Qur'an itself (Shaikh 2003: 156).

Secular feminists maintain that 'gender equality is the measuring stick of the broader concerns for social justice and pluralism' (Safi 2003: 11), linking women's rights with human rights and democracy. They argue that enforced sex-segregation and veiling are human rights issues. Secular feminists believe that Muslim women should be able to participate fully in all the cultural, social, and political affairs of their communities and to that end contest the gendered ideologies, politics, and legislation in their respective countries. The greatest barrier in the quest for women's rights is perceived by them to be the influence of religious conservatives.

However, Tohidi (2002) argues that to polarize secular feminism and Islamic feminism is essentially divisive and 'can only benefit reactionary patriarchal forces, be they traditional, new Islamist, or secular modern' (p. 13). She explains that the term Islamic feminism is controversial – opposed by right-wing conservative Islamists who hold strong anti-feminist views, and by secular feminists who hold strong anti-Islamic views and that, 'Both groups essentialize Islam and feminism and see the two as mutually exclusive' (p. 14). Alternatively, Muslim feminism can encompass differing perspectives and still remain distinct from Western feminisms and associations with imperialism and First-World, white, middle-class women. Al-Faruqi (2005) makes the point that, 'If feminism is to succeed in an

Islamic environment, it must be an indigenous form of feminism, rather than one conceived and nurtured in an alien environment with different problems and different solutions and goals.'

The global power of Islamist discourse has compelled many Muslim women to try to advance their cause 'within an Islamic framework'. Tohidi (2002: 14) sees such struggles as 'a faith-based response . . . against the old (traditionalist patriarchy) on the one hand and the new (modern and post-modern) realities on the other'. Those who promote female sport and exercise – characterised as Muslim sport feminists – have to negotiate this stark contrast between tradition (enforced veiling/female-only sport) and modernity (sexualized sportswear/mixed sport). In common with Islamic feminists, they refer directly to the Qur'an in their quest for gender *equity* in sport – a term they use to mean 'equivalent to', replacing *equality*, meaning 'the same as'. Their position justifies single-sex activities and leaves the politico-religious state unchallenged.

The danger of a religious-based discourse is to divert attention away from 'societal opposition to the economic, social, and cultural conditions brought about by nearly two decades of Islamization' (Moghadam 2002: 1148), and to ignore, exclude or silence non-Muslim, religious-minority women or those with a secular orientation (Tohidi 2002: 15). It is argued that real democratization can come about only from outside a religious framework (Moghissi 1999). Moghadam (2002: 1162) explains that, 'Civil society . . . guarantees protection of civil and human rights regardless of gender, religion, ethnicity, and class. An Islamic state cannot and will not undertake this because it defines citizenship rights on the basis of sex and religion.'

Given that most Muslim feminists are pragmatic and struggle for change within the Islamic framework, it is recognised by those who seek a secular politics that it is essential to nurture a dialogue with them. The resultant increased communication between the two groups is described as a 'popular feminist consciousness' (Moghadam 2002: 1145) even although Middle Eastern feminists are predominantly from the urban middle classes and cut off from the grass roots of society (Ahmed 1992: 225; Goodwin 1994: 169). Some of them are state feminists (Moghadam 2002: 1158) – those who have connections with government and accept status quo politics in order to lobby for women's rights. For example, Faezah Hashemi (former member of parliament and daughter of the former President of Iran, Ali Akbar Hashemi-Rafsanjani 1990–7) has been at the forefront of the development of sport for Muslim women.

The importance of human agency is clear. Referring to the concept of hegemony and the interrelationship between feminists, Islamists, and the state, Karam (1998: 24–6) explains that, 'the state gains legitimacy through the manufacture of consent'. She is referring to Egypt, but there are many Muslim women who consent to gender inequalities in all the countries of the Middle East. But while these women may help to reproduce the system of male privilege, other women oppose it. In the specific case of female sport and exercise, the struggles and negotiations of Muslim sport feminists – albeit within an Islamic framework – have undoubtedly resulted in changes and advances for girls and women.

It is difficult to gauge the extent of women's sense of oppression or their opposition to it. In the most repressive Islamic states, if women speak out openly, they can quickly become labelled as infidels. Most outspoken Muslim feminists live in Western countries, such as Canada, the UK and the US, some of whom have had a fatwa[4] issued against them, making other Muslim women from countries where fundamentalist Islamists are powerful, such as the Gulf states, fearful of speaking out.

Although women's physical bodies are at the centre of cultural control and contest, 'mainstream' Muslim feminists are concerned with what they see as priority issues – for example, legal rights, female suffrage, domestic violence, children's rights – and have done little to address problems of sexuality and compulsory veiling, take notice of arguments about the importance of health-giving exercise, or engage with the Muslim women's sport movement. Furthermore, most Muslim sport feminists teach physical education in girls' schools and teacher training colleges and their interventions are mostly contained within their institutions (Al-Haidar 2004; Hargreaves 2000).

Lobbying for the provision of facilities and opportunities for health-giving exercise and sport for Muslim women is potentially one of the most radical feminist initiatives. The physiological, psychological, and social benefits of exercise have been thoroughly researched (Wells 1995; Ogden 2001; Hargreaves 1994) and publicly acknowledged across the world, and Muslim sport feminists – many of whom have been educated in the West – have brought the importance of exercise for Muslim girls and women to the attention of politicians and policy-makers in their respective countries (Abdelrahman 1991; Al-Haidar 2004; Daiman 1994). As a result, in some countries – for example, Bahrain, Egypt, Iran and Kuwait – a substructure of girls' and women's sport has been established, although there remain huge disparities between resourcing for boys and girls and for men and women. Because conservative Islamic ideology dictates that Muslim females can only participate in single-sex settings or in public venues wearing Islamic clothing, the situation is complex. Furthermore, Muslim sport feminists never argue for secular sport for Muslim women (Dastgir 2005), but turn to the Qur'an to advocate female exercise. Al-Haidar (2004: 45) believes that, 'all good practising Muslims in modern-day Islamic societies should carefully maintain their bodies and use them to the maximum – to exercise them, train them, master them, make them supple, strong and beautiful . . . a true believer will strive for the ideals of physical strength, mental and physical harmony, beauty, and virtue'.

Doctrinaire interpretations of the Qur'an, laid out in an essay by Sr. Hikmat Beiruty entitled, 'Muslim Women in Sport', are cautionary. First, Beiruty outlines the dress rule: 'When participating in sports, the clothing must be Islamically acceptable. This would therefore exclude shorts, t-shirts, leotards, swimming costumes etc.' Then she explains sex-segregation: 'It is very important to ensure that there are no males watching. Mixing of sexes is forbidden in normal situations . . . let alone in a sporting arena or exercise facility.' She continues, 'In most female-only schools, there are always male teachers around. Hence wearing even body suits is not sufficient, therefore to remove yourself from this activity is the only solution.' Beiruty goes on to warn that even some all-female venues, such as swimming complexes, are also taboo since Muslim women should not mix with non-believers, 'because contact with them might easily lead to disastrous results.' She cites the holy scriptures to support this claim: 'That is why the Khalif 'Umar wrote to Abu 'Ubaidah Ibn al-Jarrah, the Governor of Syria, to prohibit the Muslim women from going to the baths with the women of the Ahl al-Kitab (the People of the Book).' Beiruty concludes: 'This distinction between women on grounds of character and religion is intended to safeguard Muslim women against the influence of women whose moral and cultural background is either not known or is objectionable from the Islamic point of view.'

Yet another interpretation is that there is nothing in the Qur'an that disallows women who are faithful to Islam from taking part in open sport competitions and in Western-style sportswear. This is the position taken by the Algerian runner, Hassiba Boulmerka, who won a gold medal in the 1500 metres at the World Athletic Championships in 1991 and then at the Olympics in 1992. But with the strengthening of fundamentalism in Algeria, a public disavowal of Boulmerka was issued because she had run in vest and shorts. For fear of her life, she was forced to leave her country and move to Europe – a poignant reminder of the powerful links between the Muslim female sporting body, politics, and religion. Boulmerka is a symbol of resistance and progress for Muslim sportswomen, representing a form of Muslim feminism built on affirmative readings of the Qur'an, and reflecting the potential for Muslim women to develop their interests in the modern world without rejecting their Muslim faith. She refused to choose between Islam and modernity and, later, as a member of the IOC, became a spokesperson for Muslim sportswomen throughout the world. Sadly, other young Algerian runners are fearful of fundamentalist retribution, and many of them experience harshly unequal gender relations of power in the family context when fathers and husbands forbid them from pursuing athletic careers (Hargreaves 2000: 61–4). Muslim sportswomen with secular views have no legitimacy or power, and almost always remain silent. That is why the Atlanta-Sydney Plus initiative, run by a non-Muslim European women's rights activist group (originally Atlanta Plus), demanded that the IOC should ban from Olympic competition all those countries that disallow women from taking part in the Games (Hargreaves 2000: 72–4). Parvin Darabi (2006) is a secular feminist who collaborates with Atlanta Plus. She runs the non-profit Dr Homa Darabi Foundation that focuses 'on defending the rights of women against religious, cultural and social-based abuse'. Together with Atlanta Plus and representatives of NGOs, Darabi met Mr Rogge, the President of the IOC, during the Athens Olympics to discuss the issue of 'gender apartheid'. But the Foundation is located in California, USA, and Darabi struggles on behalf of, but not in close liaison with, Muslim women living their everyday lives in Islamic states.

In general, Muslim sport feminists are followers of state ideology. Several of them who are in senior positions in schools and colleges have attended conferences as representatives of their country (for example, the first-ever international conference on women and sport in Brighton, England, in 1994, and the first conference on Muslim women in sport in Alexandria, Egypt, in 1995). In interviews these delegates were generally supportive of the political status quo in their countries and critical of the commercialized and sexualized bodies of sportswomen in the West. Their discourse about Muslim girls and women in sport is based always on the assumption that the context is Islamic. Although these women have been integrated into the International Women's Sport Movement (Hargreaves 2000: 215–33), and meet with Western sport feminists in sisterly friendship and camaraderie, there is no mention of secular sport for Muslim women, but, rather, a respect and sensitivity to difference. Nor is there any discussion of the wider political issues that impinge on sporting experiences and opportunities. And the senior professionals seem to be unaware of the frustrations of those who are younger. For example, when Egyptian physical education students were interviewed by a young research assistant, they admitted to feeling very envious of those of us from the West who were jogging in the park in shorts and swimming in the sea, while they were obliged to wear scarves and long cloaks.

However, Muslim sport feminists have had notable successes working within the Islamic system. The exemplar is Faezah Hashemi who has been an outspoken advocate of girls' and women's rights to engage in sport and whose inspiration resulted in the successful establishment, in 1993 in Iran, of a four-yearly multi-event competition for Muslim women, in order to give female athletes from Muslim countries the opportunity to compete internationally without violating Shariah law. The fourth games, re-named the Islamic Countries' Women's Games, were held in 2005 when women from over 30 different countries competed in 18 sports, and disabled women and non-Muslim women were included for the first time (Dastgir 2005; Steel 2005). The rapid advances made in sport for Iranian women, started during Rafsanjani's presidency (1990–7), were exceptional, and Iran has become the leading Muslim nation for women's sport. During the opening ceremony of the 2005 Games, all contestants wore Islamic clothing and Iranian spectators were carefully controlled and forbidden to applaud. But once the stadium was securely closed to all men, the *Muslim* women transformed into *sportswomen*, leaving their abayas in the changing rooms, putting on competitive sportswear and moving their bodies freely and aggressively, muscle-against-muscle, struggling and sweating to win their events. Newspaper articles tell us that the Iranian futsal[5] squad were supported by the government, had a

Brazilian coach, trained intensively to the point of obsession, and their skills, fitness, and team play were absolutely breathtaking (Dastgir 2005). But they are prevented from honing their skills further because they are banned from competing in elite international competitions, such as the Women's World Football Championships. A decision taken by the Iranian government just before the Games, to limit women's sports in the country, threatens both the future of the Games and Hashemi's leadership (ibid.).

The struggles over Muslim sport are highly complex and there is no certainty about the outcome. Muslim feminism is a highly contested term, and although Muslim sport feminists have made progress in all the countries of the Middle East and have created specialist organizations, such as the Islamic Federation of Women's Sport (1992), and the Sport Association for Arab Women (1996), they have done so within Islamic rules, hence, mostly behind closed doors. Their inroads into physical culture have therefore been limited: they have not encroached on male sporting spaces to any extent, nor have they threatened significantly the prominence and power of men in sport. Nevertheless, it has been claimed that whenever Muslim women such as Hassiba Boulmerka are seen actively pursuing sport careers, it has greater impact on the thinking of ordinary Muslim women than the actions of militant educated women. With the advent of mobile telephones, computer access to the internet, e-mail communication, satellite television, and travel to the West, Muslim women have been made more aware of the extent of their cultural restrictions than ever before.

Muslim female Olympians

In 1984, Nawal El Moutawakel from Morocco became the first Muslim (and simultaneously, the first Arab) to win an Olympic gold medal. Then in 1992, Hassiba Boulmerka from Algeria won an Olympic gold. Since then only a tiny number of Muslim women have been Olympians, most of whom were given a wild card by the IOC (because they had not achieved Olympic standards), only to get knocked out in the first round. Highly critical of the brazen images of female athleticism in international competitions, Islamic ideologues castigate the IOC for their 'cruel violation of human rights' in not providing Islamic-rules' female competitions. At the same time, Western spokespersons claim that it is Muslim leaders who are breaking human rights' standards because *they* ban their women from taking part in open competitions. Aspiring Muslim sportswomen are in the middle of a deadlock situation – denied a high enough standard of training and competition in their own countries to reach international standards, and banned from international events unless they wear Islamic clothing. The bodies of elite Muslim sportswomen are less skilled, fit, strong, fast, and prepared for high-level events than their Western counterparts – not through lack of will or desire, but because there are structures of control that prevent progress.

Muslim nations send at most one or two women to the Olympic Games.

For example, at the 1996 Games, Saudi Arabia sent 23 men and no women, Kuwait 32 men and no women, Iran 34 men and 1 woman, and Pakistan 26 men and 1 woman. According to officials in Athens, the number of Muslim women participating in the 2004 Olympics was the lowest since 1960 (Raad 2004). Almost always Muslim female Olympians take part in sports that allow them to wear traditional dress (e.g. canoeing, kayaking, shooting, archery, equestrian events), but surprisingly, there were some sprinters and swimmers at the Athens Olympics. Predictably, times for the sprinters in the opening heats of the women's 100 metres track and field were very slow by comparison with those of top sprinters from non-Muslim nations: Rakia Al-Gassra from Bahrain (11.49 seconds), Alaa Jassim from Iraq (12.7 seconds), Dana Al Nasrallah from Kuwait (13.92 seconds), and Rubina Muqimyar from Afghanistan (14.4 seconds). However, their Islamic identities were on show and their participation alone on the global stage of athletics was viewed as a triumph.

Referring to Iran, Gorji (2004), points out that Islamic clothing require-ments prohibit women from competing in most Olympic events; in others where it is possible to wear robes and headscarves, their performances are poor. In the 2004 Olympics, Iranian sportswomen were banned from com-peting in most female sports and unable to meet the Olympic standard in Taekwondo and canoeing. As a result, only one Iranian female competitor – Nassim Hassanpour – was able to go to Athens. She competed in the 10-metre air pistol event because she is banned from international competition in gymnastics, which is her real passion. In common with other Muslim women, Nassim was channelled into a sport which requires very different usages of the body – a compromise allowing her to compete at the Olympics.

The question of clothing affects all Muslim sportswomen who aspire to be elite competitors. Al-Gassra, a devout Muslim influenced by fundamentalists in her village, was covered from head to toe when she ran the 100 metres in searing heat in Athens, with a scarf around her head, a long-sleeved, loose-fitting T-shirt, thick black tights, socks and track shoes. Muqimyar was required by the Afghan Olympic Committee to wear a tracksuit so that she did not show her legs (James 2004). However, Al-Nasrallah from Kuwait – at only 16 years of age – was wearing shorts and a T-short. In contrast to the men in the Kuwaiti team, no sports kit was provided for her by the Kuwaiti Olympic Committee and so she had to buy something to run in. Al-Nasrallah is at home with Western sports culture and not unduly influenced by Kuwaiti Islamists, having attended the American School in Kuwait and now she is at a high school in the USA. She told me, 'In Kuwait out of respect to the others I wear shorts, which is OK as long as they are not too brief . . . I also wear a T-shirt that is not sleeveless because I think it would be disrespectful for people that have different beliefs than I do.'

Advances in sportswear manufacture may help to boost the participation of Muslim women in the future. Thirteen-year-old Rubab Raza, the first Pakistani female to swim at an Olympics (2004) – with a wild card – wore a

Figure 4.1 Rakia Al-Gassra from Bahrain in the 100-metre heats at the Athens
Olympics, 2004. Permission of Getty images

full length body suit (the sort worn by Western swimmers for its ability
to cut down water resistance) (BBC 2005). So her performance was not
impeded, even although her modesty was supposedly protected. But in running events clothing has a modifying impact on the heat-regulating function
of the skin, and permeability would be a vital factor in ensuring that Muslim
women could run full out without risk of overheating (Zhang *et al.* 2002),
especially in middle- and long-distance events. Bahrainian officials met with
Nike representatives to consider a 'swift suit' for Al-Gassra – similar to the
one worn by Cathy Freeman from Australia when she won the gold medal in
the 400 metres in Sydney 2000 (Hinds 2004). But the holes on the back and
legs of the suit reveal skin, which breaks conservative Islamic rules, requiring
Nike to submit a new design. Ironically, the swift suit – intended by the
Bahrainians to hide from men's eyes any vision of the 'real' woman inside –
hugs the body, and accentuates the feminine shape of the breasts, the hips,
and the waist. It is a reconstructed yet open embrace of rigorous female
physicality and muscularity.

The greatest immediate deterrent to the participation of Muslim sportswomen at major events is the opposition that continues to face them from Islamist leaders who wield power in their local communities. All forms of participation attract critical religious commentary from conservative Muslim clerics, based on the notions of Divine revelation and absolute truth. They encourage feelings of guilt and sometimes fear in young Muslim sportswomen who are ignorant of alternative Qur'anic definitions of womanhood. Sometimes the influence of religious leaders can be very persuasive. For example, after Bahrain's Olympic Committee had selected a young swimmer to compete at the Sydney Olympic Games in 2000, religious leaders visited her parents and warned them against their daughter appearing in front of so many people in a swimsuit. As a result, she was forced to stay at home (Zinser 2004). A later example of Islamist opposition to female sport relates to post-Taliban Afghanistan, where there are still a number of strongly conservative Mullahs in the government. Abdul Matin Mutasem Bilal is one of these. Referring to Muqinyar running in Athens, he asked the question, 'When I tell you that her neighbour shouldn't see all her face, how should thousands of foreigners, non-Muslims, in a big stadium be allowed to see her body?' Like Hassiba Boulmerka, both Muqinyar and her team-mate Friba Razayee (judo) believe that their athletic quest is not un-Islamic in any way. Muqinyar stated that her anger against the previous restrictions of the Taliban was channelled into her running in Athens (BBC 2004b). Even although Western clothing is allowed in Kuwait, Al-Nasrallah was interrogated in an interview about why she was running in shorts. When I asked her why there are so few other young Kuwaiti women pursuing sport to a high level, she answered that negative attitudes to female sport are intrinsic to traditional culture as much as to religious zeal.

Islamists also exercise control over Muslim female Olympians via the media, by preventing other Muslim women from knowing about, or seeing, their performances. At the Sydney and Athens Olympics, state-owned television networks in many Muslim countries were instructed to keep coverage of women's events to a minimum. A leaked circular from the Ministry of Islamic Guidance and Culture in Tehran directed that there should be no live images of women, that programmes should be carefully vetted and that, 'Editors must take care to prevent viewers from being confronted with uncovered parts of the female anatomy in contests' (cited in Taheri 2004a) – a virtual ban. In Kuwait, Islamist member of parliament, Waleed al-Tabtabai, complained about the 'obscene display of women's bodies during televised coverage of women's beach volleyball, diving and synchronized swimming' at the Sydney Olympics in 2000. He continued, 'Showing such competitions cannot be accepted as sports because they only reflect Western standards which do not provide a woman's body with the sanctity, honour and protection that Islam does' (Carnell 2000). Another Kuwaiti MP described television coverage at the Athens Olympics as a 'great catastrophe'. He was angry about the adverse effects of 'revealing and indecent' sportswear on the morals of Kuwaiti society and threatened action against the Information Minister and other senior officials (*Iran Daily* 2004). Some theologians argue that all women's sport should be banned – from the screen and in practice because of the 'sinful consequences' that result. Similar statements made by theologians in countries throughout the Middle East have influenced Mohsen Sahabi, a Muslim historian, to claim that, 'The question of how much of a woman's body could be seen in public is one of the two or three most important issues that have dominated theological debate in Islam for decades . . . More time and energy is devoted to this issue than to economic development or scientific research' (cited in Taheri 2000b).

The constant attention paid to the bodies of Muslim women in sport constitutes an extreme form of surveillance, limiting Olympic participation and pointing to the ways in which personal bodies are radically controlled by religious and political discourses. In contradiction, the Olympics also provide a space for the construction and celebration of Muslim identity and nationhood. Although all the Muslim female sprinters at the Athens Olympics were eliminated in the first round, together they aroused a great swell of Muslim pride. Nawal El-Moutakwakel identified herself especially with Al-Nasrallah and Gassra, as a Muslim, as an Arab, and as a woman, when she said, 'To see two girls coming from the Gulf states makes me really happy . . . I came all the way down to shake their hands, because it's a proud moment for us' (Raad 2004). All the sprinters were hugely proud of representing their respective countries in the most prestigious of all international competitions (Moore 2004). Muqimyar and Rezihi were the first-ever women to represent Afghanistan at the Olympics, and Al-Nasrallah was the first Kuwaiti female Olympian (Elias 2004). Muqimyar explained: 'The most important thing for me is that I am taking part in the Olympics . . . When people see the Afghan flag in the Olympics, I'll be proud' (Moore 2004). Gassra became a symbol for the celebration of Bahraini identity when she was invited by King Shaikh Hamad bin Isa Al Khalifa to his court to express the affection and esteem of the country (Taheri 2004b). Kuwaiti women who were spectators at the Athens Olympics said they were proud and excited because they were seeing the first-ever *Kuwaiti* female taking part in an Olympic competition, and because she symbolized the possibilities for other *Muslim women* in the future.

The appearance of all the female Muslim Olympians in Athens had symbolic value. They were intrinsic to constructions of 'nation' and also symbolic of a reconstruction of Muslim womanhood. They symbolized, too, the mixing of local versions of Islam with global structures and the changing, unstable relationship between state and religion, with women's bodies at the centre of struggles and changes. Because female Muslim Olympians are tiny in number, they represent the exceptional, but they also symbolize the possible.

Negotiating the local and global: grasping the possible

The question of Muslim women in sport is inextricably linked to the debate among Muslim feminists about whether women's lives should be compulsorily linked to Islam, or whether religious affairs should be a personal choice so that women could have freedom to participate in cultural activities as they wish. There is little chance that secular states will replace Islamic ones, and as long as Islamism remains influential both locally and globally, opportunities for Muslim women to use their bodies freely and healthily will remain limited, often minimal, and in many situations, nonexistent. Although in many Islamic states there is official recognition of the values to health and psychological well-being of exercise and sport for girls and women, there are marked discrepancies between government policies supporting gender equity (within a separate development arrangement) and huge differences between resources for males and females – at schools, in universities, clubs and other recreational facilities, in both the state and private sectors (Al-Haidar 2004; Hargreaves 2000). Restrictions are regularly imposed on women, but not on men. For example, in Saudi Arabia women suffer forced unhealthiness and bodily containment whereas men can enjoy healthy and sensous freedom of movement. Goodwin (1994: 222) makes the following observation: 'At the Sheraton's outdoor swimming-pool café, and in the 100 degree-plus evening heat and humidity, women shrouded completely in black lift their *niqab*[6] flaps to sip cappuccino while men, the chosen gender, swim back and forth past them.' There are Saudi women who speak in private about their hatred of the *abaya*, about being banned from using hotel gyms, about the obligation for them to be accompanied by a male relative and, regardless of soaring temperatures, having to wear the *abaya* and *hijab*[7] if they speed-walk to keep fit. But they say nothing in public. Another example occurred in Iran in 2000 when a ban was imposed on women riding bicycles or motorcycles because of the fear that doing so would activate their thighs and legs, thus arousing 'uncontrollable lustful drives', and because men watching them could be 'led towards dangerous urges' (cited in Taheri 2004a) – an example of biological determinism reminiscent of attitudes towards women in nineteenth-century Europe and North America (Hargreaves 2000; Vertinsky 1990). Also in Iran – in 2003 – plans for a new women-only sports stadium with 12-foot high surrounding walls to ensure privacy were scrapped when critics claimed that being close to an airport men on planes flying above would be able to view the women below (Taheri 2004a).

Examples like these are often used as symbolic representations of the 'Islamic community' and compared with the supposed freedom experienced by women in the West. But Shaikh (2003: 149) warns us that the dichotomous categorization of 'Islam versus the West . . . results in monolithic constructions that efface the complex nature of realities and multiple ethical discourses prevalent in both Muslim and Western societies'. The reality is that the lives of Muslim women are different, depending on location and social and religious backgrounds. For example, the position of Muslim women in certain countries is excessively harsh, as in Afghanistan where some women are suffering from a Taliban resurgence (Ulph 2005), whereas in Kuwait, for example, there is a high percentage of women with university degrees, the highest female work-force in the Gulf region, and women can wear Western clothes, drive cars, travel, and study abroad. However, there are marked social divisions between Shi'a and Sunni Muslims[8] and other religious groups, 'between the rich and not-so-rich, between *badu* (tribal populations) and *hadhar* (city dwellers), and between *bidun*[9] and citizens' (Tétreault and al-Mughni 2000: 153). Kuwaiti nationals, all of whom are Muslims, comprise a minority of the population, whereas non-Kuwaitis are the largest and most vulnerable group. Wealthy, educated, and professional women can respond creatively to the pressures of global cultures, whereas poor, dispossessed women lack the educational and cultural capital to do so. The status of poor women is entirely dependent on their relationship with men (ibid.: 158) and they remain mostly at home 'invisible' in their family and labouring roles. Women who are Kuwaiti nationals were finally given full political rights in 2005, but will not be able to vote in the parliamentary elections until 2007 (BBC 2005). It is these women who have the potential to campaign for the health and exercise needs of the underclasses. Alqudsi-Ghobra (2005) makes the point that, 'Kuwaiti women's groups need to draw their own basic agendas, with their own priorities and demands, and follow through accordingly.'

Members of the elite Islamic upper classes in all countries in the Middle East have the advantages and relative autonomy to carve out cultural opportunities for themselves (Al-Hadair 2004; Goodwin 1994). They often lead a 'double life' negotiating differences between local and global cultures. Many of them embrace Western culture, including sport. They send their children to American or European schools and universities where, like Dana Nasrallah, they play sports alongside their school and university peers. Nasrallah has participated in soccer, basketball, baseball, horseback riding, and ice-skating, and has competed in track and field and cross country. Elite Muslim women travel to holiday resorts where they can enjoy mixed sports and fitness facilities; they watch American television programmes about dieting and keep fit; and they consume fashion and sportswear images. At home, they also have time and energy and opportunities to devote to exercise and sport with (immigrant) servants to run their homes. They go to expensive, private, all-women spaces where they work out or do aerobics; or to foreign hotels where they enjoy mixed swimming or tennis. Elite women cope with cultural barriers by grasping agency and reinventing the rules. Even in Saudi Arabia where conservative dress codes and movement restrictions are strictly applied, behind the scenes, in female-only locations, rich women remove their *abayas* to show off designer jeans, expensive jewellery, and trendy hair styles. They live comfortable lives with chauffeurs to deliver them to all-women health spas. The focus is on their bodies, one minute dressed in black from head-to-toe, then, like a chrysalis, transformed into sexualized and expensively commodified bodies in the latest fitness gear. These are the women who holiday in the more liberal Egypt or Lebanon, or on the beaches of Southern Europe. I interviewed a young Saudi woman in London who talked about 'living two lives' – studying and travelling in Europe, wearing Western dress and 'working out', and then returning to Riyadh to a veiled life. She was very cautious about her European lifestyle in case she was 'discovered', and claimed she would deny that she exercised in mixed venues.

There is no problem of denial for devout Islamist women. After puberty, most of them will take no exercise of any sort. And from adolescence, all young Muslim women are pressured to conform. In Kuwait where whole families use public beaches for recreation, no Muslim women are seen swimming. In some locations, women go into the sea wearing a full *abaya*.

Muslim women negotiate the conflict between East and West traditionalists and modernists, by constructing and using their bodies in very different ways. What could be characterized as an incipient sports movement for Muslim women incorporates believers who are contesting male domination in sport within Islam *and* secularists who want gender equality within a democracy. Sport is attractive to Muslim women (as it is to non-Muslim women in countries all over the world), and they are active agents grasping opportunities in various ways. Tohidi's (2002) shift of analytic focus from gender oppression to resistance and empowerment fits the empirical evidence about Muslim women in sport. For example, the exclusion of men from sport – specifically, the Islamic Countries' Women's Games, discussed earlier – is seen as a major triumph by Muslim sportswomen who boast of the benefits of organizing their sports in a women-only environment, whereas in the West, they argue, sport is always dominated by men. They claim that the Games have allowed them to emerge from isolation and enjoy a sense of solidarity with other Muslim women (Anvari 2001).

More women are taking part in mixed-sex sports, usually in full body covering. In 2005, two of a group of five Iranian women reached the summit of Mount Everest. They were breaking new ground – firstly, as members of a mixed-sex team and, secondly, for climbing outside Iran (Halpern 2005). But the advances that Muslim women have made in sport have not taken place without difficulties, struggles, or setbacks, and the way forward is by no means certain. In some cases, young women have used sport as a focus for their opposition to imposed restrictions. For example, Iranian women skiers joined a protest against the closure of the country's leading ski resort on the anniversaries of the deaths of the Prophet Muhammad and his grandson Hasan. Skiing provides a feeling of bodily and social freedom lacking in everyday life, explained as follows by young Iranians: 'It gives you a beautiful feeling'; 'It is one of the few ways we can spend our energy and not see many law enforcement agencies.' They complain that 'It is wrong that someone died 1,400 years ago and here we have to worship not just him, but his grandchildren as well.' Subverting the official dress code, female skiers wear gaudy headbands and hats and even go entirely without any head covering (Tait 2005). In Pakistan, female runners have also been subverting tradition by running in mixed-sex races and openly resisting opposition. In December 2004, in Lahore, Pakistani men and women ran together for the first time in a full marathon, but although the women were wearing the traditional dress of Pakistan – *shalwar kameez* and *dupatta*[10] – the event sparked off violent opposition from MMA Islamic extremists[11] at a mini-marathon held shortly afterwards. A mob of MMA supporters wielded batons, threw petrol bombs, and torched cars, forcing the government to make a ruling that all future mini-marathons would be single-sex events or be cancelled. The women responded by demonstrating outside the national parliament against the 'Talibanisation' of Pakistan, one of whom said, 'These mullahs want us to just stay home, have children and God knows what else.' Although Pakistani sportswomen have suffered from the growing influence of right-wing politics, they have successfully gained ground in some sports. For example, after years of struggle for recognition from the Pakistan government and the Pakistan Cricket Board, in 2005 the national women's cricket team (with a strict dress code of long trousers and shirts) played an international match on home soil for the first time, later playing for the first time in the Women's Asia Cup. The first-ever women's football match was played in Pakistan in 2004, and in 2005 the first-ever women's international squash tournament was held (Dyson 2005; Walsh 2005).

Over the past two years, Muslim fundamentalists have organized a campaign against women's sports in Bangladesh as well. Bangladesh is a predominantly Islamic nation of 140 million people, but governed by secular laws, and women regularly take part in a growing range of sports, including handball, hockey, judo, karate, shooting, swimming, taekwondo, track and field, and volleyball. Nevertheless, the country's first-ever women's wrestling competition was cancelled as a result of threats from fundamentalist groups claiming that female wrestling is vulgar and indecent and would hurt the religious feelings of the 100 million Muslims in the country. Even although officials gave assurances that all competitors would be decently dressed, no shorts would be worn, and there would be no offence to Islamic codes, the fundamentalists claimed that they were 'even ready to sacrifice life, if necessary, to protect any kind of indecent sports to be held in the country'. Threats to people's safety also forced the Bangladeshi government to stop women taking part in a long-distance river swim (Ahmed 2004; Buerk 2004). Even in this country with a secular government, Islamists have a powerful hold over the political system and women's sports have become highly politicized. Women who take part in outdoor sports are easy, vulnerable targets; doing so has become a public political act.

Ironically, there are fewer problems for the first-ever group of female boxers from the Middle East. They live in Jordan – a constitutional monarchy with an ongoing process of political development. Unswayed by the opposition of Islamists, King Abdulla openly supports the women's boxing team as part of the government's promotion of women's rights. Following verbal attacks from conservative clerics, one of the boxers responded, 'I am not a bad girl and I don't want people to think I am a bad girl. I just like the sport.' In line with global developments in women's sport, the female boxers in Jordan fit well into the macho-dominated muscled atmosphere, wearing protective helmets and singlets, and idolizing Leila Ali, daughter of former World Heavyweight Champion, Mohammed Ali (Brabant 2004).

In some cases, Muslim sportswomen integrate into the world of Western sports. However, if they are successful and recognised in the global media, they remain vulnerable to Islamist opposition. For example, Sania Mirza was the first Indian player to enter the fourth round of a grand slam tennis tournament at the US Open in 2005. She rose at a fantastic rate to be ranked 34 in the world, becoming 'overnight' an icon of youth and modernity, Islamic emancipation and Indian pride, and was conferred with the Padma Shri, India's fourth highest civilian award. Because Mirza is a Muslim (in a country that has the second highest number of Muslims in the world at 140 million), she has attracted the attention of Islamist clerics who issued a religious diktat saying that her tennis skirts are 'un-Islamic' and 'corrupting'. An ultra-radical group declared that she would be 'stopped from playing' if she did not wear 'proper clothes'. For her safety, she now has a team of bodyguards and wears slightly more conservative on-court outfits. In support of Mirza, the Chairman of the All-India Shia Muslim Personal Law Board, and the general secretary of the Muslim Council of Bengal, have both argued in contradiction to the right-wing clerics, praising Mirza for being an inspiration and a role model for the many deprived people in the Muslim community and in the country (http://www.sania-mirza.net; Sikka 2006). Mirza's story highlights controversy over women's bodies among Islamic officials themselves – those that reflect what Gellner (1994: xii) describes as 'the conspicuous fundamentalist trend in Islam', and the more moderate, liberal position that is less audible and less visible on the global stage.

The case of Dina Al-Sabah is more extreme. Al-Sabah is a Kuwaiti citizen and a member of the Kuwaiti royal family, although she has lived much of her life in other countries and lives today in the USA. She says that she feels culturally Muslim and Arabic, that her family is her heritage, but she does not follow their traditions. The Muslim culture that dissuades young girls from exercising made no sense to her, but she felt immediately at home in the West, pursuing and competing in a range of sports. Now she is a professional IFBB[12] Figure competitor with her own website (http://www.fitdina.com), describing her as 'The Internet's Sauciest Female Fitness Model'. Al-Sabah is very serious about her sport, training and dieting to hone her body to perfection. A bikini is required for competitive Figure routines that include various gymnastic, strength, flexibility, and dance moves. Al-Sabah's body topography is described as 'complete with wild hairpin curves and cobblestone abs' (O'Connell 2005: 220). She claims to be an athlete first, proud of her body and for being a role model for other women to get fit and healthy. But her explicitly exposed and sexualized body is morally reprehensible to Muslim leaders in Kuwait who have refused to renew her passport unless she gives up her sport and removes her website. Most members of her family refuse to communicate with her and much of the hate-mail that she gets from Arabs around the world comes from distant relatives who feel she has sullied the family name. But she also receives messages of support from Muslim women across the world – made possible by the internet. Al-Sabah's case is unique, but it demonstrates that the display of female flesh in a physique sport of the sort that is hugely popular with men throughout the Middle East, is considered to be so un-Islamic as to warrant the removal of a woman's national identity and freedom to return to her homeland.

The new constructions of Muslim femininity and selfhood outlined above override conventional caricatures and stereotypes of Muslim women disseminated in the media. They are the products of tensions between Muslims and non-Muslims, and between Muslims with differing perspectives about the significance of women's bodies in Islam. They show, too, the variety and complexities of a world community of Muslim sportswomen.

Conclusion

Leila Ahmed (1992: 248) argues that, 'The sum of what is currently known about women and gender in Arab societies – the many different Arab societies and cultures that there are – is miniscule. The areas of women's lives and the informal structures they inhabit that are still unexplored are vast.' In relation to women's bodies in exercise and sport, this statement remains absolutely true today, a decade and a half later. And this chapter adds only *some* details, and analysis of *some* situations, to the minuscule amount previously written.

The increased rate of modernization in the Muslim world has incorporated unprecedented improvements in female education followed by increasing engagement in political, cultural, and social life, including women's exercise and sport. But throughout the Muslim world, the individual female body and the social body are cemented together, and whether from the elite classes or from the lower classes and non-national groups, women's sporting (and non-sporting) bodies are undeniably politicized and controlled by male power. But the concrete reality for Muslim women is that their bodies are malleable – there is imposition of an order on the body, but at the same time women have become significant agents of change and have shown resistance to barriers. In other words, there is tension in women's sports between structure and control, development and progress.

As we have seen, much of the debate about the character and usages of the bodies of Muslim women in sport is infused by antagonisms between East and West. Muslim women are sucked into political debates within their own countries and become increasingly vulnerable to bodily controls when tensions between local liberal and fundamentalist factions increase and/or when local–global tensions increase. This chapter is about struggles over culture and female embodiment. Leila Ahmed (1992: 245) urges that, 'Arab Muslim women need to reject . . . the androcentrism of whatever culture or tradition in which they find themselves', and then goes on to caution, 'but that is quite different from saying that they need to adopt Western customs, goals and lifestyles'. It is certainly the case that in their struggles for bodily autonomy and empowerment through exercise and sport, the expectations of different Muslim women from different locations and backgrounds vary greatly and they are compelled to negotiate the imbalance between Islam and the West in various and creative ways.

Notes

1   Sport is used throughout this chapter to include all forms of physical exercise for Muslim women, such as team sports and games, swimming, keep fit activities, body building, outdoor recreation, hiking, and walking.
2   The Qur'an (Koran) is in Muslim belief the book revealed by God. The Hadith are extensive and detailed recordings of what the Prophet Mohammed said and did. Together, they have shaped Muslim ethics and values.
3   Shariah is the Arabic word for Islamic law – a system based upon the Qur'an, Hadith, and the work of Muslim scholars in the first two centuries of Islam. Shariah draws no distinction between religious and secular life. Applied fully, it is a code for living that all Muslims should adhere to, including prayers, fasting, and donations to the poor. Shariah is the totality of religious, political, social, domestic and private life. Wikipedia en.wikipedia.org/wiki/Sharia 13/01/2006.
4   A fatwa is a legal pronouncement, issued by a religious law specialist on a specific issue. Wikipedia *http://en.wikipedia.org/wiki/Fatwah 13/01/2006*.
5   Futsal is an original type of five-a-side football playing on a marked pitch and with a smaller, heavier ball than in conventional football.
6   *Niqab* is a face veil worn over a headscarf so that the whole of the woman's face is covered, leaving only a small slit for the eyes.
7   *Abaya* is an overgarment. It is the traditional form of *hijab* (the Arabic term for dressing modestly) for many countries of the *Arabian* peninsula. Traditional *abaya* are black, and may be either a large square of fabric draped from the shoulders or head, or a long black kaftan. The *abaya* should cover the whole body save face, feet, and hands. It can be worn with the *niqab*. Saudi Arabia requires women to wear *abaya* in public. *Hijab* is also used to mean headscarf.
8   In Kuwait, approximately 69.9 per cent of the population are Sunni Muslims and 20 per cent Shi'a Muslims – the rest are Christians, Hindus, Buddhists and non-believers (Al-Haidar 2004: 23).
9   *Bibun* can be defined as a stateless class of persons – expatriate workers and their families, some of whom have lived in Kuwait for over ten years and over 40 per cent of whom were born in Kuwait (Tétreault and al-Mughni 2000: 151).
10 *Shalwar kameez* is the national dress for both men and women in Pakistan. *Shalwar* are loose, pyjama-like trousers, and the *kameez* is a long shirt or tunic. *Dupatta* is a headscarf.
11 Muttahida Majlis-e-Amal (MMA) is a powerful alliance of Islamic political parties spearheading the rise of the religious right in Pakistan, and considered to be aligned to the Taliban.
12 International Federation of Body Building.

Bibliography

Abdelrahman, N. (1991) 'Women and sport in the Islamic society: an analytical study of some Islamic Ulamas and physical education specialists', unpublished paper presented at the First Islamic Islamic Countries Sports Solidarity Congress for Women, University of Alexandria, Egypt.

Ahmed, F. (2004) 'Bangladesh calls off women's wrestling event', *Indo-Asian News Service*, 4 June, online, available HTTP: http://www.wrestlegirl.com/gnews1202.htm.

Ahmed, L. (1992) *Women and Gender in Islam*, New Haven, CT and London: Yale University Press.

Ahmed, A. and Donnan, H. (1994) 'Islam in the age of postmodernity', in A. Ahmed and H. Donnan (eds) *Islam, Globalization and Postmodernity*, London: Routledge, 1–20.

Al-Faruqi, L. (2005) 'Islamic traditions and the feminist movement: confrontation or Cooperation?, online, available HTTP: http://www.jannah.org/sisters/feminism.html (accessed 10 March 2005).

Al-Haidar, G. (2004) 'Struggling for a right: Islam and the participation in sports and physical recreation of girls and women in Kuwait', unpublished Ph.D. thesis, London: Brunel University.

Alqudsi-Ghobra, T. (2008) 'Women in Kuwait: educated, modern and Middle Eastern', online, available HTTP: http://www.kuwait-info.org/Kuwaiti_Women/women_in_kuwait.html (accessed 12 December 2005).

Anvari, H. (2001) 'Games beneath the veil uncovered', *The Guardian*, 26 October.

Badran, M. (2002) 'Islamic Feminism: what's in a name?', in *Al-Ahram Weekly Online No. 569*, online, available HTTP: http://weekly.ahram.org.eg/2002/569/cu1.htm (accessed 8 January 2006).

BBC (2004a) 'Pakistani girl makes Olympic history', *BBC News*, 20 August, online, available HTTP: http://news.bbc.co.uk/1/hi/world/south_asia/3582788.stm.

BBC (2004b) 'Afghan women's Olympic dream', *BBC News*, 22 June, online, available HTTP: http://news.bbc.co.uk/2/hi/south_asia/3826673.stm.

BBC (2005) 'Leaders hail Kuwait women's votes', *BBC News*, 17 May, online, available HTTP: http://news.bbc.co.uk/2/hi/middle_east/4554381.stm.

Beiruty, H., Sr. (no date) 'Muslim women in sports', rep. from *Nida'ul Islam Magazine*, online, available HTTP: http://www.zawaj.com/articles/women_sports.html.

Brabant, M. (2004) 'Jordan's female boxers go for glory', *BBC News*, 14 July, online, available HTTP: http://news.bbc.co.uk/2/hi/middle_east/3892797.stm.

Buerk, R. (2004) 'Bangladesh stops women swimmers', 30 November, online, available HTTP: http://banglacricket.com/alochona/viewthread.php?tid=7987&page=1.

Carnell, B. (2000) 'Kuwaiti politician, feminists agree – women's bodies should be hidden', online, available HTTP: http://www.equityfeminism.com/archives/years/2000/000049.html.

Carroll, R. and Borger, J. (2005) 'US relents on Islamic law to reach Iraq Deal', *The Guardian*, 22 August.

Daiman, S. (1994) 'Women, sport and Islam', *The Magazine of the Sports Council*, May/June, London: The Sports Council.

Darabi, P. (2006) 'Muslim women and the Olympic games', Dr Homa Darabi Foundation, online, available HTTP: http://www.homa.org (accessed 4 January 2006).

Dastgir, M. (2005) 'Tehran inaugurates women's Islamic competitions: maybe for the last time', online, available HTTP: roozonline.com/11english/010443.shtml (accessed 29 September 2005).

Dyson, J. (2005) 'On tour in Pakistan', *The Guardian*, 18 December.

Elias, D. (2004) 'Conservative Kuwait sends its first woman to the Olympics', *Associated Press*, 11 August.

Gellner, E. (1994) 'Forward', in A. Ahmed and H. Donnan (eds), *Islam, Globalization and Postmodernity*, London: Routledge.

Goodwin, J. (1994) *Price of Honour: Muslim Women Lift the Veil of Silence on the Islamic World*, London: Warner Books.

Gorji, M. (2004) 'Olympics 2004: gender apartheid for Iranian women because of Islamic fundamentalism', *E-Zan*, 15 August, Vol. 3.

Halliday, F. (1994) 'The politics of Islamic fundamentalism', in A. Ahmed and H. Donnan (eds), *Islam, Globalization and Postmodernity*, London: Routledge.

Halpern, O. (2005) 'Iranian women triumph on Everest', *Jerusalem Post*, 14 June.

Hargreaves, J.A. (1993) 'Bodies matter! Images of sport and female sexualization', in C. Brackenridge (ed.), *Body Matters*, Leisure Studies Association Publication, 47: 60–6.

Hargreaves, J.A. (1994) *Sporting Females: Critical Issues in the History and Sociology of Women's Sports*, London: Routledge.

Hargreaves, J.A. (2000) *Heroines of Sport: The Politics of Difference and Identity*, London: Routledge.

Hinds, R. (2004) 'From behind the veil', 23 August, online, available HTTP: http://www.arabwomenconnect.org/hdocs/mainform.asp?p=news/readNews&id=620.

Iran Daily (2004) Online, 25 August, available HTTP: http://www.iran-daily.com/1383/2072/html/politic.htm#3084.

James, S. (2004) 'War-zone competitors who beat the odds to reach Athens', *The Guardian*, 29 July.

Kanneh, K. (1995) 'The difficult politics of wigs and veils: feminism and the colonial body', in B. Ashcroft, G. Griffiths and H. Tiffin (eds), *The Post-Colonial Studies Reader*, London: Routledge.

Karam, A. (1998) *Women, Islamisms and the State*, London: Macmillan.

Mahdi, A. and Carroll, R. (2005) 'Under US Noses, Brutal Insurgents Rule Sunni Citadel', *The Guardian*, 15 September.

Mahl, M. (1995) 'Women on the edge of time', *New Internationalist*, August: 14–16.

Mernissi, F. (1991) *The Veil and the Male Elite: A Feminist Interpretation of Women's Rights in Islam*, New York: Perseus Books.

Mernissi, F. (1993) *Women and Islam: An Historical and Theological Enquiry*, Oxford: Blackwell.

Mernissi, F. (2003) *Beyond the Veil: Male–Female Dynamics in Muslim Society*, London: Saqi Books.

Moghadam, V. (2002) 'Islamic feminism and its discontents: toward a resolution of the debate', *Signs: Journal of Women in Culture and Society*, 27(4): 1,135–70.

Moghissi, H. (1999) *Feminism and Islamic Fundamentalism: The Limits of Postmodern Analysis*, London: Zed Publications.

Moore, K. (2004) 'Olympics 2004: Muslim women athletes move ahead, but don't leave faith Behind', 6 August, online, available HTTP: http://www.parstimes.com/news/archive/2004/rfe/ olympics_ muslim_ women.html.

Morgan, W. (1998) 'Hassiba Boulmerka and Islamic Green: international sports, cultural differences, and their postmodern interpretation', in G. Rail (ed.) *Sport and Postmodern Times*, Albany: Suny.

Nagata, J. (1994) 'How to be Islamic without being an Islamic State: contested models of development in Malaysia, in A. Ahmed and H. Donnan (eds), *Islam, Globalization and Postmodernity*, London: Routledge.

Nomani, A. (2005) 'A gender Jihad for Islam's future' *The Washington Post*, 6 November, online, available HTTP: http://www.washingtonpost.com/wpyn/content/article /2005/11/04/ AR2005110402306.html.

O'Connell, J. (2005) 'Too hot to handle', *Muscle & Fitness*, August: 218–24.

Ogden J. (2001) *Health Psychology: A Textbook*, Buckingham: Open University Press.

Raad, Z. (2004) 'Gulf women sprinters fail to qualify', *Middle East Online*, 20 August, online, available HTTP: http://www.middle-east-online.com/english/?id=11028.

Roberts, J. (1980) *The Pelican History of the World*, Harmondsworth: Penguin.

Safi, O. (2003) 'Introduction', in O. Safi (ed.), *Progressive Muslims: On Justice, Gender and Pluralism*, Oxford: Oneworld Publications.

Sardar, Z. (2002) 'Islam: resistance and reform', *New Internationalist*, 345: 9–13.

Schlein, L. (2004) 'Iranian Islam apologist (Shirin Ebadi) Pleas for Women's Rights in Islamic Countries', online, available HTTP: www.iranian.ws/iran_news/publish/article (accessed 13 December 2005).

Shaikh, S. (2003) 'Transforming feminisms: Islam, women, and gender justice', in O. Safi (ed.) *Progressive Muslims: On justice, gender and pluralism*, Oxford: Oneworld Publications.

Sikka, B. (2006) 'India's most wanted', *The Observer Sport Monthly*, February: 55–61.

Steel, J. (2005) 'Sport and the scarf', BBC Radio 4, 9 September.

Taheri, A. (2004a) 'Muslim women play only an incidental part in the Olympics' *Gulf News*, 18 August.

Taheri, A. (2004b) 'Muslim women at the Olympics', *Lane 9 News Archive*, 21 August, online, HTTP: http://www.swimmingworldmagazine.com/lane9/news/7934.asp

Tait, R. (2005), 'Religious mourning casts pall on Iran's once carefree ski Slopes', *The Guardian*, 11 April.

Tétreault, M. and al-Mughni, H. (2000) 'From subjects to citizens: women and the nation in Kuwait', in S. Ranchod-Nilsson and M. Tétreault (eds), *Women, States, and Nationalism*, London: Routledge.

Tisdall, S. (2005) 'World briefing: band of brothers', *The Guardian*, 9 December.

Tohidi, N. (1991) 'Gender and Islamic fundamentalism: feminist politics in Iran', in C. Mohanty, A. Russo and L. Torres (eds), *Third World Women and the Politics of Feminism*, Bloomington, IN: Indiana University Press.

Tohidi, N. (2002) 'Islamic feminism: perils and romises', *Middle East Women's Studies Review*, Fall and Winter, 16(3/4): 13–15, and 27, online, available HTTP: http://www.amews.org/review/reviewarticles/tohidi.htm

Tremlett, G. (2005) 'Muslim women launch "gender jihad" ', *The Guardian*, 31 October.

Turner, B. (1984) *The Body and Society*, Oxford: Basil Blackwell.

Ulph, S. (2005) 'Taliban resurgence in Afghanistan', *Terrorism Focus*, 18 October, 2(19).

Vertinsky, P. (1990) *The Eternally Wounded Woman: Women, Exercise and Doctors in the Late Nineteenth Century*, Manchester: Manchester University Press.

Walsh, D. (2005) 'Mullahs target women runners', *The Guardian*, 12 April.

Walter, N. and al-Faisal, R. (2005) 'Veiled hopes', *The Guardian Weekend*, 5 February.

Watson, H. (1994) 'Women and the veil: personal responses to global processes', in A. Ahmed and H. Donnan (eds), *Islam, Globalization and Postmodernity*, London: Routledge.

Wells, C. (1995) *Women Sport and Performance: A Physiological Perspective*, Champaign, IL: Human Kinetics.

Zhang, P., Gong, R., Yanai, Y and Tokura, H. (2002) 'Effects of clothing material on thermoregulatory responses' *Textile Research Journal*, 72(1): 39–43.

Zinser, L. (2004) 'Swimming: breaking down barriers for women', *International Herald Tribune*, 24 August.

5 Producing girls

Empire, sport, and the neoliberal body

Leslie Heywood

Introduction

In the years since Title IX, the Education Act of 1972 which mandated equal
funding in high school and college sport and which is widely held to have
inaugurated the widespread development of girls' and women's sport in the
US, the global economic structure has undergone two major shifts. First,
following the collapse of state socialism and the worldwide consolidation of
capitalism, along with the rapid spread of information technologies, the phenomenon of globalization was increasingly explained by the belief that (for its
affluent inhabitants) the world was a shared social and economic space,
centred on the decline of the nation-state and the growing influence of the
multinational corporation; and second, following the events of 11 September
2001,[1] there has been a reassertion of geopolitics and state power, but within
the context of an already globalized world constructed according to the main
tenets of neo-liberalism: (i) that there is no substitute for the market economy;
(ii) free trade will benefit the poor; and (iii) that less-developed countries
simply lack development capital and that such capital can only flow to these
countries in sufficient quantities via private capital markets (Brown 2003:
571–2). This economic context raises a particular set of questions for the
discussion of contemporary girls and women in sport in the US: first, to
what extent are contemporary definitions of 'girlhood' in affluent countries
dependent upon the definition of young women as a metaphor for positive
social change? To what extent have young women become the poster image of
the 'opportunities' increased privatization offers – an economic structure in
which there is supposedly no further need for feminism? How does the strong,
healthy image of the athletic female body reinforce this definition? Second, to
what extent do women's sports advocacy organizations (which, with the severe
curtailment of public sources are increasingly dependent on private funding)
further the ideology of Empire, making girls' success in sport the projection
of their future success in the corporate world? And third, to what extent
might it be said that the image of the powerful, athletic female body functions
as the representation of health, success, and the physical representation of
these 'opportunities' the new economic structure supposedly provides?

Using the most recent research from Girl Studies, a subdivision of
Women's and Gender Studies that focuses on youth cultures and the

sociology of youth specific to girls, I will look at how girls are 'produced' as girls in the United States, how sport is being used to further that particular form of production, and how even advocacy organizations with progressive, radical interests can become trapped in a cycle where their advocacy is impossible without using the language of globalization and Empire. This specific contradiction within women's sport advocacy discourse today is a pressing example of what theorists of the global economy typically formulate as the all-encompassing nature of this system, how there is no 'outside' position from which to manoeuvre and oppose its work. As Manuel Castells writes, 'any node that disconnects itself is simply bypassed, and resources (capital, information, technology, goods, services, skilled labour) continue to flow in the rest of the network ... within the value system of productivism/consumerism, there is no individual alternative for countries, firms, or people' (2003: 330). Castells claims that there is literally no outside, no individual or institution that can fail to participate. But this is not to say that there can be no change from within – for example, liberal feminists in the 1970s and 1980s used Title IX to significantly transform the horizon of women's sports, and perhaps new strategies to transform the influences of global consumerism are evolving today. As I will argue, one such strategy may involve an examination of a popular image of the female athletic body in the context of the neoliberal ideology that supports globalization.

Empire and the 'future girl': the do-it-yourself subject and the subjection of feminism

In *Empire*, Hardt and Negri's (2000) oft-cited work on the new political order of globalization, the authors argue that today's global Empire is fundamentally different from older forms of imperialism and capitalist expansion. They go on to claim that unlike the imperialism of the nineteenth and early twentieth centuries based on a straightforward model of dominance and control, the contemporary global Empire makes use of aspects of US constitutionalism and its decentralized traditions of frontier expansion and hybrid identities. Hardt and Negri use the term 'Empire' to mean not rule by a dominant power over subjugated territories and peoples, but rather to mean 'systems of global regulation that have no boundaries but which nonetheless embody relations of domination and subjugation' (Held 2003: 53). Hardt and Negri identify 'a new logic and structure of rule' characterized by the erosion of the nation-state: 'a decentred, deterritorializing apparatus of rule that progressively incorporates the entire global realm' (2000: xi–xii). Further, their formulation of Empire as an economic structure that 'creates the very world it inhabits' (2000: xv) and in which power works largely through mechanisms of self-policing and people's active participation in consumer culture, in turn helps to explain some of the formulations in *Future Girl: Young Women in the 21st Century* (Harris 2004a). Here Australian sociologist Anita Harris makes the argument that since the 1990s, a convergence of neoliberal and feminist discourses has emerged to radically reshape the categories of, and social ideas about, girls. The convergence of the needs of the new economy with some of the successes of second-wave feminism such as the expansion of opportunity for girls and women in education and some forms of employment in the developed countries of the North[2] has resulted in discourses that construct girls in terms of a 'can-do' or 'girlpower' model, and a seemingly opposite model based on girls 'at risk'.

In a Western economic structure based on deindustrialization, decentralization, the expansion of global communications, technology, and service sectors, Harris and girl studies' theorists like Angela McRobbie (2004) argue that girls rather than boys or youth generally are being constructed as the ideal subjects of Empire. Harris (2004a: 1) argues that, 'In a time of dramatic social, cultural, and political transition, young women are being constructed as a vanguard of new subjectivity . . . power, opportunities, and success are all modelled by the "future girl", a kind of young woman celebrated for her "desire, determination, and confidence" to take charge of her life, seize chances, and achieve her goals.' In fact, according to Angela McRobbie (2004: 6), 'young women are championed as a metaphor for social change' – a metaphor that disavows the need for feminism and other social justice struggles. For while 'future girl' subjectivity and the goals that accompany it might sound like a positive construction, Harris points out that this discourse obscures the fact that 'many girls bear the full impact of economic rationalism, new security concerns, and the dismantling of welfare. Young women appear to have it all, and yet many constitute those hardest hit by the effects of the new global political economy on jobs, resources, and community' (Harris 2004a: xvii). Furthermore, this construction of girls as the new possibilities for success works to produce subjects who see their lives as DIY[3] projects and who will take personal responsibility for their failure rather than looking to the larger economic structure or to the state. 'Late modern times', Harris writes, 'are characterized by dislocation, flux, and globalization, and demand citizens who are flexible and self-realizing. Direct intervention and guidance by institutions have been replaced by self-governance; power has devolved onto individuals to regulate themselves through the right choices' (2004a: 2) and 'public policy often employs the language of individual responsibility and enterprise to fill the gap left by deregulation' (2004a: 4). The notions of responsibility, agency, and choice operate to accomplish what Hardt and Negri describe as 'the first task of Empire . . . to enlarge the realm of the consensus that supports its power' (2000: 14).

What better way to achieve consensus than through an appeal to individual power, particularly to young women who, even a generation or two earlier, were admonished to perform the effacements of traditional femininity? As Jennifer Drake and I argue, because the gender wage-gap in the 20–24-year-old demographic has disappeared in the US (although it grows the further you get up the economic ladder), in terms of her immediate surroundings, some 'future girls' see the equality that second-wave feminism promised, and see their chances as unlimited (Heywood and Drake 2004: 14). Harris writes that 'the enormous discursive clout of "Girl Power" is . . . frequently used in government and non-government services and programs for young women that are related to health, sexuality, education, sports, business knowledge, and self-esteem' (2004b: 166). This larger context of Empire and Western girls' supposedly new place in it has wide-ranging implications for the analysis of sport.

Girls' sport advocacy in the age of neoliberalism

Due to cutbacks of state support for physical education or sports and physical activity programming of any kind, and the growing shift in state funding toward militarization ostensibly connected to the 'war on terror', for its continued efficacy and survival women's sport advocacy discourse in the US is seen to participate in what Harris (2004a) calls the 'can do/at risk' paradigm for girls in marketing its otherwise progressive programmes. This paradigm creates a contradictory condition in which the discourse used to sell the programming seems also to serve the interests of 'the new economy', producing 'ideal' girls as self-made, flexible consumer subjects who are self-monitoring and adaptable to change, and which blames girls designated 'at risk' for their 'failures'. 'At risk' girls are, according to Harris, disproportionately 'unlikely to be middle class, and are generally of particular ethnic minorities' (2004a: 25). Yet this is exactly the structural problematic that women's sport advocacy programming is designed to address. Its marketing approach weds the discourse of liberal feminism with that of neoliberalism, constructing sport as a space where girls learn to take responsibility for their own lives – a responsibility that has care of the body for health and 'success' at its core. Girls thus become the ideal subjects of Empire, part of the new global economy that relies on individuals with flexibility who are trained to blame their inevitable 'failures' on themselves rather than the system their lives are structured within. But it is a discourse clearly at odds with the intent of 'activist' sport programming – programming that has girls' interests, not the market's interests, in mind.

However, in order to successfully obtain enough funding to continue programming and make an impact, women's sport advocacy organizations such as the Women's Sports Foundation (WSF), the largest organization of this kind, structures some of its marketing along these lines, positing a direct connection between sport participation and successful self-production. An example of this is the section directed toward adults in the WSF GoGirl World website created for GoGirlGo!, their capstone advocacy project, in which WSF presents itself as the gateway organization that will serve to convert 'at risk' girls into 'can do' girls. The WSF GoGirlGo! programme is very much part of a larger trend in this regard, for as Jane Victoria Ward and

Beth Cooper Benjamin point out, 'as concern about girls became more widespread, interest in marketing to girls (in the form of girls' programs, sports, Websites, toys, pop idols, etc.) grew alongside it' (2004: 21).

Such marketing points to the necessity of participation within the discourse of the 'can do/at risk' paradigm. Participation, however, does not make the Foundation's activities reducible to that discourse, but rather points to the inescapability and pervasiveness of that discourse, and to the fact that participation in activities that might show some of the disadvantages of globalization in the context of the current global economy is increasingly difficult and contradictory. Harris writes that, 'activists struggle with the problem that structural explanations for their differential circumstances are losing ground in the face of pervasive discourses of Girl Power, self-invention, and meritocracy' (2004b: 171). Also, Castells suggests, above, that to participate successfully in the global economy today – because it is global, and because there are few if no viable alternatives – is to adopt its terms, or risk being bypassed entirely. As Hardt and Negri put it, 'it is false to claim that we can (re)establish local identities that are in some sense *outside* and protected against the global flows of capital and Empire' (2000: 45).

My point is that participation in this discourse is unavoidable, and that at the same time, this participation has ideological consequences in terms of the message it sends. I want to make it clear that the Foundation has done and continues to do a tremendous amount to promote the cause of women in sports. This can be seen in the Foundation's mission statement, which seeks to help produce a society in which:

- Girls and women of all ages fully experience and enjoy sports and physical activity with no barriers to their participation.
- Girls and women are confident and comfortable identifying themselves as athletes.
- Everyone believes that sports and physical activity are important to the health, leadership development, and well-being of all girls and women.
- Everyone agrees that society benefits when females reach their full potential.
- Boys and girls are assumed to have equal opportunity and ability in sports.
- Sports for males and females embrace positive values, such as cooperation and respect for others.
- Equal opportunity is assured and equal ability is assumed in the sports workplace.
- There is extensive interest in, and quality media coverage of, women in sports.

(WSF 2003: 1)

However, in the current context, activism of the sort outlined here might be seen to require new terms. The pervasiveness of neoliberalism in the functioning of the global economy means that in order effectively to garner resources to further the activist mission, the Foundation's discourse in selling the GoGirlGo! project can be seen to occupy a complicated, contradictory position that fits Harris's descriptions and that seems to disregard some of the institutional barriers that girls will face and not necessarily be able to overcome solely due to their sport participation. Furthermore, due to the current shift away from the New Deal initiatives and later civil rights struggles, non-profit organizations and community-based organizations increasingly have to rely on a 'personal responsibility' rather than a civic responsibility discourse to further their missions.[4]

In my analysis of the marketing of the GoGirlGo! project, I am walking a line where, as Jennifer Eisenhauer says of the artwork *I'm Not Just a Girl*, 'critique and the object of critique do not form neatly into an opposition' (2004: 87). Any object, discourse, or programme can function positively in some contexts while necessarily functioning negatively in others, and this does not mean that the negative cancels the positive out. In the case of GoGirlGo!, the programme functions very positively in the context of health and proposing sport as a means to attain it, but in its marketing strategies can be seen to participate in the production of new femininities that are market-driven consumer femininities that sometimes disregard structural differences between women. That does not mean, however, that in its actual programming functions these differences are disregarded. This contradictory aspect of the 'GoGirlGo!' marketing is a good example of the way structural explanations are not marketable or saleable in the context of the pervasiveness of neoliberalism, and do not work as effective tools to generate funding for programmes. Since financial support is forthcoming from few sources except the private sector, marketing must partake of the discourse most operational in that sector. Therefore, 'empowerment' in the context of GoGirlGo! sometimes seems to be formulated in the sense that, as Harris puts it, 'strong and empowered girls are those that have and spend money' (2004b: 167). Indeed, if many of the current theorists of the global economy are right, activists need to rethink the traditional dualisms between working inside or outside the system to promote social change. In the current situation, as Hardt and Negri write, 'we should be done once and for all with the search for an outside, a standpoint that imagines a purity for our politics' (2000: 46). However, a lack of 'purity' does not mean that no change is possible, but rather that the notion of what constitutes change needs to be reconceptualized. WSF's complicity on one level with the terms of neoliberalism indicates not a 'selling out', but is rather an indication of the broader, more complicated horizon that activists today are working within, a horizon that critical thinkers and activists everywhere must more fully confront by dropping the notion of an 'outside' to the system and the possibility of ideological purity.

We can begin to see some of these complications at work in the WSF position paper, 'Benefits – Why Sports Participation for Girls and Women'

(WSF 2005a). Available on the website and originally formulated as a grant-getting device to help with funding, the paper begins the ideal construction of girls that Harris's research describes on three levels: (i) it is prescriptive about what girls should and should not do – i.e. 'risky behaviours' such as the consumption of drugs and alcohol and pregnancy are constructed as negative practices that sport can 'solve'; (ii) it offers sport as a solution to anything that would make a girl less productive, get her 'off track', such as depression, negative body image, or low self-esteem; and (iii) it claims to give girls the tools they will need to succeed in the corporate world. According to the paper:

> high school girls who play sports are less likely to be involved in an unwanted pregnancy; more likely to get better grades in school and more likely to graduate than girls who do not play sports. Girls and women who play sports have higher levels of confidence and self esteem and lower levels of depression. Girls and women who play sports have a more positive body image and experience higher states of psychological well-being. Sport is where boys have traditionally learned about teamwork, goal-setting, the pursuit of excellence in performance and other achievement-oriented behaviours – critical skills necessary for success in the workplace. In an economic environment where the quality of our children's lives will be dependent on two-income families, our daughters cannot be less prepared for the highly competitive workplace than our sons. It is no accident that 80 per cent of the female executives at Fortune 500 companies identified themselves as having played sports.
>
> (WSF 2005a)

The message here is clear: in addition to experiencing the health benefits of sport, 'success' means successful participation in the corporate world and consumer economy, and this is stated as if we all agree with the assumption that girls' life goals should be to join such a company, that there is no alternative pathway to success. The message to adults from whom they are seeking donations is that sport is a perfect vehicle for normalizing girls to occupy some of the higher managerial positions in the consumer economy, thus ensuring this particular definition of 'success'.

The GoGirl World website (WSF 2005b) provides an example of these aims. Harris writes that 'the new watchfulness in youth research, policy, and popular culture seeks to shape conduct through perpetual everyday observation and to elicit self-monitoring in youth themselves' (2004a: 6). They are not only obliged to manage their own life trajectories, but are enticed to display this management for the scrutiny of experts and observers. The website performs exactly these functions. The webpage for *GoGirl World* has a split screen, with a cartoon image of a funky, ethnic, hip-hop girl with unlaced sneakers, leather wrist cuffs, and a key hanging from a chain around her neck. Inside, there are places for girls to ask the 'sports diva' questions, and her answers unerringly sell sport as a solution to all problems. Under the 'School' button, text pops up that reads:

> Cheer up! We come from the school that girls rule! This higher learning joint is about the places where sport and your life intersect. Read about how your favourite athletes deal with life's curve balls. Learn the tricks to being a stellar leader. Figure out what you might want to do with your life.

Functioning explicitly as a 'life coach', in *GoGirl World* there are places for girls to exhibit their sport stories, to share how sport has reshaped their lives. And there are sidebars where girls can click to find a 'Guide for Life', and a 'Future Focus'.

The image on the other side of the split screen on the page for *GoGirl World* is directed to adults, a photograph of four well-dressed, carefully ethnically diverse adults who look like they are on a coffee break from the board meeting at Gatorade. The text box reads: 'Adults – concerned about the health and well-being of American girls? Join GoGirlGo! National Campaign and help bring physical activity into a girl's life.' When you click on that link, it brings you to a page that makes use of the risk statistics quoted earlier, and which includes a button you can click on to 'get a girl active'. According to the pitch, getting a girl active is important because 'active girls have a better chance of successfully navigating the heavy emotional and social pressures of girlhood. Improving girls' health and wellness depends on YOU. Click on

Figure 5.1 The GoGirlGo! homepage, www.gogirlgo.com. Reproduced by permission of the Women's Sports Foundation (USA)

one or more of the four action buttons at the top of this page and start making a difference today!' Underneath the images, the logos of WSF's corporate sponsors change every few seconds from Gatorade, a sports drink company, to Advanta, a provider of small business services, to Wrigley, the chewing gum company, to Moving Comfort, a women's sport apparel manufacturer. The visual message is striking: funky girl becomes corporate girl though her sport participation.

As we have seen, WSF uses the risk discourses of health and wellness to make this argument. Such use points to the impossibility of the economic viability of any clearly oppositional message, as well as the continuing reliance on the public health discourse of responsibility and individual behaviours. In the reports, WSF conflates the social discourses around what Harris identifies as the 'can do girls', who tend to suffer from 'crises of identity and self-esteem', and 'at risk' girls, who are said to be more likely to engage in 'risky behaviours' such as substance abuse and an active sex life (2004a: 33). Not taking into account the structural differences between the usually white, wealthy 'can do' girls, and the non-white, non-wealthy 'at risk' girls, the GoGirlGo! website conflates these discourses and offers sport as a solution to problems of both kinds. In this sense, 'a broader and more systemic analysis of young women's circumstances is lost' (Harris 2004a: 33). It is a good example of 'Girl Power' discourse at work. In its fundraising efforts, GoGirlGo!'s description of sport as a panacea of solutions, in Jessica Taft's words, 'reflects the ideologies of individualism and personal responsibility, and has a noticeable disregard for social systems and institutions . . . it hides both the material and the discursive forces shaping identity and the ways these gendered, raced, classed, and sexualized identities may give girls privileges or pose challenges' (2004: 73). On one level, that of the broader public discourse where such notions lose or gain credence, to sell an activist campaign without attention to these issues – as one must do in order to be funded – may also have the unintentional effect of legitimizing rather than questioning the way these ideologies function in the contemporary global economy. The solution becomes part of the problem – the pervasiveness of the neoliberal ideology of responsibility and self-determination requires that those who oppose it adopt its terms, further consolidating its terms.

Yet, as established earlier, if Castells and other theorists of the global economy are right, to question rather than to adopt its terms results in being left behind: 'any node that disconnects itself is simply bypassed' (2003: 330). Given the difficulty of viability within this particular political, economic context, one might argue that how one markets one's programming may well reinforce the ideology of neoliberalism on one level, but that within this reinforcement, cracks and fissures also begin to appear. This is the way Hardt and Negri formulate the activist horizon today:

> in the postmodern world, the ruling spectacle of Empire is constructed through a variety of self-legitimating discourses and structures . . . [our

job is to] bring to light the contradictions, cycles, and crises of the process because in each of these moments the imagined necessity of the
historical development can open toward alternative possibilities. In
other words, the deconstruction of the spectral reign of global capitalism
reveals the possibility of alternative social organizations.

(2000: 47–8)

According to Hardt and Negri, as well as many other academics and
thinkers dealing with problems connected to the global economy such as
environmental impacts and fundamental inequalities, what currently *seems*
all-encompassing may not be so. This can be extended to the case in point:
while dominant discourses are today producing girls as the ideal subjects of
Empire, and while even oppositional activist organizations seem to be working in accordance with this, the limits to the neoliberal programme of globalization and bottom-line economic expansion are becoming increasingly clear.
The affluent consumer lifestyle of developed countries, and the growing
disparity of wealth and resources between those countries and developing
countries, does not bode well for the continuance of this programme. The
devastating environmental impacts and the problems of sustainability are
increasingly discussed, as is geopolitical instability due to the growing consolidation of resources toward the top.[5] So while at this particular historical
moment activist discourses around girls increasingly take the neoliberal line,
this does not necessarily mean that the girls who experience the programming that is sold in this way will adopt it, nor does it mean that the
programming itself necessarily works in accordance with these terms.

Powerful bodies–powerful lives: marketing, implementation, and the neoliberal body

Along these lines, one might raise the question of differences between the
marketing of a programme, and the content of the programming. It is at this
juncture that the contradictory position of contemporary activist organizations becomes clear. Does the pitch to potential funders negate or even prob-
lematize a programming content that has different aims? In the case of
GoGirlGo! there are two separate programmes, one directed to third through
eighth graders, the other to high school girls.[6] The programming guide for
group leaders specifies that each GoGirlGo! session runs as follows: each
session begins with a famous athlete's story, which is read aloud and focuses
on a particular issue. This is followed by reactions and discussion. Then
information is provided about each issue, and an activity that centres around
it. After the session, each girl is encouraged to keep a journal for reactions
and feelings about the issues raised. Each session focuses on a different topic.
These include leadership, body image, acceptance and respect, smoking,
emotions, nutrition, bullying, families, sleep, drug and alcohol use, anger,
'hooking up', and harassment. A physical activity follows each discussion

session. Packs for group leaders include 'six concrete things an adult can do to help a girl', which range from 'focusing on who she is rather than on appearance' to 'encouraging her to take risks, share her thoughts and opinions, and get involved in a sport' (WSF 2004: 65). Programming is very flexible, and can range in time from one afternoon to twelve days. Girls are to be encouraged to make use of the GoGirl World website beyond the programming sessions. Adult leaders are supposed to provide an open forum for discussion and communication, using the athlete's stories as a point of departure for discussion.

Each story is fairly neutral in terms of its ideological content. Soccer star Julie Foudy, for instance, writes about why she and other good athletes don't smoke. Paralympic track athlete, Aimee Mullens, talks about why she doesn't drink and how to resist pressure. Basketball star Tamika Catchings writes about being different – how prejudice works and how to not participate in it yourself. Swimmer Darra Torres discusses body image in similar terms. While one might say that these stories are prescriptive, encouraging particular behaviours and norms, one might also say that this discussion cannot be analyzed in similar terms to the marketing campaign: there are no pitches equating success with participation in the corporate world, there is no emphasis on any particular economic goal. 'Love yourself, and don't let others or ideal media images push you around' seems to be the central message. However, the message of each story is that sport helped each woman to overcome her particular problem, whether it was abuse, depression, prejudice, or pressure to engage in risky behaviour.

While this is certainly a positive message and a positive incitement to participate in sport and thereby receive its health benefits, the 'love yourself/ reject the system' message itself might not be the most effective strategy in a system such as Empire in which there is no simple outside or point of rejection. Indeed, this 'love yourself/reject the system' message may be generational to the extent that the pervasiveness of ideals and media images was for pre-Title IX generations not as pervasive is it is for girls now. Susan Bordo points to this discrepancy when she discusses audience reactions to her work:

> My generation . . . still believes it is possible to 'just turn off the television.' They are scornful, disdainful, sure of their own immunity to the world I talk about. No one really believes the ads, do they? Don't we all know these are just images, designed to sell products? . . . Now, I simply catch the eye of a twenty-year-old in the audience. They know. They understand that you can be as cynical as you want about the ads – and many of them are – and still feel powerless to resist their messages. They know, no matter what their parents, teachers, and clergy are telling them, that 'inner beauty' is a big laugh in this culture.
>
> (Bordo 2003: xxvii)

The GoGirlGo! programming model does seem to take what Bordo refers to as a generational view that is different from that of its target audience. 'Love yourself' is empty rhetoric in a culture that is continually evaluating and judging, and presenting ideal images that girls have to measure themselves against. They cannot 'just turn off the TV' – they would also have to turn off the world wide web, not look at magazines or billboards, not go to movies . . . in short, they would have to stop participating in dominant culture entirely. If GoGirlGo! and programmes like it really want to offer a safe space for girls where they are motivated to make exercise a regular part of their lives through discussion of resisting pressures, a simple message of 'love yourself' will not do. Some systematic analysis of where, exactly, the 'pressures' to conform come from is needed, and discussion of media images of the female athlete and prescribed body ideal is part of that. Furthermore, as I will develop below, part of my point is that the media images of the athletic female body that at least partially inform the context of the GoGirlGo! programming and that consciously or not serve as one of the motivations to 'get a girl going', are themselves linked in the larger culture to success in the consumer economy.

For these reasons, perhaps more than any others, within the programming itself attention could be called to the *image* of female athletes and their ideal bodies that this programming uses to sell itself. An explanation of how the new 'girl power' thesis and female athletes' place within it are linked to the way Empire has absorbed women's sport into its definitional frame might be the most educational of all in terms of developing girls' awareness about their place within the global economy. A discussion of how this large, seemingly abstract issue is actually inscribed on their physical bodies, or at least inform the body ideals to which they might aspire as athletes, may well function as one of the most powerful ways to achieve this kind of awareness. This would help girls to, as Susan Bordo writes, 'recognize that normalizing cultural forms exist', and help them to achieve one important activist goal that currently seems missing from the GoGirlGo! programming:

> enhanced *consciousness* of the power, complexity, and *systemic* nature of culture, the interconnected webs of its functioning . . . in our present culture of mystification – a culture which continually pulls us away from systemic understanding and inclines us toward constructions that emphasize individual freedom, choice, power, ability – simply becoming *more conscious* is a tremendous achievement.
>
> (2003: 30, original emphasis)

I would argue that, since images are so compelling and persuasive, and communicate so powerfully on levels that are not always conscious, a discussion of what the image of the female athlete means and communicates might be one of the most effective ways to help girls recognize their embeddedness in the culture, the ways it shapes their lives, and what agency they do have to resist it.

This would be a particularly effective strategy, because as I noted earlier, the marketing discourse used to sell GoGirlGo! to some extent participates in this culture of mystification in the way it weds the discourse of liberal feminism with that of neoliberalism, presenting sport as a space where girls learn to become the ideal subjects of a new global economy that relies on individuals with flexibility who are trained to blame their inevitable 'failures' on themselves rather than the system their lives are structured within. But the *image* of the female athletic body is perhaps even more powerful than the *discourse* about success, health, and personal responsibility. And it is the image that arguably best represents the contradictory situation that characterizes women's sport in the US: the very corporate forces that have brought women's sport greater attention, and help make sport programming possible (such as the fact that the dollar sales of women's athletic footwear in the US topped men's for the first time in 1994, and in 1995 women spent $6 billion compared to men's $5.6, therefore creating a corporate interest in women's athletics that did not previously exist) are also the forces that may make girls' lives the most difficult (see Wallenchinsky 1996: 47). While corporations like Nike have provided a host of idealized images of female athletes that have had a powerful cultural function, that function is both positive and negative (Heywood and Dworkin 2003, esp. Prologue and Ch. 2). In some cases, when the image serves, female athletes are no longer 'deviant', they are normalized, serving as 'role models', the 'can do' girls who have gotten it right. Connected to this 'girl power' image, in the assumptions behind it, the transformed body of, and ideas about, the female athlete become the perfect representative agency for this idea of success, the 'can do' mapped directly onto her biceps and supple lines of her flexible, lean shoulders. We can see this in images of female athletes throughout the mass media, such as this one from the Roxy sportswear website.

The girls in the Roxy image show a sculpted, lean-muscled femininity that is obviously the product of athletic training, whether that training is obtained on a surfboard or in the gym. They look happy, healthy, and strong, good consumers of the 'extreme sports lifestyle' as well as its embodiment. While more traditional sports require less flexible bodies, extreme sports require a body that can adapt to any situation, whose strength is not in its bulk but in its adaptability to changing circumstance, much as the global economic context requires adaptation to constantly shifting parameters. The image fits. Empire's symbolic reliance on images and narratives of female athleticism to advance its aims is the more complicated reason behind 'the rise of the female athlete as cultural icon' outlined in *Built to Win* (Heywood and Dworkin 2003) in addition to the appeal to young women as an important consumer market, the ideal image of female athletes perfectly incorporates the ideal of the new, can-do, DIY, take responsibility-for-yourself subject. As Harris writes, 'today [girls] are supposed to become unique, successful individuals making their own choices and plans to accomplish autonomy . . . To be girl-powered is to make good choices and to be empowered as an individual' (2004a: 6). Girl-power images such as those in the Roxy photo of girls who participate in extreme sports are a central part of the cultivation of that image of uniqueness, strength, and autonomy. That image is meant and perhaps is interpreted by viewers (if the advertising works successfully) as a synecdoche for the successful life. While it is clear that all audiences do not read images the same way, and that they are often read counter to their intended message and reappropriated for oppositional ends, this does not mean that the images do not simultaneously communicate messages that normalize – in this case, the idea that the athletic female body is representative of the success a young sporting girl will have in her life, and part of that success is as a member of consumer culture who consumes Roxy.[7] For instance, Bordo notes that today muscles and athleticism, once coded as male and working class, 'frequently symbolize qualities of *character* rather than class, race, or gender status' (2003: 24, emphasis mine). The 'character' a young female athlete demonstrates with her body is that of the powerful, self-determining consumer subject, the image of health and happiness that comes through successful participation in the neoliberal ideology of the DIY lifestyle.

One can see the connection made even more clearly in the 'alternative' sportswear catalogue marketed for women called – not insignificantly – Title IX. Making use of the idea of girl/woman power in their very name, this woman-owned and operated company explicitly couples sport participation with career success with images of everyday female athletes on each of its pages (not models or celebrities) with accompanying text identifying the athletes' sports and careers and whatever products they are modelling. One page of the summer 2005 catalogue, for instance, features 'Malia: orthodontist and surfer', selling the 'wrap-it-up skirt', next to 'Brigid, pharmaceutical rep. And runner', selling the 'no-brainer skirt'. Here, successful careers are explicitly linked to sport participation that is visually demonstrated by the women's fit bodies, and, significantly, by carefree images that clearly communicate that 'I'm doing my own thing despite (or because of) my job'. A crucial part of this messaging is that 'success' and the body and career represented by it is a personal choice, and it is a choice available to all.

I focus on images that are part of the larger culture rather than specifically on GoGirlGo! because it is specifically this cultural context that GoGirlGo! uses and defines itself in relationship to. Both corporations and advocacy organizations make use of the image of the female athlete. It is the larger cultural context and dominant meanings that help determine how the image will function, and the athlete image largely communicates a message of personal success and control. This image is particularly contradictory in that while on one level, an athletic body and the training it takes to achieve it *does* give one increased health, discipline, and a set of skills (like goal-setting, etc.) that are applicable to the business world, at the same time it also makes one an enthusiastic participant in a particular set of behaviours and practices (daily athletic training, and income-getting and spending). Serious athletic training does give one a sense of power and control, but this sense may have another dimension. In the sense of its participation in a particular aspect of consumer culture (the gym/sport/health/apparel industries), and in dedicating one's life to the kind of career necessary to generate the income that allows one to participate, one might say that, as Bordo explains,

> contemporary disciplines of diet and exercise [are] . . . practices which train the female body in . . . obedience to cultural demands, while at the same time being *experienced* in terms of power and control . . . thus, the heady experience of feeling powerful and 'in control,' far from being a necessarily accurate reflection of one's social position, is always suspect as itself the product of power relations whose shape may be very different.
>
> (2003: 27, original emphasis)

This is not to say that being healthy and athletic is in any sense 'bad' or that we should not participate in these practices, but rather that as we do, we should also be aware of the larger cultural forces that shape these practices and our own choices to participate in them.

Therefore, GoGirlGo!'s aim to 'get a girl moving' is multifaceted. As we have seen, one of the implicit messages in the GoGirlGo! marketing makes precisely this point: the healthy, powerful female body in sport becomes the prerequisite for power and success in life. The female athlete and female athleticism and strength are the literal embodiments of Girl Power, the subject who is, through her accomplishment and good lessons she learns in sport, supposed to develop her strength, health, and self-confidence and apply these to her career goals. Her athletic body becomes the visual image of and figure for career success, and girls' successful participation in the consumer economy that this career would ensure. An awareness of the cultural work that images accomplish could surely be added to any advocacy programming that both wants to bring girls on board and get them to think and act further. The way the image can function as a masking device that obscures the structural inequalities girls face every day could easily be added to the discussions proposed in the GoGirlGo! curriculum.

This is all the more important because confronting this larger framework of social and economic inequity is implicit in one of the key objectives of GoGirlGo!, which is to provide the opportunity to play to all girls. As the website homepage reads, 'Not all girls get to play. Unless a girl's school or parents can afford to pay for her physical activity, chances are she will grow up inactive. Over the past 30 years, the physical education curriculum in the United States has been repeatedly cut in grades K–12, putting girls from underserved populations at an even higher risk' (WSF 2005b).[8] Yet while it is true that if these girls do get to participate in sport regularly, they will have health benefits, the aspect of the equation that simple participation does not address is that even the lives of girls who are active face very real challenges in what Matt Bai calls 'the rise of the Wal-Mart economy' (2005: 40).

What nexus of 'value' and 'self-esteem' does sport in the sense marketed here promote and produce? In encouraging strength and self-determination through sport, as well as health benefits, can this discourse realistically address the needs of those girls who, economically, will never get to compete? Women's sport advocacy promotes a number of admirable goals, but does its insistence on sport as a solution to individual problems over-emphasize sports' capabilities? What if a girl is unable to fix her life through sport? What if she makes the right 'choices', does not smoke and is healthy, but has to work 38 hours a week for the minimum wage and no health insurance benefits at Wal-Mart? And another 38 hours a week job without benefits on top of the first job just to make ends meet? And will she have the time or energy to participate in any kind of physical activity then?

GoGirlGo!, like other health and girls' advocacy programmes, is not asking this kind of question. This is important in that the substantiated claim that regular participation in sport and physical activity has positive health outcomes needs to also be situated in terms of the actual life circumstances of many Americans who, due to the structural changes associated with globalization, tend to either be chronically overemployed or underemployed, both situations affecting their ability to participate in sport (see Schor 1993; Ehrenreich 2002). Yet is it possible to point this out in the current climate, in which the way 'selling' a message to the public is, in the context of what Robert McChesney (2003) calls 'the new global media', necessarily reduced to a single sound bite that does not allow for complications? This helps explain what sometimes seem to be overstated claims. Simply to function in the current context of discourse marketability, claims have to be overstated, and complications effaced. In the public marketing of these campaigns, the message must stay simple, but in the content of the programming, these issues might be more substantively raised.

The image of the female athlete's body is a powerful visual complement to the rhetoric I have discussed, and can serve as a focal point for this kind of discussion. It is no accident that the female athlete image first became embraced by corporations and a part of mainstream advertising in the early 1990s, the time of NAFTA, GATT, and the widespread practice of downsizing and outsourcing in the US.[9] While the stars of the first generation post Title IX, such as Mia Hamm and Brandi Chastain of the US Women's World Cup soccer team, were first coming into their full athletic potential as female athletes and gaining corporate endorsements, the corporate world that was also supposedly opening up to women started to shut down many of its domestic opportunities. The benevolent father image that corporations like

IBM had presented in earlier decades – the idea that you could have one corporate employer for life who would function as a substitute family and take care of you – was replaced by the lean, mean corporate model that paid its Chief Executive Officers exorbitant salaries while keeping its domestic staffs as small as possible. Workers were expected to be flexible and mobile, moving and travelling wherever required, and adapting to the idea that one will have many careers in a lifetime. The dot.com phenomenon[10] emphasized the same things: flexibility, self-determination, and the willingness to sacrifice everything to one's career.

Habituated to sacrifice and determination but never part of the huge institutional sport infrastructures that their male counterparts enjoyed, female athletes fit this new model more closely than did the men, and this ideology was sold to women through the image of the athletic body as a radical ideal for women and girls. Power and success in all areas, the image said, is what you can aspire to. It is without question a more positive image than many other relentlessly sexualized and feminized images so pervasive today. Indeed, the positive aspects of the female athlete image are what hooks a viewer – who wouldn't want to be powerful, healthy, and happy?

I am not arguing against power, health, or happiness, nor am I suggesting in any way that one should not be an athlete. However, as I hope to have shown, this image also masks an implicit endorsement of neoliberalism and its attendant assumptions. The image of the female athlete body does the cultural work of advertizing equal opportunities – anyone can achieve this look if they just work hard enough (and anyone can 'succeed' on all levels if they just work hard enough) – that masks the growing structural inequalities characteristic of the global economy and the erosion of and even active dismantling of New Deal support networks in the US.[11] The image of the female athletic body also supports a whole lifestyle industry based on the idea of self-determination and personal choice. Like the contortions of current advocacy strategies, the image itself is contradictory. I am not saying that anyone intentionally uses the image as a symbol of neoliberalism, but rather that in the current context so dominated by these normalized ideologies, the image can't help but signify in these terms, at least to some. Clearly our most positive image in terms of gender norms, the female athletic body both signifies literal power and health at the same time that power and health serve to mask the conditions that make this body possible (or not) in the first place.

Notes

1 11 September 2001 marks the destruction in New York of the Twin Towers of the World Trade Center.

2 In globalization discourse, 'the North' is now used to refer to what used to be called 'the first world' or 'the developed world', and 'South' is used for the 'third/fourth world' or the 'developing world'.

3 DIY is the abbreviation for 'do it yourself'. In girl culture, it first came to currency

with the Riot Grrrl movement in the early 1990s in the US, Britain, Canada, and Australia but was quickly co-opted by market forces. See Garrison (2000).

4 New Deal Initiatives in the US are associated with President Roosevelt in the 1930s, and included the Fair Labor Standards Act of 1938, which banned child labour and established a minimum wage, and the Social Security Act, which established a system that provided old-age pensions for workers, survivors benefits for victims of industrial accidents, unemployment insurance, and aid for dependent mothers and children, the blind and physically disabled. The 'New Deal' is known as establishing a 'safety net' for workers and putting the concerns of the people on par with the concerns of corporations. It is a system under attack in the US today. Civil rights struggles in the US are associated with the struggles for racial equality in the sixties, women's rights in the seventies, and gay and lesbian rights in the seventies and later.

5 See the various debates centred around environmental sustainability and relationships between globalization and growing inequality in Held and McGrew (eds) (2003). See also Middleton (2003).

6 Grade 3 to Grade 8 includes girls aged from 8 to 13 years of age, and high school girls are aged 14–17 years of age.

7 On the ways consumers read images against the grain of their dominant messages, see the introduction to Fiske (1996).

8 According to the Center for Disease Control and Prevention (1995), while physical education in US schools was once an established part of the curriculum, currently in grades K–12 (normally 5–17 years of age), only 25 per cent of students have access to daily physical activity programmes.

9 NAFTA (North American Free Trade Agreement) established a much expanded free trade zone in 1994 that extended the influence and reach of corporate America. GATT (General Agreement on Tariffs and Trade) was first signed in 1947, but was greatly expanded in the 1990s, and now includes 110 countries. It was designed to provide an international forum that encouraged free trade between member states by regulating and reducing tariffs on traded goods. These two agreements greatly facilitated economic globalization.

10 During the 1990s, companies set up to use the Internet as their primary trading platform became known as 'dot.coms'. Young people with little or no business experience but with innovative ideas received significant investment capital and made fortunes seemingly overnight. The 'dot.com phenomenon' resulted in the inflation of the stock market, especially Internet stocks, but by the end of the 1990s, most of these business ventures had failed.

11 See Castells (2003), Stearns (2003) and UNDP Report '1999' (2003).

Bibliography

Bai, M. (2005) 'The new boss', *The New York Times Magazine*, 30 January: 40.

Bordo, S. (2003) *Unbearable Weight: Feminism, Western Culture, and the Body*, rev. edn, Berkeley, CA: University of California Press.

Brown, C. (2003) 'A world gone wrong', in D. Held and A. McGrew (eds) *The Global Transformations Reader*, Cambridge: Polity Press.

Castells, M. (2003) 'Global informational capitalism', in D. Held and A. McGrew (eds) *The Global Transformations Reader*, Cambridge: Polity Press.

Castells, M. (2003) 'The rise of the fourth world', in D. Held and A. McGrew (eds) *The Global Transformations Reader*, Cambridge: Polity Press.

Center for Disease Control and Prevention (1995) 'Youth risk behaviour survey', *CDC Surveill. Summ.* 45: 33–5.

Ehrenreich, B. (2002) *Nickel and Dimed: On Not Getting by in America*, New York: Owl Books.

Eisenhauer, J. (2004) 'Mythic figures and lived identities: locating the "girl" in feminist discourse', in A. Harris (ed.) *All About the Girl: Culture, Power, and Identity*, New York: Routledge.

Fiske, J. (1996) *Media Matters*, Minneapolis, MN: University of Minnesota Press.

Garrison, E. K. (2000) 'US feminism grrrl style: youth (sub)cultures and the technologies of the Third Wave', *Feminist Studies*, 26 (1): 141–70.

Hardt, M. and Negri, A. (2000) *Empire*, Cambridge, MA: Harvard University Press.

Harris, A. (2004a) *Future Girl: Young Women in the 21st Century*, New York: Routledge.

Harris, A. (2004b) 'Jamming girl culture: young women and consumer citizenship', in A. Harris (ed.) *All About the Girl: Culture, Power, and Identity*, New York: Routledge.

Harris, A. (2004c) *All About the Girl: Culture, Power, and Identity*, New York: Routledge.

Held, D. (2003) 'Understanding globalization', in D. Held and A. McGrew (eds) *The Global Transformations Reader*, Cambridge: Polity Press.

Held, D. and McGrew, A. (eds) (2003) *The Global Transformations Reader*, Cambridge: Polity Press.

Heywood, L. and Drake, J. (2004) 'It's all about the Benjamins', in S. Gillis, G. Howie and R. Munford (eds) *Third Wave Feminism: A Critical Exploration*, New York: Palgrave Macmillan.

Heywood, L. and Dworkin, S. (2003) *Built to Win: The Female Athlete as Cultural Icon*, Minneapolis, MN: University of Minnesota Press.

McChesney, R. (2003) 'The new global media', in D. Held and A. McGrew (eds) *The Global Transformations Reader*, Cambridge: Polity Press.

McRobbie, A. (2004) 'Notes on post-feminism and popular culture: Bridget Jones and the new gender regime', in A. Harris (ed.) *All About the Girl: Culture, Power, and Identity*, New York: Routledge.

Middleton, N. (2003) *The Global Casino*, London: Arnold Publishers, online, available HTTP: http:www.roxy.com (accessed 16 April 2005).

Schor, J. (1993) *The Overworked American*, New York: Basic Books.

Stearns, J. (2003) 'Globalization and gendered inequality', in D. Held and A. McGrew (eds) *The Global Transformations Reader*, Cambridge: Polity Press.

Taft, J. (2004) 'Girl power politics: pop-culture barriers and organizational resistance', in A. Harris (ed.) *All About the Girl: Culture, Power, and Identity*, New York: Routledge.

UNDP Report 1999 (2003) 'Patterns of global inequality', in D. Held and A. McGrew (eds) *The Global Transformations Reader*, Cambridge: Polity Press.

Wallechinsky, D. (1996) 'Vaults, leaps, and dashes: women's sports go the distance', *New York Times Magazine*, 23 June: 47.

Ward, J. and Cooper Benjamin, B. (2004) 'Women, girls, and the unfinished work of connection: a critical review of American girls' studies', in A. Harris (ed.) *All About the Girl: Culture, Power, and Identity*, New York: Routledge.

Women's Sports Foundation (2003) *Women's Sports Foundation Annual Report*, New York: WSF.

Women's Sports Foundation (2004) *GoGirlGo!, Official Coach and Group Leader's Guide for Third to Eighth Grade Girls*, New York: WSF.

Women's Sports Foundation (2005a) 'Benefits – Why Sports Participation for Girls and Women', Women's Sports Foundation Position Paper, online, available HTTP: <http://www.womenssportsfoundation.org/cgibin/iowa/issues/body/article.html> (accessed 16 April 2005).

Women's Sports Foundation (2005b) 'Go Girls Go', website, accessed 1 October 2005.

6   Entertaining femininities

The embodied exhibitions of striptease and sport, 1950–1975

Becki L. Ross

In Kitimat [British Columbia], there were Greek sailors at the local nightclub. I did a Middle Eastern gypsy type of act. I balanced the beer on my head and I wore a coin belt and coin robe with a little vest and a long gypsy skirt; I brought out a tambourine and they went insane. They loved me so much, they treated me like a princess. Men would tell me, 'Don't take this the wrong way, but taking your clothes off ruins it. You have a beautiful body and we're coming here to watch you dance'.

(Sarita Melita, retired striptease dancer, 2004)[1]

You have to be the All-American girl, with little smiles all the time. At the championships, they watch everything you do. You can't make a face, and if you kick the ice during a practice session, forget it. A skater's reputation off the ice has a lot to do with it, too. So you can't run around with boys. And you can't run around in blue jeans, and you can't say how you really think or how you really feel. You just have to pretend that you're little Miss Goody Goody.

(Dorothy Hamill, retired figure skater, 1975)[2]

Immediately after World War II, the industry of commercial female striptease flourished in cities across North America. *Vancouver Sun* newspaper reporter Patrick Nagle recalls a 'show business railway' that moved performers, including showgirls, up and down the Pacific coast from Los Angeles to Las Vegas to the seaport city of Vancouver, British Columbia.[3] Already well known for its earlier history of raunchy, risqué, bootlegging brothels, and burlesque, Vancouver embraced the revived industry of 'bump and grind' (Salmi 2000: 17). In this chapter, drawing from archival and interview data, I explore retired striptease dancers' complex stories of their agency, craft, expertise, and gifts as physically talented, sexy performers in an era that preceded split beavers, table dancing, lap dancing, stage fees, champagne rooms, and the Canadian government's short-lived 'Exotic Dancers' visa programme (1998–2004).[4] Rather than remember themselves as objectified, degraded victims of men's super-sonic lust, ex-dancers narrate tales of how they resisted and accommodated conventions of proper, lady-like femininity. Their observations suggest fruitful comparison and contrast with elite female athletes – golfers, figure skaters, and tennis stars during the same time period, 1950–75. Indeed, I discovered myriad, intriguing parallels across two seemingly unrelated fields of professional entertainment: striptease and sport. At the same time, inspired by theorist Judith Butler (2002), I found that hierarchies of legitimation and illegitimation installed the intelligibility, recognizability, and state sanctification of some women's performing bodies, and not others.

The embodied skill, strength, and overt sex appeal of stripteasers

The decades immediately after World War II heralded the growing profitability of female striptease driven by the increasing commodification of sex in North American popular culture. Bawdy comic books, *Playboy* magazine (launched in 1953), pin-up calendars, pulp novels, trashy tabloids, and mainstream Hollywood movies flirted with the edges of decency.[5] Striptease queens – Gypsy Rose Lee, Tempest Storm, Lili St. Cyr, Evelyn West, Ricki Covette, and many others – staged sensational exaggerations of femininity and played up the rigid gender prescriptions of the era. They mined the rich reservoir of symbols of white glamour, pageantry, and feminine magnetism emblemized by Jayne Mansfield, Elizabeth Taylor, Kim Novak, and Marilyn Monroe, straight from the silver screen and Las Vegas's sin strip. And at the same time, stripteasers across Canada, Europe, and the United States were trendsetters in their own right: they invented numerous artistic, cultural, athletic, and musical innovations and interpretations, daringly tweaking the conventions of female propriety. Their styles were cutting-edge and their brazen sexiness was widely copied and adapted, albeit in sanitized fashion, by many mainstream female entertainers.

While the majority of North American women in the 1950s wrestled with opposing messages that mixed together 'little girl innocence' with sensual but restrained sophistication leveraged to attract and keep a man, extraordinary bump-and-grinders openly communicated non-conformist sexual suggestiveness via multiple techniques (Johns 2003: 20). Dancers were bombshells, and a bombshell, to quote Kristina Zarlengo, was a 'deeply desirable, unattainable woman with an inflated body and intense sexuality – a steadfast atomic age feminine ideal . . . who represented raw power of a kind frequently associated with the atom bomb' (1999: 927).

In Vancouver, predominantly white American headliners and, by the mid-to-late 1960s, an increasing number of local dancers, were professionally managed, commanded celebrity status, and invested a significant chunk of their earnings in expensive gowns, dance lessons, choreography, props, wigs, hairpieces, shoes, music, and make-up. The city's top-drawer West End nightclubs expected dancers to assemble an elaborate wardrobe and props.

Sumptuous fabrics of silk, velvet, organza, tulle, satin, and chiffon were spun into magnificent gowns, over-coats, hats, shawls, jackets, capes, dusters, and Frederick's of Hollywood-inspired negligées, all with specialized snaps, clasps, and zippers for easy removal. Dancers coveted Springolater shoes sold at Pike Market in Seattle: spiked heels with a steel shaft, 'they were Barbie doll shoes' says April Paris, 'made for strippers'.[6] Striptease dancers cunningly peeled off their sequined gowns, furs, and peekaboo devices to reveal sparkly pasties and g-strings (often worn layered over one another, up to three at a time). The g-string, Italian American striptease legend Ann Corio slyly observed, 'was a tiny jewel-like bauble on a string around the waist covering up its specific subject' (Corio and DiMona 1968: 76). As well, notes choreographer Jack Card, under g-strings, some dancers experimented with rhinestone clips in the 1950s and 1960s: v-shaped and glittery, made of sprung steel, they fitted over the pubic area and inserted into the vagina.[7]

In addition to clothing, dancers further customized their acts by experimenting with elements of magic, puppetry, theatre, gymnastics, pantomime, comedy, and jazz, modern, tap, and Latin dance. Some incorporated props such as electric trapezes, parrots, live doves, Siberian tigers, cockatiels, roller skates, boa constrictors, fireballs on stage, and glow-in-the-dark body paints, while others made creative use of bird cages, oversized fish bowls, seven-foot tall champagne glasses, fog and bubble machines. More than half of the nineteen retired dancers I interviewed had dance and/or gymnastics training prior to entering the industry – the other half learned the ropes on the job.

A self-taught deaf dancer with movie star aspirations, Princess Lillian learned moves and gimmicks from choreographer Jack Card at Isy's Supper Club in the late 1960s: 'I had tassels, and I'd make them twirl like an airplane propeller. I used to have a snake in my show – 110 pounds. I played the drums and accordion on stage; I worked with a baton, I had a belly dancer costume, I did some Scottish dancing. I had a biker theme: leather and a whip. People LOVED my show. I was very Las Vegas, and my show was very classy. I was an entertainer.'[8]

Tarren Rae described what made her act in the early 1970s unique and popular: 'I was really good at gymnastics. I started really young, I was very flexible. I learned how to balance. Everybody did headstands at Gary Taylor's Show Lounge. Everybody did splits, everybody did walk-overs. Strippers weren't doing that – they were strutting, barely touching the floor. So I took the two cultures and meshed them together. I had a lot of dance and theme shows like a Cabaret show, a Glen Miller show, a hippie girl thing, and a Star Wars show.'[9]

Shelinda studied ballet for a year as a girl, and when she started her professional striptease career, she took jazz dance classes at a dance school on Hamilton Street. There, she recalls, she learned special moves, including spins and stretches. 'I could do a high kick, and I'd have to make sure my shoe didn't hit me in the nose. I was very athletic . . . a "healthy looking brunette". I'd wear my hair up, and it would come down on the last song.'

Like other white striptease dancers who entered the business in the early-to-mid 1970s, April Paris opted for 'artsy and innovative' routines that incorporated yoga, acrobatics, gymnastics, jazz, and the 'free-flowing philosophy' of 'nakedness is beautiful'. Influenced by women's liberation movement, hippie culture, and a growing fitness and aerobics industry, dancers invented new styles that blended dance moves and overt athleticism. April Paris explained the shift away from old-fashioned bump and grind:

> The burlesque dancers – most of them were from the States – strutted. They always wore their heels, and lots of make-up, which was very strange. They had costumes they brought in steamer trunks. Bras with rhinestones and big t-bars that go up the hip and then you just flip them off and underneath you've got a g-string, which is just the little triangle with elastic up the butt encrusted with rhinestones. We felt that we had to get down there on our hands and knees on the hardwood floor. We couldn't do three or four songs standing up – we would get down on the floor in bare feet or our Capezzio shoes, our Danskin bodysuits, and we would do our gymnastic splits, stand on our head, spin around the poles.
>
> I was yogic, I could stand on my head – I was like a corkscrew. My head was there and my legs were swirling around. That was my move. You can't steal a move – that was your livelihood.[10]

Her dream of the Canadian National Ballet dashed – 'my bones were too big and my turn-out wasn't good enough' – Jasmine Tea choreographed her own original routines for small, cramped hotel stages in the early 1970s: 'I used to do the splits against the wall, backwards, and then go up into a handstand on the wall, and then go into a one-arm handstand in the splits. I took off an outer g-string with my one hand, while I was up on the other hand . . . I danced hard, I liked to sweat, and I enjoyed the applause: it was my creative outlet.'[11] Believing in dance as 'the most beautiful art form there is,' Jasmine Tea showed her audience 'another side of dance'. She developed a secretary set with a three-piece suit, eye glasses, and her hair in a bun. A regular customer at vintage and thrift stores, she made a bird costume from a black unitard, and she danced as a raven. She also noted some dancers from local jazz and modern troupes would supplement their poor wages by taking shifts on striptease stages.

The constrained 'marketability' and resilient stereotypes of dancers of colour

Hierarchies of race and class stratified commercial striptease as they did the world of professional sport. Many of Vancouver's black dancers in the postwar decades were promoted as 'novelty acts' much like African American Josephine Baker in Paris during the 1920s and 1930s (Stuart 1999). Choo Choo Williams, Miss Lovie, and Lottie the Body were hired to dance in lower end, 'B-list' clubs in the working-class, East End neighbourhood of Chinatown/Main Street. In the eyes of the vast majority of white North Americans in the postwar era, black stripteasers epitomized what Yvette Abrahams has termed the lascivious sensuality and wild rhythms presumed 'natural' to their race (Abrahams 1998: 227). In the late 1950s, Choo Choo Williams developed a Carmen Miranda persona and danced the limbo to a Latin beat at the Harlem Nocturne, a small black nightclub on East Hastings Street that she operated with her husband, trombonist Ernie King.

None of the dancers of colour attained the marquee status enjoyed by white headliners, though as Choo Choo Williams commented, light-skinned or 'high yellow' dancers were more likely to reach higher heights in the business than darker-skinned women.[12] Racist stereotypes of black women as mammies, washerwomen, laundresses, and maids, compounded by ideals of white female beauty, compromised black dancers' 'marketability'. They had more difficulty than white dancers in securing top-paying gigs, purchasing expensive costumes, dance lessons, props, and promotional photographs. Even if black women possessed the material resources necessary to achieve headliner billing, the colour line persisted, dividing the lavish, white-owned West End supper clubs from the down-scale, rough East End cabarets rented by men of colour, and dividing white headliners from 'novelties' of colour (Ross and Greenwell 2005).

Born in Texas, raised in Chicago, Miss Lovie moved permanently to Vancouver in 1964. A former paediatric nurse, she developed an act in which, bikini clad, she sat on the floor facing away from her audience and rhythmically twitched the muscles in her legs and buttocks to the beat of Conga drums. She explained her signature act: 'I made things happen with my body. I'd sit on the floor, I'd stick my legs up high, up above my head, and I'd make my butt pop. I made my buttocks work like drums through muscle control. I could move around the floor like a clock, in a circle. I did the splits. I used to do a lot of black light dancing, and I used to wear a lot of glitter all over my body. That use to be my thing: I glittered.'[13] In her trademark leopard and zebra bikinis and anklets, Miss Lovie was popular at East End nightclubs where she was promoted as 'the world's foremost exponent of Afro Cuban dancing' and an 'Artist of Rhythm'. Like Choo Choo and Josephine Baker, Miss Lovie was expected to embody what Anne McClintock terms anachronistic African primitivism and hypersexuality (McClintock 1995: 40). Similar to white racist projections on the black athletic bodies of American bodybuilder Carla Dunlap in the 1980s (see Brady 2001; Boyle 2005), figure skater Surya Bonaly of France in the 1990s, and American tennis stars, Venus and Serena Williams in 2005 (see Spencer 2004), Miss Lovie was expected to exhibit a raw, animalistic physicality. And, like other black performers, Miss Lovie both capitulated to and interrupted the terms of white voyeurism.[14]

Sarita Melita was one of the few Latina striptease dancers to live and work in Vancouver. Originally from 'the war zone of east Los Angeles', the eldest of nine children raised by a single, working-class Puerto Rican mother, Sarita Melita fled to Vancouver with her draft-dodging boyfriend and was granted landed immigrant status in 1973. She began dancing in local nightclubs and on the road in 1975 at nineteen after years of poorly-paid secretarial, service, and clerical jobs. She recalled, 'In those days, you had to be blond, and you had to be white, tall, long legs, big boobs. I was exotic. I had long black hair, I had darker skin, I had a darker look – a Middle-Eastern look, and my look was not in.'[15] Sarita's mother – 'a mango in a white man's land' – had also been an exotic dancer in Los Angeles, and from her trials and tribulations Sarita learned that 'Hell would have frozen over' before a black, Puerto Rican, or Mexican Hispanic woman was granted marquee status.[16] In spite of similar economic and racial barriers to achieving her own headliner status, Sarita, like her mother before her, successfully appropriated orientalist signifiers for her own purposes, emphasizing her Latin roots, her love of dance, music, costuming, applause, and the physicality and grace of movement. 'I put gold greasepaint all over my entire body, and with the Queen Nefertiti costume I looked like an animated statue. I used authentic Egyptian music, it was haunting, and had very sexual rhythms. Then, I did a salsa, because I'm Puerto Rican – it was a tribute, and I did a 'West Side Story' thing. I had a tight red ballroom-dancing gown, and I did a lot of mambo, rumba – it was music right from Puerto Rico – hot Latin music. I also did an Arabian dance with the veils and belly dancing; I would balance a candle or a drink on my head and I would dance and do floor work.'[17]

The embodied skill, strength, and cheesecake of female athletes

After World War II, striptease dancers – both white and non-white – were not the only female performers to be rewarded for pandering to the titillation factor. Professional female figure skaters with the Ice Capades, Ice Follies, and Canadian Ice Fantasy,[18] female trapeze artists, magicians' assistants, beauty pageant contestants, cheerleaders, and baton-twirling majorettes also donned scanty costumes and traded in their heterosexual allure (Kaufman 1998). Jazz historian Sherrie Tucker found that female big-band, jazz, and swing instrumentalists in the 1940s and 1950s were made to 'look like strippers' with 'gowns revealing plenty of bosoms' (Cayler, cited in Tucker 2000: 58–9). Baseball players for the All American Girls Professional Baseball League (1943–54) were mandated to wear short-skirted uniforms and attend Charm School (Browne 1993). In the 1940s and 1950s, these players were chaperoned by older, mature women hired to safeguard the security and innocence of 'their girls' on the road. Prohibited from dating, the all-white baseball stars were, after all, expected to keep themselves pure for the revered nation-building pursuits of marriage and maternity.[19] Betsy Rawls, a top female professional golfer from the late 1940s to the mid 1970s, remembers that 'we were conscious of needing to dress properly and look and act

ladylike, and we always did' (Rawls, quoted in Kort 2005: 16). Historians
Patricia Vertinsky and Gwendolyn Captain show that African American
athletes Wilma Rudolph (track and field) and Althea Gibson (tennis/golf)
were coached to cultivate an attractive, feminine image (1998: 545).

Named in the media as the dainty 'Ice Princess' and the 'blond beauty on
blades', figure skater Barbara Ann Scott won Canadian, North American,
European, and World Championship titles between 1944 and 1949, and an
Olympic gold medal in St Moritz, Switzerland in 1948. Born in Ottawa,
Ontario in 1929, she was deemed 'Canada's national heroine' and 'Canada's
sweetheart', and she later skated professionally as a headliner in the
Hollywood Ice Revue, travelling internationally until retirement in 1955.
Modelling for money and wearing little more than striptease queen Tempest
Storm in the 1950s, Scott was captured on film with cheesecake appeal coyly
felating an ice-cream cone.

Twenty years after Barbara Ann Scott's reign, white tennis player 'Chrissie'
Evert, 'America's sweetheart' (Bodo 1995), was described in the mainstream
press as cool and delicate looking, a lithe blond who wore traditional dresses,
make-up, bows, earrings, nail polish and hair ribbons during her matches
(Festle 1996: 152). Tennis player Renée Richards (formerly Richard Raskind)
was a male-to-female transsexual whose 'distinctly' feminine attributes were
lauded in the *New York Times*: 'Dr. Richards displays . . . high cheek bones,
shapely legs, graceful gold pierced earrings and peach nail polish.'[20] And in
the 1970s, members of the Ladies Professional Golf Association (LPGA),
Australian Jan Stephenson and American Laura Baugh, were touted as blond
buxom bombshells on the links. Like both white and non-white women in
the postwar modelling industry who embodied prerequisites of charm,
poise, and elegance, female sportswomen on and off competitive terrains
were expected to be paragons of well-groomed, manicured, styled, and
fetching femininity (Haidarali 2005).

In mainstream news stories, the physical and mental toughness, extraordinary discipline, courage, work ethic, and excellence of female professional athletes were qualities routinely overshadowed by commentary that
emphasized their conventional attractiveness to the 'opposite sex'. Indeed,
as feminist critics such as Leslie Heywood and Shari Dworkin (2003) and
Laura Robinson (2002) argue, the sexualization of female athletes has a long,
vexed history. However, the respectability of female athletes was virtually
guaranteed by the legitimizing stamp of their participation in family-oriented
entertainment in reputable venues.

'Family-oriented' venues vs. 'sleazy' nightclubs

For mainstream female athletes and their promoters, community arenas, golf
courses, and tennis stadiums were perceived as wholesome community
venues for the entire family to enjoy. These publicly subsidized sites and
their healthy, fun-filled activities were vigorously promoted to appeal to

spectators of both genders, all ages, and a wide array of consumer tastes. For example, England's Wimbledon tennis tournament has been described as evocative of 'the moral purity and tranquillity of the suburban garden, a slice of the rural idyll, nature cultivated and made safe' (Kennedy 2001: 61). In the post-war era, most women's professional golf, tennis, and figure skating events were staged during the daytime or early evening in order to draw from a wide spectrum of fans, including parents with children. The events were often a celebrated, much anticipated occasion for local communities and volunteers: the 'tour stops' and their 'stars' were widely advertized on radio and colourful posters, in newspapers, and on television; players were interviewed by reporters; tickets were sold at newsstands, community halls, retail outlets, and on site. The venues themselves, while varying in seating, typically included kiosks that sold souvenirs, pro-grammes, and non-alcoholic beverages and snacks. For communities long-acquainted with the history of travelling circuses, carnivals, and concerts, a sporting event was touted as a special, memorable opportunity to witness 'the best female athletes in the world'. Attendance spelled several hours of reasonably priced, exciting amusement and family-bonding, sunshine and fresh air (at golf and tennis tournaments), and a boosted sense of civic spirit and pride. The athletes themselves sought to 'deliver the goods' by maximiz-ing the 'entertainment value' for hard-working, honest fans: a dazzling tennis serve, a hole-in-one, or an elaborate spin or tricky jump on ice, were awe-inspiring feats to strive for.

By contrast, female bump-and-grinders self-consciously marketed and sold their overtly sexualized persona on the darkened, night-time stages of burlesque halls, strip clubs, and girlie shows at summer carnivals such as the Pacific National Exhibition (Stencell 1999). Unchaperoned, striptease performers' premeditated, primary purpose was to sell sexual thrills to increasingly male-only audiences in sex-saturated spaces where alcohol flowed freely until well past midnight. Indeed, the majority of Vancouver's nightclubs were unlicensed bottle clubs until the late 1960s: patrons brought their own booze in brown bags and bought set-ups – mix and ice – from the bar.

It was widely believed that male nightclub owners were shady, low-life mobsters, bookies, and pimps who stimulated and exploited other men's desire for 'exotics', bootlegged liquor, and working girls. Although Vancou-ver's hotspots were never shut down en masse as they were in New York City in the 1930s,[21] clubs such as the State Burlesque Theatre, the Penthouse Cabaret, Harlem Nocturne, New Delhi, Smilin' Buddha, and Kublai Khan were forever at risk of incursion. All operated by non-Anglo immigrant men, these nightclubs were routinely caricatured as raunchy breeding grounds for rapists, sex perverts, and murderers (Adami 1982: 29). Vancouver police exercised significant discretionary power to lay charges of 'lewd and obscene public exhibition', illegal alcohol sales and consumption, gambling, minors on the premises, and prostitution-related offences.[22] Commercial striptease was staged behind closed doors in nightclubs associated with forbidden, quasi-criminal actors and activity; by extension, dancers – even famous, internationally renowned striptease queens – were stained by their presumed involvement in dodgy, underworld goings-on.

In spite of the creative athleticism and artistry consistently displayed by female striptease dancers in the postwar era in Canada and elsewhere, these performers were roundly scorned by many as drug-addicted whores and home-wreckers. While 'mannish' female athletes were seen to traverse the male/female binary in dangerous ways, dancers were punished for exceeding the social norms of demure femininity. Both white and non-white dancers were denied claims to bourgeois feminine respectability especially after 'bottomless' performance – full nudity – was decriminalized in British Columbia in 1972. To Canadian ex-dancer Margaret Dragu, striptease performers played the role of conscientious objector by bravely testing and defying society's sexual limits, and they experienced outsider status as 'sexual offenders' (Dragu and Harrison 1988: 53–7). Even in the context of the sexual revolution, women's liberation, and the relaxation of some gender and sexual mores in the late 1960s, erotic dancers provoked shock, anxiety, and moralizing judgment. At the same time, not one of the nineteen retired dancers I interviewed considered herself a powerless dupe of patriarchal control or a sullied victim of men's sexist and racist appetites.

Non-traditional money-making for 'girls'

Only a small number of women in corporations and in the professions of law and medicine earned as much as top-drawer white striptease queens following World War II. By the late 1960s throughout the 1970s, dancers' wages ranged from $500 a week to $4,000 a week. Like prostitution, striptease was so removed from the dominant culture of gender-appropriate roles that dancers' wages were not depressed like those of mainstream working women. In fact, headlining dancers were well compensated in part due to the significant value of their industry to the local economy combined with the lack of competition from women prepared to take similar risks.[23] Like players for the B.C. Lions professional football team (1954) and the Vancouver Canucks – the city's National Hockey League franchise (1970) – strippers were professionals in gender-segregated entertainment. Only men were paid to play football and hockey, and until the advent of male strippers – Chippendales in the late 1970s – only women were paid wages to strip.[24] However, while football and hockey stars were attributed the lionized status of heroes and modern-day gods, strippers were reviled by some and adored by others. To quote ex-dancer Bonnie Scott, 'What was ironic was being looked upon as lesser than life and getting the best salary you could get out there. Not too many people made more money than we did. We got paid very highly to be the object of men's desire.'

Striptease dancers in the postwar era had little trouble attracting well-paying male spectators in large part because they catered directly, and without apology, to their customers' desire for staged sexual fantasies that matched and often exceeded representations of cheesecake in popular culture. By contrast, most high-performance female athletes, particularly those whose sports demanded vigorous strength, body contact, and speed, toiled in obscurity without a secure income and often under a veil of suspicion because they were seen as trespassers on men's terrain. In the immediate postwar decades, few sports administrators, funders, coaches, or promoters believed that women's athletics were as marketable or as deserving of media attention as men's athletics. Even today, serious women's sports are 'missing in action' on televised news broadcasts, on radio, and in mainstream newspapers and magazines; what coverage exists is often trivializing and peppered with sexualized humour (Bishop 2003). As Messner *et al.* argue (2000), ESPN's 'SportsCenter' offers to heterosexual male viewers consistent, almost seamless images of sport as an exclusive territory set up by and for men. Now in its eighth year as the second-class 'sister-ship' to the (men's) National Basketball Association (NBA), the Women's National Basketball Association (WNBA) is routinely packaged by the media (and by some players) as a vehicle for constructions of normative femininity, heterosexuality, maternity, and respectability (Banet-Wiser 1999: 404).

Decades ago, the few female athletes who earned a decent livelihood were exceptional figure skaters, tennis stars, and golfers. Founder of the Women's Tennis Association (WTA), and consummate advocate for women's professional tennis (and prize money equivalent to men's), Billie Jean King became the first woman to earn over $100,000 when Virginia Slims became the major corporate sponsor for women's tennis in 1971 (Lumpkin 1984: 94; see also Festle 1996). And yet in comparison to sportsmen, professional sportswomen endured shorter seasons, negligible TV and print reportage, a smaller fan base, less income, and fewer (if any) product endorsements. Still, sportswomen worked hard to reassure mixed-gender audiences of their wholesome, non-threatening femaleness, and media references to a female athlete's credentials habitually included (and still include) mention of boyfriends, husbands, and children (Stevenson 2002). For instance, much ink was spilled chronicling the 1938 marriage between pro wrestler and promoter George Zaharias and the incomparable, multi-sport 'muscle moll' Babe Didrikson. Profiled in *Life* magazine in 1947, a world-class champion in ten sports, a co-founder of the LPGA, and long rumoured to be gay, Didrikson was said to have finally learned to wear nylons, cook for her husband, wear lipstick, and grow her hair (Postman 2000).[25] Details about male athletes' (hetero) sex appeal, facial traits, hygiene, hair styles, jewellery, outfits, or lovers were rarely if ever deemed worth mention, much less ranked as the main or singular rationale of newsworthiness.

Queer-baiting vs. 'lezzie duos'

Fearful of negative financial and professional consequences of coming out publicly, closeted lesbian athletes struggled to accommodate dominant perceptions of femininity and heterosexuality (Griffin 1998; Lenskyj 1986, 1997; Cahn 1994; Robinson 2002). As Pat Griffin argues, the lesbian label was used to control, intimidate, and discredit women in sport (1998: 86). The spectre of butch lesbianism shadowed the careers of all female athletes, particularly those whose passions and muscled corporeality contradicted the conventions of hetero-marital womanhood and maternity (Caudwell 1999). The lesbian sexuality of tennis stars Billie Jean King and Martina Navratilova was lampooned and sensationalized throughout the 1970s and 1980s.[26] Similarly, members of the Ladies Professional Golf Association (LPGA) were regularly scrutinized for worrying signs of mannish, 'dyke-y' style and comportment, particularly as the sport gained greater TV coverage and corporate sponsors (especially food and cosmetics industries). In the fifty-five year history of the LPGA, only three players – Muffin Spencer-Devlin, Patty Sheehan, and Rosie Jones – have come out openly as lesbians, all near the end of their careers. For decades, tour players have been the target of nasty, homophobic bile by pundits such as CBC-TV announcer Ben Wright who, in 1993, was quoted as saying 'lesbians in the sport hurt women's golf' (cited in Kort 2005: 21). In the face of pressure by the tour's commissioner and corporate sponsors to 'keep up appearances' and be 'fan friendly', closeted lesbians remain ambivalent about the pronounced presence of thousands of lesbian spectators and partiers at the infamous annual Dinah Shore Weekend and major golf tournament in Palm Springs, California (Kort 2005: 90–1).

Decades ago, lesbianism within the postwar striptease business was similarly assumed to be widespread. In 1971, Canadian journalist Marilyn Salutin stated that, according to her informants, seventy-five per cent of female strippers were lesbians – a figure she argued reflects 'an occupational contingency' born of an 'understandable contempt for men' (Salutin 1971: 16). While Salutin's estimate lacks empirical rigour, on the striptease stage, 'girl-on-girl' duos in the 1970s mirrored 'same-sex or lezzie spreads' in commercial straight male pornography. The duos were intended to 'double men's viewing pleasure', and they were enthusiastically applauded by aroused male customers at nightclubs. Contrary to the anti-lesbian strictures intrinsic to high-profile female athletics, striptease dancers were rewarded for stoking rather than unsettling hetero-masculinist myths of female sexual availability. Whether striptease dancers were lesbians or not did not seem to matter; they accepted the contract to appeal overtly and unapologetically to men's desire for enactment of sexual fantasies on men's terms. At the same time, the ex-dancers I have interviewed spoke at length of the sexual control and empowerment they experienced on stage as they manipulated their own *and* their clients' sexuality for profit.[27]

Showgirls strut their stuff to different tunes, for different crowds

Across North America from 1950 to 1975, headlining stripteasers and professional female athletes were celebrities, albeit celebrated for different reasons, by different audiences, in different social spaces. An eclectic mix of ethnographic and auto/biographical narratives reveals that professional female figure skaters, tennis players, golfers, *and* striptease dancers were 'showgirls' – entertainers who toured for a living, earned a decent income, hired agents, sold their training and skills, displayed their athleticism, donned costumes for fans, performed with injuries, and had relatively short careers.[28] Touring meant long days and nights far from home and loved ones, sizeable telephone bills, reliance on the good will of strangers in unfamiliar cities, and hotels with uneven accommodations, laundry, and food service (particularly for vegetarians!). Time 'off stage', out of the limelight, was devoted to rigorous rehearsals or practice sessions, career management, and physical fitness regimes (which intensified for dancers and sport stars with the explosive boom of aerobics classes, weight-training, and muscle toning in the 1980s (see Lloyd 1996 and Morse 1988)). Independent contractors or freelancers in competitive fields, these showgirls engaged in unsteady, insecure, non-unionized employment, and were ineligible for vacation pay, unemployment insurance, maternity leave, compensation for illness, or pensions (Ross 2006).[29] At various points throughout their careers, they were hampered by nagging, chronic pain, the fear of aging bodies, and overzealous (usually male) fans; all dancers told rueful tales of insufficient or poor financial/investment advice during their peak-earning years. Because of the extraordinary premium placed on physical appearance and (hetero)attractiveness typically monitored by male sponsors, administrators, coaches, agents/ promoters, and choreographers, showgirls felt compelled to enact hypervigilance about their weight, personality, body shape, coiffure, couture, use of cosmetics, sexual preference, and relationships.[30]

All showgirls navigated occupational hazards and yet the benefits they accrued were significant, though mediated by the differentials of class and race/ethnicity built into sharply stratified industries. Top-drawer performers ploughed a hefty percentage of their earnings back into their bodies' capabilities and their careers to enhance their marketability, fame, and fortune. The most successful skaters, tennis players, golfers and headlining dancers netted higher incomes than other working women in the 'pink-collar ghetto', they appreciated the flexibility of scheduling, and they revelled in 'being their own boss'.[31] They also expressed the joy of polishing their skills and focus, developing the artistry and the mastery of their craft, as well as basking in the addictive 'high' of applause and the adventure of travelling to 'see the world'.

Fans of postwar women's sport and striptease likely experienced elevated levels of intensity and excitement, escapism, increased heart rate, emotional (and possibly sexual) arousal, and loyalties to favourite performers. However, golf, tennis, and figure skating – in contradistinction to striptease – were socially acceptable, white, middle-class, sports of a certain pedigree and heritage cultivated in the luxurious confines of posh, privately owned country clubs. The well-off women who excelled at skating, tennis, and golf were expected (then, as now) to publicly exhibit lady-like decorum, glamour, and humanitarian interests. In the third-quarter of the twentieth century, the exhibition of sporting skills and post-competition charm by athletes such as Barbara Ann Scott and Chris Evert was judged to affirm gender-congruent ideals of modest, graceful, agile, artistic femininity, beauty, and, more broadly, upstanding, patriotic and heteronormative womanhood indispensable to the health of the Nation. Even 'masculine' women such as Babe Didrikson, Billie Jean King and Martina Navratilova commanded (often grudging) respect for their muscularity and competitive drive, and Navratilova's concessions in the 1970s – bleached blond hair, make-up, frilly underpants, and earrings – made her more palatable to critics (though still repellent to corporate sponsors) (Navratilova and Vescey 1985: 214). Both Babe and Billie Jean dabbled in show business – Babe starred in a vaudeville show in which she hit golf balls into the audience, ran on a treadmill, sang and played the harmonica, while Billie Jean defeated chauvinist Bobby Riggs in a Las-Vegas-style 'battle of the sexes' tennis match made for television in 1973. Yet neither ever included striptease in her repertoire.

By the late 1960s, the best female golfers, figure skaters, and tennis players in North America were predominantly white women who made a decent livelihood in their individual (as opposed to team) sport, and the prize money increased dramatically with greater television revenues and corporate sponsorships in the 1970s. On occasion the targets of sexist, homophobic, and racist commentary, these sportswomen were (and are) ultimately shielded by the gender-appropriate, distinguished character of golf, tennis, and figure skating, as well as by their concerted efforts to exemplify clean, ethically upstanding, and empowering lifestyles: a 'girls next door' image. In immeasurable ways, parents tended to support and approve of their athletically gifted daughters' entry into a respected, decent career, albeit most viewed professional sport as a pit-stop on the road to eventual marriage and motherhood.[32]

Very few female athletes outside of tennis, skating, and golf were able to earn a stable living in large part because their games (and bodies) were deemed inferior to men's, or too much like men's, hence less newsworthy and, most importantly, less marketable. Still today, elite female soccer, baseball, rugby, football, hockey players, boxers, wrestlers, and bodybuilders are unable to translate their skills and savvy into widespread popularity, full-year salaries, benefits, and merchandising deals (Boyle 2003; Patton 2001).

By contrast, women who pursued a full-time striptease career in the 1950s, 1960s and 1970s had little trouble attracting (male) spectators eager to pay handsomely for their talents. But dancers did not earn sizeable incomes without penalty. The women I interviewed spoke of lying about their careers to family and friends for fear of ostracism; some were refused credit at banks, rental accommodation, and 'square' employment upon exiting the business. Several dancers' religious parents attacked striptease as 'Satan's work', and many mothers who danced were threatened by social workers with the removal of their children. Sexual harassment in strip clubs at home and on the road was common place. While high-paid female athletes in the early 1980s routinely donated dollars to charities, members of Vancouver's Exotic Dancers Association (VEDA) who stripped to raise money for needy children were told to direct their 'dirty dollars' elsewhere.[33] In Vancouver, black dancers were exoticized in white racist myths as licentious jungle bunnies confined spatially and cognitively to the 'immorality' and 'spice' of Chinatown/Main Street nightspots in the city's run-down East End. No striptease dancer, white or non-white, was offered lucrative endorsement fees, invitations to ribbon-cutting ceremonies, a commemorative stamp, a street or park in her name, a doll manufactured in her image, public speaking engagements, or the Order of Canada.[34] No striptease dancer – unlike high-profile female athletes – was ascribed the status of nationally-sanctioned heroine, esteemed and emulated by adoring girls across the nation.

Striptease dancers in the postwar era understood the cultural imperative: no self-respecting, virtuous, white Canadian woman undressed in smoky, liquor-soaked, quasi-licit nightclubs past midnight with the principal object-ive of sexually arousing men for a living. Those who did, according to popular lore, were surely drugged and/or coerced by gangsters or pimps, or victimized by poverty, broken families, and histories of abuse. Unlike serious female athletes, dancers – especially middle-class ones – could never have chosen striptease in spite of ex-dancers' vociferous claims to the contrary. Harshly judged for what they did, where, why, when, and for whom they did it, white and non-white striptease dancers were refused membership in the larger community of decorated, athletic female performers. Consigned to geographic and symbolic spaces marked by marginality and otherness, dancers' bodies were, in Foucauldian terms, subjected to capillaries of sur-veillance by politicians, clergy, social workers, women's groups, urban plan-ners, and Morality Squad officers (Foucault 1980: 24). Indeed, dancers' bodies were disciplined and administered in ways that worked concomi-tantly to re-install the iconic status of 'home and garden' mavens Betty Crocker, Donna Read, and June Cleaver.

In the postwar public imagination steeped in ideologies of feminine domesticity, sexual modesty, and suburban bliss, dancers' unholstered breasts, bare legs, rhinestoned stilettos, peekaboo gimmicks, sexy music, and smouldering erotic aura shook the foundations of culturally mandated female respectability and reserve. Baldly put, in a period of more conti-nuity than change in commercial striptease culture from 1950 to 1975, the commodified stripper-body signified working-class degeneracy, anti-authoritarian irreverence, and excess. In effect, the physical and moral regulation of strippers as ungovernable, abject objects was hinged to, and contingent on, the veneration lavished upon 'classy' professional female golfers, skaters, and tennis stars whose triumphs stirred local and national pride. In spite of evidence outlined above that the careers of striptease performers and sports stars were much more similar than they were different, a fierce collective investment in preserving the dichotomy of abject dirty dancer versus revered sweetheart athlete worked to assuage cultural anxieties about gender transgressions, the decline of the family, the 'race', and the Nation.

Both erotic dancers and elite athletes succeeded in an era of postwar economic affluence, an ever more celebrity-obsessed popular culture, and mounting consumer thirst for both 'live' and televisually mediated drama. Indeed, female sporting and stripping spectacles stirred feelings of wonder, satisfaction, and thrill in both performers and their admiring fans. However, the popular myth of female striptease as criminally tinged degradation in sleazy nightspots, and strippers as unskilled, desperate high school drop-outs with unruly, subversive ambitions, buttressed the truism that a 'peeler' was not, and would never be, 'one of us'.[35]

Crossing over and getting burned

Today, decades later, the line separating athletes from strippers is conspicuously blurred in our hyper-consumer age: coverage of the 2004 Olympics in Athens highlighted skin-tight bathing suits in the pool, synchronized swimmers in burlesque-style costumes and theatrical make-up, and female beach volleyballers in bikinis. Over the past five years, white glamour girls – tennis stars Ana Kournikova, and Maria Sharapova, figure skater Katarina Witt, middle-distance runner Katie Vermeulen, and swimmer Amanda Beard – have posed nude or semi-nude in *Playboy*, *Maxim*, and *FHM*. Members of the Canadian women's water polo and Nordic ski teams have undressed for fund-raising calendars (Robinson 2002: 29). Female professional wrestlers (many of whom are former strippers), bodybuilders, ice dancers, and fitness queens reveal more than a little soft-core flash of flesh.[36] Sex sells, and female athletes feel the pressure to test the limits of feminine heterosexiness as a strategy to secure sponsorship deals and spin-offs.

But can a sportswoman go too far and 'cross the line?' In February 1999, Leilani Rios, a 21-year old working-class Latina track star for the California State University at Fullerton was purged from the school's track and field team. Several members of Fullerton's male baseball team in university-funded Titans caps and sweaters witnessed Rios's striptease act at the Anaheim Flamingo Theatre and reported her performance to authorities. Handed an ultimatum by her coach John Elders to choose between her sport and her job as an erotic dancer, Rios elected to keep dancing because as a non-scholarship athlete, she needed the money. In a written statement, coach Elders opined: 'I determined that Ms. Rios's decision to remain an exotic dancer would detract from the image and accomplishments of her team-mates, the athletics department, and the university' (Lin 2000: F4). The baseball players were neither reprimanded nor expelled – their consumption of striptease did not besmirch the university's reputation. Rather, the well-worn adage 'boys will be boys' afforded them not only protection from rebuke, but in some quarters, authenticated their status as 'real' men. Rios, by contrast, was reminded by men that good, (white), obedient girls who keep their noses clean, their shorts on, and their loyalties straight, get team membership, praise, and the promise of future dividends. Bad, (non-white), disloyal girls like Rios who embarrass and shame an entire school, state, and nation by executing private acts in disreputable public spaces get dumped as immoral, disgraced traitors.[37]

In the end, Rios's experience signals a cautionary tale: skin, sex, athleticism, race, performance, and entertainment mix in greater proportions in the twenty-first century. However, female labourers who entertain for a living remain haunted by the punishing discursive logic of the whore stigma. While all showgirls are measured by the criterion of heterosex appeal, only those who, like professional strippers, are perceived as flagrantly specializing in whorish acts in vice districts are condemned for irreparable breach of what I term the decency covenant. As such, offenders are expected to forfeit all claims to the coveted 'role model for little girls everywhere' so utterly foundational to the world of women's professional golf, tennis, and figure skating, then and now.

Acknowledgements

I would like to thank research assistants Erin Bentley and Genevieve Lapointe, as well as the Social Sciences and Humanities Research Council of Canada and the Hampton Fund at the University of British Columbia for timely financial support. Patricia Vertinsky and Jenny Hargreaves are my inspirational mentors. I am grateful to narrators who generously shared their stories with me, and to anonymous readers who provided careful feedback. I dedicate this chapter to 'sporting women,' past and present.

Notes

1 Sarita Melita interview with Becki Ross, Vancouver, BC, 15 December 2004.
2 Dorothy Hamill, quoted in Klemesrud (1975: 42).
3 Patrick Nagle interview with Becki Ross, Victoria, BC, 28 January 2000.
4 For insight into the contemporary striptease scene, see Bruckert (2002), Burana (2001), Eaves (2002), and Atkinson (1995).
5 For selected work on the sexualization of postwar commercial culture, see McLaren (1999), Adams (1997), Friedman (2003). On histories of stripping, see Schteir (2004), Jarrett (1997), and Dragu and Harrison (1988).
6 April Paris, interview with Becki Ross, Vancouver, BC, 30 August 2000.

7 Jack Card, interview with Becki Ross, Kim Greenwell, and Michelle Swann, Vancouver, BC, 28 January 2000.

8 Princess Lillian, interview with Becki Ross, Vancouver, BC, 26 January 2001.

9 Tarren Rae, interview with Becki Ross, Vancouver, BC, 5 December 2000.

10 April Paris, interview with Becki Ross, Vancouver, BC, 30 August 2000.

11 Jasmine Tea, interview with Becki Ross, Kelowna, BC, 24 July 2000.

12 Choo Choo Williams, interview with Becki Ross, Vancouver, BC, 4 February 2002.

13 Miss Lovie, interview with Becki Ross and Kim Greenwell, Vancouver, BC, 22 September 2000.

14 Notably, the alleged African/Cuban origins of Miss Lovie and the African origins of Surya Bonaly were invented by their promoters. See Brady (2001) who argues that in the pseudo-documentary *Pumping Iron II*, that African-American body-builder, Carla Dunlap's routines open and close to a jungle soundtrack with blaring elephant noises and roaring tiger sounds.

15 Sarita Melita, interview with Becki Ross, Vancouver, BC, 15 December 2004.

16 On the negative stereotyping of Asian golfers on the LPGA since the late 1990s, see Hang Shin and Nam (2004).

17 Sarita Melita, interview, 15 December 2004.

18 On the careers of the Canadian Ice Fantasy skaters, from 1952 to 1954, see Scott (2002).

19 Varsity female athletes at the University of British Columbia and other universities across North America were similarly chaperoned out-of-town while varsity male athletes were not. See Ross and Bentley (2004).

20 For an intriguing account of how the media used the 'Richards' story' to enforce boundaries between woman/female and man/male based on essentialized conceptualizations of sex, gender, and difference, see Birrell and Cole (1990).

21 On twentieth-century raids and closures of burlesque and striptease venues, see Friedman (2000) and Ross (2003). On the policing of striptease in North America during the 1980s and 1990s, see Hanna (1998) and Lewis (2000).

22 On mid-century prostitution in Vancouver see Freund (2002).

23 For insights into the economic agency of early-twentieth-century prostitutes see McMaster (2002).

24 On male strippers, see Petersen and Dressel (1982). For a more contemporary account, see Smith (2002).

25 For additional biographies of 'Babe', see Freedman (1999) and Cayleff (1995). Jewish Canadian all-around sports legend Fanny 'Bobbie' Rosenfeld was the subject of similar rumours and sexist, anti-Semitic criticisms in the 1920s and early 1930s. See Levy *et al.* (1999).

26 For elaboration of media representation of Martina Navratilova as both lesbian and communist threat, see Spencer (2003).

27 The same point is made about the contemporary context of female strippers in Bruckert and Frigon (2003).

28 Comparisons with other female entertainers of this era – comedians, non-striptease dancers (ballet, modern, jazz, African, etc.), circus stars, singers, and actors – merit further exploration. Brace-Govan (2002) claims that ballet dancers she interviewed relinquished control over their bodies to choreographers and dance company directors, which suggests they had less professional autonomy than striptease dancers.

29 On striptease dancers' efforts to unionize, see Ross (2006).

30 Female gymnasts have been especially vulnerable to disordered eating, amenorrhea and a host of injuries and abusive authority figures. See Ryan (1995).

31 Coco Fontaine, interview with Becki Ross, Vancouver, BC, 20 September 2000.

32 Commenting on the meteoric rise of Korean golfer Se Ri Pak in the late 1990s,

Hang Shin and Nam (2004) note that multi-million dollar contracts with Cheil Jedang and Taylormade 'assuredly shaped a role model out of Se Ri Pak to girls and parents alike'.

33 On 28 November 2004, Delanies' Exotic Show Pub in Surrey, BC held its twelfth annual Christmas Strip-A-Thon: proceeds from the night including strippers' pay amounted to $4,000 and thirty strippers intended to donate the money to the Surrey Firefighters Foundation and Charitable Society; however, the Foundation declined the donation. See McMartin (2004).

34 In 1948 after having won the Olympic gold medal for figure skating at St Moritz, Switzerland, Barbara Ann Scott became the inspiration for a 'Barbara Ann Scott Doll' manufactured by the Reliable Toys Company in the United States. In 1996, Canada Post Corporation issued a stamp honouring Fanny 'Bobbie' Rosenfeld as a past Olympic champion.

35 For a provocative analysis of 'proper' bodily performance of class and gender in figure skating see Foote (2003).

36 On the recent scandal of scanty costumes and risqué, 'gynecological lifts' in the culture of international ice dancing see Reilly (2002).

37 For insightful link between the Rios case and the regulation of nudity in Pennsylvania in 2000 see Foley (2002).

Bibliography

Abraham, Yvette (1998) 'Images of Sara Bartman: sexuality, race and gender in early-nineteenth-century Britain', in Ruth R. Pierson and Nupur Chaudhuri, *Nation, Empire, Colony: Historicizing Gender and Race*, Bloomington, IN: Indiana University Press.

Adami, Hagh (1982) 'Strippers continue to take it off, despite Goulbourn's new bylaw', *Ottawa Citizen*, 3 November.

Adams, M. L. (1997) *The Trouble with Normal: Postwar Youth and the Making of Heterosexuality*, Toronto: University of Toronto Press.

Atkinson, D. (1995) *Highways and Dancehalls*, Toronto: Knopf.

Banet-Wiser, Sarah (1999) 'Hoop dreams: professional basketball and the politics of race and gender', *Journal of Sport and Social Issues*, 23(4): 403–20.

Birrell, S. and Cole, C. (1990) 'Double fault: Renee Richards and the construction and naturalization of difference', *Sociology of Sport Journal*, 7(1): 1–21.

Bishop, Ronald (2003) 'Missing in action: feature coverage of women's sport in *Sports Illustrated*', *Journal of Sport and Social Issues*, 27(2): 184–94.

Bodo, P. (1995) *The Courts of Babylon*, New York: Scribner.

Boyle, E. (2005) 'Flexing the tensions of female muscularity: how female bodybuilders negotiate normative femininity in competitive bodybuilding', *Women's Studies Quarterly*, 33(1 & 2): 134–49.

Brace-Govan, J. (2002) 'Looking at bodywork: women and three physical activities', *Journal of Sport and Social Issues*, 26(4): 403–20.

Brady, J. (2001) 'Pumping iron with resistance: Carla Dunlap's victorious body', in M. Bennett and V. Dickerson (eds) *Recovering the Black Female Body: Self-Representation By African American Women*, New Brunswick, NJ: Rutgers University Press.

Browne, L. (1993) *Girls of Summer*, Toronto: Harper Collins.

Bruckert, C. (2002) *Taking it Off, Putting it On: Women in the Strip Trade*, Toronto: Women's Press.

Bruckert, C. and Frigon, S. (2003) 'Making a spectacle of herself: on women's bodies in the skin trades', *Atlantis*, 28(1): 58–9.

Burana, L. (2001) *Strip City: A Stripper's Farewell Journey Across America*, New York: Talk Miraxax Books.

Butler, J. (2002) 'Is kinship always already heterosexual?', *Differences: A Journal of Feminist Cultural Studies*, 15(1): 14–44.

Cahn, S. (1994) *Coming On Strong: Gender and Sexuality in Twentieth Century Women's Sport*, New York: The Free Press.

Caudwell, J. (1993) 'Women's football in the United Kingdom: theorizing gender and unpacking the butch lesbian image', *Journal of Sport and Social Issues*, 23(4): 390–402.

Cayleff, S. (1995) *Babe: The Life and Legend of Babe Didrikson Zaharias*, Urbana, IL: University of Illinois Press.

Corio, A. and DiMona, J. (1968) *This Was Burlesque*, New York: Madison Square Press.

Dragu, M. and Harrison, A.S.A. (1988) *Revelations: Essays on Striptease and Sexuality*, London, Ontario: Nightwood Editions.

Eaves, E. (2002) *Bare: The Naked Truth About Stripping*, New York: Knopf.

Festle, M. J. (1996) *Playing Nice: Politics and Apologies in Women's Sport*, New York: Columbia University Press.

Foley, B. (2002) 'Naked politics: Erie, PA v. the Kandyland Club', *NWSA Journal*, 14(2): 1–17.

Foote, S. (2003) 'Making sport of Tonya: class performance and social punishment', *Journal of Sport and Social Issues*, 27(1): 3–17.

Foucault, M. (1980) *The History of Sexuality, An Introduction*, vol. I, New York: Vintage Books.

Freedman, R. (1999) *Babe Didrikson Zaharias: The Making of a Champion*, New York: Clarion Books.

Freund, M. (2002) 'The politics of naming: constructing prostitutes and regulating women in Vancouver, 1939–1945', in J. McLaren, R. Menzies, and D. Chun (eds) *Regulating Lives: Historical Essays on the State, Society, the Individual and the Law*, Vancouver: UBC Press.

Friedman, A. (2000) *Prurient Interests: Gender, Democracy, and Obscenity in New York City, 1909–1935*, New York: Columbia University Press.

Friedman, A. (2003) 'Sadists and sissies: anti-pornography campaigns in cold war America', *Gender and History*, 15(2): 201–27.

Griffin, P. (1998) *Strong Women, Deep Closets: Lesbians and Homophobia in Sport*, Leeds: Human Kinetics.

Haidarali, L. (2005) 'Polishing brown diamonds: African American women, popular magazines, and the advent of modeling in early postwar America', *Journal of Women's History*, 17(1): 10–37.

Hang Shin, E. and Nam, E. A. (2004) 'Culture, gender roles and sport: the case of Korean Players on the LPGA', *Journal of Sport and Social Issues*, 28(3): 223–44.

Hanna, J.L. (1998) 'Undressing the first amendment and corseting the striptease dancer', *The Drama Review*, 42: 38–69.

Heywood, L. and Dworkin, S. (2003) *Built to Win: The Female Athlete as Cultural Icon*, Minneapolis, MN: University of Minnesota Press.

Jarrett, L. (1997) *Stripping in Time: A History of Erotic Dancing*, London: HarperCollins.

Johns, M. (2003) *Moment of Grace: The American City in the 1950s*, Berkeley, CA: University of California Press.

Kaufman, M. (1998) 'Gaining an edge', in L. Smith (ed.) (1998) *Nike is a Goddess: The History of Women in Sport*, New York: Atlantic Monthly Press.

Kennedy, E. (2001) 'She wants to be a sledgehammer: tennis femininities on British television', *Journal of Sport and Social Issues*, 25(4): 436–40.

Klemesrud, J. (1975) 'Dorothy Hamill prepares for stardom', *Woman Sports*, 42.

Kort, M. (2005) *Dinah!: Three Decades of Sex, Golf, and Rock 'n' Roll*, Los Angeles, CA: Alyson Publications.

Lenskyj, H. (1986) *Out of Bounds: Women, Sport and Sexuality*, Toronto: Women's Press.

Lenskyj, H. (1997) 'No fear? Lesbians in sport and physical education', *Women in Sport and Physical Activity Journal*, 6(2): 7–22.

Levy, J., Rosenberg, D. and Hyman, A. (1999) 'Fanny "Bobbie" Rosenfeld: Canada's woman athlete of the half-century', *Journal of Sport History*, 6(2): 392–6.

Lewis, J. (2000) 'Controlling lap dancing: law, morality, and sex work', in R. Weitzer (ed.) *Sex for Sale: Prostitution, Pornography and the Sex Industry*, New York: Routledge.

Lin, J. (2000) 'Three strips and she's out', *Vancouver Sun*, 30 March, F4.

Lloyd, M. (1996) 'Feminism, aerobics and the politics of the body', *Body and Society*, 2(2): 79–98.

Lumpkin, A. (1984) *Women's Tennis: A Historical Documentary of the Players and Their Game*, New York: Whitston Publishing Company.

McClintock, A. (1995) *Imperial Leather: Race, Gender and Sexuality in the Colonial Context*, New York: Routledge.

McLaren, A. (1999) *Twentieth-Century Sexuality: A History*, Oxford: Blackwell Publishers.

McMartin, P. (2004) 'When charity comes with a g-string,' *Vancouver Sun*, 11 December, B1 and B10.

McMaster, L. (2002) 'Representing Vancouver's working girls, 1880–1930', unpublished Ph.D. thesis, Department of English, University of British Columbia.

Messner, M., Dunbar, M. and Hunt, D. (2000) 'The televised sports manhood formula', *Journal of Sport and Social Issues*, 24: 380–94.

Morse, M. (1988) 'Artemis Aging: exercise and the female body on video', *Discourse*, 10(1): 50–3.

Navratilova, M. and Vescey, G. (1985) *Martina*, New York: Knopf.

Patton, C. (May 2001) ' "Rock hard": Judging the female physique', *Journal of Sport and Social Issues*, 25(2): 119–21.

Petersen, D. and Dressel, P. (1982) 'Equal time for women: social notes on the male strip show', *Urban Life*, 11: 185–208.

Postman, A. (2000) 'Athlete of the century: Babe Didrikson', *Women's Sport and Fitness*, 3(2): 110–18.

Reilly, R. (2002) 'Dirty dancing', *Sports Illustrated*, 96(3): 80.

Robinson, L. (2002) *Black Tights: Women, Sport, and Sexuality*, Toronto: HarperCollins.

Ross, B. (2003) 'Striptease on the line: investigating trends in erotic entertainment,' in D. Brock (ed.) (2003) *Making Normal: Social Regulation in Canada*, Toronto: Nelson.

Ross, B. and Bentley, E. (2004) 'Gold-plated footballs and orchids for girls, a "palace of sweat" for men', in P. Vertinsky and S. McKay (eds) (2004) *Disciplining Bodies in the Gymnasium: Memory, Monument, and Modernism*, New York: Routledge.

Ross, B. and Greenwell, K. (2005) 'Spectacular striptease: performing the sexual and racial other', *Journal of Women's History*, 17(1): 137–64.

Ross, B. (2006 forthcoming) 'Troublemakers in tassels and g-strings: striptease dancers and the union question in Vancouver, BC, 1960–1980', *Canadian Review of Sociology and Anthropology*.

Ryan, J. (1995) *Little Girls in Pretty Boxes: The Making and Breaking of Elite Gymnasts and Figure Skaters*, New York: Doubleday.

Salmi, B. (2000) 'Hooker history: 125 years of illegal sex and the city', *Georgia Straight*, November, 17–19.

Salutin, M. (1971) 'Stripper morality', *Trans-Action*, 8(8): 12–23.

Scott, M. (2002) 'The original blade runners', *Vancouver Sun*, 2 February: I8.

Shteir, R. (2004) *Striptease: The Untold History of the Girlie Show*, New York: Oxford University Press.

Smith, C. (2002) 'Shiny chests and heaving g-strings: a night out with the Chippendales', *Sexualities*, 5(1): 67–89.

Spencer, N. (2003) ' "America's sweetheart" and "Czech-mate" ', *Journal of Sport and Social Issues*, 27(1): 18–37.

Spencer, N. (2004) 'Sister act IV: Venus and Serena Williams at Indian Wells: "sincere fictions" and white racism', *Journal of Sport and Social Issues*, 28(2): 115–35.

Stencell, A.W. (1999) *Girl Show: Into the Canvas World of Bump and Grind*, Toronto: ECW Press.

Stevenson, D. (2002) 'Women, sport, and globalization: competing discourses of sexuality and nation', *Journal of Sport and Social Issues*, 26(2): 209–25.

Stuart, A. (1999) 'Josephine: looking at Josephine', in A. Stuart (ed.) (1999) *Showgirls*, London: Jonathan Cape.

Tucker, S. (2000) *Swing Shift: 'All Girl' Bands of the 1940*, Durham, NC and London: Duke University Press.

Vertinsky, P. and Captain, G. (1998) 'More myth than history: American culture and representations of the black female's athletic ability', *Journal of Sport History*, 25(3): 532–61.

Zarlengo, K. (1999) 'Civilian threat, the suburban citadel, and atomic age American women', *Signs: Journal of Women in Culture and Society*, 24(4): 925–58.

7 The social logic of sparring
On the body as practical strategist[1]

Loïc Wacquant

Initiation (15 October 1988)

I enter the gym from the back. DeeDee's sitting in the office, along with big Butch and three youngsters. I greet everyone and shake hands (we always do: it's a daily ritual and a much-valued mark of respect). Right away DeeDee asks me: 'Louie, you got yo' mouthpiece withchou?' 'Yeah, I got it, *why*?' The old coach nods slowly with his chin, a gleam in his eye. I realize that today is my baptism by fire: I'm going to do my first tryout in the ring! I hadn't expected it and I'm worried about not being in very good shape; what's more, I still have a tenacious pain in my right wrist. But I just can't back out now. Besides, I'm eager to get it on; after all, I've been waiting for this moment for weeks – is it not strange to get all excited at the prospect of getting smacked in the noggin? . . .

I scope the place out to see who's going to give me my first thrashing in the ring. Will it be Butch? Just then Olivier walks in through the back door. DeeDee tells him that he's going to spar too and so he should get ready . . . It is indeed Butch who's going to break us in. He's warming up on the floor, ripping through the air with ferocious punches in his sleeveless blue jersey. At the thought of discovering him across from me between the ropes I suddenly find him even more muscular than usual, a veritable colossus even: Butch is almost a head taller than I; his torso and arms are like rolling balls of ebony glistening under the gym's pallid ceiling lights. [. . .] Is it really reasonable to climb into the ring with such an athlete?

I ask DeeDee to wrap my hands; better have him do it this time, when it counts. I get going with a round of shadowboxing in front of the mirror. I do one round on the speed bag to loosen my right wrist but as I start in on another set in front of the mirror (jab-right moving forward, pivot and left hook, jab and a step back), DeeDee shouts to me: 'Louie, what d'hell you doin? Don't wear yourself out like that or you won't have no energy left for sparrin. You're gonna get knocked flat on yo' ass right away.' He's gonna knock me on my ass anyway. The old coach calls me into the back room to put on my cup: the thick leather breeches that protects the groin and pelvis resembles a rigid harness; you put your legs through it then lace it up and tie it behind your waist. I have trouble squeezing my ass into it. DeeDee then hands me a small head guard that looks more like a net shopping bag than the real heaume that Butch is wearing – a massive half-cylinder that covers his entire face, with two cross-slits that show only the eyes, nose, mouth and chin. I sink my head into the head gear and buckle it up; too tight and . . . backwards! I turn it around, re-buckle it, and DeeDee adjusts it. 'Is that tight enough? Where's your mouthpiece?' I hook my white plastic mouthpiece onto my upper teeth, which makes me feel like an animal being readied for the slaughterhouse.

DeeDee instructs me to slather my face with grease. I dip two fingers into the jar and start nervously spreading the Vaseline on my temples, my cheekbones, my brow. I put on way too much, which gets a laugh out of DeeDee: '*Not so much*! Just on your nose and above your eyes, do it in front of d'mirror.' I remove the excess Vaseline and spread it carefully along the ridge of my eyebrows and then my nose – I better not get it broken during training! 'Does that ever happen', I ask? 'Sure does', says DeeDee . . . From the metal cabinet in the corner, the old coach digs out a pair of big red gloves into which he makes me slip my wrapped hands – enormous, overpadded red mittens, twice as long as my hands (competition gloves are much thinner and lighter). He has me make a fist inside the glove, then laces it up for me, carefully going underneath my wrist before closing the glove up with the help of a big piece of silver-grey duct tape, which he skilfully sticks over the laces.

Back in front of the mirror, I feel like I'm hallucinating when I see myself for the first time outfitted in the gear of the complete boxer. Is that really me, decked out like that in this black leather belt girdling my hips halfway up my belly, with my spindly legs sticking out below in purple sweat pants? My gigantic red gloves make me feel as if I had artificial limbs; the leather helmet squeezes my head and collapses my field of vision; the mouthpiece sticking through my lips gives me the features of a Cro-Magnon. A total metamorphosis! I am at once stunned, impressed, and incredulous. [. . .]

No more time to anguish: Olivier is stepping out of the ring, doubled over from exhaustion, it's my turn. I quickly climb the little step-stool and slip through the ropes – just like in the movies. I'm tense and at the same time furiously eager to see what it's going to be like. Submerged in a hyper-acute awareness of my own body, of its fragility, in the carnal sensation of my *corporeal integrity* and of the risk at which I'm putting it. At the same time, the leather shell into which I've been strapped gives me the unreal sensation that this same body has escaped from me – as if it had mutated into a sort of human tank. The cup is sawing at my abdominal muscles and slowing down my movements. The head guard is gripping my skull. Instead of hands, I have two large appendages like soft hammers at the ends of remote-controlled arms which respond to my commands only imperfectly.

DeeDee's hoarse voice resonates, '*Time*!', and we're off on a three-minute journey into the unknown! I crouch and walk toward Butch, who does the same. We touch gloves in the centre of the ring. An exchange of friendly jabs. Feint, approach, back up, feint, we're checking each other out. I attempt a jab-right combination, only to immediately collect Butch's big yellow glove smack in the chops. First hit absorbed without too much damage. Phew! it comes fast! I move forward hesitantly and jab, Butch slips; another jab, another slip. I march resolutely onto him, but he slides away, avoids me with a simple twist of his upper body, pivots and disappears from my field of vision. So begins a race-chase that will last a good half of the round. I follow him step for step, jab-jab-jab; he parries my fists with ease, sends me back a straight right that I counter with my right glove, another that I block ... with my nose. I try to get in closer and, like the conscientious student that I am, repeat the moves that I've executed a thousand times in front of the mirror. I attempt a straight left followed by a right, like I do on the bag, only to get pasted with three juicy jabs. It feels like I've got hot coals up my nose. I beat a hasty retreat, chased by Butch, who now seems truly gigantic to me. His reach is too long and he moves too fast: I've hardly thrown my jab before his head is no longer there and he's punching my ticket with his left at will. *Ouch*! I always see his big yellow fist coming too late. *Pow*! Another right in the puss! I react with a few reckless jabs and finally land a left to his chest, yippee! But nine-tenths of my punches catch nothing but air or else curl up and die in his gloves. Butch stands me up with a mean right that snaps my head back. Afraid he's really rung my chimes, he interrupts the action: 'You okay?'; I signal him to keep going and readjust my head guard as best I can. I strain to advance on him, trying to execute my moves properly, aim, hit, pivot, but it's all in vain: I'm incapable of putting my combinations together while taking into account his movements and anticipations. '*Time out*!' Whew! Catch your breath, quick.

I go back to my corner, sucking in great gulps of air. Inexplicably, I am already completely wasted. Sparring looks easy from the outside, but once you're in the ring, it's not the same thing. Your perimeter of vision shrinks and gets saturated in the extreme: I'd be frankly incapable of saying what's happening outside a circle of about two yards around me. You've got to move constantly and sensory tension is at its peak, which is why I'm already drenched in sweat from head to toe. The perception of your opponent is warped: Butch's gloves seem to have become so enormous that they fill up the entire ring; and when by chance I manage to get close enough to him, I can't discern any place to hit him between his belt and his big yellow paws. My own body also seems different to me and doesn't obey me as promptly as I would wish. The punches don't really hurt (because we're not banging away) but they are irritating: it's vexing to 'eat' several jabs in a row and you have the unpleasant sensation of having your mug swelling up.

I've barely caught my breath when DeeDee bellows '*Time*!' again from the back room. . . . My apprehension has left me and I resolve to put pressure on Butch. But he sees that I'm getting bolder and he too kicks it into higher gear –

Figure 7.1 Busy Louie sparring with Ashante. Picture taken by Jimmy Kitchen and published here for the first time

just enough to keep me constantly off balance. . . . A second later, I collect a cement-truck right full in the face which makes me meditate on my mistake. Things are speeding up, yet these three minutes are truly in-ter-mi-na-ble. I feel like my gloves are too heavy, too bulky, they hamper me. I'm having trouble seeing behind my guard and following my opponent's movements. I'm always one beat behind, if not two: by the time I've made out that Butch is throwing a jab, it's already landed in my kisser.

I'm getting a first-class ass-whipping. Butch is landing every punch he throws – fortunately he's not hitting hard, otherwise I would have been knocked down and out eons ago. . . . I step back and then lunge at him fearlessly – the hell with the jabs in the mug: I've got to get my licks in, too, after all. I manage to land several soft jabs and suddenly, divine surprise, I hit the bull's eye, a straight right dead-centre in Butch's mug. Instinctively, I almost say 'sorry!' out loud to Butch – but it's impossible with my mouth-piece in. I feel vaguely guilty about having bopped him right in the schnoz, since I don't have any intention of hurting him. But mainly I fear his retali-ation. And in fact things start moving faster, blows are coming in from everywhere now. Butch is circling around me like a buzzard and landing every punch. I feel my fists flailing haphazardly while he lards me with sting-ing jabs. . . . '*Time out!*' The voice of deliverance!

I've had enough: I am de-ple-ted! I jump out of the ring to collapse into the waiting arms of Eddie, who's chortling with delight. 'You still alive? You *survived*? How many rounds?' 'Two, this is the first time I've ever sparred'.... I truly don't understand how the pros can last ten and twelve rounds, while heaving truckloads of cinderblocks at each other to boot. Butch steps down out of the ring, I slap his gloves as a sign of thanks. Olivier tells me that my face is all red. My brow and nose are flaming but when I look in the mirror I'm pleasantly surprised to discover that my face isn't as swollen as it feels.

If the typical professional boxer spends the bulk of his time outside the ring, endlessly rehearsing his moves in front of a mirror or on an assortment of bags so as to hone his technique, increase his power, and sharpen his speed and coordination, and even outside the gym eating up miles and miles of daily 'roadwork', the climax and yardstick of training remains the sparring. The point of sparring – one also says 'putting on the gloves' and 'moving around' – is to approximate the conditions of the fight, with the difference that the boxers wear protective headgear and heavily padded gloves and that, as we will see, the brutality of the confrontation is greatly attenuated. Without regular practice in the ring against an opponent, the rest of the preparation would make little sense, for the peculiar mix of skills and qualities required by fighting cannot be assembled but between the ropes [. . .]

Sparring, which has its own tempo (unless he is about to fight, a boxer should 'put on the gloves' lightly or at distant intervals so as to minimize the wear and tear on his body), is both a reward and a challenge. First, it represents the tangible payoff for a long week of hard and dull labour – it is on Saturday that most of the amateur boxers of the Woodlawn Boys Club tangle between the ropes. The gym's trainers pay close attention to the physical condition of their charges and do not hesitate to bar from sparring those who are in their eyes culpable of having neglected their preparation. 'Little Anthony ain't puttin' no gloves on today, DeeDee', brays Eddie one hot afternoon in mid-August. 'He don't do no runnin', he got no gas, no stamina. It's a waste a-time to get him up in there. It's a disgrace.'

Next, sparring is a redoubtable and perpetually renewed test of strength, cunning, and courage, if only because the possibility of serious injury can never be completely eliminated, in spite of all precautions. Two boxers got their noses broken while sparring in the year after I joined the gym. I suffered the same fate as a result of two particularly rough sessions three days apart. . . . Some boxers become 'punchy' (i.e. develop the medical syndrome of the 'punch-drunk fighter', *dementia pugilistica*, sometimes confused with Parkinson's disease) not so much from beatings suffered during official bouts as from the cumulative effect of the blows absorbed in the gym during sparring. Cuts to the face are rare owing to the protective headgear worn for that purpose (and not to cushion the shock of the blows), but black eyes, bruised cheekbones and swollen lips, bloody noses, and battered hands and ribs are the habitual lot of those who put on the gloves on a regular basis. Not to mention that every time a boxer steps into the ring, be it to 'shake out' with a novice, he puts a fraction of his symbolic capital at stake: the slightest failing or slip-up, such as a knockdown or a sloppy performance, brings immediate embarrassment to the fighter, as well as to his gym-mates who hasten to assist his 'corrective face-work' so as to restabilize the fuzzy and labile status order of the gym (Goffman 1967: 19–22). Boxers have at their disposal a variety of socially validated excuses for this purpose, ranging from minor health hassles ('I been battling the flu, man, it's killing me') to imaginary injuries (a damaged knuckle, a sore shoulder) to the alibi most readily called upon, especially by trainers: a breach of the sacrosanct code of sexual abstinence during the phase of training nearing a fight (Wacquant 1998: 342–5). [. . .]

Choosing a partner

Everything in sparring hinges on the choice of partner, and for this reason it must absolutely be approved by DeeDee. The matching of opponents has to be adjusted in a manner such that both boxers benefit from the exercise and the risks of physical injury are kept below an acceptable level. Considerations of honour reinforce these technical reasons: ideally, one does not spar with an opponent who is too superior for fear of 'getting a good ass-whuppin', or one so feeble that he cannot defend himself (for fear of being accused of taking advantage of a weakling). However, vagaries in attendance and divergences in the training and fighting schedules of club members can make it difficult to find a steady partner who fits the threefold rubric of weight, skill, and style. [. . .] In sum, sparring partners are part of the specific social capital of pugilists.

In the absence of adequate sparring partners, one turns to boxers of lesser calibre to make do, or even to beginners as a last resort. Nonetheless, one must always *maintain a measure of equilibrium*, even if it requires deliberately handicapping one of the protagonists. In the case of an overly uneven matchup, the more experienced fighter tacitly commits himself to 'holding back' his punches and to working on his speed, footwork, and defensive moves while the weaker boxer concentrates on offence and hard punching. When one of them is a novice, it is essential to select an 'initiator' who has a perfect command of his punches and emotions. [. . .]: 'Gotta be somebody who can control hisself. I don' want just any guy to get up there withchyou and knock the hell outa you, Louie. He gotta know how to control hisself.' Certain boxers have a style or a mentality that makes it difficult to 'move around' with them in the ring because they do not know how to adapt to their partner. [. . .]

Much as one does not spar with just anyone, one does not spar just any old way either. The brutality of the exchanges between the ropes is a function of the balance of forces between partners (the more uneven this balance, the more limited the brutality) and of the goals of the particular sparring session, i.e. its coordinates in the twofold temporal axis of training and competition. As the date of the fight draws nearer, sparring sessions become more frequent and last longer (up to eight or ten rounds a day during the final week, with a letup in the final two or three days to make sure that you 'don't leave your fight in the gym'), the confrontation more intense, and inexperienced boxers are temporarily kept away from the ring. On the eve of an important bout, sparring can become almost as brutal as the fight itself. While gearing up for his much-awaited confrontation with Gerry Cooney, the latest 'Great White Hope', heavyweight world champion Larry Holmes offered a bounty of 10,000 dollars to the sparring partner who would send him to the canvas, as a way of enticing them to slug away without compunction (Hauser 1986: 199). Yet, as with every well-run training camp, those sparring partners had been carefully selected to give Holmes a clear advantage so as to preserve his strength and bolster his confidence for the fight.

A controlled violence

During a session, the level of violence fluctuates in cycles according to a dialectic of challenge and response, within moving limits set by the sense of equity that founds the original agreement between sparring partners – which is neither a norm nor a contract but what Erving Goffman calls a 'working consensus' (Goffman 1959: 21). If one of the fighters picks up his pace and 'gets off', the other 'instinctively' reacts by immediately hardening his response; there follows a sudden burst of violence that can escalate to the point where the two partners are hitting each other full force, before they step back and jointly agree (often by a nod or a touch of the gloves) to resume their pugilistic dialogue a notch or two lower. The task of the coach is to monitor this 'fistic conversation' to see that the less accomplished fighter is not being silenced, in which case he will instruct his opponent to diminish pressure accordingly ('Circle and jab, 'Shante, I told you not to load up! And you keep that damn left hand up, Louie!'), or that the two partners do not let the intensity of their exchanges drop too far below that of a fight, which would defeat the very purpose of the exercise ('What you be doin' up there, *makin' love?* Start workin' off that jab, I wanna see some nice right hands and counters off the block').

> I return to the back room and ask DeeDee, who is finishing a precooked noodle soup in a plastic cup, comfortably seated in his armchair: 'DeeDee, Saturday, if I can, I'd like to put on the gloves. Maybe I can move 'round with Ashante?' 'I dunno, Louie, I dunno 'cause them guys are gettin' ready for that card next week [at the Park West], so they

don' need to be playin' around right now: they need to be hittin', and hittin' hard'. And he punches the palm of his left hand with his clenched right fist.

(Field notes 1 December 1988) [. . .]

The principle of reciprocity that tacitly governs the level of violence in the ring dictates that the stronger boxer not profit from his superiority, but also that the weaker fighter not take undue advantage of his partner's wilful restraint, as I discovered at the end of a vigorous sparring session with Ashante. On 29 June 1989, I am dumbfounded to learn that Ashante complained to DeeDee that I hit too hard and that he is forced to respond by firing back solid shots right in the mug. 'He told me he cain't have fun withchyou no more, you hit too hard. You made enough progress now, he gotta be careful not to let you land your punches or you can hurt him. If you hit him clean, you can knock him down. [. . .] See, when you started out, he could play withchyou without worryin' but now you're gettin' stronger, he gotta watch out.'

The coach obviously plays a major role in the regulation of this mutually consented violence. If the boxers from Woodlawn measure their punches with such attention, it is because DeeDee, out of respect for his art, will not tolerate all-out 'slugging'. But it is also because each phase of sparring calls for an appropriate level of intensity which is useless (and dangerous) to exceed and below which one must not fall, lest the benefits of the exercise vanish. This optimal level cannot be determined before stepping into the ring; it varies according to the partners and the circumstances (fatigue, motivation, time left before the fight, etc.). It is up to the boxers to set it by jointly feeling their way – in the literal as well as figurative sense – to it with the assistance of DeeDee. Ever attentive to what is transpiring in the ring, the latter is swift to give a good dressing down to a pugilist who allows himself an immoderate use of his punching power or to exhort another to display more aggressiveness. [. . .]

Thus, what has every chance of looking like a spree of gratuitous and unchecked brutality in the eyes of a neophyte is in fact a regular and finely codified tapestry of exchanges which, though they are violent, are nonetheless constantly controlled and whose weaving together supposes a practical and continual collaboration between the two opponents in construction and maintenance of a dynamic conflictual equilibrium. Properly educated boxers relish this ever-renewed duel that is sparring, but they know that this clash is, at every moment, bounded by 'non-contractual clauses' and that it is quite distinct from a fight, even though it approximates it, in that it entails an element of 'antagonistic cooperation'[2] that is expressly banned from a bout. Curtis expresses this distinction thus:

I don't dislike anythin' [about sparring]. I like it all, 'cause ya learn at the same time. In a gym you not tryin' to win a fight, you in here *learnin'*. It's all about *learnin'*. Practicin' on doin' what you wanna do when d'up-comin' fight come, ya know . . . I cain't hurt my opponent – [smiling coyly] I mean my sparrin' *partners*. They helpin' *me* out, just like I helpin' *them* out. They not gonna get in there and try and hurt me . . . Here and again, now an' then, ya know, ya have your little flashy stuff, where he might hit you hard, you might get caught with a nice punch and you gonna try and retaliate and come back with somethin'.

Many boxers need a long phase of adjustment before they bend to these tacit norms of cooperation, which seem to contradict the public principle and ethos of unlimited competition. . . . They will have to be taught *in actu* how to 'read' the discreet cues whereby their partners enjoin them either to back off and to soft-pedal and when, on the contrary, to increase pressure so as to make them work harder. [. . .]

Sparring as perceptual, emotional, and physical labour

As a hybrid figure between training – which it extends and accelerates – and fighting – to which it is a prelude and a sketch – sparring completes the thorough re-education of the body and mind during which is forged what Foucault calls a 'multi-sensorial structure'[3] quite specific to boxing that can be articulated or discerned only in action (Foucault 1973: 165). Ring experi-ence decuples the boxer's capacity for perception and concentration; it forces him to curb his emotions; and it refashions and hardens his body in preparation for the clashes of competition. In the first place, sparring is an education of the senses and notably of the visual faculties; the permanent state of emergency which defines it effects a progressive re-organization of perceptual habits and abilities.

To realize this, one need only track the transformation that occurs in the structure and scope of one's visual field as one climbs the hierarchy of sparring. During the very first sessions, my vision is obstructed in part by my own gloves, saturated by the stimuli that are rushing at me from all sides with neither order nor meaning. The advice DeeDee shouts at me, and the sensa-tion of being armoured in my cup and headgear, not to mention the muffled but omnipresent anguish about being hit, all contribute to exacerbating this feeling of confusion. I experience then the utmost difficulty in fixing my gaze on my opponent and seeing his fists coming at me, especially as I am uneducated about the clues that are supposed to help me anticipate them. From session to session, my field of vision clears up, expands, and gets reorganized: I manage to shut out external calls on my attention and to better discern the movements of my antagonist, as if my visual faculties were growing as my body gets used to sparring. And, above all, I gradually acquire the specific 'eye' which enables me to guess at my opponent's attacks by reading the first signs of them in his eyes, the orientation of his shoulders, or the position of his hands and elbows.

Slugging it out with Ashante

3 June 1989. I warm up by moving around in front of the mirror. My body has gotten used to being in boxer's gear and I no longer have that feeling of being shelled in bothersome trappings. I climb the little ring stool and slip through the ropes. . . . I bounce up and down across from Ashante. . . . He's glistening with sweat after the four rounds he's just done with Rodney. [. . .] We have a few seconds to observe each other and I still surprise myself by wondering what in the world I'm doing in this ring facing this stocky, nasty little guy who may become welterweight champion of Illinois at the end of the month!

'*Time!*'. . . . We touch gloves. I move on him right away and badger him with quick jabs, which he parries. He stops me in my tracks to tell me, 'If you're comin' at me, keep yo' han's up or I'm gonna' deck you.' Thanks for the advice, which I take into account by swiftly raising my guard. . . . I'm determined to hit harder than usual, even if this means that Ashante's also going to hit harder – and that's exactly what happens. We test each other out. I try to find my distance. A few jabs and a few rights, blocked on both sides. I land a jab to the body, then jump on him with a left-right-left hook combination. *Boom!* In the mug! Ashante backs up and immediately counters. Instead of withdrawing, I stand fast and try to parry his punches. He hits me with a straight left flush on my mouth. I get him in a clinch and catch him out thanks to my favourite trick: a feint with the jab and a wide right cross to the face just as he moves to his left to slip away from my left. *Pow!* My fist pings right into his cheek. He nods 'okay' to me. He seems surprised that I'm boxing so energetically and picks up the pace.

Ashante's walking onto me, mouth deformed by his mouthpiece, eyes bulging with concentration. I back up and jab to try to protect myself. He fakes a straight left and throws a sharp right directly to my side: I reel under the blow and beat a hasty retreat. . . . I chase him down into a corner, jab, right, jab, and catch him with a nice right uppercut when he leans over to avoid my jab. Nonetheless he's blocking most of my hard punches very effectively: I see the opening just fine but in the time it takes for my fist to get there, he's closed up the passage or moved away by rotating his torso. (Ashante anticipates where my fists are about to go so well that it's almost like we're dancing a ballet together.) He suddenly kicks into higher gear and drills my head with short straight punches that I scarcely see coming. . . . I stagger under the blow and decide (actually, I don't decide anything, it's just a formula, I do it, that's all! Everything moves much too fast, you react instinctively) to march onto him but he stops me dead in my tracks with several hard jabs to the body. '*Time out!*' DeeDee's voice resounds.

We separate, I return to my corner and catch my breath. I'm not too tired, but it's only the first round. Big Earl advises me, 'Keep him away with your jab: jab, jab, don't let him get under your guard. Like [Sugar Ray] Leonard. Want some water?' He climbs onto the table, directs the straw of the water bottle toward my mouth and shoots me a stream of warmish water, which I swallow (something a real boxer never does).

'*Time in*!' Second round, both of us go on the attack from the get-go, without even touching gloves in a display of friendliness. Ashante is boxing faster. I struggle to keep up with his cadence, but I react better and protect myself more effectively than the previous times. He starts to punch for real: three hooks to the sides cut though my guard like butter and knock the wind out of me. *Whew!* That hurts. I counter with a few jabs but he dodges them by moving his head just enough for my fist not to reach him. Ashante traps me several times against the ropes and lards me with pointed and heavy hooks. One of his attacks even makes me lose my head and I let my defences down for a second. Luckily, he spares me and interrupts the hailstorm of punches, satisfied with letting me know that I'm wide open. I then launch an awkward attack, as I no longer have good control over my coordination. Ashante greets me with a right-left-right combination flush in the face which reddens my nose; I feel my bottom lip start to swell. I respond wildly, but still manage to sting him in the snout with a right followed up with a short left hook right on target. He always tries to duck down to his right and I catch him with two hooks straight in his head guard. *Yahoo*! Which makes him react immediately. He cuts the ring off, marching straight onto me, not even bobbing and weaving, to show me that he's going to throw punches and couldn't care less about my counters. He fakes me with both hands in turn until I leave myself open and *boom*! A wide left hook sends my head snapping back. I stagger under the punch, but wave to him, 'Okay, it's alright.' We find ourselves face to face again, both a bit surprised at so much viciousness. . . . He lands another punch on my face, a right that makes my headgear turn sideways. DeeDee growls: 'Move your head, Louie!' I'm trying! Things are really heating up now. Ashante machine-guns my torso, then knocks the wind out of me with a mean right uppercut to my side. (I'll remember that one for awhile.) I get him in a clinch again. He shoots me some short punches to the ribs and even to the back, as if we were in a real fight. . . . '*Time out*!'

We shake each other's fists briefly, to reaffirm the controlled nature of the exchange. 'Tha's good, Louie, you're doin' good, you're punching har' today, keep it up.' 'Yeah, the only problem is I'm not sure I can hold out for another round at this pace.' I'm really wore out, both by Ashante's punches and by the tempo of the session, which is much too brisk for me. I catch my breath as best I can, leaning on the ropes.

'*Time in*! Work!' The third round goes just as fast and I absorb a bushel of punches. [. . .] The level of violence rises little by little, but in a reciprocal and graduated manner – meaning that, near the end, when I don't have enough strength left to simply keep my guard up properly and respond even feebly to his punches, Ashante pretends to be boxing me but is only hitting me super-ficially, whereas if he kept on punching as hard as he was at the beginning of the round, he would send me rolling to the canvas. [. . .] I get him in a clinch again but don't have the strength to return his punches. Shoot, it should be over with by now! This round's so damn long! I keep whining to myself in my head: 'Time out! Time out!' Come on, DeeDee! Fuck, what's the matter, has he forgotten us or what? We must have been boxing for a good five minutes! '*Time out!*' Oooofff!

I'm so exhausted from this sparring session that I'm incapable of copying all my notes until the next day. My chin hurts and my entire face is sore (as if it were swollen on the inside), my bottom lip is puffed up and I have a superb reddish bruise under my left eye. But it was especially the blows to the body that wore me down. The uppercuts to the ribs have left me with a large mark that will veer imperceptibly from red to black to yellowish over the course of the next dozen days. Tonight, as I type these lines, I'm dead tired, my hands are numb, my forehead and nose bone are on fire (as if my entire face were throbbing in the manner of a ventricle) and I've got aching spots across my chest that stab me at the slightest movement. Just the craft getting pounded in.

But sparring is not only a physical exercise; it is also the means and support of a particularly intense form of 'emotion work'.[4] Because 'few lapses of self-control are punished as immediately and severely as loss of temper during a boxing bout', it is vital that one dominate at all times the impulses of one's affect (Lorenz 1966: 281). In the squared circle, one must be capable of managing one's emotions and know, according to the circumstances, how to contain or repress them or, on the contrary, how to stir and swell them; how to muzzle certain feelings (of anger, restiveness, frustration) so as to resist the blows, provocations and verbal abuse dished out by one's opponent, as well as the 'rough tactics' he may resort to (hitting below the belt or with his elbows, head-butting, rubbing his gloves into his opponent's eyes or over a facial cut in order to open it further, etc.); and how to call forth and amplify others (of aggressiveness or 'controlled fury', for instance) at will while not letting them get out of hand. [. . .]

A boxer must exercise not only a constant inner surveillance over his feelings but also continual 'expressive control' over their external 'signalling' (Goffman 1959: 59–60) so as not to let his opponent know if and when punches hurt him, and which one. Legendary trainer-manager Cus D'Amato, the 'discoverer' of Mike Tyson, sums up the matter thus: 'The fighter has mastered his emotions to the extent that he can conceal and control them. Fear is an asset to a fighter. It makes him move faster, be quicker and more alert. Heroes and cowards feel exactly the same fear. Heroes react to it differently' (cited by Brunt 1987: 55). This difference has nothing innate about it; it is an acquired ability, collectively produced by prolonged submission of the body to the discipline of sparring. Butch explains:

BUTCH: You have to stay in control, because yer emotions will burn up all yer oxygen, so you have to stay calm and relaxed though you know this guy's tryin'to knock yer head off.

LOUIE: Was it hard learning to control emotions, like to not get mad or frustrated if a guy is slippery and you can't hit him with clean shots?

BUTCH: It was hard for me. It took me years-an'-years-an'-years to git that and *juuus'* when I was gittin' it under control real goo', then thin's, hum, started movin' for me.

LOUIE: Is that something that DeeDee taught you?

BUTCH: He kept tellin' me to stay calm, relax. Jus' breathe, take it easy – but [his pace picks up] I foun' it har' to stay calm and relax when this guy's tryin' to kill ya over in the next corner, but eventually it sunk in and I understood what he was sayin'.

Indeed, the deep imbrication among gesture, conscious experience, and physiological processes – to recall Gerth and Mills's (1964) distinction between the three constituent elements of emotion – is such that a change in any one triggers an instantaneous modification of the other two. Failure to tame the sensory experience of punches flying at you amputates your ability to act and by the same token alters your corporeal state. Conversely, to be at the height of physical fitness allows you to be mentally ready and therefore to better master the feelings triggered by the flow of blows.

Finally, the strictly physical aspect of sparring should not be neglected on account of being self-evident: one must not forget that '[b]oxing is more about getting hit than it is about hitting'; it is 'primarily about being, and not giving, hurt' (Oates 1987: 25, 60). [. . .] Now, beyond one's congenital endowment, such as an 'iron chin' or the mysterious and revered quality called 'heart' (which also holds a central place in the masculine street culture of the ghetto), there is only one way to harden yourself to pain and to get your body used to taking blows, and that is to get hit regularly. For, contrary to a widespread popular notion, boxers have no personal predilection for pain and hardly enjoy getting pummeled. [. . .] What boxers have done is to elevate their threshold of tolerance for pain by submitting to it in graduated and regular fashion.

This learning of indifference to physical suffering is inseparable from the acquisition of the form of sangfroid specific to pugilism. The adequate socialization of the boxer presupposes an endurance to punches, the basis for which is the ability to tame the initial reflex of self-preservation which would undo the coordination of movements and give the opponent a decisive advantage. More so than the actual force of the latter's punches, it is this gradual acquisition of 'resistance to excitement [*résistance à l'émoi*]' as Mauss (1973: 85) says, which one is hard pressed to ascribe either to the realm of will or to the physiological order, which exhausts the novice during his first sparring sessions as well as inexperienced fighters during their bouts. This is because, in addition to the hyper-acute attention demanded by the duel in the ring, one must fight at every moment one's first reflex, which is to shell up on oneself, and forbid one's body to disobey by turning away from one's opponent, by coming undone, by running away from his flying fists in a mad dash for safety. [. . .]

Pugilistic cultivation and the body strategist

To learn how to box is to imperceptibly modify one's bodily schema, one's relation to one's body and to the uses one usually puts it to, so as to internalize a set of dispositions that are inseparably mental and physical and which, in the long run, turn the body into a virtual punching machine, but *an intelligent and creative machine capable of self-regulation* while innovating within a fixed and relatively restricted panoply of moves as an instantaneous function of the actions of the opponent in time. The mutual imbrication of corporeal dispositions and mental dispositions reaches such a degree that even willpower, morale, determination, concentration, and the control of one's emotions change into so many reflexes inscribed within the organism. In the accomplished boxer, the mental becomes part of the physical and vice versa; body and mind function in total symbiosis. [. . .]

It is this close imbrication of the physical and the mental that enables experienced boxers to continue to defend themselves and eventually rebound after skirting being knocked out. In such moments of quasi-unconsciousness, the body continues to box on its own, as it were, until they regain their senses, sometimes after a lapse of several minutes. [. . .] In the famous 'Thrilla in Manila',[5] one of the most brutal battles in the history of the Manly art, both Joe Frazier and Muhammad Ali fought much of the bout in a state bordering on unconsciousness. Several years later, after the third contest between the two great rivals of the decade, 'Smokin' Joe' recalled how, by the sixth round, 'I couldn't think anymore. All I know is the fight is there. The heat [nearly 104 degrees], the humidity [of the Filipino summer] . . . That particular fight, like, I just couldn't think, I was there, I had a job to do. I just wanted to get the job done'. He would continue to march onto Ali, drunk with punches and blinded by the swelling around his eyes, until his trainer, fearing that he was going to get himself killed in the ring, threw in the towel at the bell for the fifteenth and final round. [. . .]

Pugilistic excellence can thus be defined by the fact that the body of the fighter computes and judges for him, instantaneously, without the mediation – and the costly delay that it would cause – of abstract thinking, prior representation, and strategic calculation. As Sugar Ray Robinson concisely puts it: 'You don't think. It's all instinct. If you stop to think, you're gone' (cited in Hauser 1986: 29). This same opinion is confirmed by trainer Mickey Rosario: 'You can't think [. . .] out there [in the ring]. You got to be an animal' (cited in Plummer 1989: 43). And one might add: a *cultivated* instinct, a *socialized* animal. It is the trained body that is the *spontaneous strategist*; it knows, understands, judges, and reacts all at once. If it were otherwise, it would be impossible to survive between the ropes. [...]

Thus the strategy of the boxer, as product of the encounter of the pugilistic habitus with the very field that produced it, erases the scholastic distinction between the intentional and the habitual, the rational and the emotional, the corporeal and the mental. It pertains to an embodied practical reason which, being lodged in the depths of the socialized organism, escapes the logic of individual choice. [...] This is what Joyce Carol Oates recognizes well when she writes: ' "Free" will, "sanity", "rationality" – our characteristic modes of consciousness – are irrelevant, if not detrimental, to boxing in its most extraordinary moments' (1987: 108). Once in the ring, it is the body that learns and understands, sorts and stores information, finds the correct answer in its repertory of possible actions and reactions, and in the end becomes the veritable 'subject' (insofar as there would be one) of pugilistic practice.

Notes

1 This chapter is extracted and adapted from L. Wacquant (2004) *Body and Soul: Notebooks of an Apprentice Boxer*, New York: Oxford University Press: 77–99, with permission from Oxford University Press.
2 I borrow this notion from W.G. Sumner, *Folkways*, Boston, MA: Ginn, 1940.
3 My translation. This expression is wrongly rendered as 'multi-sensorial' in the translation of Foucault listed below.
4 On the notion of 'emotion work', see A. Hochschild (1979) 'Emotion Work, Feeling Rules and Social Structure', *American Journal of Sociology*, 85(3): 551–75.
5 'The Thrilla in Manila' videotape of the Ali–Frazier heavyweight title fight, NBC Sports Venture, 1990.

Bibliography

Brunt, S. (1987) *Mean Business: The Rise and Fall of Shawn O'Sullivan*, Harmondsworth: Penguin.
Foucault, M. (1973) *The Birth of the Clinic: An Archaeology of Medical Perception*, New York: Pantheon Books. Originally published in French in 1963.
Gerth, H. and Wright-Mills. C. (1964) *Character and Social Structure*, New York: Harcourt, Brace, Jovanovich.
Goffman, E. (1959) *The Presentation of Self in Everyday Life*, Harmondsworth: Penguin.
Goffman, E. (1967) *Interaction Ritual: Essays on Face-to-Face Behavior*, New York: Pantheon.
Hauser, T. (1986) *The Black Lights: Inside the World of Professional Boxing*, New York: McGraw Hill.
Lorenz, C. (1966) *On Aggression*, New York: Harcourt, Brace and World.
Mauss, M. (1973) 'Techniques of the body', *Economy and Society*, 2(1): 70–88 (orig. published in French in 1935).

Oates, J.C. (1987) *On Boxing*, Garden City, New York: Doubleday.

Plummer, W. (1989) *Buttercups and Strong Boys: A Sojourn at the Golden Gloves*, New York: Viking.

Wacquant, L. (1998) 'The prizefighter's three bodies', *Ethnos*, 63(3): 325–52.

8 Disabled bodies and narrative time

Men, sport, and spinal cord injury

Andrew C. Sparkes and Brett Smith

Introduction

We live time *in* and *through* the materiality of our individual fleshy bodies as biological entities. We *feel* it in our bones. Yet, time is also a social and collective experience. As Adam comments, 'Time is lived, experienced, known, theorized, created, regulated, sold and controlled. It is contextual and historical, embodied and objectified, abstracted and constructed, represented and commodified. In these multiple expressions time is an inescapable fact of social and cultural existence' (2004: 1).

Given the ways in which the body, the self, society, and time are intimately connected it is interesting to note how the latter has received little attention within the social sciences in general, and sports-related studies in particular. Collinson states that, 'to date there has been relatively little sports literature that takes time as the focus of the analysis' (2003: 331). Accordingly, little thought has been given to how time is experienced in ways that link the individual body, be it sporting or otherwise, to the social body.

Against this background of neglect, narrative studies and autobiographical research have made sustained efforts to grapple with how time is constructed and experienced in relation to body-selves that are constituted through personal storytelling. We draw on this approach in this chapter to explore how time is experienced and narrated by three men when they live in and through different kinds of bodies. Harry, Jamie, and David (pseudonyms) have suffered spinal cord injury (SCI) and become disabled through playing the contact sport of rugby football union.[1] This traumatic injury was the result of one moment in their life that propelled them from the world of the able-bodied into the world of disability where they remain to this day.

Even though all bodies are embedded in time, Seymour (2002) emphasizes that when a person becomes disabled due to SCI, time takes on a more imperious position in their lives. For her, 'Disability disrupts life's narratives and expectations . . . Living with a disability is living a life dominated by time. Rehabilitation is a lifelong process of re-embedding time into corporeal practices and self-identity, a process that is never settled but always vulnerable to disruption' (Seymour 2002: 136–8).

By focusing on how Harry, Jamie, and David narrate and experience time pre-SCI when they constructed and inhabited certain kinds of bodies, as opposed to post-SCI where each experiences time very differently as a disabled man,[2] in this chapter we hope to illustrate the complex process of reintegrating time with the body and the body with time. In particular, we seek to illuminate through their stories how the restitution, chaos, and quest narratives as described by Frank (1995) operate post-SCI to shape the ways in which Harry, Jamie, and David re-embed time into their corporal practices and self-identities. This process reveals the ways in which personal experiences of embodied time are framed by and embedded within larger socio-cultural constellations of meaning. Finally, we reflect on the wider implications of these three narrative forms for how disability is understood and constructed within Western societies.

Three men and SCI

Harry, Jamie, and David are white, heterosexual, and born in the United Kingdom. All were very physically active people and heavily involved in rugby football union. During this period they lived in and through disciplined and dominating bodies as described by Frank (1991). Following SCI they define themselves as disabled and do not take part in any sporting activity. Each claims disability benefit and a mobility allowance.

Harry, now forty years of age, lives in a rural community with his wife and young daughter. After leaving school at sixteen, he worked full-time on his parents' farm. Harry married in 1987 and became a father five years later. In 1994, at the age of thirty-one, the scrum twisted in a rugby match and his spinal cord was damaged at the level C5. Here, 'C' denotes cervical vertebrae, and the '5' indicates the neurological level of damage causing paralysis in Harry's legs and the lower part of his body. He is currently unemployed and spends most of his days at home.

Jamie, forty-four years old with three young children, was a crane driver in a dockyard. In 1994, when he was thirty-five years of age, as a result of a tackle in a rugby game, Jamie's spinal cord was damaged at the level C2. Here, 'C' denotes cervical vertebrae, and the '2' indicates the neurological level of damage. He has the highest level of SCI within the sample of men here and the severity of his spinal trauma is such that he requires artificial life support and breathes using a ventilator. Jamie has no sensation or movement below the neck. Shortly after the SCI, Jamie's wife divorced him. He is currently unemployed, lives in a new bungalow, his children visit him fortnightly, and he has two female personal assistants.

David is twenty-eight years old and a teaching assistant. He was a talented all-round sportsman and enjoyed participating in a number of physically demanding sports. In 1990, at the age of seventeen, while still at school, he acquired a C5 (cervical vertebrae, level 5) SCI following the collapse of a scrum. Like Harry, he is paralyzed in his legs and the lower part of the body.

Nearly two years after leaving formal rehabilitation and the spinal injury unit, David returned to his studies with the support of his family. He went on to gain a university degree, and later a teaching qualification. David now lives with his long-term girlfriend and identifies himself as a 'disabled activist'.

Time prior to SCI

Prior to SCI, Harry, Jamie, and David, not uncommonly, often took time for granted. When time was acknowledged it was defined as *cyclical* in Brockmeier's (2000) terms.[3] This is a narrative model or map of auto-biographical time that depicts life as if it were a repetitive structure. Here, time is experienced as a series of events, repeating themselves. Brockmeier acknowledges that in 'real time' there is no identical repetition. However, he suggests that this narrative model offers a particular vision of the course and direction of time that, in turn, help frame, and structure storytelling. For example, the seasonal nature of farm work meant that Harry's experiences of time were connected with the cycle of the seasons, as well as the use of clock time in organizing his working day: 'Farming revolves around the seasons, how I spent my days depended really on the time of year . . . I suppose farming is a repetitive lifestyle, but I loved it.'

As for many athletes, cyclic time was also experienced in relation to periodic recurrences that characterize sport. For example, the organization of the year in relation to the seasons particular sports were played in, and also the organization of the week in relation to match days, training schedules, and social events that revolved around a sports club. As David commented, 'a lot of time back then was taken up with sport and more sport . . . My time, especially during the rugby season, was pretty much spent around rugby.'

Closely connected to the experience of cyclic time was that of *linear* time. For Brockmeier (2000), in this model time is viewed as if it were a continuous line of chronological marks and is experienced as an irreversible process. Athletes are particularly familiar with this notion of clock, calendar, or linear time. That is, time based on standardized invariable units. For Shogan (1999) the technologies associated with the machinery for adding up and capitalizing time in sport actually penetrate individual bodies as part of a disciplinary process. As Collinson (2003) notes, this kind of time marks runners, etching itself onto their bodies, as they gauge their progress by time. They also optimistically and uncritically arrange their future by it, assuming that training in a certain manner for a specific period of time will result in a level of fitness that will translate into predictable performances at a given distance. Indeed, she suggests, many athletes *become* their times, and identify others by their times in specific events.

For David, Harry, and Jamie, their involvement in rugby led them to conceive of linear time as controllable and linked to specific 'objective' outcomes associated with enhanced performance, such as, improved fitness levels and more efficient skill execution. Talking of his training sessions pre-SCI, David commented:

> I was running faster as well, and found that half way through the season, before I broke my neck, I'd shaved a few seconds off a circuit I used to run. Knowing that made me train more . . . I was very dedicated to improving my game and I think that because I could see the outcome of the hours that I put in training then that made me even more dedicated. I suppose it was like having some control over your destiny.

Besides connecting these men to cyclic and linear time, their comments also reveal the manner in which *disciplined* time is experienced and developed via their involvement in rugby and how closely this is connected with the characteristics of the disciplined body described by Frank (1995) and the disciplined sporting body described by Shogan (1999). The masculine practices associated with rugby and its organization and structure provide a context and framework for the socialization of individuals that influence not only how their bodies are used but also the types of bodies they develop over time. As part of this process, their bodies become disciplined in time and time becomes disciplined in their flesh. As David explained:

> It's about disciplining the body, you work at it for what you want to do . . . what it could *do*, see how far I could push it. I was always one of the fittest . . . I worked hard at my fitness, watched what I eat, put the hours in the gym, it all helped tune the body.

For David, Harry, and Jamie, specific forms of disciplined time, cyclical time and linear time were experienced in and through their bodies as they engaged in their sporting and working lives. As part of this embodied process, a strong athletic identity and masculine sense of self were developed in a taken-for-granted manner (Sparkes and Smith 2002). Then came the fateful moment in their lives.

The fateful moment

The moment David, Harry, and Jamie suffered SCI playing rugby is vividly remembered and is *immortalized* in time. As Seymour points out, spinal injuries are 'injuries embedded in time. The body becomes a perpetual memorial to the split second of time in which the spinal cord was severed' (2002: 138). Shortly after the incident of SCI, and following the stabilization of the fracture and the ensured maintenance of essential bodily functions (e.g. respiration and urination), the men entered formal spinal injury rehabilitation. In this context, time, and the ongoing relationship between the objective body and the subjective living body in time, are suddenly thrown into sharp relief and are ruptured.[4]

David, Harry, and Jamie each experienced ruptured time and then went through similar processes of re-embodying time *within* rehabilitation. However, *outside* the context of rehabilitation their experiences of time in relation to their bodies evolved in very different ways as three powerful cultural narratives began to exert their influence on their lives post-SCI.

Time post-SCI and the restitution narrative

According to Frank, the plot of the restitution narrative has the basic story-line: 'Yesterday I was healthy, today I'm sick, but tomorrow I'll be healthy again' (Frank 1995: 77). For Harry, this translates to: 'Yesterday I was able-bodied, today I'm disabled, but tomorrow I'll be able-bodied again.' This narrative has an affinity with the *restored* self and the *entrenched* self as described by Charmaz (1987) that involves the belief that they will make a 'comeback' and return to their former livers and physical selves. One of the ways in which Harry experiences biographical time reverberates with what Crossley (2000) terms a *philosophy of the future*. With respect to disability, this is a temporal orientation that embodies a strategy of minimization insofar as the person is determined not to let SCI 'ruin' the plans that they had in the past, or held for the future. People who develop this temporal mode of living also decline to relinquish their routine future orientation, thus refusing to entertain the possibility that they might not walk again. This is evident in the following comment by Harry:

> My aim now is to focus on the future and the light at the end of the tunnel . . . I try and think about what the future has in store, look to there, and wait until a cure is found. I don't think that's strange, because that's what I want, and you know, it's not how I want to live, like this . . . I want to, and will walk again, and not far in the future a cure will be found, and it's only there that I see myself.

Framed by the demands of the restitution narrative for themes relating to the technology of a cure and the restorable body-self, a narrative connection is made to the basic temporal orientation of living in the future. However, if we explore further the complexity of the future in relation to the past and present in Harry's life story then, like Roberts (1999) suggests, we find that the future takes on different meanings. Other comments made by Harry illustrate how he shifts between three time tenses connected through the future: the *Past in the future*, the *Present in the future*, and the *Future in the past*.

Making reference to the *Present in the future*, Harry said: 'Well, it's like this. I don't see any use in thinking about the present, my priority is the future . . . and that is because I see medical advancements being made, even now as we speak.' Later in the same interview, however, he made connections with the time tense of the *Past in the future* when he commented, 'When I first came home I'd got very little use in my arms, I'm the strongest I've ever been now . . . In maybe ten or fifteen years time, I will be as good as new.' Finally, talking of the *Future in the past* as he waits for a cure that will return him to an able bodied state of being and to his former self, Harry states:

> Keeping who I was in the past, keep it in mind is something that I need to do if I am to get myself back. If, as I believe, disability is a temporary situation for me, then I want my old self back because I liked myself then . . . It's knowing that a cure will be available which helps me to keep my perspective on time in the future. So I look to the future, knowing that the past will return, and recapturing what I had can only be accomplished through what lies in medical advancements, progress. It's a matter of believing that. I just know those days will come back. But the problem is the waiting. I sit here. I can hardly get up and walk can I [laughs]. Just waiting. Waiting for the future. Waiting for the day when I can walk again and be myself.

These comments signal how Harry narrates time in relation to the future by utilizing different time tenses. They also highlight how defining SCI as temporary fosters a sense of what Charmaz (1991) terms *waiting time*. That is, the restitution narrative evokes feelings of boredom and time is lost while waiting for the body-self to be restored by advances in biomedicine. Waiting time also means a loss of control over time. This loss, in turn, extends to the loss of spontaneity and flexibility due, in part, to the time-consuming nature of managing life as a disabled person in the context of a disablist and disabling society.

According to Seymour (2002), *consumed time* is an active and ongoing process whereby quantifiable time becomes a scarce resource that must be re-embodied and constantly managed in order for the body to remain healthy, to conform to social imperatives, and to achieve satisfaction in life's activities. In doing so, time becomes a commodity and large amounts of time debits must be set against the value of the outputs. For Seymour (2002), evoking the concept of consumed time may serve to direct attention to the severely diminished opportunities for social participation for individuals 'who must lead a highly time-consuming lifestyle. Once time is seen as a resource, it affects our relationship to death, our understanding of reality, and our practices of work, leisure and sleep. Our bodies are different because of it' (Seymour 2002: 139). Consumed time is reflected in the following comment made by Harry:

> What you have to remember is that doing the simple things that I never gave much thought about when I could walk, simple things like making a cup of tea, now take up a lot of my time and energy . . . Being disabled is also a very frustrating existence because any spontaneity is lost. On a nice sunny day I'll say, 'I wonder how my father and the farm are coming along. I'll just go and see them.' But I can't simply do that. I would have

to wait for someone to drive me, assuming that I could get hold of someone. I might need time to relieve the bowels, and then, of course there is the time it would take for me to get ready and to transport myself into a car. So, I stay at home.

In restitution, for Harry, the future is colonized by the past. Stories are told to the self and others of a future that is predicated on restoring the self via medical advances so that the body's former predictability is regained. In this scenario, disability is an aberration, a blip in the otherwise linear or 'normal' passage of time. With a sense of concrete hope hinging on a trajectory directed toward the future, the present is unrewarding (Smith and Sparkes 2005a). Indeed, the plot of the restitution narrative does not lie in the present because the body-self revealed in the present is considered undesirable. Living in the present would mean accepting that medical science can disappoint and that the former disciplined body-self cultivated in an able body may be lost forever. As such, the present is filled with stories of what is being done in order to restore the body-self to what it used to be. In these ways, Harry narrates his life in the future as he waits for a cure that will return him to an able-bodied state of being. As a consequence, he seeks a restored self, and his current sense of self is *entrenched*, wedded to a body-self conception situated in the past (Charmaz 1987). In this situation, other future possible selves are ignored and the potential for Harry to develop different senses of self and explore other identities as a disabled man are limited.

Time post-SCI and the chaos narrative

According to Frank (1995) *chaos narratives* are the inverse of restitution narratives because here the plot imagines life never getting better. These stories are chaotic in their absence of narrative order. They are told as the storyteller experiences life and their body: without sequence or discernible causality. As Frank notes, chaos means 'an *anti-narrative* of time without sequence, telling without mediation, and speaking about oneself without being fully able to reflect on oneself' (1995: 98). As Jamie commented, 'Well, I, feel, nothing. Feel, it's shattering, shattering [ten second silence]. The whole thing is just completely shattering. Life has been beaten out of me.'

When chaos moves into the foreground of one's self narrative, the past, present, and future are under ontological threat. Time becomes defined as an *empty present*. This temporal orientation, according to Crossley (2000), refers to time experienced as a stream of overpowering events. Here, people live without hopes, possibilities, or aspirations. They do not think about, plan, or commit themselves to future possibilities because they are afraid of disappointment. The anxiety associated with such fears means that they fail to commit themselves to various projects and possibilities, and therefore lose all sense of meaning and coherence in their lives. Finally, time caves in.

It is not enough to simply appreciate that in chaos time is experienced as an empty present. For Jamie, embodied experiences of time also encompass a *time tense* of the *Future in the present* (Roberts 1999). Here, a future is storied as existing in the chaos of the present and this makes it extremely difficult to compose a future. The future is uncertain and feared since it is imagined as more chaos, or even worse. Narrative wreckage then engulfs the present. The past loses its order and a culturally derived sense of being propelled through time erodes. According to Jamie:

> Life moves on without me, but, then, I just survive. I don't have ambitions or a future. See the kids grow up, but well it's not the same, then, then what? . . . I don't do anything of importance. Watch television, not a lot I can do. Nothing [five second pause]. A void, just existing. Then, well, life has stopped. Just, I don't know. Exist in the present, no tomorrow, nothing. I don't know where my life is going. Then, but, it's difficult because time means nothing now . . . Not a lot to live for . . . time is, is distorted. Just nowhere. I don't know where I am.

Jamie further suggested that the over-determination of his situation led to his experiences of time being connected to, and shaped by a narrative model or map of time associated with a *static* view of life. This view of life, as described by Brockmeier is a 'state of mnemonic paralysis, overpowered by all experience that, like a psychological black hole, absorbs all possible development, all movement that could lead the autobiographical process away from this all-consuming experience' (2000: 68). This unchanging story of life, the stretched quality of static time that engulfs the person in a sea of dimensionless time, is displayed by Jamie in the following comment:

> I can't really see a future – I can't. Thinking about it, if I could, would be just too overwhelming. I just can't . . . The point is that you, Brett, can fill your day. I don't know what you do, but the point is you can. There are probably not enough hours in the day for you. But, for me it is different. Life has stopped. Time is frozen. Days, weeks, just merge into one. Nothing changes. I don't know. Things take an eternity to do. So you don't try to do anything anymore. That's why I'm stuck in a rut. In my life nothing changes. Nothing.

For Jamie, therefore, chaos is a non-identity, with neither future nor past able to guide the self in any meaningful way. With no narrative map to use as a guide, and with no foreseeable replacement, biographical time stops. In the chaos narrative, Jamie has lost a central resource that any storyteller depends on: a sense of temporality. His story is wrecked because, in part, its present is not what the past was supposed to lead up to, and the future is barely thinkable. The body-self is swept along, without control, by life's fundamental contingency. Narrative time in embodied and chaos is, subsequently, narrative wreckage.

Time post-SCI and the quest narrative

According to Frank (1995), *quest narratives* meet suffering head on, accepting illness or disability and seeking to use it. Here, becoming disabled is the occasion for a journey that becomes a quest. What is quested for may never be wholly clear, but the quest is defined by the person's belief that something is to be gained from the experience of becoming, and being, disabled.

Within a quest narrative, there is a re-embodiment of time that points to new opportunities and a chance to remake a life. One important aspect of this process includes *reclaimed time*. For Seymour (2002), a serious disruption in life's prospects and expectations can offer people an opportunity to remake themselves and reclaim time that has passed. The reality of irrevocable change, the acceptance of contingency as part of the fundamental contingency of life, and the prospect of an unknown future may give immediacy to life that was formally taken for granted. For Seymour, 'By repossessing the past a person may abandon or rework an earlier life script: the "cleaned slate" may enable the person to reconstitute him or herself in a more purposeful manner' (2002: 139). Echoing these points, David notes:

> Now I appreciate time more, know that I won't live forever, and I try and savour the moment. See, it's a journey, and the time aspect is not something that I take for granted now . . . Certainly I don't see disability as a tragedy . . . I've changed, have been reborn, and have become a better person since the accident . . . As well as the social and access problem . . . disability is also about living within the limitations, the functional ones, not thinking that you can beat them. See that's the point again. You know some people spend all their time trying to do more, but I think you can waste time like that. We all only have so much time and wasting it, throwing yourself into doing more, trying to walk again. I don't want to sound negative, each has their own way, but sometimes it's best to accept it, use it, and try and enjoy the moment.

The notion of reclaimed time draws, in part, on the *fragmentary model* of time identified by Brockmeier (2000). This is a timeless model that recognizes the unpredictable nature of human life and the complexity of the body-self. Thus, David does take *a* path, which leads to *a* future, however unknowable and unpredictable. For instance, investing in relationships, financial independence, and pursing a career remain worthwhile practices for him. The future, for David, is not completely uncontrollable, but simply less amenable to control. As such, he recognizes and challenges the myth of control in relation to the body that prevails in Western cultures.

Importantly, rejecting the myth of control and recognizing that the future cannot be totally controlled does not lead David to despondency, or a sense of powerlessness. It simply means that contingency is now accepted as part of the fundamental contingency of life that is influenced by numerous factors, many of which are beyond the control of the individual. Here, as Frank (1995) suggests, bodily predictability comes to be regarded as exceptional, and contingency comes to be accepted as normative.

> I take life as it comes. I don't worry about what the future holds. I can't control it, not totally anyway, what life throws at you. Impossible. So I tend to live in the present, in the here and now. We don't live forever, so take pleasure in the moment, as long as it doesn't hurt people. But don't get me wrong, I do think about the future, but what I don't do is pin all my hopes on it. I don't know what's in store do I? Anything could happen. Disability teaches you these things, makes you recognize how fragile the future is. Again it's about control and how much people believe that they have control over it. If I thought I could control the future, instead of living for today, then, it's like a ladder. The higher you climb, the bigger the drop. If what I planned didn't work out in the future and I've pinned all my hopes on it, then the damage would probably be pretty severe . . . So, I take each day as it comes.

Such comments not only connect David to a fragmentary narrative model of autobiographical time described by Brockmeier (2000), but also signal certain types of 'time tenses' identified by Roberts (1999). Making reference first to the *Past in the past* and then shifting to a time tense of the *Future in the future*, David remarked: 'The past is in the past and the future, well, as I say you have to recognize that the future is too far ahead, but you are still moving.' Later in the interview, however, his accounts of disability were embedded within the *Present in the present*, as the following comments indicate.

> I live in the present . . . I do think that if I lived in the past or thought too much about the future, and even if that was concerned with a cure, I don't think that's a good strategy. Why? Well, for starters the present is much more fun . . . But if I did become preoccupied with the future or even the past, then I think that places a limitation on who you can be . . . For instance, if I was concerned with the future, then I would probably lose sight of the present and who I am, or becoming. In that sense, I don't think I would develop as a person because, living in the past or future requires you to have a very specific focus and restricts your opportunities to try out different roles, or experiment with who you are. And in the end I probably would not enjoy the present, not like I do now . . . At the end of the day, I live for the here and now and don't take notice of the past, what it meant to me.

These comments not only signal a life lived in the present, but also suggest that an over-emphasis on the past or future might, for some people, lead to a situation that restricts their opportunities to engage with the possible or potential identities that are a necessary aspect of becoming a *developing* self (Charmaz 1987). Yet, as we mentioned earlier, this process of engagement is not easy. Accordingly, as if to challenge the ways in which notions of a quest story might romanticize SCI, David made comments that pointed toward a number of embodied dilemmas and problems associated with *consumed time* (Seymour 2002). His reflections on *ingested time* that involves forging a new and always fragile relationship between ingestion and the body acts as a further antidote to any tendency, by others, to oversimplify his experiences of SCI and the reconstruction of self within any one particular narrative form (see Seymour 2002; Sparkes and Smith 2003).

In summary, for David, memories of being able-bodied are situated in the past while living as a disabled person occupies the present and helps shape a future. Therefore, time horizons stay close and neither past nor future assumes priority. The present is attended to and feels fully lived. According to Charmaz (1991), the self in the present emerges from the type and quality of events in the present. A sense of passion, communion, and involvement distinguishes the intense present. Furthermore, Charmaz argues, with the intense present comes a sense of urgency: urgency to act, to experience, and to bond or commune with other bodies. The certainty of the body's contingency and one's mortality, and its imminence, also casts a vivid light on the present. In such ways, the present is embedded in the flesh and a more communicative relationship with the body is encouraged (Frank 1991, 1995). Thus, when living in the present SCI may become an opportunity, albeit a difficult one, to develop both different and differently valued body-self relationships and forms of embodiment.

Reflections

The words of Harry, Jamie, and David have illustrated the intimate connections between body, time, self, and society and the central role that narrative plays in how individuals make sense of these connections as they construct personal stories that give meaning to their lives. As Frank states, 'People build their own stories on the narrative scaffolding that their local worlds make available, and these scaffoldings constrain the kind of story that can be told, even as they enable storytelling. To put the issue in political terms, people are subject to stories others tell about them' (2004: 178).

According to Sparkes (1996, 2004), just what kinds of body-self relationships and experiences are constructed over and in time depend on the cultural repertoire of stories available for synthesis into personal stories, and the access people have to this repertoire within a political economy of developmental opportunities. Therefore, while the individual stories told by Harry, Jamie, and David, along with the ways in which time plays a pivotal role in each of them is unique to them, it is shaped and given meaning via the narrative resources at their disposal within a cultural setting. Their opportunities to (re)construct their body-selves, and how they interpret events in their lives now as disabled men, are shaped by specific narrative forms.

Harry's life, as a disabled man, is shaped by the restitution narrative. Clearly, we have no wish to denigrate the restitution narrative or under-estimate its value in certain sets of circumstance. However, there are a number of dilemmas that go with this storyline that need to be acknowledged in terms of how it connects the individual body to the social body. This is particularly so given that, with regard to disability (and illness), this narrative is the most prominent and culturally preferred in Western cultures. As Frank points out, the 'cultural power of these stories is that their telling reflects one of the best impulses in modernity: the heroism of applied science as self-overcoming' (1995: 92). That is, in Western cultures disabled people and physicians are often lauded as heroes when they attempt to overcome or 'beat' disability and return the individual to an able-bodied state of being. Talking of illness, Frank points out that the heroism of the ill person is invariably tied to the more active heroism of the healer.

> The respective heroisms of physicians and patients are complementary but asymmetrical. Each heroism is required by the other, but physicians practice an active heroism, while patients accept a passive heroism. This asymmetry is not a problem – it may be the only sensible arrangement – but the ill person who adopts this narrative as his own self-story thereby accepts a place in the moral order that subordinates him as an individual.
>
> (Frank 1995: 93)

For Harry, and other men like him whose experiences of time and their bodies are shaped by the restitution narrative with its desire for a restored self located in the (able-bodied) past, a close allegiance to and a reliance on medical science is formed. This has the potential to subordinate them as individuals to a medicalized view of the world that colonizes them as embodied beings. Here, the restitution narrative supports and promotes a complicity with biophysical notions of 'normality' and cultural ideals of the 'perfect' body. This leads to a 'successful recovery' from SCI and disability being defined in relation to a bodily aesthetic that is narrowly prescriptive in terms of posture and gait. As Paterson and Hughes note, 'Consequently, the hegemonic notion of the disabled body constructs it in terms of corporeal or intellectual "deficit". To overcome this deficit, the disabled body requires the services of scientific medicine and rehabilitation' (2000: 33). They argue that rehabilitative and therapeutic approaches to disability and impairment centre on the concept of individual adjustment and, therefore, concentrate on rectifying a perceived mental or physical 'flaw' that prevents and hampers an individual's ability to function 'normally'.

The restitution narrative, and the manner in which it frames the body-self and time feeds into dominant notions of SCI that view becoming dis-abled through sport as a personal tragedy, with disability being defined as an individual 'problem' to be rectified via a scientific cure. It privileges a specific version of 'health' and promotes being able-bodied as the normal condition that people ought to both aspire to and have restored when things 'go wrong'. As part of this process people are provided with a way of identifying and defining what is assumed to be a 'natural' and 'normative' experience in relation to becoming disabled through sport. These storylines, like other internalized 'master' narratives, tend to act as a blueprint for all stories and become vehicles through which people comprehend not only the stories of others, but crucially, of themselves. As such, the restitution narrative does little in the way of challenging the ideologies that inform an ambulist and disabling culture. It is unable to acknowledge that it might be society that requires rehabilitating within a politicized social model of disability rather than the individual who is oppressed within a disabling culture (Barnes *et al.* 1999; Oliver 1996).

Certainly, as a 'master' narrative that can be drawn on and internalized to frame the experiences and identities of people, restitution stories can be inspirational and useful for some who become disabled though SCI. It can serve particular purposes, such as, generating concrete hope for the future (Smith and Sparkes 2005a). However, this narrative can also be constraining. In part, this is because the plot of this story can funnel people into a narra-tive cul-de-sac and lock them into one pattern of response to SCI. Such a response reduces their access to other counter-narratives available within the culture that might lead to the emergence of new understandings of time as well as different and perhaps more satisfying body-self relationships. This is particularly so when the restitution narrative is linked with notions of heroic masculinity. As Kleiber and Hutchinson (1999: 152) emphasize, 'Portraying recovery as aligning one's actions with those of the physically heroic not only creates an unrealistic ideal that most individuals cannot live up to, it also directs the course of recovery in personally limiting ways.'

A further limitation of the restitution narrative noted by Frank (1995: 94) 'is the obvious but often neglected limitation of the modernist deconstruc-tion of mortality: when it doesn't work any longer, there is no other story to fall back on'. Problems, therefore, arise when the disabled person does not find restitution, when the body is not fixed or cured. Further problems arise when people become fixated on one kind of body and sense of self in circum-stances where the restitution narrative is not appropriate (Sparkes 1996, 2003). Another limitation highlighted by Frank is that restitution is increas-ingly a *commodity* that some can purchase and others cannot. Here we might imagine the individual finding that a 'cure' for SCI has been found but is unable to afford this cure. As Frank notes (1995: 95): 'High-tech medicine offers more and more restitutions that fewer and fewer people will be able to afford.' Therefore, the restitution story as a *generalized* narrative of disability and illness is likely to become increasingly restricted in its availability.

In contrast to Harry, Jamie's chaos story takes us into the world narrative wreckage. As Kleinman and Seeman note, this type of narrative tends to be chosen by those individuals and groups in society 'who actually have lost (or, more correctly, been denied) control over the events that define their lives and deaths' (2000: 238). This narrative is often grounded in the power politics of local settings in ways that deflects criticism from the structures of social oppression that can instigate and maintain chaos in the lives of individuals.

In relational terms, those with power often deny, ignore, or actively silence chaos narratives in their unwillingness to hear them and listen attentively. In view of this, one important way to alleviate and move out of chaos is by telling stories and having those stories heard by others. As Frank (1995, 2004) argues, storytelling can play an important role in repairing narrative wreckage as the body-self is gradually reclaimed in the act of telling. Thus, as a wounded storyteller, Jamie needs the opportunity and the support to recover and reclaim the voices that SCI has taken away from him. In effect, he needs to be granted narratibility. This means his life, voices, and experience of events must be affirmed as being worth telling and thus worth living and reclaiming. This demands an enhanced tolerance for chaos as a part of his life story by all those connected to Jamie. As Frank (1995) emphasizes, if the chaos story is not honoured, the world in all its possibilities is denied. To deny a chaos story is to deny the person telling this story, which means that they cannot be cared for. It also sentences them to narrative silence. As Frank points out, 'people can only be helped out when those who care are willing to become witnesses to the story. Chaos is never transcended but must be accepted before new lives can be built and new stories told' (1995: 110).

This process is not easy or straightforward. Frank (1995) acknowledges that chaos stories are anxiety provoking, threatening, and difficult to hear. This is because of their lack of any coherent sequence or plot which means that the teller is not understood as telling a 'proper' story. Another reason hearing is difficult, Frank suggests, is because the 'chaos narrative is probably the most embodied form of story. If chaos stories are told on the edges of a wound, they are also told on the edges of speech. Ultimately, chaos is told in the silences that speech cannot penetrate or illuminate' (1995: 101).

Furthermore, given that the disabled are one minority group that anyone can join at any time, and given the indistinctiveness and permeability of the boundaries between the able-bodied and the disabled, the chaos narrative is fear provoking for the able-bodied. As Couser notes, 'the border is patrolled vigilantly by "normals" more out of fear that they might stray over it than out of fear of transgression by those on the other side' (1997: 178). Part of this patrolling involves defining and legitimizing from the perspective of the able-bodied just what constitutes an 'acceptable' story involving the body, self, time, and hope. Thus, for the able-bodied the hope for a restored body-self in the future that restitution narratives offer is preferred to the lack of hope, disorder, and the static empty present that goes with the chaos narrative. As Mattingly (1998) notes, therapists and others work to construct 'success' stories: 'They presume that patients will not be committed to therapy without success, for success breeds hope, and hope is essential' (1998: 79). Accordingly, in Western societies to despair, to lose hope, and not 'move forward' are frowned upon as strategies for dealing with SCI. Moreover, as Mattingly comments, the unacceptability of the chaos narrative to listeners is closely linked to the issue of desire.

> The essential place of desire in a narrative model is particularly striking when we realize not only that the story hero but even the story listener is drawn to desire certain story outcomes and fear others . . . When a story is told, if that storytelling is successful, it creates in the listener a hope that some endings (generally the endings the hero also cares about) will transpire . . . We hope for certain ending; others we dread. We act in order to bring certain endings about, to realize certain futures, and to avoid others.
>
> (Mattingly 1998: 93)

Finally, in quest narratives as evidenced by David's story, SCI is reconfigured as a challenge and an opening to other ways of being as part of a developing self and a more communicative body. Here, becoming disabled through sport can provide an opportunity for people to develop a different set of body-self relationships and experiences of being in time than they had before. In this sense, David's quest story operates as a counter-narrative to restitution and chaos stories because it is framed and enabled by what Swain and French (2000) describe as an *affirmative model of disability*.

Building on the liberatory imperative of the social model outlined by Oliver (1996), Swain and French (2000) define the affirmative model as a non-tragic narrative of disability and impairment which encompasses positive social identities, both individual and collective, for disabled people grounded in the benefits and life experiences of being impaired and disabled. By deviating from standard plots and dominant assumptions about disabled people (e.g. disability is a tragedy that ruins a life), this model resists and challenges the mainstream stories that people attempt to fit their lives, and the lives of others into. Therefore, as a counter-narrative, the affirmative model has revelatory, liberatory, therapeutic, and transformative possibilities for the individual and the community by making available and legitimizing different ways of living as a disabled person.

Accordingly, quest stories like those told by David, and their potential links with an emancipatory politics, are about being transformed in ways that liberate individuals and groups from constraints that adversely affect their life chances and experiences. Importantly, the teller has been given something by the experience of disability that is then passed on to others in the telling as an act of witness. This passing on or sharing, Frank suggests, involves the disabled person in an act of *extrospection* in which the 'unfinished project is a new vision of oneself in a previously unimagined relation to others' (2002: 170). Defining the experience of becoming disabled through sport as a positive force that changes body-self relationships and a sense of time provides a challenge and a counter-narrative to presumptions that disability is *always* a tragedy and acts as a point of resistance against the dominant master narratives revolving around notions of a medical cure that are so persuasive and powerful in Western cultures. This resistance, and sharing of stories, signals the emergence of a communicative body acting *for* others, and connecting in a dyadic fashion with them, rather than acting against others. In this situation there is a potential to generate communal and collective stories of disability that instigate social as well as individual change in the face of oppressive structures.

There are, however, potential problems with the quest narrative. For example, Frank (1995) notes how they can easily become stories to reassure the healthy that just as the author has risen above disability or illness, they too can escape. He also points out that quest stories risk romanticizing illness: 'The risk of quest stories is like the risk of the Phoenix metaphor: they can present the burning process as too clean and the transformation as too complete, and they can implicitly deprecate those who fail to rise out of their own ashes (1995: 135). Likewise, a potential limitation of the affirmative model is that it may disembody the experience of disablement, siphoning out experiences of the body and its fleshy physicality in favour of a political-structural analysis that focuses solely on barriers to participation and an affirmation of a positive identity. Some might also see this model as depicting the disabled as a homogeneous group. Hence, there is the risk of excluding or avoiding multiple forms of impairment and their effects, ignoring those who do not see themselves as part of the collective disability rights movement, disregarding those who covet a cure, and thereby negating diversity and difference.

Notwithstanding such issues, it would seem that the quest narrative has empowered David to alter the trajectories of his life and infuse his history with new meaning and complexity. The quest storyline provides narrative scaffolding that allows him some flexibility to adapt to an uncertain future. It is also helpful in terms of enhancing his ability to explore different body-self relationships and experience time differently as a disabled man.

For Harry, Jamie, and David as disabled men, their experiences of time and the manner in which they are shaped by particular narratives has profound implications for how they, and we, live our lives as embodied beings. Their words illustrate that being a body-self in and through time is a sociologically significant component of life that deserves greater analytic attention in the future. In closing, we would like to thank Harry, Jamie, and David for their act of generosity in sharing their stories with us and hope that in this chapter we have presented their stories respectfully and done justice to the complexity of their experiences.

Notes

1   Harry, Jamie, and David were involved in a study that explored the life histories of a small group of men (n=14) who have suffered spinal cord injury (SCI) and become disabled through playing rugby football union. Details of the methodology, the various forms of analyses applied to the data, and the key issues that emerged in this study are available in Smith and Sparkes (2002, 2004, 2005a, 2005b), Sparkes (1998, 1999, 2005), Sparkes and Smith (2002, 2003).

2   Another crucial period in the lives of these men is immediately following SCI during rehabilitation. For details see Seymour (2002), and Sparkes and Smith (2003).

3   In our analysis of time we draw in an eclectic manner from the work of scholars in a variety of disciplines. In adopting such an approach, we seek not to conflate the categories of chronic illness and disability for the reasons discussed by Barnes and Mercer (1996), Couser (1997) and Sparkes and Smith (2002, 2003).

4   For details of immortalized time and ruptured time see Seymour (2002) and Sparkes and Smith (2003).

Bibliography

Adam, B. (2004) *Time*, Cambridge: Polity Press.

Barnes, C. and Mercer, G. (eds) (1996) *Exploring the Divide: Illness and Disability*, Leeds: The Disability Press.

Barnes, C. Mercer, G. and Shakespeare, T. (eds) (1999) *Exploring Disability*, Cambridge: Polity Press.

Brockmeier, J. (2000) 'Autobiographical time', *Narrative Inquiry*, 19(1): 51–73.

Charmaz, K. (1987) 'Struggling for a self: identity levels of the chronically ill', in J. Roth and P. Conrad (eds) *Research in the Sociology of Health Care: A Research Manual*, 6, Greenwich, CT: JAI Press Inc.

Charmaz, K. (1991) *Good Days, Bad Days: The Self in Chronic Illness and Time*, New Brunswick, NJ: Rutgers University Press.

Collinson, J. (2003) 'Running into injury time: distance running and temporality', *Sociology of Sport Journal*, 20(4): 331–50.

Couser, T. (1997) *Recovering Bodies*, Madison, WI: University of Wisconsin Press.

Crossley, M. (2000) *Introducing Narrative Psychology*, Buckingham: Open University Press.

Frank, A. (1991) 'For a sociology of the body: an analytical review', in M. Featherstone, M. Hepworth and B. Turner (eds) *The Body: Social Process and Cultural Theory*, London: Sage.

Frank, A. (1995) *The Wounded Storyteller*, Chicago, IL: University of Chicago Press.

Frank, A. (2002) 'The extrospection of suffering: strategies of first-person illness narratives', in W. Patterson (ed.) *Strategic Narrative*, New York: Lexington Books.

Frank, A. (2004) *The Renewal of Generosity*, Chicago, IL: University of Chicago Press.

Kleiber, D. and Hutchinson, S. (1999) 'Heroic masculinity in the recovery from spinal cord injury', in A. Sparkes and M. Silvennoinen (eds) *Talking Bodies: Men's Narratives of the Body and Sport*, SoPhi: University of Jyvaskyla, Finland.

Kleinman, A. and Seeman, D. (2000) 'Personal experience of illness', in G. Albrecht, R. Fitzpatrick and S. Scrimshaw (eds) *Handbook of Social Studies in Health and Medicine*, London: Sage.

Mattingly, C. (1998) *Healing Dramas and Clinical Plots*, Cambridge: Cambridge University Press.

Oliver, M. (1996) *Understanding Disability: From Theory to Practice*, London: Macmillan.

Paterson, K. and Hughes, B. (2000) 'Disabled bodies', in P. Hancock, B. Hughes, E. Jagger, K. Paterson, R. Russell, E. Tulle-Winton and M. Tyler (eds) *The Body, Culture and Society*, Buckingham: Open University Press.

Roberts, B. (1999) 'Some thoughts on time perspectives and auto/biography', *Auto/Biography*, 7(1 & 2): 21–5.

Seymour, W. (2002) 'Time and the body: re-embodying time in disability', *Journal of Occupational Science*, 9(3): 135–42.

Shogan, D. (1999) *The Making of High Performance Athletes: Discipline, Diversity and Ethics*, Toronto: University of Toronto Press.

Smith, B. and Sparkes, A. (2002) 'Men, sport, spinal cord injury and the construction of coherence: narrative practice in action', *Qualitative Research*, 2(2): 143–71.

Smith, B. and Sparkes, A. (2004) 'Men, sport, and spinal cord injury: an analysis of metaphors and narrative types', *Disability and Society*, 19(6): 509–612.

Smith, B. and Sparkes, A. (2005a) 'Men, sport, spinal cord injury and narratives of hope', *Social Science and Medicine*, 61(5): 1,095–105.

Smith, B. and Sparkes, A. (2005b) 'Analyzing talk in qualitative inquiry: exploring possibilities, problems, and tensions', *Quest*, 57(2): 213–42.

Sparkes, A. (1996) 'The fatal flaw: a narrative of the fragile body-self', *Qualitative Inquiry*, 2(4): 463–95.

Sparkes, A. (1998) 'Athletic identity: an Achilles' heel to the survival of self', *Qualitative Health Research*, 8(5): 644–64.

Sparkes, A. (1999) 'Exploring body narratives', *Sport, Education and Society*, 4(1): 17–30.

Sparkes, A. (2003) 'From performance to impairment: a patchwork of embodied memories', in J. Evans, B. Davies and J. Wright (eds) *Body Knowledge and Control*, London: Routledge.

Sparkes, A. (2004) 'Bodies, narratives, selves and autobiography: the example of Lance Armstrong', *Journal of Sport and Social Issues*, 28(4): 397–428.

Sparkes, A. (2005) 'Narrative analysis: exploring the *whats* and *hows* of personal stories', in I. Holloway (ed.) *Qualitative Research in Health Care*, Milton Keynes: Open University Press.

Sparkes, A. and Smith, B. (2002) 'Sport, spinal cord injury, embodied masculinities and the dilemmas of narrative identity', *Men and Masculinities*, 4(4): 258–85.

Sparkes, A. and Smith, B. (2003) 'Men, sport, spinal cord injury and narrative time', *Qualitative Research*, 3(3): 295–320.

Swain, J. and French. S. (2000) 'Towards an affirmative model of disability', *Disability and Society*, 15(4): 569–82.

9 'It's not about health, it's about performance'

Sport medicine, health, and the culture of risk in Canadian sport

Nancy Theberge

Introduction

Sport is one of the key sites for the exercise of physical power in modern life. This is true both in the sense that sporting activity involves the enactment of bodily power, and that the athletic body is a site on which disciplinary power is exercised, for example in training regimes and in scientific testing and monitoring of bodily processes (Shogan 1999). Another form of disciplinary power in sport is the medicalization of the sporting body. There are now recognized specializations in sport in a number of health professions, for example, clinical medicine, surgery, physiotherapy, chiropractic, and massage therapy. Such is the penetration of medical intervention in sport that Waddington (1996: 179) has suggested that athletes today are understood to require routine medical supervision, not because they have a clearly defined pathology but simply because they are athletes.

The roots of sport medicine lie at the turn of the twentieth century, when medical researchers studied the bodies of male athletes, not with a particular interest in sport, but in order to understand the 'biological wonders presented by the high performance athlete' (Hoberman 1992: 8). Over time this concern gave way to an interest in the application of medical science to improving athletic performance. Waddington (1996: 176) describes this as the 'conjuncture' between processes of medicalization and the increasing competitiveness of sport. The main impulses for this development were rising nationalism in the Cold War era of the 1950s leading to greater emphasis on performance in sport as a way to foster national pride, and increased commercialism leading to greater material rewards from sporting excellence. In this context, and in concert with more general processes of medicalization in modern life (Zola 1972), sport medicine became more directly concerned with improving performance, and more institutionalized, with the formation of organizations such as the British Association of Sport Medicine and the American College of Sport Medicine (established in, respectively, 1953 and 1954; the Canadian Academy of Sport Medicine was not established until 1970) and the recognition of sport medicine by national and international sporting bodies such as the Canadian Olympic Committee and the International Olympic Committee.

While the rise of sport medicine as a research specialty and the evolution of its focus on performance enhancement has been well documented (Hoberman 1992; Waddington 1996, 2000), less attention has been focused on the clinical practice of sport medicine. Discussions of the involvement of practitioners in the administration of doping regimes (Hoberman 1992; Waddington 1996, 2000) make an exception to this trend. Another avenue of inquiry concerns the involvement of health practitioners in the culture of injury and risk in sport. In a series of papers that explored this topic, Nixon (1992, 1993, 1994) employed the concept of 'sportsnets'. Borrowing from social network theory, Nixon (1992: 128) defined sportsnets as 'the webs of interaction that directly or indirectly link members of social networks in a particular sport or sports related setting'. He proposed that under certain circumstances sportsnets may 'entrap' athletes in the culture of risk; these circumstances include when they have 'asymmetric relations favoring coaches and other sportsnet gatekeepers, bridges, stars and authorities' (Nixon 1992: 132). While Nixon does not specify which groups belong to the sportsnet, his work suggests that membership includes not only athletes and coaches but also administrators and sport medicine personnel. (For an assessment and comment on Nixon's work, see Roderick 1998.)

Nixon's work has been the basis for several analyses of the practice of sport medicine in a number of settings. Walk (1997) examined the experiences of student athletic trainers in US university sport. Safai (2003) studied the negotiation of treatment between clinicians (physicians and physiotherapists) and athletes in a large Canadian university. Two studies in Britain have examined professional sport: Waddington *et al.* (1999) have examined the role of the club doctor and physiotherapist in football, while Malcolm and Sheard (2002) have studied the management of injuries, including access to health care, in rugby union.

Taken collectively, this research and related work on athletes' experiences of pain, injury, and the culture of risk in sport (Young 2005; Roderick *et al.* 2000; Howe 2004; Pike and Maguire 2003) have begun to shed light on medicalization processes in sport. This research suggests that the conspiratorial nature of the sportsnet suggested (but never specifically indicated) by Nixon is exaggerated. Rather, health professionals working in sport negotiate the tensions between their professional obligation to safeguard athletes' health and well-being and the emphasis in sport on performance, manifest both in the toll exacted on athletic bodies by intense training and in pressures to return injured athletes to activity. Safai's (2003) research in Canadian university sport led her to conclude that while the culture of risk is a defining feature of the negotiations between athletes and sport medicine practitioners, it is countered by a culture of precaution that resists the acceptance of pain and injury in sport in its attention to the health and safety of athletes. The dialectic between the cultures of risk and precaution provides the main context in which negotiations between athletes and practitioners occur.

In the Canadian context, the history of sport medicine has been marked by a striking contrast. On the one hand, Canada was a leader in developing procedures for the delivery of high-quality medical services at international competitions, such as the Olympics and Pan American Games (Safai 2005). Yet another chapter in the history of Canadian sport concerns a darker side of medical practice. Following Ben Johnson's positive drug test at the 1988 Seoul Olympics, the Canadian government commissioned Mr Justice Charles Dubin to examine the 'Use of Drugs and Banned Practices Intended to Increase Athletic Performance'. Convened in January 1989, the Dubin Inquiry was broadcast live on cable television, and offered a 'compelling and easily consumed melodrama' (MacAloon 1990: 43) on the evolution, not only of a culture of drug use among some athletes in some sports (testimony focused mainly on athletics and weightlifting), but also on the organization of the high performance sport system in which this culture emerged. Testimony also recounted in detail the central role played by a physician, Dr Jamie Astaphan, in the doping programme followed by Johnson and others who trained with him under coach Charlie Francis. While the disclosures that followed Johnson's positive drug test never gave evidence of widespread involvement of medical and other health professionals, the revelations nonetheless were a dramatic and highly publicized example of the underside of medical practice in Canadian sport.

Although the Dubin report tended to attribute responsibility for drug use to individuals who had 'lost the way', other observers emphasized the influence of broader structural conditions (MacAloon 1990; Burstyn 1990). Chief among these was the state-supported high performance sport system that emphasized results in international competitions. This emphasis translated into rewards, both symbolic and material. Among the material rewards was eligibility for living stipends provided by the federal sport agency, Sport Canada, to athletes who were highly ranked internationally. Following the release of the Dubin Report, the 1990s saw the emergence of a discourse that questioned the emphasis on performance in sport. This discourse, however, merely competed with and never replaced the emphasis on performance, which had resumed centre stage by the end of the decade. In 2001 a National Summit on Sport issued a report in which recommendations for funding excellence in sporting performance featured prominently (Coakley and Donnelly 2004: 406–7; see also Green 2004).

This chapter explores the medicalization of the athletic body through an examination of the clinical practice of sport medicine. The specific context of the research is the Canadian high performance sport system. The analysis concerns the practice of sport medicine in a context in which performance is a defining feature. To this end, the discussion explores two aspects of the work of sport medicine practitioners: how they negotiate the relation, and tensions, between performance and health; and how the focus on performance is the basis for a 'consumer oriented' model of professional practice (Johnson 1972).

The primary data for the analysis were generated from interviews with six physicians and eight physiotherapists who work with high performance athletes, supplemented by data from interviews with two administrators who are each responsible for the coordination of sport medicine services at a Canadian Sport Centre (CSC). The CSCs are a network of eight training facilities across Canada that provide support for high performance athletes and coaches in a variety of areas, including sport science and sport medicine. The CSCs are one pillar of the Canadian high performance sport system that also includes the Canadian Olympic Committee (COC), the Coaching Association of Canada and Sport Canada. In addition to coordinating the provision of sport medicine and sport science services, the CSCs assist in funding some health care services, for care not covered by public health insurance programmes. As the administrators responsible for overseeing these activities, these respondents serve an important mediating role in the delivery system of sport medicine to elite athletes.

The practitioners who were interviewed were identified in several ways. The first was through referrals from administrators at Canadian Sport Centres, who were asked to suggest names of practitioners who work with national team athletes. Additional respondents were identified from lists of practitioners at recent Olympic Games posted on the website of the Canadian Olympic Committee. A third means was a snowball technique whereby participants were asked to suggest the names of other practitioners who work with high performance athletes, who might be interviewed. In all cases, the manner of recruitment was to send an information letter about the research to potential respondents, requesting their participation. The interviews covered a wide range of topics concerning the practice of sport medicine, working relationships between practitioners in different disciplines, and the experiences of working in different settings, which are explained below. The interviews were tape recorded and later transcribed.

Health care practitioners work with athletes in a variety of settings, including private clinics and through formal affiliations with national team programmes, either in a home training base or during travel to training camps and competitions, and appointments to the medical missions at Major Games, such as the Olympics and Pan American Games. Among the practitioners interviewed for this research, all of the physicians have experience working at Olympic Games as well as World Championships in a variety of sports, and all have worked with national team programmes. Among the physiotherapists, all have worked with national team programmes and at Major Games; the majority have worked at Olympic Games. The sports in which the respondents have worked are varied, and include both contact and non-contact, team and individual, and men's and women's sports. (In the interests of preserving participants' anonymity, the sports they worked with are not identified.)

Before proceeding to the exploration of the clinical practice of sport medicine, some background information is provided in the observations of administrators on the place of sport medicine in the high performance sport system.

The purpose of sport medicine: administrators' accounts

Both of the administrators provided extended accounts of the mandate of their position as coordinators of sport science and sport medicine for high performance athletes. Their observations illuminate the context in which clinicians work, and within this context, both the emphasis on performance and the costs exacted on athletes' health in the pursuit of performance. In discussing his/her position, one respondent said:

> The default position or my default position is always the same, and that's high performance. That's the goal here. Now obviously not at the expense of someone's life or health but the idea is that our default position is always high performance. So what is in the interests of this athlete's or this team's performance . . . That's the culture I want to develop across the board. This is really about performance.

At a later point in the interview, the respondent returned to the theme of health and performance:

> I was being interviewed before one of the Olympics, I think it was Barcelona, and the interviewer asked me what it was like to be part of this movement, this sort of tremendous health movement where you're hanging around the healthiest people on the planet and I said 'Well, I want to make a distinction here. This is all about performance. This is not about health.' These are not healthy people that we are sending to Barcelona or wherever it was. These are incredibly high performers and there's a major distinction. If you looked at the medical file of each and every one of these people you would be horrified at the kinds of things they get exposed to. They get sick more often, they get injured more often, they get depressed more often. There's this total scope of the sort of medical concerns or paramedical concerns of these individuals [and it] is very, very broad and very, very deep. So, it's not about health. It's about performance. Now, does that mean we sacrifice people to the point where they're destroyed? We kill them? Or that they are crippled for the rest of their life? In some cases yes but in most cases no. There is a balance that needs to play. How well the physician or physiotherapist or the nutritionist or sports psychologist understands that context is extremely valuable.

A similar account is provided by the second administrator:

Performance is at the centre of our model. So there's no doubt that performance drives everything, but health, health is not unimportant. We don't want someone to win a gold medal and injure themselves and adversely affect their health for the long term. But saying that, we talked [earlier in the interview] about the definitions of health for an elite athlete and the general public. I think they're quite different. And you start training four, five times a week, you're not training for health. You're training for something else. You're training for performance.

Health and performance: practitioners' accounts

The interviews with practitioners explored how they work in a context where performance is the 'default position'. One way this was pursued was by asking respondents to discuss the 'purpose' of sport medicine. In common with the administrators' accounts, the responses confirmed the focus on performance, and the specific understandings of health that operate in the world of high performance sport. One physician said, 'To me, sport medicine is getting that athlete on the podium.' The respondent then expanded:

And the athlete that gets on the podium is the one that hasn't been injured. Or has been injured and gone into an appropriate rehabilitation programme early. So, if you got an injury, getting rehabilitated early so you can get back into play safely. But the whole thing comes down ultimately to trying to prevent those injuries.

In addition to this pointed statement about the purpose of sport medicine, throughout the interview this respondent indicated how in his/her practice with athletes, there is attention to a broad range of health concerns. For example, the respondent said that when on tour with a team, 'we [the respondent and a physiotherapist] will see them from soup to nuts, whatever happens to be the problem. Whether it be diarrhoea or menstrual dysfunction or headaches or depression or an Achilles problem.' For this respondent, the goal of 'getting the athlete on the podium' was realized by attending to a broad range of concerns in order to keep athletes healthy and injury-free or to return athletes to health or activity as quickly as possible following an injury.

Another physician envisioned the purpose of sport medicine as a spectrum, ranging from illness and eventually death at one end, to absence of disease in the middle to 'the other end where people are now achieving personal bests and they're optimizing what their genetics has given them, so that they're performing at an optimal level for them'. The physician continued:

For the Olympic athlete, they measure health, quite honestly, by how well they do in performance . . . We're going to have 373 athletes out of

33 million in [the 2004 Olympics in] Athens. And it is a specialized section of the world but you know, those people think about health differently than you or I think about health . . . I just look at health as a bigger picture. And optimizing health to allow maximal performance is within the sphere of what I consider good health care.

One physician spoke at length about the relationship between health and performance in high performance sport, and how this conditioned professional practice. The physician began by commenting on the health status of elite athletes in detail:

We have this concept that somehow athletes are the healthiest of the bunch and in fact they're not. They're so on the edge that the small things destroy them. So, they're not – they may be at a peak of a certain type of performance but they're not healthy in the way you think of health as resilient or able to resist all other kinds of stresses. They can't . . . I'm pretty convinced there's some element of resilience that they lose when they peak for performance. So already we've compromised their health in order for performance. But the most striking example of that is psychological. Some of these athletes are really weird psychologically. And if you fix 'em, they're no longer competitive.

Question: How do you mean, 'weird'?

Well, oh, what can I say? Not normal. They're certainly not normal psychologically. Some of them are very high maintenance psychologically. Some of them are borderline personality – I can actually get into DSM designations if you want [i.e. the Diagnostic and Statistical Manual of Mental Disorders, the diagnostic reference of mental health].[1]

The respondent went on to comment on working in this context.

I'm certainly aware hugely my function as a physician is keeping this abnormal pile of explosive destructive elements wrapped together as well as possible to get them through competition, where if I was a family practitioner and they walked into my office I would be wanting to realign everything so that they could go home and veg out. And yet every time I've seen it, where people have undertaken, or their devils have got to the stage where they can't tolerate them anymore, that as soon as they get it sorted out to some kind of reasonable degree they're no longer competitive. I find that fascinating. But it's one that illustrates the conflict between performance and health to a tremendous extent.

I then asked the respondent 'What's that like for you as a physician to work through? Or, do you?'

Your sense is it's temporary. And there is a sense of collaboration and understanding which I must say is tacit most of the time between you and the athlete, that this is in fact the way to do it.

Question: Meaning engage in activities that are not optimal for health?

Yeah. And they're well aware of the fact that as they're peaking – before the taper, for example, they feel horrible . . . And they know that during that week they're more susceptible to infection and all the rest of it. So it's a – the only underlying contract that they have with you is that ultimately, like 20 years down the road, what you have or *should* have is that they'll be okay. Once they stop training and so on, they will go back to being normal and they'll be able to attain that.

One of the main risks of high performance sport is compromised health due to overtraining. Physicians attempt to enable athletes to negotiate the precarious balance between optimal training and overtraining, with not only an understanding but an acceptance that at times health will be compromised. At the same time, they attempt to safeguard health, although key here is the understanding that this refers to long-term health and specifically, the avoidance of debilitating conditions.

Another major health risk in sport is injury. While physicians often are involved in the diagnosis and treatment of injuries, and most particularly in surgical repair, injury management and rehabilitation is primarily the domain of therapists. The discussion now turns to the observations of physiotherapists on the purpose of sport medicine, and their place as health care practitioners in high performance sport.

Health and performance: physiotherapists' accounts

Performance also figures centrally in physiotherapists' understandings of sport medicine. One physiotherapist said the purpose of sport medicine is

to enable the athlete to achieve their genetic potential . . . Getting the most that's possible out of that person . . . I think ultimately it boils down to performance and results and I think sports medicine is the tool for that person, in their quest to achieve those results.

Another physiotherapist indicated there are several purposes of sport medicine: 'to help people heal faster from injury', 'prevention of injury', and 'lastly, is increased performance'. The physiotherapist then explained the connection between these concerns: 'I think by helping people recover, by preventing injuries, you're now getting into the next realm, which is bettering their performance.'

While physicians typically made recurring references to health as well as performance in discussions of the purpose of sport medicine, physiotherapists typically made no mention of health until asked specifically. One of the most striking illustrations of this occurred in the interview with the physiotherapist quoted above who cited three purposes of sport medicine. Following this observation, I asked 'Where does health fit into this?' As indicated in the following annotated transcription, the respondent struggled to make sense of my question:

> Is sports medicine about health? Well, yeah to me that is all health. But maybe I have a skewed view. I was going to say I may have a skewed view because of the realm I work in. Um, you're right. Average person down the street, health would be, um [pause]. I can see your question now [chuckles]. Sorry, that kind of caught me [laughs].

The respondent then provided an extended account of the range of health statuses, from life-threatening conditions, which was described as being 'below' health, to being healthy, to the condition of being a high performance athlete, which the respondent described in the following way:

> I think when you look at the realm of sport and sport medicine, it's *above* health because these people have now pushed themselves to train bigger, faster, stronger . . . So if you're up in this realm here, do you ever, are you ever not healthy? Well, yes, you can have traumatic injuries that put you [*sic*] not healthy. But a lot of the injuries you have, you're still above the average health level. That's kind of the way I see it. But no, I wouldn't have put health with sports medicine. That's funny.

While the majority of physiotherapists described the purpose of sport medicine as enabling athletes to return to activity after an injury, one physiotherapist took a quite different approach. When asked about the purpose of sport medicine, this respondent said

> To be there as a resource, addressing any injury or health-related issue. But I think it goes further than that in terms of providing the athlete the education to be both accountable and educated and active in their own rehab process. I really do not like the 'we will fix you' sort of attitude and I think we're at risk of that sometimes in all the disciplines.

The respondent went on to explain how s/he tries to educate athletes to understand 'the nature of their condition' and the 'process that will facilitate' healing, so they will then be able to take responsibility for their rehabilitation, and long-term injury prevention.

While this account of the purpose of sport medicine was striking for the emphasis on education and patient responsibility, many of the other physiotherapists indicated that there is a need for greater attention to injury prevention. The contrast in the accounts of most of the physiotherapists and the one who emphasized patient education and injury prevention may be due to the contexts in which they practise. The majority of respondents are affiliated with national team programmes and in this position face particular pressures around returning athletes to activity. The respondent whose depiction emphasized educating athletes to be accountable has worked with national team programmes but at the time of the interview operated an independent practice, in which s/he works with elite athletes outside a sport programme. Many of the athletes in his/her practice have chronic conditions and therefore the therapeutic task is not 'simply' return to play but to resolve an underlying problem. Many of the practitioners who worked with sport programmes indicated that while patient education and injury prevention were important, it was difficult to find the time and resources to invest in these concerns. It is likely that the broader conception of the purpose of sport medicine offered by one respondent is enabled both by his/her working in a context that provides some distance from the pressures to return athletes to activity that many of the other physiotherapists interviewed face, as well as the kinds of conditions s/he treats, in that by the time athletes make their way to this therapist, it often is clear that what is called for is not a 'quick fix' but resolution of an underlying problem.

Athletes as consumers of sport medicine

High performance sport is the context for a particular model of professional practice in sport medicine, which may be described as consumer focused. This was described by one of the administrators interviewed:

> What we're trying to do is [develop a system] where it's essentially an athlete-driven – if that's the right word – an athlete-driven approach to accessing sport medicine, sport science support. Maybe a bit of coach involvement there. Athlete–coach driven. I don't necessarily want to take that away. Or maybe I do in the sense that I think athletes and coaches need to have input but sometimes they don't have the perspective, I believe, to make all the right decisions in terms of accessing the expertise they need to make [these decisions] and so, we need some systems in place to help them make the right choices.

It is significant that in the above account, the description of an athlete-driven model of sport is based on the understanding of the purpose of sport medicine as the optimization of performance. Put simply, it is the athlete who performs and administrators seek to rationalize the system of heath care provision in order to optimize performance. One of the challenges in this effort arises from what several respondents discussed as the particular characteristics of athletes as consumers of sport medicine services, which derive from the intense focus on performance. The administrator quoted in the previous excerpt indicated that athletes are a 'special' kind of people, who 'tend to be obsessive' about their health and physical conditioning, and 'will try anything' when they have an injury.

The other administrator said 'athletes are very superstitious. They get sometimes very panicky about their performance.' The administrator continued by indicating that

> If they have a problem and it doesn't work they'll see a physiotherapist and if that doesn't work they'll see a chiropractor or an acupuncturist or you know, whatever, shiatsu massage. They'll go through the whole gamut to try to solve a problem that they perceive.

For both of the administrators, these characterizations were offered as indicators of their perceived need to rationalize the delivery of sport medicine services and care. In this light, the previous respondent continued by saying:

> I want to orchestrate that a little bit, because this isn't about panicking and it's also about giving a particular modality or a particular profession the opportunity, the time frame required in order to see the change that they're looking for.

This respondent's depiction of athletes as prone to seeking the service of multiple practitioners, and the problems associated with this, was echoed by a number of respondents. A physiotherapist who works extensively with a national team programme said:

> Athletes are always looking for the quick fix and if it's not going quick enough with what we're doing then sometimes they start taking matters into their own hands as well [sighs] and they can sometimes get so many people involved, including acupuncturists, naturopaths, the whole gamut. And if you start to have them seeing a massage therapist the same day they may be seeing a chiro and the next day they're seeing an acupuncturist then the problem is you're never sure exactly what is helping or hindering it. And you can actually end up sort of over-treating an area where nothing is going to help because you've got *too* much going on in the area.

Elsewhere in the discussion the respondent elaborated on the pressures that lead athletes to seek quick fixes. These include not only the highly visible and dramatic moments of Olympic competitions, but more routine challenges such as attaining and then maintaining a place on a national team. Making the national team is extremely important in Canadian sport because this brings a number of benefits, including stipends and funding for some health care services. Like the administrators who attempt to rationalize the provision of health care, practitioners also try to bring some order to situations where, facing performance pressures, athletes are seeking a 'quick fix'.

The previous account of athletes seeking treatment from multiple therapists refers to working with athletes in the course of an ongoing relationship. Another context where the issue of rationalizing treatment arises is during competitions. One of the defining features of the provision of medical support at Major Games is the presence of a multi-disciplinary team, including physicians, chiropractors, and therapists from several disciplines: physiotherapy, athletic therapy, and massage therapy. Yet another defining feature of these settings is the competitive pressures. Several respondents spoke of how these two features interact to produce the consumer-driven practice of sport medicine.

A succinct description of the athlete focus in the provision of sport medicine at Major Games was provided by a physician who has worked at Olympic Games. This respondent said that at these competitions 'there's a lot of just giving way with what the athlete wants, because ultimately that's what really matters'. This point was echoed by a physiotherapist who indicated that clinicians were explicitly directed by the administrative body responsible for medical missions at the Olympics, the Canadian Olympic Committee (COC), to adhere to a client-centred model.

> The COC says to us [the medical staff] 'Give the athletes what they want.' So if the athlete is used to having chiropractic care, the athlete is going to get chiropractic care. Now if we feel that there's another intervention that might be, that perhaps should be considered, we might come to the table and say, 'Listen, you know, is there not a more global approach that we could use here?' But it's not a situation where we're going to grandstand and say, 'Well listen, you know, we've got some very good manual therapists here that could probably do every bit as much for you than what a chiropractor does.'

A number of respondents indicated that chiropractors have assumed a place of prominence in sport medicine 'because the athletes want them'. As well, many respondents, including the physiotherapist quoted above, felt that athletes are drawn to chiropractic treatment because it produces quick and discernible results. For this respondent, these results were problematic:

> I think that chiropractic represents an intervention that is very, very quick, that provides an immediate and in my opinion perhaps not a lasting result, but certainly enhances the athlete's performance on the given point in time. So for instance if you get [an athlete] that is going to compete in a big race, they'll probably want to be adjusted prior to that particular race. I'm not too sure . . . That's fine. Okay. They're probably going to perform better because of that, okay. There's probably physical

benefits to it, psychologically they believe they've been done a good service. That's not the way that I think that their, you know, core dys-function should be managed, if that's sort of their underlying problem. So there I would say that there's another intervention that should be brought into place. Unfortunately probably the Games is not the place to do that. And that's another one of the issues, okay, where you give the athlete what they want.

A physician described how chiropractic treatment is incorporated into the menu of services available at Major Games, and how the athlete's (consumer's) experience conditions the provision of therapeutic treatment:

What we try to do for the chiropractors is try to fit them into the model somehow. What we've done at *some* games is say if the person's had chiropractic treatment for that problem before, they can go without being seen by a physician. But if they've not had chiropractic treatment before they need to be assessed by a physician and the decision is made as to who they [will see]. Using new techniques and things, especially at a Major Games it will cause a problem. So that's, in general, you wouldn't use a total untried medication. You would try and stick with things that are [familiar].

Another physician provided an extended account of athletes as patients and the workings of the consumer-focused model of care, with specific reference to chiropractic. S/he began with a description of high perfor-mance athletes that echoes the earlier comments of the sport medicine administrators:

They're not a typical patient. They are high-strung, judgmental, experi-mental. They're – if I was going to do [sic] one characteristic, they're self-validating in the sense that if they do something and they have a good performance then that something is obviously the key to doing a good performance.

The respondent connected self-validation to superstition, with the link being the process of visualization:

And they're all trained, they have all undertaken mental training. Okay? Mental training involves extensive rehearsal, which means you visualize your end visualization [sic]. So you visualize your entire – you don't just visualize your performance. You visualize your entire day from the moment of wakening through to the end of the performance. So what happens is that various aspects get incorporated into that. And unfortunately that includes a lot of stuff like having massage or having your back cracked or a whole series of physiological interventions. So that's one pressure once they're driven to this self-validation model. And it's, in other areas and other worlds it's called superstition. It becomes superstitious.

The respondent continued by explaining how this affects medical practice:

The physician is in a position where somebody's already incorporated a certain process or set of processes into their [routine], then a physician is no longer in a position to say 'Look, that doesn't work.' What's the point? Unless they're dealing with, you know, there are athletes that are skeptics. But most of the time you just accept and work with and manipulate as gently as possible this series of concepts. I'd say, 'Look, we are not bringing a massage therapist for this next competition. Therefore, you should get used to the idea of not having massage surrounding competitions so therefore what you have to do is wean yourself off massage now and when you start doing your competition visualizations, visualize it without massage because it's not going to be there.'

The respondent provided another example involving chiropractic:

And you would have situations – I can remember one clearly in which they were told, no they weren't going to have a chiropractor along with them, so pre-competition manipulation was not going to be part of the pre-competition routine but one or two of them getting absolutely desperate that they have to have their back cracked and they go off on their own and find practitioners. And the first one they meet to crack their back – they'll go through five or six practitioners in a flurry of pre-competition desperation to get their back cracked. Once they feel that pop then suddenly everything's all right again. Except the poor practitioners that couldn't pop their back and the physician who says it's not gonna make a difference are all *wrong*. And the one that did pop their back, because it relieved their anxiety, is the right one. You know what I mean? So that becomes, it's a diff – I'm not trying to be critical. I'm trying to give a context in terms of which a physician works.

At a later point, the respondent gave an assessment of the chiropractic 'crack'. The respondent began by saying 'The crack itself's no big deal . . . Our joints can withstand manipulation extensively without ill effect.' With the 'crack',

What happens is the athlete's sense of what their body is at rest gets readjusted to the idea that the popped body is the, you know, the normal resting body. Those who don't get popped on a regular basis, their regular body is just a regular body and they can make it feel better by doing a slight stretch. So what happens [with athletes who regularly receive chiropractic manipulation] is you become dependent on an altered state, which is not a negative state, it's just an altered state. But once you've established that, you're going to have to keep it going, do you know what I mean? Or, you're going to have to face a weaning process.

The incorporation of chiropractic into sport medicine illustrates the historical struggle around its place in the broader system of health professions. This struggle has been marked by efforts to exclude chiropractic from acceptance as a 'legitimate' health profession, based largely on the argument that it had no basis in research and theory. Despite this, chiropractic has survived because people used it (Coburn 1993). Similarly, in sport medicine, while there is some scepticism among practitioners in other disciplines, chiropractic has not only survived, but in some sports, thrived, because athletes 'want it'.[2] Moreover, even practitioners who are sceptical about the scientific basis of chiropractic endorse its utilization, if sometimes begrudgingly, especially when a 'quick fix' is called for. The main example of this is when athletes are facing the immediate pressures of competition. In the consumer-focused world of high performance sport, the wishes of athletes are a significant factor driving the provision of health care.

There are, to be sure, limits to 'giving the athletes what they want', where the culture of precaution overtakes the culture of risk. The physician quoted above on 'giving way with what athletes want' elaborated on the challenges of the consumer-driven model of care.

> It's just that you want to do it [accommodate athletes] in a way that doesn't put them at risk. You want to have some chance to try to convince them. I've also seen athletes have an injury and go completely alternative and not get their injury under control and I'm sitting there a bit frustrated because if they'd only, you know, allowed us to treat it traditionally we actually could've brought it under control. And it's not that I'm anti-alternative. We might've been able to do both. Athletes, I find, you know, aren't really very, like, evidenced-based medicine and the concept of science dictating what they do is not part of what athletes do . . . You know, they just figure out for themselves what works.

Sport medicine practitioners, the sportsnet, and the culture of risk

The preceding discussion of the medicalization of the athletic body has examined some of the main ways in which the focus on performance conditions the practice of sport medicine. Practitioners understand that health has a different meaning for high performance athletes than for the 'normal' population; within this understanding is an acceptance that being a high performance athlete inevitably means compromising health. Additionally, the demands of high performance sport yield a model of professional practice in which 'there's a lot of just giving way with what the athlete wants'. This giving way may involve treatment that, in other clinical contexts, would be seen as unnecessary, 'superstitious', and even ill advised, as in the case of a quick fix, rather than resolution of an underlying problem. But the 'special' nature of athletes, which arises from the demands made upon the body by intense training and competition, yields a particular model of professional practice.

Further insight into how the clinical practice of sport medicine is implicated in the culture of risk in sport was offered by one of the administrators, who had competed internationally as a coach and athlete. I asked the respondent to 'paint a picture for me about how the sport science/sport medicine professions may or may not be complicit in athletes putting their health at risk through such things as training practices, approving athletes going back into training [prematurely], freezing injuries, and so forth. Do they violate 'first do no harm'? The respondent began by saying 'I don't think people do it knowingly but I think in some cases they do it unwittingly.' The respondent then provided an example that involved pressure to return an injured athlete to activity prematurely. Following a lengthy and technical discussion of physiological, biomechanical, and neurological problems that arise when an injured body attempts to compensate for substandard function, the respondent summarized the outcome:

> So you get an athlete working harder and harder so they can cover the effects of a particular injury but they don't eliminate the injury. So now they've got an inflamed area, they've got calcium deposits, they've got scar tissue that's developed because their body hasn't been allowed to heal properly. And the end result is that you've got stuff now that instead of taking six weeks to recover from will take six years, ten years. Or maybe you'll never recover from it. So, your question was 'how complicit are our sport science personnel in this process. They're complicit without knowing, without understanding the sport.'

The respondent went on to explain the last point, by discussing the pressures to perform:

> It's easy for them to not understand because there's pressure on them. 'What can you do for me?' If I go in there, I'm a competitive athlete and I go in to you as my physician and ask you, I say 'I have a competition in two weeks, I need to be ready.' And you know, the person tells me I've got a stress fracture in my fibula. So normal healing time for that? Six months. 'I've got two weeks.'

The respondent then returned to how sport medicine practitioners figure in this process.

I want to make it very clear that I don't think there's one party that has the level of control that would be required consistently across the board, across all sports, to *be* the driving force behind this abuse. I think that there are individual athletes that push themselves *way* beyond what is considered acceptable. I think there are coaches that push their athletes way beyond what is appropriate. And I think there are sport science professionals who are not as actively interactive and allow situations to occur where they shouldn't. So I think it occurs across the board. I think that coaches primarily have more responsibility than they have been willing to accept for this. And I think they are in an ideal position to regulate the abuse. Meaning that there are parents that push their children too hard. So that coaches can regulate the input of sport science practitioners and they can regulate the input coming right from the athlete themselves.

Conclusion

The preceding quotation represents an account of how the 'sportsnet' proposed by Howard Nixon (1992) operates in the context of Canadian high performance sport. This net is comprised of several key players of whom the respondent suggests that coaches are particularly powerful. Sport medicine practitioners are also a part of this net, but they are not the driving force. One of the topics dealt with in the interviews, and only briefly touched upon here, is the need to improve the 'orchestration', or administration and provision of sport medicine. Many respondents, both administrators and practitioners, emphasized the need for greater professionalization of sport medicine; by this they meant moving from arrangements where practitioners are hired on a short-term basis, say to work at a training camp. One outcome of this type of arrangement is an absence of continuity in care, which limits the ability of individual practitioners to exercise extensive control. Both groups also spoke of the need to rationalize the provision of health care, so that athletes do not 'therapist hop', a practice which also limits practitioners' control. Another recurring theme was the need for increased funding of sport medicine and sport science to provide better access, as well as increased attention to injury and illness prevention. Canada's disappointing performance at the 2004 Olympics, as well as the awarding of the 2010 Olympics to Vancouver–Whistler, will yield considerable pressure to improve the funding of high performance sport, including increased support for the rationalization and professionalization of sport medicine. By enabling the deeper integration of sport medicine practitioners into the high performance sport system and thereby intensifying the medicalization of athletic bodies, these developments may heighten the challenge of managing the tensions between the cultures of risk and precaution in sport.

Acknowledgement

This research was funded by a grant from the Social Sciences and Humanities Research Council of Canada.

Notes

1   At a later point in the interview, this respondent returned to the point of athletes 'normality' and elaborated on the comments quoted in this chapter and indicated that it would be inaccurate to convey the view that athletes with personality disorders are the norm. Rather, the respondent said, 'weird' athletes are exceptional and 'the majority of athletes are normal'.

2   In this discussion of a consumer-focused model, the several references to chiropractic point to additional issues which are explored in the larger study on which this chapter draws, but for reasons of space cannot be examined here (see Theberge, forthcoming). Historical tensions around the place of chiropractic in the system of health professions are evident in sport medicine. In this discussion of chiropractic manipulations as an illustration of athletes' utilization of chiropractic, no discussion is provided of the broad scope of practice of sport chiropractic.

Bibliography

Burstyn, V. (1990) 'The sporting life', *Saturday Night*, March, 42–9.

Coakley, J. and Donnelly, P. (2004) *Sports in Society: Issues and Controversies*, First Canadian edition, Toronto: McGraw-Hill Ryerson.

Coburn, D. (1993) 'State authority, medical dominance, and trends in the regulation of the health professions: the Ontario case', *Social Science and Medicine*, 37: 841–50.

Green, M. (2004) 'Power, policy, and political priorities: elite sport development in Canada and the United Kingdom', *Sociology of Sport Journal*, 21: 376–96.

Hoberman, J. (1992) *Mortal Engines*, New York: Free Press.

Howe, P.D. (2004) *Sport, Professionalism and Pain*, London: Routledge.

Johnson, T. (1972) *Professions and Power*, London: Macmillan.

MacAloon, J. (1990) 'Steroids and the state: Dubin, melodrama and the accomplishment of innocence', *Public Culture*, 2(2): 41–64.

Malcolm, D. and Sheard, K. (2002) ' "Pain in the assets": the effects of commercialization and professionalization on the management of injury in English rugby union', *Sociology of Sport Journal*, 18: 149–69.

Nixon, H. (1992) 'A social network analysis of influences on athletes to play with pain and injuries', *Journal of Sport and Social Issues*, 16: 127–35.

Nixon, H. (1993) 'Accepting the risks of pain and injury in sport: mediated cultural influences on playing hurt', *Sociology of Sport Journal*, 10: 183–96.

Nixon, H. (1994) 'Social pressure, social support, and help seeking for pain and injuries in college sports networks', *Journal of Sport and Social Issues*, 18: 340–55.

Pike, E. and Maguire, J. (2003) 'Injury in women's sport: classifying key elements of "risk encounters" ', *Sociology of Sport Journal*, 20: 232–51.

Roderick, M. (1998) 'The sociology of risk, pain and injury: a comment on the work of Howard L. Nixon II', *Sociology of Sport Journal*, 15: 64–79.

Roderick, M. and Parker, G. (1999) 'Managing injuries in professional football: the roles of the club doctor and physiotherapist', report prepared for the Professional Footballers Association.

Roderick, M., Waddington, I. and Parker, G. (2000) 'Playing hurt: managing injuries in English professional football', *International Review for the Sociology of Sport*, 35: 165–80.

Safai, P. (2003) 'Healing the body in the "culture of risk": negotiation of treatment between sport medicine clinicians and injured athletes in Canadian intercollegiate sport', *Sociology of Sport Journal*, 20: 127–46.

Safai, P. (2005) 'A critical analysis of the origins, development, and institutionalization of sport medicine in Canada', unpublished doctoral dissertation, University of Toronto.

Shogan, D. (1999) *The Making of High Performance Athletes*, Toronto: University of Toronto Press.

Theberge, N. (forthcoming) 'The integration of chiropractors into the health care teams: a case study from Sport Medicine', *Sociology of Health and Illness*.

Waddington, I. (1996) The development of sports medicine', *Sociology of Sport Journal*, 13: 176–96.

Waddington, I., Roderick, M. and Parker, G. (1999) *Managing Injuries in Professional Football: The Roles of the Club Doctor and Physiotherapist*, Leicester: Centre for Research into Sport and Society, University of Leicester.

Waddington, I. (2000) *Sport, Health and Drugs*, London: E. & F.N. Spon.

Walk, S. (1997) 'Peers in pain: the experience of student athletic trainers', *Sociology of Sport Journal*, 14: 22–56.

Young, K. (ed.) (2005) *Sporting Bodies, Damaged Selves*, Oxford: Elsevier.

Zola, I. (1972) 'Medicalization as an instrument of social control', *Sociological Review*, 20: 487–504.

10 Welcome to the 'sportocracy'
'Race' and sport after innocence

Gamal Abdel-Shehid

The old American-centred specifications of black life as abjection, though tied to the immiseration of so many people, are incompatible with the new currency of black culture as commodity and cipher of vitality, fitness and health in a weightless global market that relies more than ever on blacks to supply some of its most alluring 'software'.[1]

Introduction: welcome to the 'sportocracy'

As recent events suggest, we are living today in what I call a 'sportocracy'. Our world is commonly narrated as being split into two, and all aspects of human interaction are seen as parts of a competition, where two sides are pitted against one another. The current social and political landscape bears this out. The following series of binary couplets may serve as an example: man versus nature, the battle of the sexes, Islam versus Christianity, rich versus poor, Hutu versus Tutsi, the kids versus the adults, Bush versus Kerry, Tamil versus Sinhalese, East versus West, gay versus straight.

In each of these cases, there is an operating presumption, known as Manichaeism. A Manichaean worldview thinks that the world is nicely split in two on a series of axes: be they age, religion, gender, sexual orientation and so on. In addition, this framework means that there is no room to conceive of reciprocity between these poles. Moreover, there is no room within this framework to conceive of intermingling across or between these axes. In all of these cases, the complexity of human life is reduced to a metaphoric zero-sum sporting competition, where something is winnable, and if one were to win, the other must positively lose. Moreover, each of us is interpellated, or hailed, by the sportocracy as fitting into certain categories, depending on our location in the social structure.

No doubt, in the capitalist and colonialist world we live in, this has been an organizing fiction for some time. Economic life is organized in this manner, whereby the accumulation of financial wealth is only achieved via the impoverishment of others. Karl Marx, in *Capital* (1977), referred to this process as 'surplus extraction'. Contemporary and longstanding colonial relations also take this form. In the colonial relation, wealth (often natural resources) is extracted from occupied lands in order to furnish and enrich life in the occupying countries. While the colonization of indigenous peoples of the Americas is evidence of this, think also of the Israeli occupation of Palestine and the recent United States-led occupation of Iraq and Afghanistan.

It is thus no accident that the re-emergence of United States' imperialism has taken a 'sportocratic' tone. This 'sportocratic' tone is perhaps best illustrated by what I call 'Bush-speak', where people across the globe are asked to choose sides as a way to ensure (or, as is clearly the case, not ensure) something called 'security' and 'democracy' for what is called 'the West'. In light of this, many of the policy announcements that the Pentagon makes involves narrating them in the same way as a sporting competition would be narrated. While there are many examples of this, consider George Bush's speech from a United States military ship in the Persian Gulf in the spring of 2003 announcing the cessation of official combat and a 'victory' in the invasion of Iraq. Bush's speech, it was presumed, signalled the end of the war and presupposed that the losers and winners would retire to their locker rooms.

In thinking through the 'sportocracy', and offering something with which to resist it, some Marxist critiques are very useful. These critiques deploy dialectics as their primary analytic. The dialectic, as we know, is a materialist method that is posited against phenomenological or ideological ways of seeing the world, which assume there is nothing behind the superficial level, and that social phenomena exist in the world as they appear to be. The use of the dialectic as an analytic is a useful critique against the 'sportocracy', which is a phenomenological and superficial structure *par excellence*.

Much of the work from Marxists in relation to sport, such as that of Jean-Marie Brohm (1989), considers the effect that sport has on the body. For Brohm, sport in capitalist society is, like all forms of labour, alienated. As such, sport in capitalism reproduces the world of work; and following on the work of Herbert Marcuse, Brohm suggests that sport in capitalism is possible only via the repression of libidinal or erotic energy. In addition, Brohm's use of the dialectic is to remind us that what we see in sport, i.e. camaraderie, national harmony, and the pursuit of excellence is quite the opposite of what actually occurs.

In addition to Brohm, another very poignant critique of the 'sportocracy' remains Roland Barthes' essay entitled 'The World of Wrestling' in *Mythologies* (1973). Barthes' essay is important for its suggestion that sport, or in this case wrestling, is riddled with demands for purity. Specifically, the essay suggests that wrestling offers up 'pure' signs for its spectators. He writes, 'The physique of the wrestler therefore constitutes a basic sign, which like a seed contains the whole fight' (p. 18). Barthes goes on to note that wrestling's attraction exists by virtue of its seemingly unambiguous nature. Barthes refers to this unambiguous way of seeing as *myth*. He notes that

'When (myth) becomes form the meaning leaves its contingency behind, it empties itself, history evaporates' (p. 127). In other words, history, which always has the potential to disrupt neat and tidy mythological statements, is evacuated in the 'sportocracy'.

Barthes' poetic explanation of the allure of wrestling is useful for its linking of contemporary myths with notions of truth. As Barthes suggests, much of what is truthful in bourgeois society is in fact mythical. In relation to sport, Barthes reminds us once again that the dominant representations of sport, and by extension the 'sportocracy', operate to offer truth-claims about the worlds we live in far beyond the world of sport. Speaking more specifically about sport, Toby Miller (1999) suggests that sports are often allegorized by the right wing in order to pursue their own ends. As an allegory, it stands in for several ruling narratives, such as free market capitalism, patriarchy, imperialism, and racism. What is also clear, as Miller's essay suggests, is that sport is allegorized to stand in for the truth of identity.

In addition, Miller suggests that sport is a crucial site with which to accomplish the myth of biology and natural bodies. The dominant narratives of sporting culture, as well as the emerging 'scientification' of the body, shape common-sense notions about the body, which are that it can be mastered and controlled, but moreover, that it is singular and sovereign. This is true for all of the contemporary categories of identity – such as gender and 'race'.[2] Regarding gender, Miller (1999) notes that contemporary scientific discourses of the body 'articulate gender through sport. Categorization labels certain physical and behavioural norms as male or female that are substantiated in terms of nature or society' (p. 19).

In other words, sport, according to Barthes and Miller, naturalizes all of the bodies in its purview, endowing them with particular truths. Usually these truths are seen in binary ways – male–female, good–evil, capitalist–communist. This process establishes the 'sportocratic' terrain. The 'sportocracy' accomplishes two things. First, it naturalizes the social body, or the body politic. Second, it has the power to naturalize individual bodies as representatives of a fixed and singular identity category such as male, female, black, and white.

Yet this tendency does not only exist within sporting cultures. It is also crucial to note that much contemporary discussion of identity (both from radical and conservative positions) follows this pattern of naming bodies in a singular fashion and assuming them to be in opposition to each other. For example, bodies are assumed to be black, female, gay, and so on. They are often not seen as inhabiting more than one identity category. As such, many who would see themselves as inhabiting two or more identity categories are often left off the identity map as it were. These bodies (which include most of us) trouble the existing parameters of how identity is conceived in bourgeois thought. Many have worked against this framework that posits identity in binary and antagonistic ways, which (in addition to being bourgeois) is Enlightenment and colonialist.[3]

Moreover, it is clear that notions of the sovereign self, the subject of bourgeois individualism, emerges as a result of this and has repercussions to this day in terms of how we conceive of identity. In addition, and perhaps most significantly, this naturalization has consequences for how bodies speak, or are represented, in culture. By this I mean that the 'sportocracy', and the dominant system within which it works, only reserves certain utterances for certain bodies. For example, male bodies by and large, are called on to speak the truth of masculinity, and black bodies are called on to speak the truth of 'race'. In other words, this process of naturalization has major implications for voice, or which bodies are allowed to speak and what they are allowed to say.

The tendency to naturalize and singularize the physical body into discrete categories of identity continues to dominate the intellectual and political landscape. Politically, what have been called 'the new social movements' have left us with the legacy of the singular identity category, be it gay/lesbian, black. Recent and longstanding nationalist movements have also left us with essential categories of identity – such as Québécois, Canadian, Palestinian, and so on. Intellectually, many remain invested in singular notions of identity. The unease with which many in the social sciences confront post-modernism and its injunction to trouble essentialism and meta-narratives is an example of this. Moreover, it suggests a certain naïveté around the way identity categories and human society are culturally constructed, shift over time, and the power of representation in the current context of capitalist colonialism that we find ourselves in. Moreover, I think it betrays the effects of a 'sportocratic' mindset both in our discipline – socio-cultural studies of sport – and beyond.

'Scene . . . not heard': 'race' and the 'sportocracy'

This brings me to the main point I would like to discuss in this chapter, which concerns thinking through the concept 'race', specifically blackness, outside of the confines of the 'sportocracy'.[4] Needless to say, the 'sportocracy', by virtue of singularizing and naturalizing bodies, is what Paul Gilroy calls a 'raciological' structure. By constantly representing 'race' as natural, fixed, and unmediated, the 'sportocracy' helps to shore up ideas of 'race'.[5] As a result of seeing 'race' as real, the 'sportocratic' mode fails to understand multiplicity within identity categories, or the instability or the irrationality of the concept. Within this frame, bodies are 'race'-ed and singularized. Thus the singular nature of 'sportocratic' thinking cannot consider the ways that identity cuts across all of the presumably discrete fields of identity – such as religion, history, class, 'race', and sexuality.

It is in this regard that much of the literature in the field known as 'race' and sport falls under. Despite sustained anti-essentialist positions in much of the literature on contemporary politics of 'race', including the work of Black Brits such as Stuart Hall and Isaac Julien, some in socio-cultural studies of sport continue to read 'race' as natural and fixed and more often than not, as only referring to black subjects.[6] In other words, many continue to be trapped by the category of 'race'. For example, consider the recent essay by Ben Carrington.[7] By deploying people such as Franz Fanon and Paul Gilroy to help illustrate his case, Carrington charts an interesting trajectory of both the modernist and post-modernist fascination with black male bodies in sport to argue that the black male body in sport remains over-determined, as Fanon (1967) would say, as hyper-masculine, overly sexualized, and so on.

No doubt Carrington is correct about over-determination. The black male body in sport is, by and large, in the words of Houston Baker, 'scene . . . not heard'. More to the point, the 'sportocracy', by virtue of its process of singularizing identity, is very much invested in this. Yet what strikes me in the essay is the fact it offers few ways for us to resist the 'sportocracy' and allow the black body to speak in another voice. As such, Carrington's essay stops short of its task, which is to conclude by seemingly if implicitly calling for more positive images in the representation of black male athletes. Yet the question of what is a positive image remains undefined. As many have shown, the production of positive images is indeed fraught, and within black cultural politics, positive images often mean bourgeois ones and, as such, they have often been propped up in order to silence dissident black voices – be they communist, queer, or feminist.[8] In other words, Carrington's essay leaves one asking the following question: if more positive images of black male athletes were on offer, what would there be left to critique?

The conundrum posed by Carrington's conclusion is a familiar one within the context of anti-racism. It suggests that there remains a difficulty with allowing the black body to speak as something other than the victim of racism. This is clearly the thrust of Paul Gilroy's first book, *There Ain't no Black in the Union Jack*. In that book, Gilroy was critical of the tendency of both anti-racist sociology and Afrocentrism to reproduce the 'problem/victim' dichotomy for black Britain. He suggested that both of these positions rendered the black body silent, and reduced the texture and complexity of black life to a caricature, as something that only exists in relation to racism. More to the point, he suggested that both the left and right, by virtue of this way of understanding blackness, were unable to discuss both the constant naturalization and silencing of the black body.

Gilroy's recent work has continued in this vein. And he has been a major proponent for black cultural studies as opposed to anti-racist sociology that, by virtue of its dull and unreflexive way of seeing blackness, contributes to the 'sportocratic' mode.[9] While Carrington rightly cites Gilroy's work, he seems to stop short of the more radical solutions that Gilroy offers. Both in *Against Race* (2000a) and in an essay entitled 'The sugar you stir' (2000b) Gilroy suggests that the energy we put into anti-racism might be better spent trying to imagine a political and cultural future without the category of 'race'. He writes:

[My argument] proceeds from the utopian prospect that the current crisis of 'race' and representation, of politics and ethics, offers a welcome cue to free ourselves from the bonds of all raciology in what might be a new 'abolitionist' project.

(p. 126)

The crisis of 'race' and representation that Gilroy is referring to is in effect a result of two significant and concurrent developments. The first refers to the emergence of various multiculturalisms in the West, a result of both economic and cultural globalizations, and the second is the disturbing way that black bodies are represented as 'commodity and cipher of vitality' in this new globalized imperialism. As a result, Gilroy calls upon our humanist consciousness in order to work against the 'sportocratic' idea of singularity altogether, and to focus more on the multiple and polyvalent nature of 'race' in our contemporary world. According to Gilroy (2000b: 127):

[I]f we become committed to working against the reification of identity and the trivialization of its complex mechanisms . . . we will be able to build upon the precedents of double consciousness without fear and create something far more fluid: a future oriented political mentality that is more comfortable with the idea of multiplicity.

In other words, the challenge is not simply to detail racism's horrors towards black peoples, of which there are many. Rather, the challenge is also to see how blackness has been deployed in the aid of global capitalism, and to what extent we are guilty of consuming and reproducing these images unproblematically. Moreover, the challenge is not to sanction these representations of blackness, but to find ways that we can authorize more complex and more complete representations. Gilroy's critique of 'raciology' is thus also a critique of capitalism, in the sense that capitalism deploys various representations of 'race' to pursue its ends. It is for this reason that Gilroy asks us to elaborate on DuBois' notion of 'double consciousness' in order to re-imagine the story of black bodies (in sport and elsewhere) in an increasingly multicultural age.[10]

'Race' and the end of innocence

In this section, I will argue for the introduction of another crucial concept from black British cultural studies, which is the notion of the 'end of innocence'. While many in our field have taken up Stuart Hall's work specifically with relation to representation, his work on black cultural politics has not been cited to date, such as his seminal essays 'New ethnicities' and 'What is this "black" in black popular culture?' This concept is crucial to moving away from the 'sportocratic' singularization of black male bodies in sport. Such a move would open up the discussion about sport and the making of 'race' from its currently Manichaean and 'sportocratic' mode, in order to make room for a discussion of hybridity.[11]

Moreover, I hope to use Hall's concept to offer a framework so that the black male body could speak from another place than that of the victim of racism. In addition, my aim is to open up space within the category of 'black' to make room for its multiplicities, which of course include but are not limited to, alternate forms of understanding gender, sexuality, class, and nation. Hall's concept of the end of innocence is a radical insight that threatens to undo the very foundations of the field. It also threatens to undo the very enterprise of sport in the contemporary global context, because what, if anything, is contemporary sport without black masculinity? More specifically, fantasies of black masculinity, and its physical and sexual prowess, enable the psycho-sexual world of contemporary, male, high-performance sport to sustain itself.

Stuart Hall's 1996 work entitled 'New ethnicities' is a short essay dealing with the emergence of new black British cinema of the late 1980s. Hall's main claim in the essay, a now famous one, is that these films helped to usher in the 'end of the innocent notion of the essential black subject'. The end of the essential notion of the innocent black subject, as Hall put it, refers to a series of political and economic shifts that significantly impacted the representation of black 'Britishness'. As such, we can no longer solely understand 'race' (in the essay he discusses blackness) as singular, stable, and fixed. As Hall (1996: 168) writes:

> If the black subject and black experience are not stabilized by Nature or by some other essential guarantee, then it must be the case that they are constructed historically, politically, culturally.

Hall makes the additional point, using the full weight of anti-essentialist insights behind him, that 'race' is not real (if it ever was). Rather, he sees 'race' as a highly mediated historical and political concept that only becomes intelligible via representation. Thus, troubling as it may be for some, Hall demands that we read 'race' as much for its certainties as for its uncertainties. These insights place us on a new and much more difficult terrain. First, we arrive at a terrain that demands much more from us in terms of our conceptualization of black cultural politics within the world of sport. If we accept, as Hall has, that 'the end of the essential notion of the black subject' has been upon us for some time, we have to accept that there are other means of representing blackness, both past and present. With respect to sport, we need, for example, to consider the role of 'blackness' in making identities that are inside and outside blackness as it were, i.e. across gender, class, and history, not to mention sexuality.

The other crucial concept for Hall is desire. Hall's work opens us up to questions of desire and 'race' in interesting and complex ways. His argument suggests that desire is always that which disrupts the neat and tidy categories that bourgeois culture demands of us. With regard to 'race', Hall (1996) suggests that desire, and its corollary, identification, is what threatens to undo its fixity. He writes:

> Desire [is] that deep ambivalence of identification which makes the categories in which we have previously thought and argued about black cultural politics and the black cultural text extremely problematic.
>
> (p. 168)

Hall was undoubtedly influenced here by the early work of Frantz Fanon, who, in *Black Skin, White Masks* (1986), attempted to incorporate a number of Eurocentric traditions of thought – predominantly existentialism, phenomenology, and psychoanalysis – in order to find ways to contribute to the 'disalienation of the Negro' in racist society. 'The end of the innocent notion of the essential black subject' thus necessarily involves recognition of the unstable make-up of desire and the psyche inside and outside representation.

Some will undoubtedly see the introduction of these two concepts, both of desire/identification and the end of innocence, with respect to black masculinity, as hostile. This is so, in part, because psychoanalytic concepts and the insights of anti-essentialism threaten notions of coherence and stability that informs almost all of the 'sportocratic' and foundational representation of black masculinity in sport. In other words, the split or unstable racialized subject that psychoanalysis via Fanon (and subsequently Hall) refers us to is a departure from the 'sportocratic' mode of thinking which reads black bodies as stable, singular, and as Carrington rightly points out, from the exterior gaze of anthropology.

But I suggest that the hostility should not be enough to prevent us from utilizing these insights. To continue to read black bodies from the point of view of exteriority is to once again render black bodies as silent. Once again, the matter of voice is crucial, and worth paying serious attention to. As I mentioned earlier, black bodies do not speak within the 'sportocracy' except to confirm the myths of blackness. Putting these more messy insights to work means that we can move away from the melancholy tone that too often typifies the work on 'race' and sport, which is often stuck at detailing the effects of racism on black or other racialized bodies. An anti-essentialist reading of Fanon is thus central to moving us past what I see as an impasse in contemporary theorizing of sport and 'race'. Moreover, it will enable a space for us to listen to black male athletic bodies in ways that we have not yet been open to hearing.

Close readers of Fanon's work will note that the anti-essentialist Fanon exists in tandem with the one who painstakingly details the way that black bodies are perceived and violated in racism. But in socio-cultural studies of sport, it is my claim that Fanon has not been read closely enough. We seem, strangely, more capable of citing some parts of Fanon while at the same time ignoring others, specifically those that focus on the instability of 'race'. In

'New ethnicities' Hall rightly notes that while Fanon spent a great deal of energy in his first book discussing the ways that racism constructs the black subject negatively, as either absence, ugly, evil, and criminal, he also suggests that what is crucial about Fanon's work is its demonstration of the splitting of the black subject in the context of racism. This duality, or split subjectivity, produces a psychic ambivalence in the black subject. As Hall (1996: 167) notes:

> [Racism's] epistemic violence is both outside and inside, and operates by a process of splitting on both sides of the division – in here as well as out there. That's why it is a question, not only of 'black skin, white skin' but of *Black Skin, White Masks* – the internalization of the self as other.

This repositioning enables us to understand 'race' and racism in a substantially different way. In other words, the story of 'race' and racism ceases to be limited to the familiar and melancholic one that details how black bodies are constructed negatively from the outside. The recognition that blackness is a two-sided concept (at minimum) allows us to recognize the profound complexity of racism and racialized identification. This recognition creates space for a number of voices to speak about the ways in which racism operates and how it is resisted.

Thinking about the unstable nature of identity, in this case as it pertains to racialized bodies, is a significant weapon in moving us out of the 'sporto-cratic' mode. Quite simply, it disrupts the bourgeois fantasy of singularity. If we were to create a space that could speak differently about racialized identity in sporting cultures, there are a host of urgent and pressing topics that we would need to address. For example, we would need to address the very serious questions of internalized racism among black athletes, fans, and coaches (or, for that matter, among any racialized group, including indigenous peoples, or South Asians). Moreover, we would have recourse to very rich and crucial contemporary concepts such as trauma, the unconscious, the Oedipus complex, incorporation, and the *imago*. These terms appear in Fanon's *Black Skin, White Masks* and are crucial to his conceptual framework, yet to date they have been ignored completely in socio-cultural studies of sport. They tell us much about who we are, and why we may be motivated to play or watch certain sports and not others. Moreover, they allow for a more activist entry point in our scholarship in that they may help to allow us to not solely focus on racism, but rather to focus on resistance.

As a casual perusal of black popular culture in sport will show us, beginning from the recent sexual assault trial against Kobe Bryant all the way to the outrageous outfits of Serena Williams, there is much more going on in the field of 'race and sport' than the familiar story of absence and negativity.[12] Moreover, the ways in which these athletes are being deployed semiotically in a globalized environment is also important to theorize. These new realities demand new approaches. But, as I have argued here, these approaches already exist in the longstanding and rich field of black cultural studies. These insights have forced us to pay attention to 'race' and representation, global-ization, the persistence of raciology, 'the end of innocence', and the psychic life of racism.

Feminism and queer liberation after innocence

There is another reason that is related to the repressive nature of sporting cultures that has prevented the concepts discussed above from taking hold in socio-cultural studies of sport. Specifically, this other reason concerns the all-pervasive and patriarchal myths about black masculinity that many of us, wittingly or not, hold on to. For some time now, black feminists and 'lgbt' (lesbian/bisexual/gay/trans) activists have criticized the fact that often the only response to racism is recourse to masculinist ideals, in other words, to shore up a faltering black masculinity. The criticism, which has been voiced by several, suggests that anti-racist politics privileges a hetero-normative male voice, which in the process silences those of others.

In other words, the repeated refusal to deal with questions of gender and sexuality in discussing black bodies in sport is not an innocent one. Hall (1996), in his essay, rightly suggests that feminism and queer liberation have motivated his ideas of the end of innocence quite profoundly. He writes:

> Black radical politics has been frequently stabilized around particular conceptions of black masculinity, which are only now being put into question by black women and black gay men.
>
> (p. 168)

As I mentioned before, questioning the foundations of black masculinity, and its ability to speak as the voice of blackness, disturbs the singularity that the 'sportocracy' depends on. As long as this is the case, and as long as there is a silence around questions of gender and sexuality and how they intersect with black masculinity, the 'sportocratic' fictions, including the myth of black masculinity, will prevail. The task of critics who wish to move beyond the 'sportocracy' is to engage with dissonance and read black masculinity from the inside as it were, rather than simply from the outside. Reading black masculinity from the inside requires an honest interrogation of the sexual politics of 'race'. This is occurring in other disciplines, and throughout black cultural studies, but has yet to occur within socio-cultural studies of sport.[13]

In discussing radical black politics around gender and sexuality, let me return to Fanon's work and depart somewhat from Hall's main argument. Specifically, I want to flag the recent feminist and queer critiques of Fanon in order to argue for a way in which black masculinity could be read differently within the context of sporting cultures, and the 'race' and sport literature more specifically. While there is much debate around Fanon's politics of gender and sexuality, the fact of his sexism and homophobia is well documented and, despite the efforts of some, indisputable. While this does not make him unreadable, it certainly means that unless he is read with the critiques in mind, his work is much less effective in dealing with the complexities of social difference and inequality.

While many have pointed out the ways Fanon constructs women and homosexuals in *Black Skin, White Masks*, they have not paid sufficient attention to Fanon's own conception of black masculinity. I think this is important because it works as a touchstone for some of the readings of his work that appear in socio-cultural studies of sport (and elsewhere for that matter). Quite simply, the early Fanon cannot see black masculinity as anything but a pathology. The black man's body is constantly described in the negative; it is seen as lacking or as negative in relation to the white gaze, both male and female. For example, when white women look upon black men in Fanon's text, all they see is horror and revulsion as a result of their racist fantasies. Moreover, when they look upon black men with sexual desire, Fanon constructs the women themselves as pathological or perverted.

Fanon's reading of the black male subject as pathology, and his pathologizing of black male sexuality as a result, fits into his larger framework, which is a not so subtle suggestion that black masculinity is a masculinity at war. Who the black male subject is at war with shifts – at times it is his own unconscious, at times it is with the colonizer, at times it is with the racist *imago* of black masculinity. According to David Marriott (2000), '*Black Skin, White Masks* has a particular way of imagining *la guerre noire*, that psychic, quasi-internal war of the black man battling with himself' (p. 86). This articulation of war, then, structured Fanon's theory quite fundamentally. It also prevented him from recognizing the beauty of black masculinity.

Paying attention to this element in Fanon's theory of masculinity has important implications for resisting the sportocracy, and the impact it has on physical culture. What many critics have not been able to do, including Carrington, is to recognize the beauty of black masculinity. Unless this is done, the black male body in sport and elsewhere will not be able to speak. It will remain an icon, something that is apart from us. It is no accident that some of the most important figures within the context of black cultural studies are gay men, such as Marlon Riggs and Isaac Julien.[14] These artists and others allow us a chance to gaze at black men differently, as objects of beauty. This is continually an almost invisible image in contemporary culture, yet it is there, and it requires a queer and feminist sensibility to glean it. If done, seeing the beauty of black masculinity clearly troubles the notion that Fanon and others had, that black masculinity is masculinity constantly at war. Moreover, it is a central plank with which to work against the 'sportocracy'.

Notes

1 Gilroy 2000b: 127.
2 In this regard, I am aware that there are many who would not see class as an identity category.
3 For example, consider the work of Lorde 1984.
4 As a student of black cultural studies working in Canada, I have always found the use of race without quotes to be somewhat strange, and politically very dangerous, since it threatens to box in those who are racialized and make the problem of racism permanent, with no way out.
5 Please see Gilroy 2000a: Ch. 1. According to Gilroy, these raciological ideas are increasingly in crisis, yet they continue to persist.
6 For more on Stuart Hall and Isaac Julien, see Dent 1992. In Dent's book, both of them write groundbreaking essays on anti-essentialism and black popular culture.
7 Carrington 2001: 45.
8 The critique of positive images in sport is outlined in Abdel-Shehid 2005: Ch. 5.
9 For an example of anti-racist sociology, see the work of George Dei.
10 This line of argument is continued in Gilroy's (2004) latest work, *Post Colonial Melancholia*, where the discussion is focused on rescuing multiculturalism from its post-9/11 critics, who would like to see us retreat into discrete cultures.
11 Hybridity is a concept that is still profoundly underdeveloped in our field, whereby the work of people such as Homi Bhabha has not been sufficiently interrogated. One exception is Shogan's work, *The Making of High Performance Athletes*.
12 Recall that in the 2004 US Open, Serena Williams received tremendous publicity for her outfits, which were so skin tight, that they looked, as a friend commented, 'as though they were painted on'.
13 Please see Abdel-Shehid 2005, for work in the field that takes up these questions.
14 For more, see Dent 1992.

Bibliography

Abdel-Shehid, G. (2005) *Who Da' Man? Black Masculinities and Sporting Cultures*, Toronto: Canadian Scholars' Press.
Barthes, R. (1973) 'The world of wrestling,' in *Mythologies*, London: Paladin.
Brohm, J.M. (1989) *Sport: A Prison of Measured Time*, London: Pluto Press.
Carrington, B. (2001) 'Fear of a black athlete: masculinity, politics and the body', *New Formations*, 45.
Dei, G. (1998) *Anti-Racism Education: Theory and Practice*, Halifax, NS: Fernwood.
Dent, G. (1992) *Black Popular Culture*, Seattle, OR: Bay Press.
Fanon, F. (1967) *Black Skin, White Masks*, translated by Charles Markmann, New York: Grove Press (reprinted 1986, London: Pluto Press).
Gilroy, P. (1991) *There Ain't no Black in the Union Jack: The Cultural Politics of Race and Nation*, Chicago, IL: University of Chicago Press.
Gilroy, P. (2000a) *Against Race*, Cambridge, MA: Harvard Belknap.
Gilroy, P. (2000b) 'The sugar you stir', in P. Gilroy, L. Grossberg, and A. McRobbie, (eds) *Without Guarantees: Essays in Honour of Stuart Hall*, London: Verso.
Gilroy, P. (2004). *Post Colonial Melancholia*, New York: Columbia University Press.
Hall, S. (1992) 'What is this "Black" in Black Popular Culture', in Gina Dent (ed.) *Black Popular Culture*, Seattle: Bay Press.
Hall, S. (1996) 'New ethnicities' in H.A. Baker Jr., M. Diawara and R. Lindbergh (eds) *Black British Cultural Studies*, London: University of Chicago Press.

Hall, S. (1997) 'The work of representation', in *Representation: Cultural Representations and Signifying Practices*, London: Sage.

Lorde, A. (1984) *Sister/Outsider*, Trumansburg, NY: Crossings Press.

Marriott, D. (2000) *On Black Men*, New York: Columbia University Press.

Marx, K. (1977) *Capital, vol. I: A Critique of Political Economy* (Chs 10–11), trans. by Ben Fowkes, New York: Vintage.

Miller, T. (1999) 'Competing allegories', in T. Miller and R. Martin (eds) *SportCult*, Minnesota, MN: University of Minnesota Press.

Shogan, D. (1999) *The Making of High Performance Athletes: Discipline, Diversity and Ethics*, Toronto: University of Toronto Press.

11 Race and athletics in the twenty-first century

John Hoberman

Blackness and physicality

The haunting of our integrated sports world by deeply rooted racial pre-occupations was brought home to me once again several years ago by a young black woman enrolled in my course on 'Race and Medicine in African-American Life' at the University of Texas. As we discussed stereotypes of black athletic aptitude, she described the indignation she had felt when her boyfriend, a massive lineman on the university's football team, had returned from the physical tests and interviews that are administered each year to the most promising college players by the National Football League (NFL) at its scouting combine event. This procedure had reminded both her and the athlete of the slave markets of the antebellum South, and her anger was still evident as she recounted her friend's ordeal to her classmates. Years later, in another classroom, I was present when a black former University of Texas football player described college football as a form of slavery.

The resemblance between the NFL's assessment of athletes and the assessments of slaves in the antebellum South is quite real. As Walter Johnson notes:

> Throughout the day, the traders goaded the slaves into motion so that the buyers could better evaluate the way they moved ... Around the walls of the pens, slaves were set into motion to prove their stamina and agility ... Robert Chambers remembered seeing slaves being asked to run across the sale room in Virginia. [The slave] John Brown remembered slaves dancing, jumping, walking, leaping, tumbling and twisting before the buyers' eyes, showing off that they had 'no stiff joints or other physical defects' ... Following the conventions of antebellum racism, slaves were made to demonstrate their saleability by outwardly performing their supposed emotional insensibility and physical vitality.[1]

A century and a half after the slave auctions, those hoping to join the highly paid (and primarily African-American) labour market of the NFL were required to undergo a ritual that bears comparison with the exhibitions of slave bodies in a meaningful way.

Both scenarios present evaluations of black human beings for the purpose of measuring the labour power that is latent in their bodies. While both procedures include an assessment of the temperament of the person being examined, the potential value of personality traits lies in whether they will promote the efficient functioning of the physical apparatus, whether this means picking cotton or carrying a football. In both cases, the value and identity of the person being assessed is confined to his or her body. His (or, in the context of slavery, her) identity excludes the development of the mind. This identity also excludes the full range of human emotions, as evidenced by the slave traders' interest in finding slaves endowed with an 'emotional insensibility' that would promote their productivity as labourers. A similar conception of black hardiness was evident during the 1960s as black athletes integrated college sports: 'The double standard applies to injuries', Jack Olsen pointed out in 1968. 'They figure that the Negro is Superman', says a Negro back. 'We can't get hurt', says an esteemed basketball player. 'We're supposed to be made of stone.' This is a view aired by every dissident group of black athletes that has publicly made an issue of its grievances in recent months.[2] I heard similar accounts from black college athletes during the 1990s. It should be noted that the presumption of physical hardiness (see below) includes a presumption of psychological hardiness, as well, since coping with injuries (and white authority figures' reactions to injuries) draws on emotional and not simply physical resources.

The significance of the traditional Western habit of identifying black people with their bodies has been noted by black intellectuals such as Franz Fanon and Ralph Ellison. In *Black Skin, White Masks* (1952), Fanon identifies the white person's *sense* of the black person as a *fear* ('Negrophobia') that exists 'on an instinctual, biological level'. 'To suffer from a phobia of Negroes is to be afraid of the biological. For the Negro is only biological.' 'The Negro symbolizes the biological. First of all, he enters puberty at the age of nine and is a father at the age of ten; he is hot-blooded, and his blood is strong; he is tough. As a white man remarked to him not long ago, with a certain bitterness: "You all have strong constitutions".'[3] The presumption of black hardiness includes the sexual precocity, instinctive ('hot-blooded') passion, and 'tough' resilience that are universally regarded as 'biological' phenomena and that once again exclude the life and development of the mind.

In a similar vein, Ralph Ellison lamented the reductionism inherent in seeing black people as physical specimens. Ellison saw the ' "physical" character of their expression' as a consequence of racial trauma that concealed the human complexity of black people from white observers. This state of affairs 'makes the American Negro far different from the "simple" specimen for which he is taken. And the "physical" quality offered as evidence of his primitive simplicity is actually the form of his complexity'.[4] Ellison's comments in 1945 on this theme antedate the consequences of 'black dominance' in some high-profile sports, which has reinforced the identification of black people with their bodies, so he did not apply his critique of the simplistic treatment of black people to the hyper-physical and thus truncated identity of the black athlete.

The absence of the black athlete from Ellison's treatment of the black body does not mean, however, that black athleticism was not a potent racial marker at this time. Fanon reports having carried out an informal survey of white opinion on this theme. His method consisted in administering word association tests to some 500 people in which he 'inserted the word Negro among some twenty others'. As he describes it: 'I took advantage of a certain air of trust, of relaxation; in each instance I waited until my subject no longer hesitated to talk to me quite openly – that is, until he was sure that he would not offend me.' The result of this experiment was that almost 60 per cent of his respondents reported associations with *Negro* that clustered around the following related themes: '*Negro* brought forth biology, penis, strong, athletic, potent boxer, Joe Louis, Jesse Owens, Senegalese troops, savage, animal, devil, sin.'[5] Here athleticism serves as a locus that can absorb and reformulate a variety of racial fantasies focusing on sexual, military, and even animal prowess.

The significance of the black athlete as a paradigmatic representative of his 'race' has thus persisted and even intensified over the half-century that has elapsed since Fanon elicited white reactions to the word *Negro*. Ideas about racial athletic aptitude acquire meaning within evolutionary narratives about apparently racially differential traits that might account for the disproportionate achievements of athletes of East and West African origin, respectively. The dominant performances of East African distance runners, male and female, over the past generation has stimulated much scientific and pseudo-scientific thinking about the origins of these performances. Sprinters of West African origin, primarily African-Americans and Afro-Caribbeans, utterly dominate these events; for example, no sprinter the modern world would classify as 'white' has ever run a legal time of under 10 seconds for the 100-metre event, while dozens of 'black' athletes have done so.[6]

The evolutionary narrative

The evolutionary narrative about racial athletic aptitude belongs to a cultural construct of African biology the historian of science Nancy Stepan has called 'tropical nature'. This 'imaginative construct' posits an 'untamed nature' that is regarded as a crucible of biological energy and innovation that has no counterpart anywhere else on earth. For the European imagination, Stepan writes, 'tropical nature stood for many different values – for heat and warmth but also for a dangerous and diseased environment; for superabundant fertility but also for fatal excess; for species novelty but also for the bizarre and deadly; for lazy sensuality and sexuality but also for impermissible racial mixings and degeneration'. Almost two centuries ago Alexander von Humboldt put it as follows: 'Nature in these climates appears more active, more fruitful, we might say, more prodigal of life.'[7] Africa is a biological hot-house where anything can happen. The appearance of astonishing African distance runners during the 1960s eventually gave rise to an evolutionary narrative of athletic superiority that has drawn on the positive (super-energized) aspects of tropical nature and its potential for producing 'superabundant' forms of life.

The persistence of this fantasy of extreme African biology is confirmed in a travel essay that appeared in 2004 in a distinguished German newspaper: 'It is this overwhelming freedom of the senses, this indifferent arbitrariness of being, that seizes you deep inside. For the central European who is used to inhabiting a landscape which for centuries has been subdivided and domesticated, and who knows wild animals only as a road hazard, Botswana and Africa are not just another continent: this is another world for which we lack a mythological sense . . . [it is] a maelstrom of evolution.' In this evolutionary fantasy world of unlimited possibilities the tourist 'gazes at the presence of the relentless process of devouring and being devoured' and is forced to acknowledge his own unfitness to survive. 'Everything is so intense, so full of immediacy, that at times one wants to weep with gratitude for being allowed to be here at all. And then you breathe a quick sigh of relief, because you know that you will not have to remain here forever.'[8] Confronted with the fact of his own biological inadequacy, the humbled (but also grateful) European tourist recapitulates the experience of the European athlete who makes the pilgrimage to Africa to seek (and find) that performance limit beyond which only Africans can go.

An eloquent testimonial to the natural world of Africa as an arena of biological and athletic struggle appeared in *Sports Illustrated* in 1990. The scene is the Kenyan highlands:

> On Christmas morning you awaken to the cries of hawks and the songs of children, and lie there thinking about how Africa can seem a sieve of afflictions through which only the hardy may pass. The largest, fastest, wildest, strangest beasts are here. Every poisonous bug, screaming bird and thorned shrub has arrived at this moment through the most severe competition. They have a history of overpowering more gentle environments. You think of lungfish, of killer bees, of AIDS. Of men. Of the great Repo Men, the Nandi, turned from their raiding and become runners.

But this evolutionary drama also promises the end of multiracial sport: 'In the rest of the world, sport serves as an initiation, as a true test. In East Africa, initiation is the initiation. Sport is a pale shadow of the competitive life that has gone on forever across this high, fierce, first continent. Is it any wonder that frail European varieties feel threatened?'[9]

We shall see that the world's non-African distance runners have experienced their own version of this humbling, even humiliating, confrontation with the 'superabundance' of African life forms that now include the athletic prodigies who dominate the most prestigious distance running competitions around the world. First, however, let us examine the perception of an African super-vitality that contains the potential for a prodigal athleticism.

The idea of a superabundant African human biology appeared during the 1950s in the form of reports of developmental precocity among black children and, in particular, East African (Ugandan) infants. 'The most remarkable finding', according to a 1957 report, 'was the precocity of the younger infants. The motor development was greatly in advance of that of European infants of the same age, but was not an isolated phenomenon; it was paralleled by advanced adaptivity, language and personal-social behaviour'. While it was still too early for these authors to be thinking of their athletic potential, the Ugandan babies are described as being able to run by the age of one. What is more: 'From birth, the muscular tone of the African infant is different from that of the European, and the head is held better.'[10] In 1970 there are reports of Jamaican children who 'were precocious in age of creeping, standing, and walking when compared with New Haven White children'.[11] As early as 1958, however, other authors were expressing doubts about whether such findings were real.[12] It is possible that these perceptions of African infants, like other perceptions of African athletes, belong to a larger category consisting of 'images of the naturalized and idealized African – physically perfect, naturally gifted, graceful, and able to outperform the best the Occident could offer'.[13] We have already seen that white reactions to the natural phenomena of Africa and the idea of their sheer vitality can be submissive and even reverential, and scientists and physicians too can react in this manner.

The athletic version of this evolutionary narrative also includes the precocious child-athlete of African origin. While the best known prodigies of this kind are the golfer Tiger Woods and the soccer player Freddy Adu, there are others, such as the 14-year-old African-American basketball player Demetrius Walker, whose perceived athletic ability has stimulated commentaries that recall earlier accounts of precocious African infants. 'I've never seen a combination of speed, size and coordination like this kid has', one coach says. 'He's so athletic that he can dominate without developing the fundamentals.' 'He's so advanced physically, but he still doesn't have a man's body', says another. 'Imagine when that happens.'[14] The Haitian soccer star Fabrice Noel was a professional at fourteen. 'I've been around soccer for 30 years', says his high school coach. 'I've never seen a kid like this. He was as fast with the ball as he is without it. Faster than Freddy Adu. He has so many moves, I'm not sure he has a spine.'[15] When the Tanzania Stars soccer team, made up of handicapped boys, played a handicapped Norwegian boys team in 1991, the result was a rout. 'We have a lot to learn from these boys', said the Norwegian coach. 'They are considerably more handicapped than we are, but they play soccer as though they've never done anything else'.[16]

Only time will tell whether legendary children like Freddy Adu fulfill their early promise or eventually display the diminished capacities that the traditional (racist) doctrine of precocious development predicts. In the meantime, trafficking in African children who might become the prodigies of the future has been common in parts of Europe. One Italian youth soccer official has called this trade 'a new slave market. Anyone who isn't a second George Weah [the Liberian star of the 1990s] is discarded.' The odds of any boy's making it into the Series A league is about one in 50,000. 'The Italians import our children as if they were bananas', said the president of the African Soccer Association, Issa Hayatou. He was supported in this view by the former Brazilian star Pelé, who describes a modern slave trade to Europe. Soccer-playing children are also imported into to France, Holland, and Belgium.[17]

Black 'hardiness' and racial athletic aptitude

The evolutionary narrative of black athletic aptitude belongs to a folkloric doctrine of black 'hardiness' that posits a more primitive human type that is biologically distinct from and physiologically superior to that of civilized man. The alleged traits of this more robust human organism have traditionally included a nervous system that is resistant to pain, a supernormal capacity to recover from surgery and injuries, supernormal fertility, osseous hardiness (greater bone density), dental hardiness (decay-resistant teeth), obstetric hardiness (ease of birth), cardiovascular hardiness, haematological hardiness (normal functioning with fewer red blood cells), dermatological hardiness (thicker and tougher skin), thermal hardiness (heat resistance), and immunity to some disorders. The basic premise is that blacks are endowed with a biological toughness and resiliency that constitute an enduring racial trait.

The extension of the hardiness doctrine to include racial athletic aptitude proceeded throughout the twentieth century. Indeed, a team of scientific authors writing in 1940 infers the existence of racial biological differences from different levels of athletic performance:

> The existence of physiological differences between Negroes and Whites other than those dependent on pigmentation and external anatomical features is suggested by the superior records of Negroes in track and field athletics and by the commonly expressed opinion that they have greater resistance to high temperatures than have Whites. So far, however, no one has demonstrated unique physiological characteristics of the Negro that might be related to the capacity for energy transformation.[18]

Over the past decade scientific studies of anatomical and physiological factors related to elite athletic performance have begun to shed some light on the superiority of African distance runners.[19] These studies remain virtually unknown to ordinary citizens and even athletes. Their reactions to the consequences of black athletic superiority are examined in the later sections of this essay.

Racism in European sports venues

The 'black dominance' established by athletes of African origin in some high-profile sports has provoked various xenophobic reactions among those elements of the European population that engage with multiracial sport as a political and cultural issue that can be used for propagandistic purposes.

The neo-fascist French politician Jean-Marie Le Pen, for example, has made unusually candid remarks interpreting the social and biological signifi-cance of the racially integrated sports world. At a meeting of his Front National in 1996 he declared that 'the French national soccer team did not deserve the title of national champion because of the large number of "foreigners" on the team. In addition, most of the team did not sing the national anthem or do not even know it, while the "other teams boomed theirs out" with robust voices.'[20] When asked the same year whether he believed in superior and inferior races, Le Pen replied with considerable polemical guile:

> First you have to define what a race is and what you are comparing. It is obvious that an illiterate Eskimo is superior to a European Nobel Prize winner in literature if what counts is killing a polar bear on the pack ice. The best sprinters at the Olympic Games are black, the best swimmers are white. Is it forbidden, illegal or immoral to state that those differ-ences are real? As a humanist and as a Christian, I can assure you that I believe in the equal dignity of all people.[21]

The act of comparing the killing of polar bears to the production of Nobel Prize-winning literature conveys its own sarcastic message about the relative value of savage and civilized cultures. Pointing to racially segregated athletic events carries its own message about distinct racial biologies. Posing as 'a humanist and as a Christian', the anti-Semitic and anti-immigrant politician stakes his claim to a universal humanism worthy of the United Nations Charter. Like every accomplished racial demagogue, Le Pen had learned how to cross the threshold of civilized discourse without stranding himself past the point of no return.

Three years earlier the neo-fascist Parisian newspaper *Rivarol* had ridiculed the idea that soccer was serving as a 'fantastic laboratory for [racial] integra-tion' in Marseille.[22] Anti-racist social engineering of this kind has become standard practice in the European Union, with various anti-racist groups active in this campaign. In April 2005, FARE, the European Network

Against Racism in Soccer, protested against the massive verbal harassment directed against two black players on England's national team, Emile Heskey and Ashley Cole, in a stadium in Bratislava, Slovakia.[23] Two years earlier Cole and another black player, Marcel Desailly of the French national team, had described their experiences with racist crowds in Europe. 'The racist taunts and attacks are seen as a "test of character" and not as a cause for complaint – that, Desailly said, is how black professionals were once advised to handle such incidents. "The clubs said that racists are paying customers" said the captain of the French European champions, "and that they have a right to say what they want".'[24] Racist agitation in European soccer stadiums remains a widespread problem in the EU to this day, calling into question the effectiveness of anti-racist initiatives such as FARE. Even a small minority constituting a critical mass of xenophobic agitators can transform the mood inside a stadium with racist or anti-Semitic banners (as in Rome), racist chanting, or ape-like grunting noises and showers of bananas directed at black players on visiting teams.

As these episodes make clear, less sophisticated European racialists than Le Pen are inclined to express their resentments against racial aliens directly and dramatically. In Belgium the right-wing Vlaams demagogue Bruno Stevenheydens complains that: 'The Africans are taking our jobs [in professional soccer]. The invasion must stop.' The chairman of a German soccer fan club reveals an interesting ambivalence. 'What [the Africans] do with the ball is fantastic', he says. So why does he want to replace them with (inferior) white players? 'Because they're black.'[25] In Italy pressure from right-wing racist fans intimidated the Hellas Verona soccer club to the point where it gave up pursuing a black player from Holland whom fans had hung in effigy in the stadium.[26] In Israel, where many African-American basketball players have worked, the coach of the European-champion Maccabi Tel Aviv basketball team, Pini Gershon, was quoted as follows: 'There are two shades of blacks. There's the light-skin, who are a lot smarter than the dark blacks – those are really dummies.' And: 'The dark ones are like slaves; whatever you tell them to do, they'll do without thinking about it. They usually come from the streets.'[27] These are comments (made in 2001) that could have been made by a plantation physician in the American South a century and a half ago. Once again we are reminded that even the most primitive tenets of nineteenth-century racial anthropology can flourish in the sports culture of the early twenty-first century. It thus appears that in some societies racially integrated sport confers little or no immunity against archaic ideas about racial difference.

Racism in Romanian soccer stadiums is directed most often against the Roma minority. In April 2005 one stadium announcer derided the visiting coach of a Roma-associated team as a 'miserable gypsy'. During halftime the same announcer had played over the loudspeaker system one of Romania's best-known racist songs, 'Gypsies and Ufos'. Because in Romania Roma are denigrated as 'crows', the mayor of one city raged against 'all these crows and players from the Internet who I'd put in a zoo and tell the children they should look at the apes, because they wouldn't be able to tell them apart'.[28] Here, along with the grunts and the bananas, one hears a twenty-first-century version of the evolutionary narrative of nineteenth-century racial anthropology that distinguishes between the savage and the civilized. The persistence of aggressive racism in these public venues raises questions about how much multiracial sport can do as an integrationist social strategy in a Europe that is becoming racially integrated faster than it can deal with the social stress such integration creates. The widespread violence directed against French society by immigrant youths in late 2005 marked the failure of, among other institutions, a French sport club system that counts 14 million members as well as an elite soccer league that employs stars of immigrant origin who appear to lead charmed lives far removed from the immigrant suburbs from which they came.[29]

White coping strategies

The superiority demonstrated by athletes of African origin has provoked various reactions among European, American, and Asian athletes.[30] On at least a couple of occasions Europeans have attempted to find encouragement in the idea of an African mentality that impedes performance in distance running. Thus the German coach Dieter Hogen claimed that Kenya produces few world-class marathoners because: 'They would rather run fast for an hour than slow for two hours.' In a word, they must learn to be patient.[31] In a similar vein, the Spanish marathoner Martin Fiz said in 1999: 'You can run a Spanish record in the 5,000 or 10,000 meters and not even get close to the best times of the Africans.' But in the marathon it is different. 'They run too anarchistically', he said.[32]

In the chorus of white athletes' reactions to their apparent disadvantages this sort of bravado is exceptional. Another and more respectful approach to the African runners is what might be called the pilgrimage to Africa. Perhaps the best-known pilgrim of this kind was the German runner Dieter Baumann, the Olympic champion in the 5,000-metre run at the 1992 Barcelona Games. Baumann went to Kenya to train with the world's best, and according to one German reporter: 'The result was a miracle. The only white runner who could tolerate such body- and soul-lacerating workouts without skipping a single training session reached a new level of performance. The group dynamic carried him along.'[33] Another star of the 1990s, the American runner Bob Kennedy, did not travel to Kenya but did the next best thing by training with Kenyans outside their homeland. Admiring American sportswriters noted his acculturation to the Africans' training culture. Kennedy, said one, 'is the only American to have consistently competed with the Africans and the only one to have won their respect'.[34] 'In effect', another wrote, 'he became one of them. He has been much admired by his peers as an "honorary Kenyan".'[35] It should be noted that Baumann and the American runner Bob Kennedy are the only white runners ever to break the 13-minute barrier in the 5,000-metre event.

A closer look at their careers makes it clear, however, that both men eventually developed that sense of their own limitations that has enveloped so many white distance runners over the past two decades. Baumann's wife and trainer, Isabelle, spoke in 1996 about how they had responded to the African challenge: 'Generally speaking, athletes try to do more than they are physically capable of doing. That is why we have to be careful about reacting too emotionally. We have already tried to adapt to the current trend and to ratchet up the stress level in training even higher. But we had to admit that it wasn't working.'[36] The American steeplechaser Pascal Dobert said in 1998: 'I don't expect to set World Records or anything, but maybe to be the fastest non-African ever to run his event.'[37] The talented American marathoner Keith Brantly explained his predicament in the following way: 'People think I don't train as hard as the Kenyans. I've trained with them, because I wanted to know for myself. And I found out – I do train as hard. I'm simply not as talented. I'm driving as hard as they are, but I don't have as big an engine. They just have bigger engines. Big, big engines.'[38]

Bob Kennedy tried to adapt to the Africans' superiority by telling himself and others that they were not insuperable and that a solution to his problem was to be found somewhere. 'Their dominance is not the Kenyans' fault, it's our fault', he said in 1987. 'What are they supposed to do, go slower? What we have to do is learn how to go faster, how to keep up with them.'[39] Many years later Kennedy recalled a conversation he had once with the great Kenyan runner Kipchoge Keino:

> He said just remember that the Kenyan athletes, they're just men. [You're a] man, they're men. There's nothing different except they work really hard and they want to win really badly. And if you work really hard and want to win very bad, you can be just as good as they are. And it's true. They are just human beings and there is no mystique about them. And American athletes can be as good or better than Kenyan athletes, if we get the best talent we have and that talent is committed to the task that is at hand.[40]

'There's not much that separates us', Kennedy said in 1997. 'The Kenyans respect the way I run. I race hard. I train aggressive. When I train with these guys I am not merely hanging on. Just as often I am pushing the pace.'[41] Such training did not, however, enable him to run world-class times with the Africans in international competitions.

'I'm training to be the fastest, period', the white American sprinter Kevin Little said in 1997.[42] (He did not come close to succeeding.) The Norwegian sprinter Geir Moen, who never quite made it into the world elite during the 1990s, spoke in the same vein about his superior black rivals: 'The people of color have dominated the sprints for many years. It's time for the whites to do something. I think there's an advantage to being white, because there are a lot of people who want to see a white sprinter make his move. But there's no point in being the world's fastest white man. I want to beat everyone.' The (more realistic) alternative to being a world-beater was to become the champion of his own racial category: 'There's a way to go, but I see a chance to be one of a few white Europeans under 10 seconds in the 100 metres and under 20 seconds in the 200 meters.'[43] But no white sprinter has ever run under 10 seconds in the 100-meter event under legal conditions, and Moen would not even get close to that barrier over the remainder of his career. The German sprinter Tobias Unger announced in 2005 that he had decided to pursue 'realistic goals' such as breaking the German 200-metre record set by the East German Frank Emmelmann (20.23) during the (steroid-soaked) 1980s.[44] Bob Kennedy, too, was capable of taking comfort in being at the top of his racial cohort: 'It means something to be the first non-African because they've dominated so much.'[45] 'This was a liberating event for Europe', Dieter Baumann said after he ran a good race against Africans in 1997, as if his best performances represented a kind of racial redemption for the white population of the Old World.[46] In the end, however, none of these earnest resolutions enabled white athletes to meet black standards.

The auto-suggestive recitations of these and other athletes are attempts to enlist the power of positive thinking on behalf of preserving athletic self-respect in the face of constant demoralization.[47] Alternatives to this auto-therapeutic strategy have ranged from teaching (German) sprinters the 'natural feel of running'[48] – a symbolic pilgrimage to Africa – to 'scientific' techniques that include the untested and the implausible. In 2000, for example, the Fila athletic shoe company and *Runner's World* magazine announced an initiative called Discovery USA, a programme to identify and develop world-class distance runners in the United States. The director of this scheme was Dr Gabriele Rosa, an Italian physician and coach who had become prominent developing Kenyan marathoners.[49] 'What I'm trying to do is begin a new strategy in America', said Rosa:

> It's not easy for Americans. The athletes like to enjoy outside things and want to have girlfriends and stay out, too. So it's a difficult situation. . . . In Kenya, it's a different social and economic atmosphere. At first, I wasn't sure if this idea would work in America. But now, I think it can. There's only one way to reproduce the mentality and philosophy and mission of running. This program is the way. A distance runner who participated in this program, Jeff Cox, expressed confidence that it would transform American runners into world-class competitors: 'I would put Dr. Rosa's program up against what anyone else in the world is doing.[50]

Five years later there is no evidence it has produced any runners who can compete with the world's best. The American citizens who finished third and fifth in the 2005 New York Marathon, Meb Keflezighi and Abdihakim Abdirahman, are both African immigrants. The coach of the first-place finisher in the New York race, the Kenyan Paul Tergat, is Gabriele Rosa.[51]

The more 'scientific' scheme that has aimed at producing world-class American distance runners is the Oregon Project financed by Nike and headed by the former marathon star Alberto Salazar. A description of this programme published in 2002 conveys both the technological ambition involved and the credulity enough high-tech equipment can inspire in journalists who should appreciate the role of caution in assessing such enterprises:

> Then there's the laptop loaded with some $35,000 worth of Russian software. By analyzing heart rate patterns, the software aims to take the guesswork out of training. Plug electrodes into the auxiliary box, wire up the runner's chest, and four minutes later there's an onscreen message suggesting just how intensely to work out that day. If the runner adds an electrode to his forehead, in 15 more minutes the system assesses overall health by checking the condition of his liver, kidneys, and central nervous system. [Chad] Johnson, for one, is a big believer in the software. 'It knows when I'm ready to go', he says.

Other high-tech tools available to the Oregon team include a vibrating platform to increase leg power and a hyperbaric (high-pressure oxygen) chamber to repair muscle tears. The company's goal in all this is clear: use technology to counter the increasing domination of African runners, many of whom were born and train at altitude. 'The rest of the world has gotten faster, and Americans have gotten slower', says Salazar. 'Our methods have gone awry.'[52]

The house in which these athletes live has been converted into a hypobaric ('altitude') chamber that produces extra red blood cells by simulating the lower oxygen levels of high altitude. We are told that a so-called OmegaWave Sports Technology System, developed by Russian scientists during the 1980s and 1990s, is used to measure brain waves indicating whether the athlete should rest or exert himself. The problem is that neurologists 'have never heard of the "omega waves" the system supposedly charts'.[53] Here, too, the application of a purportedly scientific technology has failed to produce athletes who can run on the same level as Africans whose training methods do not require the application of technologies beyond effective running shoes.

A very unusual 'scientific' scenario is the discovery of the prodigal white child runner whose further development can be imagined to eventually match the preternatural ability of the best Africans. Julie Aßmann is an eleven-year-old German girl whose biological development, according to the scientists who have examined her, is that of a nine-year-old child. But her blood flow of 3.9 litres per minute is 50 per cent higher than the norm for her body size. Like many of the best Kenyan runners, her legs carry significantly less muscle mass than other athletes. According to one prominent German sports scientist, she is 'an absolutely extraordinary talent.'[54] Whether she will ever develop into an elite athlete is an entirely different question. As a member of a wealthy and technologically advanced society, Julie Aßmann will never confront the brutal economic circumstances that face her Kenyan counterparts, such as Regina Jerotich, who said in 2005: 'God has given me the talent to win races and support my family.'[55] Julie Aßmann's eventual decision not to devote her youthful life to athletic training, should it come, will represent yet another failure to recruit the best 'white' talent into the losing race against the Africans.

Racial athletic aptitude and its social effects

The social impact of black athletic dominance and the racial folklore that is generated or strengthened by de facto racial segregation in high-profile athletic events, while difficult to measure in an empirical way, can be assumed to be significant in multiracial societies that have substantial black populations.[56] In China, where there is no black population that might resent or discourage speculations about racial anatomy and physiology, racial folklore about athletic aptitude has flourished. 'Black people have very good genetics', professor Tian Maijiu, vice president of the Beijing Institute of Physical Education, said in 1994. 'Compared with them, the people in Asia are very inferior.' He then proceeded to offer an inaccurate description of blood type distribution by race, linking blood type O with sprinting ability.[57] After the Chinese hurdler Liu Xiang won the 110-metre event at the 2004 Athens Olympic Games, tying the world record in the process, the *People's Daily* comment that: 'If Chinese people want to make their mark in the major Olympic competitions, they have to break through the fatalism that race determines everything.' 'Short distance races are physically intensive. They require a lot of physical abilities, like speed and sudden strength', said a researcher at the China Institute of Sports Science. 'Although we have no research data, it has been an open fact that Asians and Chinese are disadvantaged when compared to Europeans and Americans.' Stereotypes about genetic inferiority are matched by other stereotypes about high Chinese intelligence and the special training methods they devise to overcome the genetic handicap.[58]

In the United States, however, public discussions of racial athletic aptitude can be difficult and controversial, because they serve as surrogates for the larger social debate about nature versus nurture that seems to force a choice between genetic and environmental explanations for human traits and behaviours. These episodes invariably result in public statements of condemnation and considerable confusion about what is and can be known about the origins of black dominance in some sports. In November 2005, for example, the 67-year-old football coach at the Air Force Academy, Fisher DeBerry, expressed his frustration when his team was overwhelmed by a

Texas Christian University team that fielded many more black players than his team did. 'The other team had a lot more Afro-American players than we did', he said. 'It just seems to be that way, that Afro-American kids can run very, very well. That doesn't mean that Caucasian kids and other descents [*sic*] can't run, but it's very obvious to me they run extremely well.'[59]

Air Force Academy officials described these comments as 'seriously inappropriate', and DeBerry soon issued a public apology. The executive director of the Black Coaches Association declared that any mention of racial athletic aptitude was inappropriate. 'To draw any kind of inference that blacks were faster and whites were slower, that's a subject as a coach you don't go to. It should've been left alone'. And he added: 'All of that is like saying Negroes can dance. It's a racist statement. I know white players that are fast. Someone is going to have to come up with some kind of scientific or biological study that I've never seen nor read that says this is a cause or effect.'[60]

Many other observers found the charge of racism misplaced. 'DeBerry has nothing to apologize for', wrote the African-American sportswriter Michael Wilbon. Despite the discomfort caused by invoking hypothetical racial differences, 'our fear of any discussion involving race should not eliminate common-sense observations'. Wilbon also perceived differing responses to this incident from blacks and whites, respectively. 'I've heard some black dissent, but mostly I hear objections being raised by white administrators and media colleagues, a sort of misplaced white liberal guilt, if you ask me.'[61]

Absent from the public discussion of DeBerry's statements was the documented fact that no sprinter the modern world would classify (or who would self-identify) as 'white' has ever run under 10 seconds in the 100-metre dash under legal conditions, meaning a tailwind of less that 2 metres/second. All those who have done it are (wholly or partly) of West African origin. The single exception is an Australian with an Aboriginal mother who just made it through the 10-second barrier and never ran that well again. Electronic timing has been required for major races since 1977, so there are almost thirty years of reliable performance data to work with. The problem is that reliable data sets and credible scientific research do not seem to interest the media or the public that takes its cues from the media they consume. Discoveries about differences in body weight between black and white distance runners, for example, do not resonate with the emotions that feed our ideas about racial differences and what they might mean.[62]

It is the racial fixations of the nineteenth century, rather than the sciences of the twenty-first, that still exercise the greater influence over how modern societies interpret the performances of black athletes. And the focal point of the excitement is the (racial) personality, rather than the body, of the black performer. The specific anatomical and physiological hypotheses of racial biology that can be applied to the question of racial athletic aptitude appear to hold little interest for the media or the general public. The endless series of racial dramas that appear in the American sports media are soap operas that always derive their dramatic interest from the following question about racial character: Can white authorities keep unstable black men under control and make them civilized?

The current relevance of this nineteenth-century scenario was evident, for example, in a recent comment made by one of the last white running backs to succeed in the National Football League (NFL). Reacting to the media furore surrounding defiant remarks by Terrell Owens, a black NFL star, John Riggins, an NFL luminary of the 1970s and 1980s, said the following:

> You're talking about bringing a wild animal that you think you've domesticated into your locker room, and it's going to eat one of your players, maybe two of them. Don't be angry at the animal. You ought to look yourself in the mirror here and say, 'I knew what I had here, and I did allow that animal into my locker room and it killed a couple of my players'. We're not talking about criminal behavior, but we are when you talk about the social contract. Terrell Owens does not recognize a social contract that we have among human beings, that we have in a civilized society.[63]

All those years Riggins had spent playing beside his black teammates – the racial fraternizing that is supposed to make the sports world a special venue for rapprochement between blacks and whites – appear to have done little to deactivate in him the primitive stereotypes we associate with the era of plantation slavery. The equating of aggressive blacks with 'wild animals', the classic invidious comparison between the savage and the civilized – this is the racial fantasy world of the nineteenth century come back to life.

This social-control scenario has taken various forms in American sport, even as sports officials still refuse to acknowledge in public the racial origins of the tensions and conflicts that play out in their televised venues. The unending parade of high-profile black athletes who find themselves in trouble with the law reinforces the underlying premise that this population requires special supervision. The primary sports venue for these dramas is the National Basketball Association (NBA), which in October 2005 introduced a mandatory dress code to counteract 'the unflattering stereotype of the so-called hip-hop generation player [who has] braided his hair and sport[s] a multitude of tattoos, extending from both muscular shoulders down to his forearms'.[64] Yet even this crackdown on 'the urban black fashion aesthetic', as one protesting African-American sportswriter phrased it, may not be enough.[65] 'What of those fans who approve of the new dress code but object to indelible tattoos and ungrammatical speech?' asked a white sports columnist.[66] What about 'the anger in the air, palpable and ugly, a gladiatorial ambience that over the years has become pervasive in too many N.B.A. arenas'.[67] The most powerful documentation of the racial tensions that afflict the NBA is David Shields' memoir *Black Planet* (1999), which analyzes the wide range of racially awkward situations and grotesqueries that are an integral part of this professional sport. It is an exhaustive and fascinating chronicle where we encounter, among other edifying spectacles, what another writer has called 'the too-widely accepted pastime of affluent whites feeling empowered to verbally abuse half-dressed, sweaty black men' who earn far more than most of the (overwhelmingly) white spectators.[68] Such practices reproduce within the sports arena the racial imbalance of power that has long been the social norm in the larger world outside.

The global popularity of the NBA has spread anti-social and dysfunctional images of the African-American athlete around the world. In 1997, for example, a Swiss newspaper published a long article on the 'bad boys' of the American sports scene, beginning with the latest news about O.J. Simpson's legal ordeal and concluding with an extended account of the 'Basketball-Rowdy' Dennis Rodman.[69] The notorious November 2004 brawl in Detroit involving NBA players and spectators was reported at length in a major German newspaper.[70] Kobe Bryant's campaign to rehabilitate his image after being accused of rape was covered in Germany's most influential news-weekly.[71] These images belong to the larger repertory of violent black male images associated with the globalization of the hip-hop subculture.[72]

The potential social impact of dysfunctional black male images has long concerned African Americans, who have had to contend with centuries of racial defamation originating outside their communities. The 'blaxploitation' films of the 1970s that originated within the black community provoked harsh criticism from black organizations opposed to 'the continued warping of our black children's minds with the filth, violence and cultural lies that are all-pervasive in current productions of so-called black movies', as a spokesman for the Los Angeles Coalition Against Blaxploitation put it in 1972.[73] In recent years such concerns have focused on misbehaving rappers and athletes and their frequent associations with criminal or other anti-social behaviours that impede educational achievement and social advancement. This critical line of thought still contends with what remains of the traditional African-American idea that the sports world offers young black athletes an unusual degree of social mobility and an opportunity to demonstrate positive black character traits to the larger society. The problem for this traditionalist argument is that the self-styled 'hip-hop' athlete is seldom interested in conforming to such norms. The socially constructive effects that black athletes such as Jackie Robinson could have during the Civil Rights era stand in stark contrast to what the 'hip-hop' generation of athletes conveys to its domestic and now global audience.

One form of the generational conflict between Civil Rights-era African-American cultural critics and 'the hip-hop generation' that has come after them concerns the social impact of high-profile black athletes. Some older African-American commentators reject the social mobility argument and condemn the athletic exhibitionists. Brent Staples, a member of the editorial board of the *New York Times*, wrote in 2004: 'The myth of upward mobility through basketball is a cancer on the black inner city. The cliché about basketball offering a "ticket out of the ghetto" – through college scholarships and professional contracts – traps black boys into framing their lives around the sport while abandoning studies that would actually prepare them for reachable careers.'[74] Thad Mumford, a television writer and producer, protests the minstrel element that can insert itself into the NBA and NFL subcultures: 'The unsayable but unassailable truth is that the clowning, dancing, preening smacktalker is becoming the Rorschach image of the African-American male athlete. It casts a huge shadow over all other images. This persona has the power to sell what no one should buy: the notion that black folks are still cuttin' up for the white man.'[75] The novelist John Edgar Wideman commented in 2001:

> As much as basketball may be hyped as a rosy consummation of multi-cultural, multi-racial, melting-pot togetherness in ads featuring N.B.A. stars, in N.B.A. promos fronting ecstatic white fans who love that game, basketball also functions to embody racial fantasies, to prove and perpetuate 'essential' differences between blacks and whites, to justify the idea of white supremacy and rationalize an unfair balance of power, maintained by violence, lies, and terror, between blacks and whites.[76]

The African-American inventor James E. West, the holder of 250 patents and a research professor at Johns Hopkins University, 'fantasizes about a day when children hold inventors and scientists in higher esteem than hip-hop stars and professional athletes'.[77]

Sport's racial dimension in the twenty-first century will retain both its social and genetic aspects. Black dominance within important sectors of the sports entertainment industry will continue to emphasize the identification of black people with the capacities of their bodies rather than their minds. Reversing the social effects lamented by the African-American commentators cited above will not be possible in the foreseeable future, since effective opposition to the commercial interests which profit from publicizing black athletes is nowhere on the horizon. So the expressive styles of the most visible black athletes will continue to influence especially young people of colour around the globe. At the same time, the Human Genome Project will produce more and more information about varying distributions of certain genetic variations (alleles) among 'racial' populations that experience corresponding (and differing) rates of medical disorders of genetic origin. This research, as the sociological Troy Duster points out, is 'poised to exert a cascading effect – reinscribing taxonomies of race across a broad range of scientific practices and fields'.[78] In fact, the concept of biological race is already making a comeback after spending decades in disrepute. 'We should reintroduce the concept of race into science and medicine', a medical advisor to the Human Genome Project stated in 2004.[79] This evolving racial genetics may well isolate some of the genes responsible for conferring advantages on athletes who possess specific genetic endowments associated with a particular 'race'. The visibility of these performers on the Olympic stage will have the effect of both legitimizing the new genomic research and reinforcing the authority of the familiar thinking that assigns specific genes to the 'races' we have long employed to maintain a typology of human beings.

Notes

1 W. Johnson, *Soul by Soul: Life Inside the Antebellum Slave Market*, Cambridge, MA: Harvard University Press, 1999, p. 130.
2 J. Olsen, 'Pride and prejudice', *Sports Illustrated*, 1968, 28.
3 F. Fanon, *Black Skin, White Masks* [1952], New York: Grove Press, Inc., 1967, 160, 165, 167.
4 R. Ellison, 'Richard Wright's Blues' [1945], in *Shadow and Act*, New York: Vintage Books, 1972, 88–9.
5 *Black Skin, White Masks*, 166.
6 See, for example, J. Hoberman, *Testosterone Dreams: Rejuvenation, Aphrodisia, Doping*, Berkeley, CA: University of California Press, 2005, pp. 236, 340.
7 N. L. Stepan, *Picturing Tropical Nature*, Ithaca, NY: Cornell University Press, 2001, pp. 11–12, 21, 37.
8 'Der Traum von Afrika', *Süddeutsche Zeitung* (13 April 2004). This dramatic vision of African nature recalls in some respects what Abdul R. JanMohamed has described as the world as presented by colonial fiction, 'a world at the boundaries of "civilization", a world that has not (yet) been domestication by European signification or codified in detail by its ideology. That world is therefore perceived as uncontrollable, chaotic, unattainable, and ultimately evil'. See 'The Economy of Manichean Allegory: The Function of Racial Difference in Colonialist Literature', in H.L. Gates, Jr. (ed.), *Race, Writing, and Difference*, Chicago, IL and London: University of Chicago Press, 1986, p. 83.
9 K. Moore, 'Sons of the wind', *Sports Illustrated*, 26 February 1990), 79. Moore's biological panorama comprising animals, plants and people recalls JanMohamed's comment that in I. Dinesen's *Out of Africa* (1937) 'African natives can be collapsed into African animals and mystified still further as some magical essence of the continent . . .' See 'The Economy of Manichean Allegory', 87.
10 M. Geber and R.F.A. Dean, 'Gesell tests on African children', *Pediatrics*, 1957, 20: 1064, 1058.
11 J.E. Kilbride, M.C. Robbins, and P.L. Kilbride, 'The comparative motor development of Baganda, American white, and American black infants', *American Anthropologist*, 1970, 72: 1422.
12 J.C. Cobb, 'Precocity of African children', *Pediatrics*, 1958, 21: 867; H. Knobloch, 'Precocity of African children', *Pediatrics*, 1958, 22: 601.
13 J. Bale, *Imagined Olympians: Body Culture and Colonial Representation in Rwanda*, Minneapolis, MN and London: University of Minnesota Press, 2002, p. 85.
14 K.T. Greenfield, 'The fast track', *Sports Illustrated*, 14 January 2005, 61, 63.
15 R. Reilly, 'A deadly talent', *Sports Illustrated*, 17 October 2005, 72.
16 'Uslåelige afrikanere', *Aftenposten* (Oslo), 3 August 1991.
17 'Die verlorenen Kinder des Fußballs', *Süddeutsche Zeitung* (Munich), 11 November 1999.
18 D.B. Dill, J.W. Wilson, F.G. Hall, and S. Robinson, 'Properties of the blood of Negroes and Whites in relation to climate and season', *Journal of Biological Chemistry*, 1940, 136: 450–1.

19 See, for example, J. Hoberman, 'African athletic aptitude and the social sciences', *Equine and Comparative Exercise Physiology*, 2004, 31: 1–5.
20 'Le Pen sind Nationalspieler nicht französisch genug', *Süddeutsche Zeitung*, 25 June 1996.
21 'Ich bin ein Rebell', *Der Spiegel*, 11 November 1996, 174, 176.
22 'Ballon rond, noirs et blancs', *Rivarol*, 4 June 1993.
23 'Der Präsident droht Prügel an', *Süddeutsche Zeitung*, 13 May 2005.
24 'Strafen und keine Antwort', *Frankfurter Allgemeine Zeitung*, 7 March 2003.
25 'Immer fröhlich, immer lustig', *Der Spiegel*, 22 March 2004, 158, 160.
26 'In der Arena ist kein Platz', *Süddeutsche Zeitung*, 26 July 1999.
27 'Maccabi TA coach Gershon: Black players are dummies', *Jerusalem Post*, 2 July 2001 [Jerusalem Post Internet Edition].
28 'Der Präsident droht Prügel an', *Süddeutsche Zeitung*, 13 May 2005.
29 'In der sozialen Krise Frankreichs ist der Sport machtlos', *Frankfurter Allgemeine Zeitung* [FAZ.NET], 12 November 2005.
30 The gold-medal-winning (and world-record tying) performance in the 110-metre high hurdles at the 2004 Athens Olympic Games by Liu Xiang of China (12.91 seconds) inspired this Olympic champion to indulge in some revisionist talk about racial athletic aptitude and the Asian inferiority complex that had intimidated 'yellow men' who feared competing against blacks. 'Today the Chinese people showed the world they can run as fast as anybody else', Xiang told the Olympic News Service. In the same interview, however, Xiang made it clear that his own inferiority complex had not been entirely expunged. 'Because I am Chinese, and with the physiology of the Asian race, I think taking all this into consideration, this is a miracle'. See P. Berlin, 'Gold for 2 Chinese runners could be harbinger of 2008', *New York Times*, 28 August 2004.
31 'Ein wenig Zeit für tausend Episoden', *Süddeutsche Zeitung*, 30 September 1996.
32 'Sommernachtsträume', *Süddeutsche Zeitung*, 20 August 1999.
33 'Atemberaubende Dynamik unter Capitano Moses', *Süddeutsche Zeitung*, 23/24 May 1998.
34 T. Layden, 'Stretching out', *Sports Illustrated*, 7 June 1999, 140.
35 'Kennedy returns after Olympic disappointment', *New York Times*, 31 January 2001.
36 'Die Ehre des Abendlandes retten', *Der Spiegel*, 11 March 1996.
37 S. Lindstrom, 'Training with the Kenyans', *Track and Field News*, July 1998, 48.
38 J.D. Welch, 'Brantly PR-driven', *Track and Field News*, July 1998, 26.
39 J.D. Welch, 'In a class by himself', *Track and Field News*, August 1987, 58.
40 R. Quintana, 'Pre-race interview with Bob Kennedy', online, available HTTP: *http://www.fast-women.com/news/footlocker03/stories/bobkennedy*, (accessed 24 December 24 2003).
41 J.D. Welch, 'In a class by himself', *Track and Field News*, August 1987, 58.
42 'White men (and women) can't sprint?' *International Herald Tribune*, 12 March 1997.
43 'En puma fra Moss', *Aftenposten* (Oslo), 25 February 1995.
44 'Autonome Zelle' (Tobias Unger), *Der Spiegel*, 6 June 2005, 142–3.
45 'U.S. men realize mind must be prepared, too', *USA TODAY*, 17 July 1996.
46 'Dieter Baumann hetzt die Hasen vor sich her', *Süddeutsche Zeitung*, 7 April 1997.
47 On the possible role of 'stereotype threat' in discouraging white athletes, see J. Baker and S. Horton, 'East African running dominance revisited: a role for stereotype threat?' *British Journal of Sports Medicine*, 2003, 37: 553–5.
48 'Love parade in spikes', *Der Spiegel*, 25 June 2001, 177.
49 B. Hoban, 'Running on empty?' *Austin American-Statesman*, 23 April 2000.
50 'Dispensing with loneliness in long-distance running', *New York Times*, 3 November 2000.

51 'A marathon turns into a sprint, and a Kenyan wins it by just a step', *New York Times*, 7 November 2005.

52 A. Tilin, 'The ultimate running machine', *Wired*, August 2002.

53 A. Tilin, 'The ultimate running machine', *Wired*, August 2002.

54 'Anatomie eines Wunderkindes' *Der Spiegel*, 4 April 2005, 138–40.

55 'Laufen ist unsere einzige Chance', *Frankfurter Allgemeine Zeitung* (FAZ.NET), 11 October 2005.

56 See J. Hoberman, *Darwin's Athletes: How Sport Has Damaged Black America and Preserved the Myth of Race*, New York: Houghton Mifflin, 1997; J. Hoberman, 'The price of 'Black dominance', *Transaction: Social Science and Modern Society*, March/April 2000, 49–56.

57 'Avoiding competition against blacks', *Atlanta Constitution*, 17 April 1994.

58 J. Yardley, 'Racial "handicaps" and a great sprint forward', *New York Times*, 8 September 2004.

59 L. Hancock, 'Race, sports raise awkward questions', *Dallas Morning News*, 29 October 2005.

60 L. Hancock, 'Race, sports raise awkward questions', *Dallas Morning News*, 29 October 2005.

61 M. Wilbon, 'Misplaced fury over racism', *Washington Post*, 29 October 2005.

62 'Black athletes are significantly smaller and substantially lighter, often by as much as 15 kg. There may also be other anthropomorphic differences, for example, in the relative mass and length of the lower limb, but we did not specifically address that question. Clearly these differences are likely to have a strong genetic component'. See T.D. Noakes *et al.*, 'Physiological function and neuromuscular recruitment in elite South African distance runners', *Equine and Comparative Exercise Physiology*, 2004, 1: 267.

63 W.C. Rhoden, 'The colts' main brain is Dungy, not Manning', *New York Times*, 8 November 2005.

64 H. Araton, 'One year after Pacers–Pistons fight, tough questions of race and sports', *New York Times*, 30 October 2005.

65 K.B. Blackistone, 'Stern's power trip unfashionable', *Dallas Morning News*, 20 October 2005.

66 H. Araton, 'The N.B.A.'s latest edict already looks threadbare', *New York Times*, 21 October 2005.

67 H. Araton, 'One year after Pacers–Pistons fight, tough questions of race and sports', *New York Times*, 30 October 2005.

68 H. Araton, 'One year after Pacers–Pistons fight, tough questions of race and sports', *New York Times*, 30 October 2005.

69 'Böse Buben bringen die Kasse kräftig zum Klingeln', *Die Weltwoche* (Zurich), 13 February 1997.

70 'Ein negativabzug der Gesellschaft', *Frankfurter Allgemeine Zeitung*, 26 November 2004.

71 'Großer Schritt', *Der Spiegel*, 7 November 2005, 94.

72 'One of the striking things about the scenes from France (November 2004) is how thoroughly the rioters have assimilated hip-hop and rap culture. It's not only that they use the same hand gestures as American rappers, wear the same clothes and necklaces, play the same video games and sit with the same sorts of car stereos at full blast. It's that they seem to have adopted the same poses of exaggerated manhood, the same attitudes about women, money and the police. They seem to have replicated the same sort of gang culture, the same romantic visions of gun-slinging drug dealers. In a globalized age it's perhaps inevitable that the culture of resistance gets globalized, too. What we are seeing is what Mark Lilla of the University of Chicago calls a universal culture of the wretched of the earth. The images, modes and attitudes of hip-hop and gangsta rap are so powerful they

are having a hegemonic effect across the globe'. See D. Brooks, 'Gangsta, in French', *New York Times*, 10 November 2005.

73 'Blacks vs. shaft', *Newsweek*, 28 August 1972, 88. See also L. Hairston, 'The black film – "Supernigger" as folk hero', *Freedomways*, 1974, 14: 218–22.

74 B. Staples, 'Broken hoop dreams for the basketball players of Coney Island', *New York Times*, 1 February 2004.

75 T. Mumford, 'The new minstrel show: black vaudeville with statistics', *New York Times*, 23 May 2004.

76 Quoted in R. Lipsyte, 'In purest form, basketball is a playground game', *New York Times*, 28 October 2001.

77 'Not invented here', *New York Times*, 13 November 2005.

78 T. Duster, 'Race and reification in science', *Science*, 18 February 2005, 307: 1051. See also S.G. Stolberg, 'Shouldn't a pill be colorblind?' *New York Times*, 13 May 2001.

79 A. Daar, a professor of surgery at the University of Toronto, at a conference in Berlin in 2004. See 'Die neue Rassendebatte', *Der Spiegel*, 2004, 17: 186. Daar is currently director of ethics and policy at the McLaughlin Centre for Molecular Medicine, University of Toronto, Canada. He is also director of the applied ethics and biotechnology programme at the University of Toronto Joint Centre for Bioethics and co-director of the Canadian Program on Genomics and Global Health. See also: 'The concept of race may not be biologically meaningless after all; it might even have some practical use in deciding on medical treatments, at least until more complete individual genomic information becomes available. Yet in the interests of humane values, many scientists are reluctant to make even minor adjustments to the old orthodoxy. One of the more painful spectacles in modern science, the developmental biologist Armand Marie Leroi has observed, is that of human geneticists piously disavowing the existence of races even as they investigate the genetic relationships between "ethnic groups" '. See J. Holt, 'Madness about a method', *New York Times Magazine*, 11 December 2005, 28.

Bibliography

Araton, H. (21 October 2005) 'The N.B.A.'s latest edict already looks threadbare', *New York Times*.

Araton, H. (30 October 2005) 'One year after Pacers–Pistons fight, tough questions of race and sports', *New York Times*.

Baker, J. and Horton, S. (2003) 'East African running dominance revisited: a role for stereotype threat'? *British Journal of Sports Medicine*, 37: 553–5.

Bale, J. (2002) *Imagined Olympians: Body Culture and Colonial Representation in Rwanda*, Minneapolis, MN and London: University of Minnesota Press.

Berlin, P. (28 August 2004) 'Gold for 2 Chinese runners could be harbinger of 2008', *New York Times*.

Blackistone, K.B. (20 October 2003) 'Stern's power trip unfashionable', *Dallas Morning News*.

Brooks, D. (10 November 2005) 'Gangsta, in French', *New York Times*.

Cobb, J.C. (1958) 'Precocity of African children', *Pediatrics*, 21: 867.

Daar, A. (2004) 'Die neue Rassendebatte', *Der Spiegel*, 17: 186.

Dill, D.B., Wilson, J.W., Hall, F.G. and Robinson, S. (1940) 'Properties of the blood of Negroes and Whites in relation to climate and season', *Journal of Biological Chemistry*, 136: 450–1.

Duster, T. (18 February 2005) 'Race and reification in science', *Science*, 307: 1,051.

Ellison, E. (1972) 'Richard Wright's blues' (1945), in *Shadow and Act*, New York: Vintage Books.

Fanon, F. (1967) *Black Skin, White Masks* (1952), New York: Grove Press, Inc.

Geber. M. and Dean, R.F.A. (1957) 'Gesell tests on African children', *Pediatrics*, 20: 1,064, 1,058.

Gershon, L. (2 July 2001) 'Black players are dummies', *Jerusalem Post* (Jerusalem Post Internet Edition).

Greenfield, K.T. (January 2005) 'The fast track', *Sports Illustrated*, 14: 61, 63, 63.

Hairston, L. (1974) 'The Black film – "Supernigger" as folk hero', *Freedomways*, 14: 218–22.

Hancock, L. (29 October 2005) 'Race, sports raise awkward questions', *Dallas Morning News*.

Hoban, B. (23 April 2000) 'Running on empty?' *Austin American-Statesman*.

Hoberman, J. (1997) *Darwin's Athletes: How Sport Has Damaged Black America and Preserved the Myth of Race*, New York: Houghton Mifflin.

Hoberman, J. (March/April 2000) 'The price of "black dominance" ', *Transaction: Social Science and Modern Society*, 49–56.

Hoberman, J. (2004) 'African athletic aptitude and the social sciences', *Equine and Comparative Exercise Physiology*, 31: 1–5.

Hoberman, J. (2005) *Testosterone Dreams: Rejuvenation, Aphrodisia, Doping*, Berkeley, CA: University of California Press.

Holt, J. (December 2005) 'Madness about a method', *New York Times Magazine*, 11: 28.

JanMohamed, A.R. (1986) 'The economy of Manichean Allegory: the function of racial difference in colonialist literature', in H.L. Gates, Jr. (ed.), *'Race', Writing, and Difference*, Chicago, IL and London: University of Chicago Press.

Johnson, W. (1999) *Soul by Soul: Life Inside the Antebellum Slave Market*, Cambridge, MA: Harvard University Press.

Kilbride, J.E., Robbins, M.C. and Kilbride, P.L. (1970) 'The comparative motor development of Baganda, American White, and American Black Infants', *American Anthropologist*, 72: 1,422.

Knobloch, H. (1958) 'Precocity of African children', *Pediatrics*, 22: 601.

Layden, T. (June 1999) 'Stretching out', *Sports Illustrated*, 70: 140.

Lindstrom, S. (July 1998) 'Training with the Kenyans', *Track and Field News*, 48.

Lipsyte, R. (28 October 2001) 'In purest form, basketball is a playground game', *New York Times*.

Moore, K. (February 1990) 'Sons of the wind', *Sports Illustrated*, 26: 79.

Mumford, T. (23 May 2004) 'The new minstrel show: black vaudeville with statistics', *New York Times*.

Noakes, T.D. *et al.*, (2004) 'Physiological function and neuromuscular recruitment in elite South African distance runners', *Equine and Comparative Exercise Physiology*, 1: 267.

Olsen, J. (July 1968) 'Pride and prejudice', *Sports Illustrated*, 8: 28.

Quintana, R. (2003) 'Pre-race interview with Bob Kennedy'. Online. Available HTTP: *http://www.fast-women.com/news/footlocker03/stories/bobkennedy* (accessed 24 December).

Reilly, R. (17 October 2005) 'A deadly talent', *Sports Illustrated*, 72.

Rhoden, W.C. (8 November 2005) 'The colts' main brain is Dungy, not Manning', *New York Times*.

Staples, B. (1 February 2004) 'Broken hoop dreams for the basketball players of Coney Island', *New York Times*.
Stepan, N.L. (2001) *Picturing Tropical Nature*, Ithaca, NY: Cornell University Press.
Stolberg, S.G. (13 May 2001) 'Shouldn't a pill be colorblind?' *New York Times*.
Welch, J.D. (July 1998) 'Brantly PR-Driven', *Track and Field News*, 26.
Tilin, A. (August 2002) 'The ultimate running machine', *Wired*.
Welch, J.D. (August 1987) 'In a class by himself', *Track and Field News*, 58.
Wilbon, M. (29 October 2005) 'Misplaced fury over racism', *Washington Post*.
Yardley, J. (8 September 2004) 'Racial "handicaps" and a great sprint forward', *New York Times*.

Newspaper articles

'Der Traum von Afrika', *Süddeutsche Zeitung* (13 April 2004).
'Böse Buben bringen die Kasse kräftig zum Klingeln', *Die Weltwoche* (Zurich) (13 February 1997).
'Ein wenig Zeit für tausend Episoden', *Süddeutsche Zeitung* (30 September 1996).
'Sommernachtsträume', *Süddeutsche Zeitung* (20 August 1999).
'Atemberaubende Dynamik unter Capitano Moses', *Süddeutsche Zeitung* (23/24 May 1998).
'In der sozialen Krise Frankreichs ist der Sport machtlos', *Frankfurter Allgemeine Zeitung* (FAZ.NET) (12 November 2005).
'Der Präsident droht Prügel an', *Süddeutsche Zeitung* (13 May 2005).
'Avoiding competition against blacks', *Atlanta Constitution* (17 April 1994).
'Dispensing with loneliness in long-distance running', *New York Times* (3 November 2000).
'A marathon turns into a sprint, and a Kenyan wins it by just a step', *New York Times* (7 November 2005).
'Anatomie eines Wunderkindes', *Der Spiegel* (4 April 2005): 138–40.
'Laufen ist unsere einzige Chance', *Frankfurter Allgemeine Zeitung* (FAZ.NET) (11 October 2005).
'Ein negativabzug der Gesellschaft', *Frankfurter Allgemeine Zeitung* (26 November 2004).
'Großer Schritt', *Der Spiegel* (7 November 2005): 94.
'Blacks vs. Shaft', *Newsweek* (28 August 28 1972): 88.
'Not invented here', *New York Times* (13 November 2005).
'Die verlorenen Kinder des Fußballs,' *Süddeutsche Zeitung* (Munich) (11 November 1999).
'Le Pen sind Nationalspieler nicht französisch genug', *Süddeutsche Zeitung* (25 June 1996).
'Ich bin ein Rebell', *Der Spiegel* (11 November 1996): 174, 176.
'Ballon rond, noirs et blancs', *Rivarol* (4 June 1993).
'Der Präsident droht Prügel an', *Süddeutsche Zeitung* (13 May 2005).
'Strafen und keine Antwort', *Frankfurter Allgemeine Zeitung* (7 March 2003).
'Immer fröhlich, immer lustig', *Der Spiegel* (22 March 2004): 160, 158.
'In der Arena ist kein Platz', *Süddeutsche Zeitung* (26 July 1999).
'Kennedy returns after Olympic disappointment', *New York Times* (31 January 2001).
'Die Ehre des Abendlandes retten', *Der Spiegel* (11 March 1996).

'White men (and women) can't sprint?' *International Herald Tribune* (12 March 1997).

'En puma fra Moss', *Aftenposten* (Oslo) (25 February 1995).

'Autonome Zelle' (Tobias Unger), *Der Spiegel* (6 June 2005): 142–3.

'U.S. men realize mind must be prepared, too', *USA TODAY* (17 July 1996).

'Dieter Baumann hetzt die Hasen vor sich her', *Süddeutsche Zeitung* (7 April 1997).

'Love Parade in spikes', *Der Spiegel* (25 June 2001): 177.

12 Technologized bodies

Virtual women and transformations in understandings of the body as natural

Kate O'Riordan

Introduction

This chapter examines case studies of virtual bodies in popular digital culture including the Visible Human Project, interfaces, avatars, and the Human Genome Projects. By deploying concepts of the natural to read images of female bodies in digital culture, the chapter examines the ontology of the image and body/image relations. The continuous blurring of the divisions between the biological female body and the simulated one are demonstrated in the chapter and it is concluded that the visions of biotechnologies are invested in a parallel physical reductionism to those of popular digital culture.

In many UK and USA media contexts, the female body, in particular, has been conceptualized and represented as constitutive of the natural and of the flesh, to be formed, socialized, and conditioned by culture. As Kember notes, citing, Keller (1992), 'Due to the historical identification of women with nature it is a short step from the secrets of women, to the secrets of nature' (Kember 2003: 26).

However, as this quotation illustrates, through the investment in 'secrets', the experience of the female body indicates that it has never been tame; the excessive body is that which disrupts social structure, resists containment, and thus remains under investigation in scientific discourses. Through sites of investigation and explanation, particularly through reproduction, there are constant tensions between female bodies as they are represented, naturalized, and explained and as they are experienced and socialized.

It is around these tensions that the following central arguments in the chapter are developed:

- Information and communication technologies, through cyberspaces, re-produce normative simulations of naturalized female bodies and this normativity is intensified through digital forms.
- Case studies of animated virtual female bodies in digital culture reveal that parallel processes of naturalization function in relation to technologies and bodies.

- Digital cultures and biotechnologies have been positioned as sharing a constitutive framework of digitization and simulation which allows a deterministic force to be re-produced across the two fields.
- Biotechnologies, through genomics, perform a parallel reductionism.

Without polarizing experience and image, and without claiming homogeneity for either category, my aim is to explore these nature/culture tensions in relation to the digitization and simulation of information, images, and bodies. Drawing together virtually physical female bodies in a range of forms, the chapter engages with the constitution of bodies and digital cultures and examines some of the connections between digital technologies and bioinformatics. The focus that I am trying to identify is the mediation and simulation of the female body through informational means and the circuit created through the body as flesh and the body as image. This is my centre: the constitution and mediation of those designated physically natural (female bodies) through those which are designated physically artificial (digital images).

Through a highly complex, and in no-way simply causal relation, imaging technologies and material experiences are mutually constitutive sociomaterial practices (Suchman 2002).[1] This is to say that they are part of a network of elements through which identity is actualized and experience nuanced. Deconstructions of the 'effects' model in media studies (e.g. Gauntlett 1995) provide an overview of arguments against the causal models of media relations. However, it is also necessary to consider the affective properties of media and turn to contributions developed from actor network theories in social studies of science and technology, and conceptualizations of kinship and social relations in anthropology for more deeply theorized understandings of the circuits and networks of meaning that contribute to the constitution of the social world. The central productive tension is in holding open a route through and between different kinds of constructionisms and determinisms whilst producing a relational model of media interactions, interfaces, and hybrid models of social relations.

In the context of mediation and interfaces, understandings of female bodies have been continually reworked, sexualized, pathologized, mapped, imagined, contested, and transformed through imaging techniques in science, medicine, fine art, and various other forms of popular visual culture (Haraway 1997). These techniques have included technologies of etching, illustration, painting, photography, and film (Jordanova 1989; Cartwright 1995). In the twentieth and twenty-first centuries the regimes of digital imaging technologies at the interface have contributed to further technologizations of the body. Undertakings such as the Visible Human Project (VHP)[2] and the Human Genome Projects (HGP)[3] epitomize the new regimes of the digital visual cultures of bodies in popular science and continue to normalize and naturalize a limited repertoire of images and concepts of the female body. Through these regimes bodies have been rendered simultaneously penetrable, transparent, malleable, wired, networked, and normalized through discourses that approximate the specificity of bodies into an aggregate concept of 'the body'. Digital imaging techniques have been central to these processes, and the aim of this chapter is to chart some interfaces and relations between female bodies and digital imaging through the paradoxical tension of the constitution of the natural through the artificial.

The powers invested in new imaging technologies to produce this tension of natural through artificial in the production of reproduction are well documented by feminist sociologists and anthropologists. Rosalind Petchesky (1992), Carol Stabile (1993), and Valerie Hartouni's (1997) work on foetal images, for example, highlights the force that visual images of female bodies have in relation to the experience and constitution of maternity. Catherine Waldby (2000) has extensively examined the Visible Human Project, and this work, together with Haraway (1997), Keller (2000), Kember (2003), and Franklin's work on genomics (2000), examines the links between the field of digital vision and that of the normative genetic lens that now contributes to understandings of bodies.

The rich literature from feminist sources examining the relational dynamics of female bodies and imaging technologies creates feminist interventions into science, mainly through the social studies of technology and science literature. Roof (1996), Waldby (2000), Kember (2003) and others link the digital image and simulation of the body with the digital encoding of the body though the genome map. This literature examines the convergence of the medical image, the digital simulation, and the body through examples such as the Visible Human Project (Waldby 2000) and narratives of Artificial Life (Kember 2003). Equally significant are the networked convergences of popular culture and scientific images (Cartwright 1995). That the imaging techniques of art and illustration are constitutive of the vision of science and that visual culture is also constituted through technology resonates throughout this literature. The movement of this mutual constitution into the networks of digital imaging and digital science is established elsewhere (Waldby 2000; Cartwright 1995; Manovich 2001; Doyle and O'Riordan 2002; Kember 2003) and is also central to this chapter.

Technologies of visual mediation have been the most significant elements in these (Foucauldian) processes of subjecting bodies to the scopic control of informatics, biometrics, and closure. There are close affinities and overlap between the technologies employed in the technoscientific fields and those employed within popular culture (Cartwright 1995). Science as read through medical imaging on the web, for example, is a contributory factor in concepts of 'popular', whilst images of science are also rendered through fictions. This inter-relation of imaging across overlapping social fields is crucial to the solidity and flexibility of the dominant structures that are scaffolded by such images and imaginings. Drawing on visual digital culture, I outline here the ways in which technologies are intertwined with the physicality of bodies, in frames of both work and leisure, producing understandings of those bodies as movements through technologized networks.

The chapter examines some selected key instances of mediated and virtual bodies and thereby develops arguments that the simulation of female bodies in digital culture draws on very specific body types; that this model of constructing bodies has parallels in biotechnologies; and that the digital or virtual does not determine these developments but is used to re-produce specifically reductive understandings of bodies. The limitations of this chapter are clear: it draws on a case study of production, form, and image and does not deal with issues of consumption. Considerations of consumption would illuminate the aspects of irony and humour also involved in digital aesthetics and would provide richer aspects to this analysis.

Digital bodies in popular culture

Virtual female bodies are realized through a variety of mechanisms in popular culture and populate medical imaging, computer games, VR scenarios, films, websites, adverts, cartoons, and books. A fictionalized version can be found in Gibson's novels, *Idoru* (1996) and *All Tomorrow's Parties* (2000) through the character Rei Toei, a 'virtual idol' of such complexity that 'she' develops consciousness in the novel through Alife type properties.

> She is Rei Toei. She is a personality-construct, a congeries of software agents, the creation of information-designers. She is akin to what I believe they call a 'synthespian', in Hollywood.
>
> (Gibson 1997: 92)

Precursors of virtual bodies from the 1980s include the image of the computerized 'female' of *Weird Science*, who emerges from inside the computer in the plot of this film (updated for the 1990s in *Virtual Sexuality* and again in *The 6th Day* (2000)). An image from advertising is the AOL 'woman' with the digitized dress who explains, through voice, movement, and gesture, how down to earth but exciting the internet is for domestic use. This figure appeared in UK AOL advertising in the late 1990s. Games avatars such as the iconic action hero Lara Croft and audio-visual interface models such as Ananova exemplify the diversity of uses virtual female bodies can have. Virtual models, actors, and sex toys are other niche markets for the virtual female body or 'digital beauties' as dubbed by Wiedemann (2001) in a book of the same name, which catalogues such virtual women.

Gibson's fictional Idoru 'Rei Toei' was reputedly inspired by a simulated female called Kyoko Date, created in 1996. Kyoko was a computer generated 'Idol Singer' produced by Hori Productions, a Japanese music promotion company, which has a portfolio of 'real' Idol Singers geared towards the teenage market. Kyoko Date was marketed as the world's first virtual pop singer. Singles were released in Kyoko's name and there were appearances in audio-visual performances and interviews, magazine spreads, online articles, and critical appraisals. The exhibition of movement and use of speech was

Figure 12.1 'Digital beauties', as dubbed by Wiedemann (2001) in a book of the same
name, which catalogues such virtual women. Image reproduced from the
book cover of Wiedermann, Julius (ed.) *Digital Beauties*, 1st edition,
Taschen, with kind permission of Julius Wiedermann.

central to the on-screen realization of this figure. Kyoko Date was reported to
be hugely popular and enjoyed a brief but significant celebrity status in Japan
(Poole 2000; Hamilton 1997).

Just one actual example of the deployment of the label synthespian (that
Gibson uses in the fictional quotation above) is by the USA-based computing
animation company Kleiser-Walczak to describe their products which have
application in film, advertising, and computer games. Another comment
from the advertising commentary for the book *Digital Beauties* reinforces
this conflation of person and image:

> it's about time you got to know some of the 'people' you'll be coming
> across in the future on TV and even in film; one such example is
> Steven Stahlberg's lovely Webbie Tookay, the first virtual model to sign

Figure 12.2 Digital Beauties, book cover 2. Image reproduced from the book cover of Wiedermann, Julius (ed.) *Digital Beauties*, 2nd edition, Taschen, with kind permission of Julius Wiedermann.

with Elite Digital Models. Some of these digital creations have even been included in 'sexiest women' lists – along with real humans, of course!

(Wiedemann 2001)

The anchorage for these creations to be located as sexy and/or friendly physical women who can interact as bodies in space is continually repeated throughout the promotional literature on these simulations.

One of the central premises of cyber-mythology was that gender and sexuality could be re-envisioned, re-experienced, and re-configured through simulation and digital media. In some circles it appeared that cyberfeminists would inherit cyberspace (Plant 1997), in others that the ideal cybersubject could inhabit multiple identities through volitional performance (Stone 1996; Bornstein 1998). Although exciting, dynamic, and politically important moves were made through these constellations, a disruption of the performative power of the image to reiterate and reinscribe normative bodies was not an outcome. As Hillis comments in relation to virtual reality scenarios:

> Despite the promise of an infinite potential of electronically generated digital patterns, pixelations, and performances, the 'as if' geography of the virtual world is not really 'whatever' we want it to be. To date, it is rather small, both materially and experientially.
>
> (Hillis 1999: 210)

This appraisal extends to the current state of the internet, where once the rhetoric of the wilds of cyberspace promised 'new frontiers', there is now a reiteration of sameness. This is reified in commercial digital aesthetics, and there is a proliferation of publications on how to program 'digital beauties' (e.g. Wiedemann 2001 and 2002[4]) or the sexualized active female form as an aesthetic goal of digital simulation.

Digital Beauties (Wiedemann 2001), and a range of other books, provide a more exhaustive promotion, cataloguing, and taxonomy of virtual females. A few examples from these are: Ulala – a presenter, game avatar, and film character used by Britain's terrrestrial Channel 5. Ulala is a pink-haired reporter who dances and wears a pink micro skirt, thigh boots and bra top. Secondly, Mya is mobile telecommunications company Motorola's virtual persona who will talk to customers, providing a human-like interface to the internet mobile phone link. Mya simulates a blonde, white, female. Thirdly, Trina is distribution company Triumph International's virtual model who advertises underwear. Trina wears a black microskirt and bra and dances in a UK advertising campaign (June 2000). Fourthly, Webbie Tookay, the virtual supermodel promoted by the Elite modelling agency, is mentioned by Taschen. Webbie is advertised as model and presenter/entertainer. Fifthly, Sylvie is one of several Virtual Personalities Inc products. This company produces desktop Verbotsfi[5] to provide a 'friendly interface' for the computer user. Two other figures that have emerged from the computer game industry are Lara Croft and Shiori Fujisaki. Shiori, like Lara, is a game avatar that has crossed media platforms, in Shiori's case to become a singer. Lara appears in adverts, film, books, computer games, and fan sites.

This path of digital aesthetic development is about activity, movement and sound, and the simulation of bodies that appear to be physical through appearing to be in movement through space. Physical movement is a prerequisite for the simulation of flesh. This is twofold in that the viewer must both witness their physicality and also imagine physical encounter to render these icons meaningful. The possibility that the viewer's body might physically encounter them, beyond seeing and hearing them on screen, is part of the performance. They are animated figures that appear, at least minimally, to interact, thus physical characteristics such as voice, gesture, and movement are central programming challenges. In the case of Ananova, speech programming is used so that the figure becomes an audio-visual text reader. Facial expression, tone, and gesture are all considerations in the delivery of the news: a grave tone for serious news for example. With Lara Croft it is movement that is central to the character as the avatar is used to negotiate the virtual spatiality of the game world. Body shape and action is central to the 'femaleness' of these images. The sporting body of Lara Croft, who canoes, swims, runs, and hunts, has much in common with the growing popularity of the female form as active and defined through accented musculature. These figures perform a mimesis of the worked on and sculpted body of the active female 'techno-body' (Balsamo 1996: 5). These are above all, female figures in action and it is these qualities of physicality and activity that animate their virtual gender.

These figures, which cross media platforms, and have become significant in film, science fiction, and advertising, have been analyzed elsewhere. The field of games studies, for example, points to the diversity and mutability of meanings proliferating through such 'action' avatars. Schleiner (1998) and O'Riordan's (2001) work on Lara Croft highlights the multiplicity of potential readings and the diverse subject positions associated with these figures through image/reader relations. However, the press coverage of Ananova and the company profiles produced for Ananova, Lara Croft, and the other examples detailed above also signal the powerful force for normalization, containment, and literalization constituted through these figures. The contextual language used to present them anthropomorphizes the images and discursively ties them to familial and physical kinship networks of birth, origin, marriage, and ownership. The discursive power that locates these virtualizations as 'women' and the ability of the Lara Croft sign, for example, to travel across cultural forms and create a relational space for the 'woman' signified is indicative of the complexity of current networks of meaning creation in relation to media images more generally and simulations in particular.

My claim here is that the realization of virtual physical female bodies, through digital culture, is used to transform these images from fictional or metaphorical signs to simulations with ontological status. Designed to present an anthropomorphic female address, they become agents in the digital field of vision, not simply as and in new media forms, but through a widespread and multi-sited re-appearance and animation. They almost take on a life of their own. As apparently active bodies they are animated, not only as in the animation of cartoons but in the literal use of animated to mean life-like and in motion.

In this sense, the animation of virtual female bodies into moving figures can be seen as the 'mundane' of intelligent agents, robotics, and other interfaces for the question of affect or sociability in relation to machines. This issue of how the human/machine interface is constituted and re-established through affective/intelligent agents has already been raised through questions about the status of the image and its relationship to 'reality'. Debates about simulation and similitude have already been visited in relation to this terrain and Kember (1998) and Hillis (1999) thoroughly examine some of the issues of the status of the image and digital vision. However, where Hillis (1999) argues that in the field of digital 'sight' all figures are objects in the reification of digital 'space', I would argue that virtual females render the subject/object distinction problematic, especially through their claim to affective movement and sound. Unlike robotic AI, their physical dependence on context is not so swiftly exposed through closer observation (Suchman 2004). They are still vampiric puppet images that return to their coffins/boxes after the show, but they do not appear as objects in space, piles of wires, or inanimate toys, hence their boxes are rendered invisible though the theatre of digital software. The trick of rendering the technological frame (virtually) invisible is executed in relation to virtual bodies as effectively as in the televisual documentary method.[6] Their proliferation across different forms adds to such apparently independent activity.

Simulation, as opposed to the direct representation, provides a different way of understanding images of female bodies because it is understood as removed from a direct referent (Baudrillard 1983). In order that simulations appear lifelike, and affect an anthropomorphic address they must be original supplements but also achieve a specific aesthetic constellation including movement and sound. They are constituted through a mixture of copied and pasted aspects so that a familiar image of young celebrity is created but no one person is implicated. Thus simulations constitute a discursive creation that must draw on stereotypes of femininity in order to signal 'female'. They must show the details of beautiful breasts, small waists and styled hair to perform the instantly recognizable and active female form to banish ambiguity and recombine sex, sexuality, and gender into an essential moving image. The digital form, because of its unnatural connotation, already frames these simulations as ambiguous so the aesthetic must correct this, although not too seamlessly. They must be almost real but, as yet, not quite.

Virtual females contribute to the 'resolution' of informatic and virtual bodies, as actual body images through movement and form. However, the particular kinds of fixed limited and uniform images appearing as virtual female bodies reinforces and re-instates a visualization of normative bodies in popular culture. This contributes to other projects where female bodies are reduced into 'the body' of popular digital culture: contained, mapped, inverted as a template, and re-produced as a model of how bodies 'should' be, through the power of a generalized concept of normality. In this sense, virtual females are like contemporary Frankensteinian monsters, although airbrushed and male authored, which can be mobilized in relation to debates about human–computer interaction, the self and other, origin and reproduction, whilst simultaneously naturalizing particularly patriarchal modes of gender/technology relations (Turney 1998).

Thesis, antithesis, and synthesis

Understandings of biological bodies as natural have shifted, through a variety of frames, crossing the boundaries and binaries of nature/culture body/ artefact to almost infinite limits. Franklin (2000), for example, argues that nature and culture are collapsed through a constant borrowing from each other. However, discourses that normalize, contain, and understand biological bodies, as newly constituted through bio and info technologies, remain normative and reductive as they continue to speak back to an imagined origin of normality, rationality, and reality for their authority. Neo-Darwinist scientific discourses, for example, constantly return to these same poles of nature and culture for reassurance in the face of the blurring of boundaries that such technological shifts invoke (e.g. Dawkins 1976, 1990; Fukuyama 2002).

There is a common investment in transcending the limitations and constraints of physical bodies in both the field of information technologies and that of biotechnologies. The imagined potential for 'programming' a bioinformatics of the body through DNA is paralleled by the promise of an informatic body that has been developed in relation to information and communication technologies. In digital culture, where communication technology is the central figure, and translation and simulation the metaphors, the vision is that any, all, and as yet unimagined bodies, selves, and agents are possible in cyberspace and the inequalities and limitations of embodiment can be shed. In the new 'genetic imaginary' where biotechnology centres around the genome (Franklin 2000), DNA can potentially be programmed, selected, and copied to form new bodies freed from the determinants of inheritance, through the new determinism of genetic engineering and scientific control.

The future cannot be predicted, although it can be imagined, but what has already occurred, and continues to unfold, is a reiteration of a limited and fixed repertoire of understandings of the female body, through the digital image. The case studies explored here as well as other examples such as women's home pages, web cameras, internet pornography, and online advertising, from the advent of the web onwards, could be used to develop this claim. However, such broad strokes over time and genre would be misleading, I am not trying to describe a homogeneity of all images, but simply point to significant trends in specific groups of images.

The international media economy in its offline shape has appropriated the idealistic frames of cyberspace wholesale (Gamson 2003). This has occurred at the point at which the image became central to online media and this grip has intensified simultaneously to processing power increases, image data size shrinkage, and image ubiquity. The text formats used prior to the web inhibited full integration with more traditional media structures and the self-authored prose of much text communication allowed for more novel explorations of identity communication. However, as the visual image came to dominate the web, its power to constitute only the familiar was invoked. In making reference to developments in the information technology 'revolution', which I see as providing something of a cautionary tale, I argue that there is a similar pattern emerging around bioinformatics, through genomics. This pattern is one of similar and familiar desires to universalize, through logics of normativity and prescription, rather than possibility.

Female bodies are conceptualized, imaged, and constituted through a wide array of disparate discourses. However, the young, white, heterosexual body remains the normative template in digital visual culture. From medical imaging to mobile interfaces, a specific template of closure and normativity thus arises in the political economy of the digital image. There is a 'phenomenological openness' (Shildrick 2004: 161) and diversity of bio-logical bodies and the promise of infinite visual possibility in the digital image. Nonetheless the frames for visualizing the female body in contempor-ary communication and biotechnologies appear to remain locked into a closed reiteration of the young, white, heterosexual, female body as 'the (normal) female body'.

Linking the biotechnologies of genome mapping with the digital imaging techniques of entertainment/leisure industries and medical infrastructures reveals a persistent narrowing of the visual possibility of what it means to have and be a female body. Without discounting the many interventions to disrupt such normative models made through art, science, activism, and theory, it is important to underscore the conservative anxiety and repetition in the 'new', as newness continues to unfold in the emerging discourses of genomics, and other areas of bioinformatics. Judith Roof argues of the con-junction of digital imaging and genome mapping: 'dreams of genetic manipu-lation come from the digital as DNA becomes the biological version of a raster grid'[7] (Roof 1996: 176). The framework of digital bodies shifted from affective images to effective programs through the human genome map and its conceptualization as program.

The cyborg interaction of the virtual body is supplemented with interven-tions in the micro-structures of the body through the micro-technologies of genomics. The raster grid was used to map images of the body and as the framework for simulated images, thus allowing the imagined 'translation' of the body into the digital. The biological 'raster grid' of DNA comes from the other side of this coupling and reiterates the collapses of information into biology and biology into information.

Digital culture and bioinformatics

All bodies are part of networks of informational, embodied, physical, spir-itual, psychic, and symbolic nodes. Disentangling the logics of coercion, which contribute to forcing such normative meanings, becomes increasingly difficult as the complexity of the social endlessly proliferates. However, there are strong connections between developments in information technologies and those of bioinformatics in relation to conceptualizing and imaging the female body. Taking the figure of the female digital image in popular culture as an illustration, together with the contextual frameworks of the post-modern slide of informatics into bioinformatics, allows an examination of some of the ways in which understandings of female embodiment are narrowed and imprisoned through the matrixes of digital information. The focus here is on female bodies and I do not have the scope to cover issues of male embodiment, but it follows that to contain female bodies there must be a simultaneous containment of male bodies as separate and different. Particular images are created which intersect with cultural stereotypes, which reiterate and reinforce older types and stereotypes in new forms.

A central (and not original) argument here is that the media stereotype and digital metonym (Roof 1996) develop a reality ('enter history') through the proliferation of the simulated female body image. A more political point, and one that has been made elsewhere, is that the constant reiteration of templates for normality infect the current biomediation of bodies through biotechnologies that act on biological bodies now and in the future. Like the Visible Human Project, the Human Genome Project creates a template for normality (for all bodies). Where the VHP used one body to synecdochally stand in for all bodies, the HGP (like virtual female bodies) is drawn from multiple samples and creates the genome map based on a hypothetical composite of specific types, assuming 'the body' for science. It is a synchronicity, rather than coincidence, that virtual female bodies in popular culture, and the genomic body, are all composite entities, based on no(one)body.

The 'origin' of digital images and genetically engineered entities is contested: on the one hand they substantiate a legacy of technoscience and on the other they can be read as interventions into narratives of paternity. Judith Roof argues that both the digital image and the DNA code disrupt the continuity and origin of cultural frameworks as they are dislocated from a material referent and thus have the capacity to create their own meaning: 'The digital defies history by producing what has never been, even though the image, once produced, enters history' (Roof 1999: 186). However, whatever origin stories of digital culture are developed, virtual bodies, and digital images, have physical actualities and carry histories of meaning. As well as constituting material practices, they are agents for transforming metaphor into ontology, thus blurring boundaries between epistemology and ontology, as well as having become new symbolic socializing agents (Poster 2004). The digital image intersects with the flesh and the simulated images of women that are used to populate digital mediascapes resonate and interject into experiences of being and having female bodies. Through the digital economy of bodies and technologies, the normative visions of virtual bodies in cyberspace inform the delimitation of the digital bodies of biotechnology, which are similarly used to mobilize heteronormative rhetorics of perfectability, sameness, and exclusion.

A return to nature (an aside)

Discursively nature is used to mobilize ideologies of a world with an onto-logical priority and purity in relation to culture, society, and the artificial. This is a strategy evoked by ecologists, socio-biologists, and neo-conservatives alike (Soper 1996). Naturalization is a process which involves rendering social structures and power relations invisible and beyond the reach of cul-ture thus effecting determinisms and essentialisms. Elizabeth Grosz (2004) has argued that nature is the interiority of culture, the unconscious of con-sciousness, not opposed but a contained effect of culture. As already men-tioned, Sara Franklin (2000) has powerfully argued that the binary opposition of nature and culture has been collapsed through the economic logic that structures the normalization of biotechnology and delivers the flesh to the market. However, although her argument has a paradigmatic force, it is clear in evaluating popular discourses of genomics that nature has not lost its illocutionary power of value and reassurance to stand against the artificial.

Kate Soper (1996) argues that both eco-feminists (with a protectionist view of nature) and those who commercialize natural resources for economic gain make the same category error when they regard nature as something above and beyond culture. However, the resonance that this category retains needs continual exploration. Whilst accepting the force of Franklin's (2000) argu-ment, the continuing power of 'the natural' to enforce power relations remains difficult and Franklin (2000) argues also that the category keeps emerging in different forms. Whilst nature and culture have partially col-lapsed and rupture each other, it is usually a determinism of either a culture over nature or nature over culture that emerges.

It is perhaps in relation to digital culture that nature/culture dynamics and collapses have been most powerfully invoked: firstly as digital communica-tions media are used to imagine the existence of a free-flowing body, uncon-strained by the flesh and able to be indefinitely plastic; secondly, as digital mapping is used as a method for translating physical bodies, particularly through the example of the VHP and HGPs. The cyborg in its many mani-festations is of course a classic figure for these invocations. In this framework the body, identity, and technologies become infinitely malleable substances. Thacker (2004) develops a further metaphor for the conjunction of digitiza-tion, biotechnology, and the body in his thesis on 'biomedia' as a descriptive and prescriptive term.

Invoking a nature/culture collapse produces a definition or conceptualiza-tion of 'the body', which can encompass a wide understanding. For example in *Data Made Flesh*, editors Phillip Thurtle and Robert Mitchell extend their definition of the body as: 'Anything that cannot be divided without changing the fundamental pattern of its dynamics' (2004: 4). An important point here is that in the theoretical discourses around biotechnologies and digital culture there is a theoretical stretching and proliferation of bodies into 'the body' of theory. The enclosure of individual bodies into an infinite idea of the body is a multi-sited and diverse performance. Bodies that I wish to return to are individual female bodies and the infinite range that this category of experience can cover.

The digital image carries with it many traditions. Discourses of the information age evoke an ontological collapse of nature into culture through the trope of digitization. Cybernetics, informatics, and genomics combine in the powerful domin(m)atrix of the technoculture to evoke a body that is translatable and trans-substantiable through mediation. With a startling similitude, both Walter Gilbert (1992), one of the 'heroes' of genetic science, and Marvin Minsky, operating through the informatics model, argue that the human body can not only be understood as data, but is a form of information that can be exchanged into other forms whilst remaining 'essentially' unchanged. Walter Gilbert argues that the human subject can be present in a data storage format because the map of the human genome can be stored in this format, thus invoking the genome as the sum of the human. Marvin Minsky also hypothesized (as did Moravec and Kurtzweil) that consciousness could be recorded in digital formats through the coding practice of cyberspace. Extropians, transhumanists, posthumanists, and geneticists alike argue that the collapse of the human body into data redefines the natural/artificial binary and produces new kinds of bodies. However, in the face of the information age and within the dominance of technoscience, biological bodies have remained (reconfigured and understood as networks), but the materiality of biology and information alike has persisted. As fast as the body has been coded out, it has returned to challenge the informational paradigm. Through the flesh, the shadow of the natural has remained, returned, and been reproduced in different forms.

N. Katherine Hayles (1999) points out that in the context of statements like Marvin Minsky's: 'It can be a shock to remember that for information to exist, it must *always* be instantiated into a medium, whether [or not] that medium is . . . the computer-generated topological maps used by the Human Genome Project' (1999: 13).

The medium of the physical biological body remains the only socially intelligible origin point for the mediation of the person, despite the extensive mapping processes of bodies. Bodies remain visible and surplus to their mapped information, thus remaining in part naturalized media whilst simultaneously signifying something beyond the maps and data they are made to reveal. However, while there are no other human bodies that can be referred to beyond or in the various maps of the body produced thus far, there is 'the body' constituted through virtual bodies that populate the cultural horizons of sciences and popular cultures alike, as well as their inter-relational fields.

Mitchell and Thurtle (2004) argue that in establishing a viable concept of the body, a biological body bounded by flesh is one of many kinds of bodies. In this kind of theoretical context we must be careful to attend to the specificity of biological and non-biological bodies if we want this distinction to have any future meaning. I would argue that a definition of the body needs to include a concept of 'bio' as a necessary distinction for any kind of bioethics (although human specificity is not a necessary distinction as we might want to include other animals (Braidotti 2004)). However, in drawing on a definition of the body as a 'circuit' Mitchell and Thurtle's (2004) formulation is potentially helpful in pointing to the complex relations that constitute biosocial bodies and to the intersection of image and experience that I am trying to underscore.

In their formulation Mitchell and Thurtle (2004) also refer to four other conceptualizations of the human body that they reject as individual explanations but build on as composite contributions to their 'circuit'. These are described as:

- the 'naturalist body', which is 'just there' and is 'naturally determined' (p. 4);
- the culturally determined body, 'a blank slate', where culture determines bodily disposition;
- the animalistic body, where the body is 'a residue of animalistic quality in mankind' (p. 4);
- the phenomenological body, 'that is the body as perceived or experienced' (p. 5). They argue that this is a problematic formulation of the biological body in that it reduces the body to the 'zero point of experience' and does 'little to help us understand the integrity of mediated experience in linking and transforming bodily interaction' (p. 5). It is this latter aspect that is crucial to understanding how biological bodies are complex networks constituted through interactions.

The 'integrity of mediated experience in linking and transforming bodily interaction' (p. 5) is a crucial aspect of understanding the physicality of digital culture. Often described as ephemeral and set against the 'embodied', digital culture constitutes another physical frame through which fluid embodied experience is constituted. The question that this raises is that of specificity, contingency, and agency: i.e. where in the interactions of bodies and frames can these details of agency be found? Agency is performed through movement in the case of simulated female bodies. Their claim to physicality and agency is enacted through their apparent animation.

In each case, where the infinitely diverse specificity of individual bodies has been abstracted into a composite or synechdocal body, or 'the body', individual bodies are the only possible intelligible moments. 'The body' of digital culture, bioinformatics, and theory has ceased to become intelligible and has become a rhetorical force. Another way of putting this is to ask how it is possible to retrieve a force for intelligibility, agency, and difference in the generalized field of the body, how to retrieve bodies instead of 'the body'. This question, I think, provides the impetus for the (re)turn to the body that has occurred across many academic fields.

Conclusion

The purposes of this chapter have been to lay out some of the context for the theoretical consideration of how digital bodies and biological bodies have become simultaneously mutually constitutive and separate. Using a variety of examples of virtual physical bodies, including animated 'digital beauties' and how these particular digital aesthetics might apply to the digitized genome, allows a consideration of how bodies (even when they are virtual) remain the locus of the natural. An examination of mediated and virtual bodies shows how the body of bioinformatics is constituted through the digital and what this mutual constitution may imply. To return to my opening claim, it is female bodies that retain the force of the natural. As the nurturing progenitors of natural processes they remain very resonant kinds of subjects. The possibilities of digital media, simulation, and imaging techniques have been used to mobilize a discourse of liberation, optimism, and change. These utopian extremes thinly camouflage a conservative celebration of the fetish of the normatively naturalized, active, young, white, and sexualized female body. The translation of code into the body through genomics seems to imply an animation of biotech bodies. The use of women's bodies, through their reproductive capacities, as managers of these genomic codes, and of future bodies (Shildrick 2004: 154) brings us around to a naturalization of the technologies of genomics as they become secured through a further techno-naturalization of women's bodies.

As Jenny Kitzinger observes, 'Concepts of nature are always used in the performance of culture' (Kitzinger, in press). Simultaneously concepts of culture are always used in the performance of nature. What happens in this latter performance though is of course the erasure of cultural signs through the seamless performance of nature. However, the almost seamless progression from digitization to genomics and the virtualization of the body of science and popular culture through digital images and code coheres in a re-naturalized understanding of female bodies as not only perfectible in image but as managers and carriers of bodily perfectability through the plasticity of DNA as code. The seamlessness of this performance and the apparently immanent connections between genomics and digital culture require further investigation to draw out the particular interests that are implicated.

This chapter has explored the figure of the virtual physical female body, locating different examples in a range of debates about the female body, the artificial, technology, and the natural. Having looked more closely at virtual females in digital culture, I hope to have provided a discussion of how one version of the female body is constituted and reconstituted through the circuits between bodies and images, experiences and representation. Crucial to these aggregate simulations of the flesh are the physical conditions of movement, sound, and interaction.

Judith Roof (1996) argues that there is a generative ontological collapse between digital imaging techniques and the techno-scientific coding of the body through DNA simulation. This has a parallel in Thacker's (2002) claim that through biomedia, corporeal bodies and information technologies are co-constitutive in producing new figurations of what 'biological', 'technological', and 'the body' mean and can do. However, this collapse does not play out as a flattening of difference, or a collapse of the physical into the image. The continuous blurring of the divisions between the biological female body and the simulated one point to a process of continuous boundary reinforcement where the natural continues to be used to define the artificial, and vice versa, whilst the boundaries of the two are constantly redrawn around active bodies.

Roof's further argument that the origin point of the digital is obscured, and that this can disrupt the patriarchal order does not however seem to be played out in visual digital culture.

> But unlike photography, the digital image does not necessarily rely on the actual or natural. Where photography is analogous to the Frankensteinian corporeal, digital imaging is like DNA, dependent on and springing directly from a code.
>
> (Roof 1996: 175)

The digital image does not necessarily rely on the actual or natural. However, the digital image is demonstrably used to naturalize and actualize particular types of female bodies in action. The moving images that have been developed, in an attempt to simulate physical female bodies, actualize templates for physical normality in the field of digital vision. The iterative relationship between digitization and genomics allows a speculation that the force of the naturalized stereotype will permeate the micro-structures of the physical body. As Hein and Hein argue, 'If we condition ourselves to clichés we will take the means to realize them effectively' (2000: 328).

Where the simulated digital image of the physical female body has a material relation to the experience of bodies through popular culture and medical discourse, the digitized genome is intended to have an intimate relationship with the flesh of imagined bodies. These digital visions and biotechnological discourses are invested in a parallel physical reductionism and normative aesthetic to those of popular culture, where the 'genetic imaginary' (Franklin 2000), thus far, is as limited as the digital image.

Acknowledgements

The support of the Economic and Social Research Council (ESRC) is gratefully acknowledged. The work was part of the programme of the ESRC Research Centre for Economic and Social Aspects of Genomics. I am also indebted to contributions from Drs Caroline Bassett and Joan Haran, Professor Maureen McNeil and the detailed guidance from the editors, Patricia Vertinsky and Jennifer Hargreaves.

Notes

1 I cite Suchman's use of 'socio-material practices' in her online article 'Replicants and irreductions: affective encounters at the interface', because although the term is used widely in feminist research, I use it here to indicate a similar deployment as well as to reference intersecting work on affect and the interface.

2 The Visible Human and Visible Female projects (1989) are medical imaging projects currently hosted by the US National Library of Medicine. The projects produce 3D image data sets of the body where the user can navigate the interiority of the body. The images were created through a process of slicing corpses very thinly and scanning each slice, recompiling the virtual body, and providing a virtual map of the body. In this example the Visible Female was based on one corpse used to stand in for 'female'.

3 The Human Genome Project, conducted throughout the 1990s, aimed to provide a map of the complete human genome. Using samples from lots of bodies, it sought to provide a virtual map of 'the genome'. This project was also constituted through digital technology and the analysis of data and production of results was realized through this form.

4 These are just two examples of a genre of books 'celebrating' the programming mastery of producing almost lifelike simulations of female bodies for new media platforms. These all have young white females on the front cover and are illustrated with simulations of heterosexually alluring stereotypes, a fairly breathless style, and in some cases real programming instructions.

5 Verbots refer to existing 'bots' which are computer programs described as agents. Agents can perform retrieval tasks on the internet and are discussed further in Kember 2000. They are also found in IRC and MUDs where they can act as assistants or help programs. Sometimes they 'pass' for actual users and one of the goals of agent programming is to produce bots, which can pass the 'Turing Test' and present as human through a text interface. Interfacing with agents/bots has traditionally occurred through text – whilst these verbots use an audio-visual interface to present a simulation of a human interface.

6 I am indebted to Dr Joan Haran for pointing out that the hard drive is such a frame.

7 A raster grid creates the framework for pixels. Each image is created as an array of value and thus each pixel is a separate unit, which can always be located by its co-ordinates on the grid.

Bibliography

Balsamo, A. (1996) *Technologies of the Gendered Body: Reading Cyborg Women*, Durham, NC: Duke.

Baudrillard, J. (1983) *Simulations*, New York: Semiotext(e).

Bornstein, K. (1998) *My Gender Workbook: How to Become the Kind of Man or Woman You Always Thought You Could Be . . . or Something Else Entirely*, London and New York: Routledge.

Braidotti, R. (2004) 'From "bio-power" to the politics of life itself', paper presented at *What's Life Got To Do With It*, Lancaster University.

Cartwright, L. (1995) *Screening the Body: Tracing Medicine's Visual Culture*, Minneapolis, MN: University of Minnesota Press.

Dawkins, R. (1976, 1990) *The Selfish Gene*, New York: Oxford University Press.

Doyle, J. and O'Riordan, K. (2002) 'Virtually visible: female cyberbodies and the medical imagination', in A. Booth and M. Flanagan (eds) *Reload: Rethinking Women and Cyberculture*, Cambridge, MA: MIT Press.

Franklin, S. (2000) 'Life itself: global nature and the genetic imaginary', in S. Franklin, C. Lury and J. Stacey (eds) *Global Nature: Global Culture*, London: Sage.

Fukuyama, F. (2002) *Our Posthuman Future: Consequences of the Biotechnology Revolution*, New York: Farrar, Straus and Giroux.

Gamson, J. (2003) 'Gay media inc. Media structures, the new gay conglomerates and collective sexual identities', in M. McCaughey and M.D. Ayers (eds) *Cyberactivism: Online Activism in Theory and Practice*, London and New York: Routledge.

Gauntlett, D. (1995) *Moving Experiences: Understanding Television's Influences and Effects*, Eastleigh: John Libbey Media.

Gibson, W. (1997) *Idoru*, London: Penguin Books.

Gibson, W. (2000) *All Tomorrow's Parties*, London: Penguin Books.

Gilbert, W. (1992) 'Visions of the grail', in D.J. Kevles and L. Hood (eds) *The Code of Codes*, Cambridge, MA: Harvard University Press.

Grosz, E. (2004) *Nick of Time: Politics, Evolution and the Untimely*, Durham, NC: Duke University Press.

Hamilton, R. (1997) 'Virtual idols and digital girls: artifice and sexuality in anime, kisekae and Kyoko Date,' *Bad Subjects: Political Education for Everyday Life*, 35.

Haraway, D. (1997) *Modest Witness @ Second Millenium. Female Man© Meets Onco Mouse™: Feminism and Technoscience*, London, New York: Routledge.

Hartouni, V. (1997) *Cultural Conceptions: On Reproductive Technologies and the Remaking of Life*, Minnesota, MN: University of Minnesota Press.

Hayles, N. K. (1999) *How We Became Posthuman: Virtual Bodies in Cybernetics, Literature, and Informatics*, Chicago, IL: Chicago University Press.

Hein, P.U. and Hein, M. E. (2000) 'Human, mutant, machine,' *New Genetics and Society*, 19 (3): 317–29.

Hillis, K. (1999) *Digital Sensations: Space, Identity, and Embodiment In Virtual Reality*, Minneapolis, MN: University of Minnesota Press.

Jordanova, L. (1989) *Sexual Visions: Images of Gender in Science and Medicine Between the Eighteenth and Twentieth Centuries*, Wisconsin, WI: University of Wisconsin Press.

Keller, E.F. (1992) *Secrets of Life, Secrets of Death*, New York and London: Routledge.

Keller, E.F. (2000) *The Century of the Gene*, Cambridge, MA: Harvard University Press.

Kember, S. (1998) *Virtual Anxiety: Photography, New Technologies and Subjectivity*, Manchester: Manchester University Press.

Kember, S. (2003) *Cyberfeminism and Artificial Life*, London and New York: Routledge.

Kitzinger, J. (forthcoming) 'Constructing and deconstructing the gay gene', in D. Ellison *et al.* (eds) *Ethics and Diversity*, London and New York: Taylor and Francis.

Manovich, L. (2001) *The Language of the New Media*, Cambridge, MA: MIT Press.

O'Riordan, K. (2001) 'Playing with Lara in virtual space', in S.R. Munt (ed.) *Techno-spaces: Inside the New Media*, London: Cassell.

Petchesky, R. (1992) 'Foetal images: The power of visual culture in the politics of reproduction', in H. B. Holmes (ed.) *Issues in Reproductive Technology: An Anthology*, New York: Garland.

Plant, S. (1997) *Zeros + Ones: Digital Women + the New Technoculture*, New York: Doubleday.

Poole, S. (2000) *Trigger Happy: The Inner Life of Video Games*, London: Harper Collins.

Poster, M. (2004) 'Fused desire: bodies, families, and information machines' in R. Mitchell and P. Thurtle (eds) *Data Made Flesh: Embodying Information*, London and New York: Routledge.

Roof, J. (1996) *Reproductions of Reproduction: Imaging Symbolic Change*, New York: Routledge.

Schleiner, A.M. (1998) 'Does Lara Croft wear fake polygons?' *Switch, Electronic Gender: Art At The Interface*, June.

Shildrick, M. (2004) 'Genetics, normativity and ethics: some bioethical concerns', *Feminist Theory*, 5(2): 149–66.

Soper, K. (1996) 'NATURE/Nature', in G. Robertson *et al.* (eds) *Future Natural – Nature Science Culture*, New York: Routledge.

Stabile, C. (1993) 'Shooting the mother: foetal photography and the politics of disappearance', *Camera Obscura*, 28.

Stone, A. R. (1996) *The War of Desire and Technology at the Close of the Mechanical Age*, Cambridge, MA: MIT Press.

Suchman, L. (2002) 'Replicants and irreductions: affective encounters at the interface' Lancaster: Centre for Science Studies, Lancaster University.

Suchman, L. (2004) 'Signs of life in sciences of the artificial', paper presented at *What's Life Got to Do with It?* Lancaster: Lancaster University.

Thacker, E. (2004) *Biomedia*, Minnesota, MN: University of Minnesota Press.

The 6th Day (2000) Roger Spottiswoode. USA: Columbia Pictures.

Thurtle, P. and Mitchell, R. (2004) *The Data Made Flesh: Embodying Information*, London and New York: Routledge.

Turney, J. (1998) *Frankenstein's Footsteps: Science, Genetics and Popular Culture*, New Haven, CT: Yale University Press.

Virtual Sexuality (1999) Nick Hurran. USA: Columbia Pictures.

Waldby, C. (2000) *The Visible Human Project: Informatic Bodies and Posthuman Medicine*, London and New York: Routledge.

Weird Science (1985) John Hughes. USA: Universal Pictures.

Wiedemann, J. (ed.) (2001) *Digital Beauties*, Taschen Books.

Wiedemann, J. (ed.) (2002) *Digital Beauties: 2D and 3D CG Digital Models*, Taschen Books.

Index